AF703095

Data Handling Utilities in C

Data Handling Utilities in C

Robert A. Radcliffe
Thomas J. Raab

SYBEX®

Berkeley • Paris • Düsseldorf • London

Cover art by Dave Jensen
Book design by Sharon Leong

Allnet is a trademark of Allnet Communications Services, Inc.
AT&T is a trademark of American Telephone and Telegraph Co.
dBASE III is a trademark of Ashton-Tate.
IBM and PC-DOS are trademarks of International Business Machines Corp.
Intel is a trademark of Intel Corporation.
Lattice C Compiler is a trademark of Lattice, Inc.
MCI is a trademark of MCI Telecommunications Corp.
Sprint is a trademark of GTE Sprint Communications Corp.
US Tel is a trademark of US Telecom.
Zip + 4 is a trademark of United States Postal Service.

SYBEX is not affiliated with any manufacturer.

Every effort has been made to supply complete and accurate information. However, SYBEX assumes no responsibility for its use, nor for any infringements of patents or other rights of third parties which would result.

Neither SYBEX Computer Books, Inc. nor anyone else who has been involved in the creation, production, or delivery of the programs in this book shall be liable for any direct, incidental, or consequential damages, such as, but not limited to, loss of anticipated profits or benefits, resulting from the use of any program in this book.

Copyright©1986 SYBEX Inc., 2344 Sixth Street, Berkeley, CA 94710. World rights reserved. No part of this publication may be stored in a retrieval system, transmitted, or reproduced in any way, including but not limited to photocopy, photograph, magnetic or other record, without the prior agreement and written permission of the publisher.

Library of Congress Card Number: 86-61061
ISBN 0-89588-304-X
Printed by Haddon Craftsmen
Manufactured in the United States of America
10 9 8 7 6 5 4 3 2

To former associates

Joseph H. Keane
David M. Ritter
and
K.B. Wesley

whose humor convinced me that "I should buy a little spam farm, one with spam as far as the eye can C.C.C...",

my heartfelt thanks for your past support, encouragement and understanding.

Acknowledgments

My sincere thanks to Dr. Rudolph Langer, whose insight rescued this book from a stack of promising proposals and helped shape it into what we both believe should have been published fifteen years ago.

Many thanks to Thomas J. Raab, co-author and consultant, for "being there" to talk over troubling technical problems and for consistently providing suggestions and solutions with uncanny clarity and perception.

To Terrence F. Bergen, longtime friend and business associate, my thanks to you and your staff at Computerland of Lancaster, Pennsylvania for all your help.

To Dr. E.L. Bourodimos, Professor—Rutgers University—for setting a standard of academic rigor and excellence to which I still aspire.

My special thanks and appreciation to those at SYBEX who, in their own way, contributed to make this book better than any one of us could have done individually:

David Kolodney, developmental editor, for organizing the draft and encouraging us to produce better examples throughout the book.

Bonnie Gruen, line editor, for persevering through Part 2, coordinating all of the editing revisions, and staying cool when we were not sure which was what, and when, and where.

David Clark and Olivia Shinomoto, word processing, for getting the what to where, even when it wasn't.

Sharon Leong, book designer, for making a silk purse out of what would have been a sow's ear.

Brenda Walker, typesetter, for keeping straight where the ampersands were and were not.

Jon Strickland, proofreader, for catching all the errors that everyone else said were already caught.

Henri Socha, technical reviewer, for providing some excellent suggestions and catching some blunders in a draft that was at times more like a stiff breeze.

Thanks for helping us to achieve something that at times seemed impossible.

R.A.R.

Contents

Part Two: Logical Data Types

Appendixes

Introduction

This book is designed to present the standard interface definitions of a structured methodology for data entry, to provide the complete source code implementation of this methodology, and to provide functional tools for software developers who are confronted with the pressures of completing a commercial programming assignment in the C programming language.

The authors assume that you have already read Kernighan/Ritchie's *The C Programming Language* (Englewood Cliffs, NJ: Prentice-Hall, 1978) and perhaps another follow-up book such as Hunter's *Understanding C.* (Further references to Kernighan/Ritchie will list just the authors' names and page numbers.) In all likelihood you have begun to experience that sinking feeling common to everyone at the start of most new programming assignments. We hope to moderate your level of anxiety by showing you what the C programming language can do when used in conjunction with our structured data entry methodology, and to show that by using our methodology, you can also become a more effective programmer.

Clearly this book is intended to pick up where Kernighan/Ritchie and Hunter leave off, by focusing upon how C can actually be used to complete a programming assignment. This is not just another book about the C programming language itself; rather, an application programmer's sourcebook of ideas and software tools that can be directly applied to your programming assignments. This book may best be thought of as an additional C utility library from which useful ideas, functions, and tools can be extracted to fulfill a particular programming requirement. Just as quality craftsmanship results from an artisan's skillful use of available materials and tools, quality software today results from the prudent use of state-of-the-art libraries of helpful functions.

Since commercial application programming involves a high degree of user interaction and an extensive need for relatively large permanent files of information, this book concentrates on the development of sound methodologies and techniques for data entry, validation, efficient data storage, and display. Since the actual processing of information in commercial programs is generally not complex, little emphasis has been placed upon the development of processing algorithms. However, particular care has been taken to fully address error handling because the issue of error control and recovery literally dominates the software development process for today's complex microcomputer systems.

For these reasons, we focus in this book on the development of a structured approach to data entry that functionally extends the rather limited input/output (I/O) handling features of the C programming language, and we discuss how this methodology relates to the fundamental issues of file design, sorting, and software interfacing. By using our concept of logical data types (LDTs), you can develop application programs that allow both programming and user staff to work directly with common fields of information such as dates, dollars, telephone numbers, and time instead of the less familiar char, int, float, and double data types which are native to the C programming language itself. We also present a unique field mask concept for data entry and display which further exhances the flexibility of our methodology. Also with our video scratch pad technique, we show you how to independently use the interfaces we have developed and yet retain the power and flexibility of the overall methodology.

This book provides an extensive source code library of functions that includes

- The common underlying utilities that support our overall structured methodology
- The full implementation of seven logical data types (which will satisfy 95% of the data entry field types you will probably ever need)
- Other supporting data validation and utility routines
- A comprehensive set of quality assurance and test programs to verify the integrity of all source code

To those of you about to conclude that you do not need this book because you are using a database management package with a report writer, let us suggest from our experience that at least 10% of your data entry and 25% of your reports will require "custom programming." This book will be a great help to you in these instances, and is essential if you must also provide file interfaces to other software products functioning on different microprocessors and operating systems.

The materials presented in this book are practical in nature. In contrast to more theoretical books that often fail to address common software development problems, this book presents solutions to many nagging problems that have been ignored for years. Although considered an advanced book, the concepts presented here should be understandable to all readers with a basic understanding of the C programming language. The source code, techniques, and examples presented comprise a handy desktop reference for anyone involved in application programming. These materials are particularly helpful for writing filter programs to provide compatibility with other third party software, and for writing programs for interfacing with other spreadsheet, graphics, word processing, and communication software products.

Over 150 functions are included and fully documented in this book. There are helpful notes and commentary keyed to the source code to facilitate your understanding of the material and to make it possible for you to put the source code immediately to use. There are no hidden catches to prevent you from using any of the source code. In fact, to make your use of the material easier, IBM PC compatible disks containing all the source code in this book can be purchased separately (see last page of book). These disks also include 40 additional test programs that are not listed in the book but are very useful.

In Part 1 of this book, we present the concepts and framework for the development of a structured data entry approach using the C programming language. We explore the weaknesses of standard C I/O, introduce the concept of logical data types (LDTs), and develop the standard interface definitions for data encoding, decoding, and validation. We also develop a combined encode and validation interface definition, create a sophisticated getstring and companion putstring interface, and develop advanced LDT field processing interfaces. Complete provisions for error control and recovery and error logging are incorporated throughout. The interrelationship of the storage characteristics of logical data types, file design, and features of software products for file management and sorting are explored. Guidelines are also presented for the evaluation and selection of the vendor software products listed in Appendix C.

Part 2 provides the complete source code implementation of each standard interface definition described in Part 1 for the field data entry of seven different logical data types that are common to many application programs. It includes character strings, dates, dollars, integers, reals, telephone numbers, and times, with discussions and examples of how to handle ID numbers, check digits, logicals, names, soundex codes, social security numbers, zip codes, and more.

A separate chapter is devoted to each logical data type (LDT), but the outline of these seven chapters is standardized. Once you have worked with a chapter about one LDT, it will be easy to refer to and study the material presented for another LDT. Chapter 6 on dates is probably the most comprehensive in print today. Given the importance that dates play in most application programs, don't overlook it. Each logical data type chapter also includes a quality assurance test program that allows you to test each associated encode and decode function, and demonstrates how you can use the interface definitions developed in this book in your C programs. In Chapter 12 we show you how to create your own project-specific logical data types within the structured data entry framework and in Chapter 13 we explain how to implement a systemwide error and message logging file called stdlog.

We have also included 12 appendices that provide the following information and make this book completely self-contained:

- Glossary
- Bibliography
- Vendor lists of C-compatible software products
- Guidelines for performing PC-DOS interrupt functions
- ASCII character set definition
- Lattice C _main command line processor
- Complete listing of all header files (.h)

- Functions for byte reordering of native C data types
- Powers of 2^n table
- Modulus 10/11 check digit algorithms
- Native C data type characteristics
- Linker automatic response files (.lnk)

All the supporting materials that are needed to understand the concepts and source code presented in this book are included for your convenience. Both a comprehensive book index and a separate index of source code are provided to help you quickly locate the functions in the book.

We have implemented the source code in this book for the following computing environment:

IBM PC/XT, 256K memory
IBM Monochrome Monitor
PC-DOS, release 3.1
WordStar, release 3.3
Lattice C Compiler, version 2.0
  (S memory model; lc1 -a option)
IBM PC Linker, release 2.3

Should you wish to port this software to another microprocessor, operating system or vendor's C compiler, some changes to the header files (see Appendix G) and the source code dependent upon PC-DOS and Lattice C would have to be made. We have been careful to highlight which functions are dependent upon PC-DOS and Lattice C in the index of source code.

We believe that the standard interface definitions that comprise our structured data entry methodology also can be implemented in programming languages other than C. We hope that you will adapt and improve upon the source code included in this book. We know that in certain instances more compact and elegant source code could be written; however, with our methodology you have complete control over all of the source code necessary for its implementation.

So . . . change it, modify it, improve it . . . but most of all, use it!

Part One: Structured Data Entry

The Software Development Process

1

Our overall objective in this book is to develop and demonstrate how to use a *structured data entry methodology* to overcome the I/O limitations that will confront you when using the C programming language for commercial applications. We have elected to implement our methodology using IBM PC hardware, the PC-DOS operating system, and the Lattice C compiler.

Several formidable problems need to be overcome to utilize C effectively for such development. *Data entry, file processing,* and *sorting* are three crucial requirements for the success of any assignment. These facilities are not adequately handled by the C compilers and the standard libraries of utilities that are normally provided with C.

These facilities must either be developed independently or purchased from software vendors who market C utility libraries of commonly needed routines. Needless to say, no one should "reinvent the wheel" and therefore it is a good idea to purchase such needed routines. Numerous products are on the market for general utility functions, indexed file processing, sorting, and screen/window management. For your convenience a partial list of such products is included in Appendix C.

The data entry functions presented in this book are not redundant with any commercially available products. Rather, the source code included in this book is intended to serve as an additional library of C functions upon which a software developer can rely to satisfy particular programming requirements. This book is more than just a library of 150 C functions however, for it develops the source code within the context of modern software development concepts, programming techniques, and management practices.

We would like to establish at the outset a common understanding of the guidelines chosen to control the software developed for this book. The table below lists objectives we believe should be taken into account when developing any software using C. Given the continued technological turmoil anticipated in the computer industry, these objectives represent a sound set of guidelines for nearly any development project.

1. Maximizing the portability of software to accomodate future hardware developments in the microcomputer industry

2. Minimizing future software maintenance costs by making source code development more structured, and hence self-documenting, consistent, and reliable

3. Establishing standard libraries of functions with standard interface definitions

4. Carefully selecting and standardizing the software tools and techniques employed by the various members of a project team

5. Ensuring data integrity and reliability through comprehensive data editing and validation while maintaining a consistent dialog with the user

6. Providing for immediate data correction and error recovery in a consistent manner

7. Providing quality assurance and testing mechanisms prior to and independent of the user environment

It is worth noting that no mention of compilers, operating systems, specific computer hardware or project requirements is included in this list. We believe that such detailed matters are secondary.

Item number 4 reflects our belief that project managers should minimize and isolate the use of techniques that are hardware and compiler dependent. When such techniques really are called for because of performance or capability considerations, they should be formalized into project standard interface definitions so that such code is isolated for all to use, and not scattered, in an undocumented way, throughout a system.

All PC-DOS or Lattice C dependent functions developed for this book are fully documented and cross-referenced for your convenience in the index of source code files. Each is easily replaceable to make it possible to "port" this software to another operating system or another vendor's C compiler.

Item number 7 in the above list points to the need for better testing and quality assurance procedures during the software development process itself. The development of independent methods of testing source code should become a part of every project effort.

Each logical data type included in Part 2 is provided with a quality assurance driver routine (qaxxxx.c), which can be used to test that particular logical data type independent of its use in an application program. Modifications to the source code for a logical data type can be fully tested prior to being linked into an application program. Such precautions can avert costly and embarrassing Beta test results.

The index of source code files at the end of the book includes, in addition to the qaxxxx.c programs, a comprehensive set of some 40 test programs to be found on the disk available with this book (see the last page for details). Because of space limitations, only a few of these test programs could be incorporated into the text itself.

The Need for Logical Data Types

2

To understand why an alternative I/O facility is necessary, one must first understand what elementary data types are defined and thereby native to the C language itself. The elementary data types of the C programming language are char, int, float, and double. In this book we will refer to these data types as *native* or *physical data types.* They can be further broken down and described by their physical characteristics, for example: unsigned, short, and long. A full data type specification can consist of up to two adjectives and an elementary type. The following data type specifications can be found throughout the source code included in this book:

char
int
long int
float
double

The immediate problem to deal with is choosing the best way to handle common commercial programming fields of data in C such as dates, dollars, and time. The logical data type concepts presented in this book will map such common commercial field types into the physical data types available in C. Before proceeding further, let's take a closer look at the concept of logical data types.

The Logical Data Type Concept

If we agree to call the native C data types char, int, float, and double physical data types, then we would like to, from this point on, refer to the common fields of input such as dates, dollars, and time as *logical data types (LDTs)* because they are logical in a commercial application programming environment. Why should application programmers and users be forced to think directly in terms of the physical data types native to the C language specification? It is from this simple observation and to this end that we begin to develop the materials presented in this book.

Logical data types are, therefore, abstractions that are defined by a software developer in such a way that normal commercial data is "mapped" or equated to the C data types, and the translation in and out of C data types is completely transparent to the user. The logical data types presented in this book include character, date, dollar, integer, real, telephone, and time as well as instructions for creating and implementing any xxxx type that might be required for a particular software development project. Complete sections on each of these logical data types are included in Part 2 of this book.

No standard C I/O is used to directly translate keyboard character strings representing char, int, float, or double into their corresponding physical data types. Instead, we have developed a structured data entry methodology for this purpose. All user input is treated as a character string without any data conversion. User interaction for data entry is handled by the *getstring* function (see Chapter 4). These strings are passed through an *encode* routine that enforces all syntax checking, edit, error control, and physical data type conversion. The interface definition of the encode function is common to all logical data types, thereby promoting a structured approach to data entry. Additional *data validation* can be performed after encoding is complete. A common interface definition for data validation is similarly valid for use with all logical data types. The *decode* functions create character string representations of encoded logical data types. Again, the decode interface definition is common to all logical data types. Actual display of the decoded character string is performed by the *putstring* function (see Chapter 4). Clearly, the structure of this methodology is beginning to emerge. With this structure all of the objectives stated in Chapter 1 can be achieved, while overcoming the severe I/O limitations of the C programming language.

Figure 2.1 outlines the overall components of this methodology.

Before developing the details of this structured methodology, let's examine the limitations of directly using the standard I/O features provided for by the C language itself. The benefits of adopting a structured approach for data entry becomes more apparent when the deficiencies of standard C I/O are fully understood.

Limitations of C I/O Routines

There are six standard I/O format conversion routines available in the C programming language. They include scanf and printf and their companion routines fscanf and fprintf, and sscanf and sprintf. Collectively these functions provide for the conversion of ASCII character strings to native C physical data

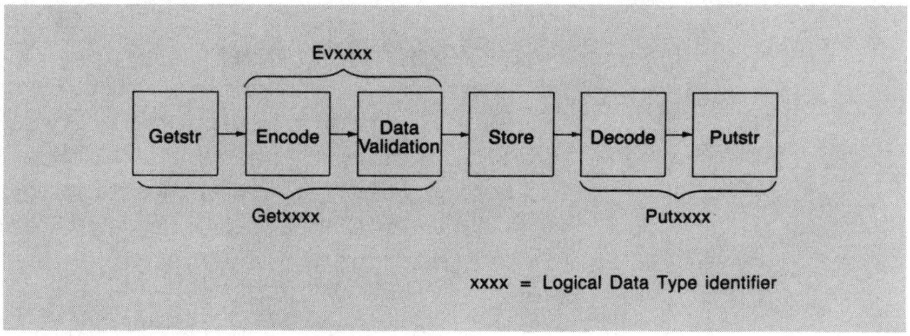

***Figure 2.1**– Flow diagram of structured data entry methodology*

formats and vice versa; however, they do so in a manner that makes them practically useless in a serious commercial programming environment.

Scanf/Fscanf/Sscanf

These routines are analogous to an encode function. Scanf accepts its input from the standard input device (stdin), normally the keyboard, whereas fscanf accepts its input from the input device file pointer specified, and sscanf accepts its input from a string located in memory. They are written in the following form:

```
erc = scanf(control, arg1, arg2, . . .)
erc = fscanf(device, control, arg1, arg2, . . .)
erc = sscanf(string, control, arg1, arg2, . . .)
```

Each function provides error return codes (erc) as follows:

−1 or EOF	Function has reached end-of-file
0	The next input character does not match the first specification in the control string
+n	The number (n) of successfully matched and assigned input items.

Printf/Fprintf/Sprintf

These routines are analogous to a decode function. Printf directs its output to the standard output device (stdout), normally the screen; whereas fprintf directs its output to the output device file pointer specified; and sprintf directs its output to a string located in memory. They are written in the following form:

```
erc = printf(control, arg1, arg2, . . .)
erc = fprintf(device, control, arg1, arg2, . . .)
erc = sprintf(string, control, arg1, arg2, . . .)
```

These functions provide no error return codes. Kernighan & Ritchie (p. 147) warn that " . . . you will get nonsense answers if there are not enough arguments or if they are the wrong type."

An input character string is processed from left to right until the specified field width or the first *white space* character is encountered. In C, white space characters are blanks, tabs, and new lines. You can suppress the actual assignment of a variable by specifying the asterisk (*) control character. When outputting a character string, you can specify field width, left or right justification, and (if appropriate) a number of decimal positions. In the case of a normal conversion, an *erc* = +*n* results (see ercs above).

Let's look more closely at how these format conversions are handled for the native C data types of char, int, float and double.

Char Restrictions

The general form of a character input string is as follows:

aaaaaaaaaa

where "a" is any non-white-space ASCII character. If the function encounters a white space character (Blank!), it generates an erc = +n message and terminates conversion at that point.

Int Restrictions

The general form of an integer (short or long) input string is as follows:

[−]ddddd

where [−] is an optional leading minus and "d" is any numeric character.

Since the C language does not have a unary plus (+) operator, you can only input an optional leading minus sign, not a plus sign. You can input only digits. If C encounters a non-digit, it generates an erc = 0 and terminates conversion at that point. If it encounters a white space character, it generates an erc = +n and terminates conversion at that point.

Overflow/underflow is not detected as an erc; rather, it causes wraparound. For example, if a positive 43520 is entered for a variable of type int (valid range −32767 to +32767), a value of −22016 results; similarly, if a −43520 is entered, a value of 22016 results. Similar problems exist for variables specified as short int and long int. Kernighan & Ritchie (p.185) simply states, "All existing implementations of C ignore integer overflows, ..."

Float and Double Restrictions

The general form of a float (long or double) input string is as follows:

```
[-]dddd[.]dddd
```

where [−] is an optional leading minus and "d" is any numeric character and [.] is an optional decimal point.

An alternate form for float, which is less useful in commercial applications, is

```
[-]dddd[.]dddE[+/-]xx
```

where E is required and stands for exponent, and an optional plus (+) or minus (−) sign may precede the xx which is a numeric character exponent value.

As with int, since C does not have a unary plus operator, you can input an optional preceding minus sign but not a plus sign. And again you can only input digits. If a nondigit is encountered, an erc = 0 is generated and conversion is terminated at that point. If a white space character is encountered, an erc = +n is generated and conversion is terminated at that point.

Overflow/underflow is not detected as an erc; but, unlike int, the results become unpredictable. However, unpredictable results occur only when a number outside the range of a float (valid from 8.43×10^{-37} to 3.37×10^{38}) is entered. This problem is highly unlikely and not of particular significance in a commercial programming environment. Similar problems exist for long float or double.

With floating point numbers however, rounding and loss of significant digits can pose a significant problem in commercial applications. During format conversion, rounding is not detected as an erc. All numbers within the allowable ranges for float and double are converted reliably only up to the number of significant digits associated with the type. No erc is detected however. Rounding-up can occur upon display of a floating point number at the least significant digit if the subsequent digit is greater than 5.

The treatment of all other floating point exceptions is unpredictable. Kernighan & Ritchie (p.185) states, " . . . treatment of division by 0, and all floating point exceptions, varies between machines, and is normally adjustable by a library function."

Other Format Conversion Functions

Additional *ATOx functions* (short for *A*SCII *TO x,* where x is a native C data type such as integer, long integer, or float) are available. The choice of ATOx functions available varies depending upon the specific C compiler and operating system under which it is implemented.

Generally speaking ATOx functions differ from scanf, fscanf, and sscanf in the following ways:

1. White space characters are ignored and do not serve to terminate format conversion. Conversion is terminated when all the digits are exhausted or a NULL delimeter is encountered.

2. Leading plus signs are allowable.

The overflow, underflow, rounding, and data exception problems discussed above remain, however, and the direct use of ATOx functions for the format conversion of logical data types is still very limited due to the syntax requirements of most commercial I/O fields.

Overcoming the Limitations

To better exemplify some of the problems of directly using standard C I/O, consider the following sample record structure for an employee record:

Field description	**Standard C I/O Problems**
Social security number	Typically this would be a character string, which is inefficient when compared to int. Or if it *is* int then it cannot allow delimiters to be entered (not numeric character) for readability.
Name, Last , First , MI	Always a problem with embedded spaces in last name (blank is a whitespace character) or with no middle initial.
Date-of-birth	Typically an inefficient character string representation requiring the user to conform to a rigid input format that is difficult to edit, and often using an abbreviate two-digit year which can be inaccurate for birth dates and causes sorting problems. Direct date math operations are impossible.
Telephone, home	Usually an inefficient character string representation requiring delimiting characters to be input, and causing sort problems if alphabetic telephone exchanges numbers are entered.
Shift start time	Usually an inefficient character string representation with no ability to perform math operations for processing timecards.
Salary, weekly	Often a double, which prevents the input or output of comma

	delimited fields and leading dollar signs for readability. Rounding problems with real numbers causes problems with accuracy to cents.
Percent bonus	User confusion often results when working with percentage fields because trailing percent signs can't be used as a helpful reminder. For example, you must type 15.00 not 0.15 to represent 15%.

Using these standard I/O routines without significant preprocessing of an input character string can have largely unpredictable results. The packaging of logical data types in the proposed encode and decode manner defined below will overcome these I/O conversion problems by providing the preprocessing that is necessary to accurately accept the common commercial field input formats and convert them into C native data types.

Encode Functionality Defined

In the structured data entry methodology that we are proposing, the encode interface definition for a logical data type is responsible for accepting an ASCII character string of input and producing the appropriate native representation in C for that logical data type. We call this operation *encoding.* Each logical data type encode function is designed to overcome the limiting I/O and format conversion features of the C programming language (scanf, fscanf, sscanf, and atox). Each encode function is intended to provide foolproof conversion of the fields of information common to commercial programs: character strings, dates, dollars, integers, reals, time, and telephone numbers. Helpful hints are also provided for handling such other common fields as IDnumbers, logicals, names, social security numbers, and zip codes. Conceptually it is intended that any encode function should accept any output character strings produced by its corresponding decode function.

All encode functions are of type int. A successful conversion will yield an encode function error return code (erc) of zero (or ERC_OK; see Appendix G: ldt.h). An unsuccessful conversion will yield a nonzero erc conforming to a desired project numbering scheme.

To promote sound software development practices, encode functions should be collected into a system-wide library and considered as standard development utilities.

Before developing the formal logical data type encode interface definition, it is important to understand what functional responsibilities we have attributed to it. The following list presents the design specifications for a logical data type encode function.

1. Standardizes field length checking (ldt.h: MAX_xxxx).
2. Converts case input format.
3. Enforces desired keyboard character-set syntax.
4. Performs character-set transformations.
5. Enforces logical data type format control.
6. Performs elementary logical data type editing.
7. Enforces mandatory/nonmandatory field specification (mflag).
8. Performs conversion or mapping to a native C data type, structure, or union, with range checking.
9. Establishes default value assignment.
10. Implements desired project error return codes (erc).

Decode Functionality Defined

In our methodology, the decode interface definition for a logical data type is responsible for accepting an encoded native C representation of a logical data type and producing an ASCII character string of output. We will speak of this operation as *decoding.* Each decode function is designed to overcome the limiting I/O and format conversion features of C (printf, fprintf, sprintf).

All decode functions are of type int. As with encode, successful conversion will yield a decode function error return code (erc) of zero (or ERC_OK) and an unsuccessful conversion will yield a nonzero erc conforming to a desired project numbering scheme.

Like encode functions, decode functions should also be collected into a system-wide library and considered as standard development utilities.

The following list presents the design specifications of a logical data type decode function.

1. Standardizes field length checking (ldt.h: MAX_xxxx).
2. Converts case output format.
3. Controls justification over destination output field (jflag).
4. Establishes default value assignment.
5. Implements desired project error return codes.

Data Validation Functionality Defined

The data validation interface definition is responsible for accepting an encoded logical data type and returning a function error return code of zero if the validation test is satisfied, or a nonzero erc conforming to a desired project numbering scheme if the validation test is not satisfied. All data validation functions are of type int.

Data validation is applied after encoding and it enforces additional constraints for a logical data type beyond those provided by the encode function itself. Typically, data validation checks for errors based on range checks, table lookups, interfield dependencies, calls to other dvxxxxyy functions, or additional data entry for override.

Data validation functions too should be collected into a system-wide library and considered as standard development utilities.

The following list presents the design specifications of a logical data type data validation function.

1. Performs any desired validation test(s), such as:
    - Range checks (e.g., only 1–10)
    - Fragmented limits (e.g., only 1–10 or 101–120)

- Restricted value checks (e.g., only Y or N)
- Relational checks (e.g., less than 0.00)
- Algorithm checking (e.g., check digits)
- Calls to other dvxxxxyy functions
- Checks that allow for additional data entry (e.g. confirmation or override)

2. Implements desired project error return codes.

A Close Look at C Data Types

It is important to understand how elementary C data types are physically allocated in storage (memory or disk). Although storage allocation characteristics vary depending on the machine, for this book we are using the values presented in Table 2.1, which should be representative of most 16-bit microprocessors today.

The corresponding value ranges and numbers of significant digits for the various combinations of C data types that may be specified are shown in Table 2.2.

Figure 2.2 depicts both the logical and physical bit patterning for all native C data types on the INTEL 8088/86/186 family of microprocessors. The logical bit ordering illustrates the allowable range of values associated with each data type, while the physical bit ordering is crucial for understanding file design and sorting matters.

	------	Short	Long
Char	8	n/a	n/a
Int	16	16	32
Float	32	n/a	64
Double	64	n/a	n/a

Table 2.1– Assumed bit allocations for C data types

Note that in the logical bit designation the rightmost bit is identified as bit-0 (see Appendix I: Powers of 2 Table). Bit-0 equals 2^0, bit-1 equals 2^1, etc. The bit positions correspond to the nth power of 2 and facilitate conversion of hexadecimal to binary to decimal and vice versa.

It is significant to note that the C programming language does not have a native character string data type. Neither are character string functions for assignment, comparison, concatenation etc. handled intrinsically. All character string manipulation must therefore be performed by explicitly issuing function calls. Character strings in C are defined to consist of a contiguous array of characters terminated by a trailing null (0x00 or \0) delimiting character. Later in the chapter we will fully explore the effects that character strings and all other native C data types have upon physical file design, key fields of indexed files, and collating sequences when sorting.

(INTEL 8088/86/186)

	Bits	Bytes	Value Range	Sig-Digits
Char	8	1	0 to 127 (x00 to x7F)	n/a
Short Int	16	2	−32,767 to +32,767	4–5
Int	16	2	−32,767 to +32,767	4–5
Unsigned Int	16	2	0 to 65,536	4–5
Long Int	32	4	−2,147,483,647 to +2,147,483,647	9–10
Unsigned Long Int	32	4	0 to 4,294,967,296	9–10
Float	32	4	$8.43 \times 10^{-37} \leqslant \lvert x \rvert \leqslant 3.37 \times 10^{38}$	6–7
Long Float	64	8	$4.19 \times 10^{-307} \leqslant \lvert x \rvert \leqslant 1.67 \times 10^{308}$	15–16
Double	64	8	$4.19 \times 10^{-307} \leqslant \lvert x \rvert \leqslant 1.67 \times 10^{308}$	15–16

Note: For complete details on value range computation for char, int, long int, float, and double see Appendix K.

***Table** 2.2– Value ranges and significant digits for C data types*

It is from the information provided in Table 2.2 and Figure 2.2 that nearly all variable type assignments, file design, and sorting decisions are made. We will refer back to these illustrations time and again when developing logical data types.

Your choices of elementary data types affect system design from the point of view of allowable ranges of values, significant

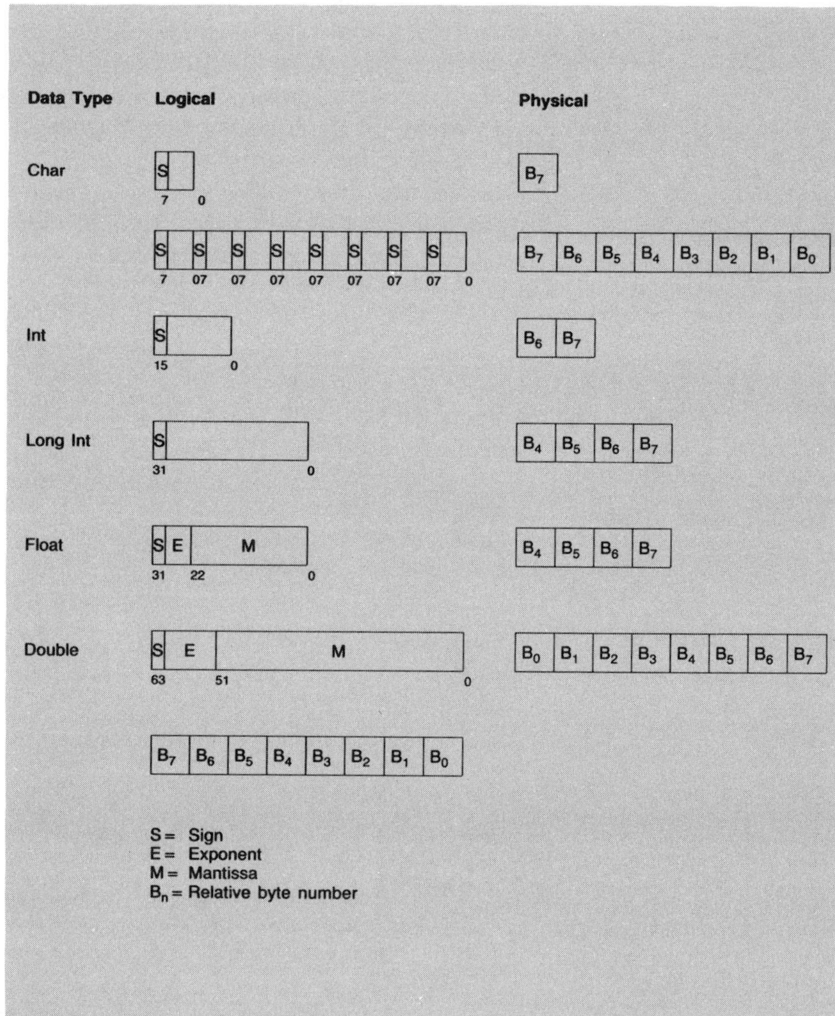

Figure 2.2– *Native C data type logical and physical bit/byte patterns*

digits preserved, boundary alignment, and memory and disk storage space allocated. In order to design a good system you must choose data types that match given size and space constraints in the least processing time.

File Design Issues

Every commercial software system involves permanent files of information. Because we don't want to duplicate the efforts of various file and database management products that are already commercially available and that extend the limited I/O facilities of the C language itself, we will focus instead on common design issues that are relevant when evaluating or selecting these products.

To do so, we will formulate a list of important features common to indexed file management products and examine their effects upon key fields of record structures. We then explore further the relationships between the native C data types that are used to represent logical data types, and their physical storage characteristics, which have a profound effect upon file design decisions. The next section highlights the important features of sorting products and explores similar effects upon collating sequences and thereby file design decisions.

File design in a commercial environment essentially consists of assembling fields of information into records to fulfill the need for permanent storage (master records) and temporary storage (transaction records). Although variable length record files and text files are used in a commercial environment, most microcomputer-based file and database management products only support fixed length record files since the overall trend in the industry seems to be leaning that way. The bulk of the discussion that follows centers, therefore, upon structured (fixed record length) files.

In the microcomputer world, disk storage space is generally limited, and processing speed is relatively slow. Under such constraints it is understandable that, if at all possible, sorting should be avoided. The scratch disk space and decreased response time associated with sorting are a premium price to pay. Files that can be accessed both sequentially and randomly while retaining overall system responsiveness are preferred. When evaluated against this set of criteria, indexed file access methods (also referred to as ISAM or B-TREE) are much more useful than text, RSAM (record sequential access method), and DAM (direct access method)—other common file access methods.

It is also important to understand the effects that C native data types have upon physical data storage and the ordering of fields in a record design. These effects can be more, or less, pronounced, depending upon the features supported by a given vendor's indexed file processing software product. It must be understood that all decisions regarding file design depend upon the features of a given vendor's product. Disregard of this fact can only result in a requirement for more disk and memory storage, and poorer overall system performance. Let's explore which product features we believe have the greatest impact on file design decisions.

Product Features that Affect File Design

Because of the distinct performance advantage of indexed file access methods, numerous products are available that provide interfaces which support C (see Appendix C). The price and included features vary considerably.

Beyond the obvious concerns of product capacity for number of records, record size, number of keys, and throughput, three critical areas of concern emerge that most directly impact file and record design:

1. Whether key definition supports segmented keys or all keys must be nonsegmented.
2. Whether key definition supports all C data types (i.e. char, int, long int, float, and double) in a transparent manner.
3. Whether segmented key definitions support segments of varying C data types or must the general type of binary be specified.

The key specification features of an indexed file management product control all field ordering decisions when constructing a file record definition. They can also affect decisions regarding choices of C data types used for keys because byte ordering characteristics vary by C data type. (Please refer again to Figure 2.2.) Because the process of key insertion (ordering) is essentially a sorting process, the physical ordering of bytes (hence bits) controls the ordering process. To achieve a desired key order for retrieval purposes, key specification and file design must work hand-in-hand.

To better understand the ramifications of the combinations of features that can result in the formulation of an indexed file management product, we will first center our discussion of keys on the two most significant features of segmented and non-segmented keys.

Segmented and Nonsegmented Keys

Nonsegmented keys must physically represent a contiguous, ascending range of bytes. In a record structure, such a key would be specified to span a range of byte offsets from byte(i) to byte(j), where (i) < = (j) within the record structure.

Segmented keys, on the other hand, can physically represent an unordered series of nonoverlapping, ascending ranges of bytes. In a record structure, such a key would be specified to respresent a series of ranges of byte offsets from byte(i) to byte(j), byte(m) to byte(n), where (i) < =(j) and (m) < = (n) within the record structure.

Key specifications generally have the following form:

KEY = (Type, Offset, Length, Order)

where the parameters are defined as follows:

Type	Native C or other data type such as char, int, float, etc.
Offset	Starting byte offset of key from byte 0 of the record description
Length	Length in bytes of the key
Order	Ascending or descending collating sequence

It should be understood that segmented keys provide for a key definition that is largely independent of the physical ordering of fields in a record structure. To accomplish a similar result with nonsegmented keys, file design must place the desired fields adjacent and logical (left to right) to reflect the desired series. Key definitions that span fields of a record are sometimes referred to as *composite keys.*

Figure 2.3 illustrates these major key differences.

Keys of Native C Data Type

The next crucial issue centers upon whether keys (segmented or nonsegmented) can be specified as being of a native C data type (char, char string, int, long int, float, double). Such a feature presumes that the actual physical ordering of bytes and sign-bit characteristics (see Figure 2.2) are known to the software product. Since the physical ordering of bytes varies depending upon machine architecture, the ability to accomodate such complete key specification is indicative of a software product that is highly machine dependent and possibly less portable. A binary type key is generally provided as a catch-all for those native data types that are not accomodated by available key specifications. A binary key is generally equated to an unsigned byte, i.e. simply treating bits 0 thru 7 as a binary unit.

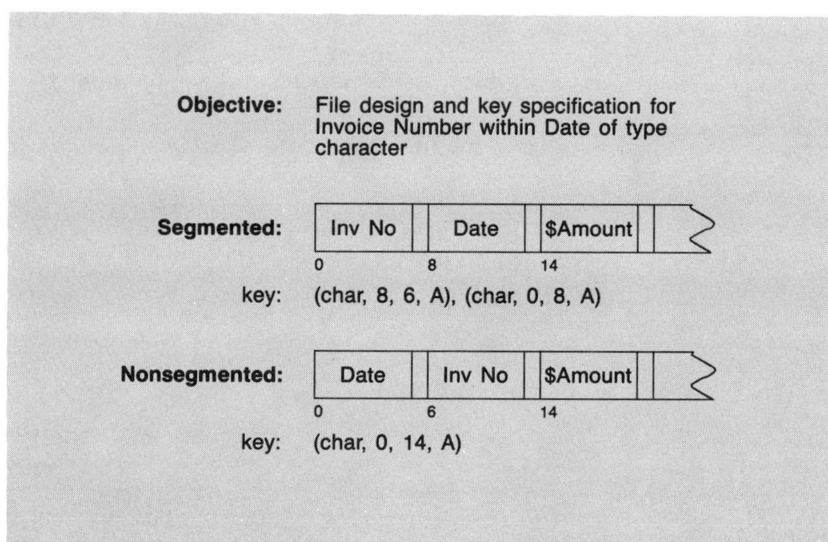

Figure 2.3– *Segmented vs. nonsegmented keys*

Segmented Keys of Mixed C Data Types

Whether key specification supports segmented keys of differing C data type again measures the flexibility of the package. The binary specification might have to be used for all components of a key specification that is composed of different C data types.

Depending upon the product, binary can imply simply a physical range of bytes, or it can imply a degree of transparency. For example, in the case of the 8088/86/186, binary can account for the fact that all physical data types except char are stored in memory from the lowest address (see Figure 2.2). Storage peculiarities such as this are largely a function of which microcomputer chip is being utilized. Whether or not this is accomodated is largely a function of which software product is chosen.

Depending upon what characteristics are attributed to binary for a given vendor's product, it might be necessary to alter the ordering of bytes associated with native C data types actually being written to a file record so that a desired key ordering results. There are four Rxy byte manipulation routines that can be helpful to overcome the limitations of a given software product (see Appendix H):

1. Function RI2: reverse int 2-bytes.
2. Function RI4: reverse long int 4-bytes.
3. Function RF4: reverse float 4-bytes.
4. Function RD8: reverse double 8-bytes.

These routines are constructed to mirror the physical data storage formats shown in Figure 2.2. Because these Rxy routines mirror the byte order of these physical data types, they can be called successively to toggle the physical representation. If a data file is written with Rxy variables, when these variables are read they should be *Rxy*ed to return them to a meaningful data representation for subsequent processing. Figure 2.4 highlights these possible binary key characteristics.

Boundary Alignment and Padding

Let's now examine native C data types, and highlight key design concerns that arise when they are utilized as fields in record structures. We will examine issues related to *boundary alignment,* automatic and intentional *padding* in record definitions. It would be helpful to refer to Table 2.2 and Figure 2.2.

It is important to understand how your compiler handles data type boundary alignment before beginning the physical file design of your application, or when interfacing with other software packages or computer systems that might handle boundary alignment differently.

These boundary alignment and padding concerns relate to any field definition, whether or not it is a key field. Fields that are not key fields are often still candidate fields for sorting purposes. When it comes to *pad* bytes, Kernighan & Ritchie (p.196) simply state, " . . . members of a structure begin on an addressing boundary appropriate to its type; therefore, there may be unnamed holes in a structure." We prefer to call the "unnamed holes" *pad* or *slack* bytes.

The "addressing boundary appropriate to its type" is dictated by the architecture of a given microprocessor and is often implemented by compiler vendors in a variety of ways.

The side-effects of pad bytes can be devastating. The sort order, for either key or sort fields resulting from the pad bytes, is often a source of surprise and embarrassment. Processing

Type	Logical	Physical	"Rxy" Physical
Char	B_7 B_6 B_5 B_4 B_3 B_2 B_1 B_0	B_7 B_6 B_5 B_4 B_3 B_2 B_1 B_0	N/A
Int	B_7 B_6	B_6 B_7	B_7 B_6
Long Int	B_7 B_6 B_5 B_4	B_4 B_5 B_6 B_7	B_7 B_6 B_5 B_4
Float	B_7 B_6 B_5 B_4	B_4 B_5 B_6 B_7	B_7 B_6 B_5 B_4
Double	B_7 B_6 B_5 B_4 B_3 B_2 B_1 B_0	B_0 B_1 B_2 B_3 B_4 B_5 B_6 B_7	B_7 B_6 B_5 B_4 B_3 B_2 B_1 B_0

***Figure** 2.4– Binary keys: logical vs. physical*

speed can be dramatically affected. The odd-address alignment of word-oriented data types can double the number of memory accesses per field.

The use of the sizeof operator returns the length of a C structure including pad bytes, but precisely where the pad bytes have been inserted to satisfy data type boundary alignment requirements is unclear. Pad bytes shift field byte offset values that are necessary for key and sort field specification. Kernighan & Ritchie perhaps aptly refer to them as "unnamed holes" because they are not initialized and therefore assume the value present at that particular memory location. We often have wondered why compilers do not allow software developers to control the value assigned to a pad byte.

For these reasons, and because most C documentation skirts this nagging problem, we will clarify *intentional* as opposed to *automatic* insertion of pad bytes in C structures and hence record definitions. This will hopefully remove the guesswork and surprise associated with specifying field byte-offset values for key and sort fields.

Because the rules for boundary alignment vary by compiler and microprocessor (and since we are concentrating upon the Lattice C Compiler and Intel 8088/86/186 chips), the material we present might not be directly applicable if you are using a different microprocessor; however, you will gain insight into how to approach this problem for your particular combination of C compiler and microprocessor.

The ramifications of boundary alignment (and hence pad bytes) for arithmetic data types (i.e. noncharacter) is derived from the data bus characteristics of a microprocessor. Most microprocessors today can be broadly categorized into three data bus groups:

Data Bus	Microprocessor
8-bit	Intel 8088
16-bit	Intel 8086/186, 80286
32-bit	Intel 80386

8-Bit Data Bus

The Lattice C compiler implementation for the 8088 microprocessor only enforces word (even address) alignment of pointers, structures and unions. Elements within a structure (record definition) for example are not padded for alignment by type within the structure. This is understandable because data can only be accessed one byte at a time with an 8-bit data bus; therefore there is no inherent advantage to automatic padding for boundary alignment.

If, however, software is being developed on an 8-bit data bus machine for ultimate use on a 16-bit or 32-bit data bus microprocessor, then for portability reasons the alignment characteristics of the target processor should dictate structure (record) design.

16-Bit Data Bus

The Lattice C compiler implementation for the 8086/186/286 microprocessor also only enforces word (16-bit, even address) alignment of pointers, structures and unions. Unlike the 8088 however, data from a structure is accessed two bytes at a time with a 16-bit data bus. Arithmetic data types should be word aligned to prevent an extra memory access from being made for odd-address aligned data types. Since odd-alignment can only be introduced by intermixing char data types of odd length, it would be a good design rule-of-thumb to make all char (or consecutive char) allocations even numbers to ensure that int, float, and double allocations begin on a even-address boundary. This process can be thought of as intentional padding versus the automatic padding enforced by the compiler itself. If, however, software is being developed on a 16-bit data bus machine for ultimate use on a 32-bit data bus microprocessor, for portability reasons the alignment characteristics of the target processor should dictate structure (record) design.

32-Bit Data Bus

Compiler implementations for the 80386 microprocessor (anticipated to be commercially available in mid-1987) will probably enforce word (32-bit, quad-word address) alignment of pointers, structures, and unions. Elements within a structure (record definition) will probably not be padded for alignment by type within the structure.

Unlike the 8088 and 8086 however, data from a structure is accessed four bytes at a time with a 32-bit data bus. Like the

16-bit data bus, arithmetic data types should also be quad-word aligned. Again, since odd-alignment can only be introduced by intermixing char data types of odd length, or short integers, you should make all char (or consecutive char) allocations even numbers, and group short ints to word multiples to ensure that int, float, and double allocations begin on a quad-word-address boundary. Figure 2.5 reiterates these data bus dependent boundary alignment rules-of-thumb.

Character Strings in Record Structures

The use of character strings in file records poses several pitfalls that can be easily overcome if the traps are clearly understood. All character strings are declared to be of a specific

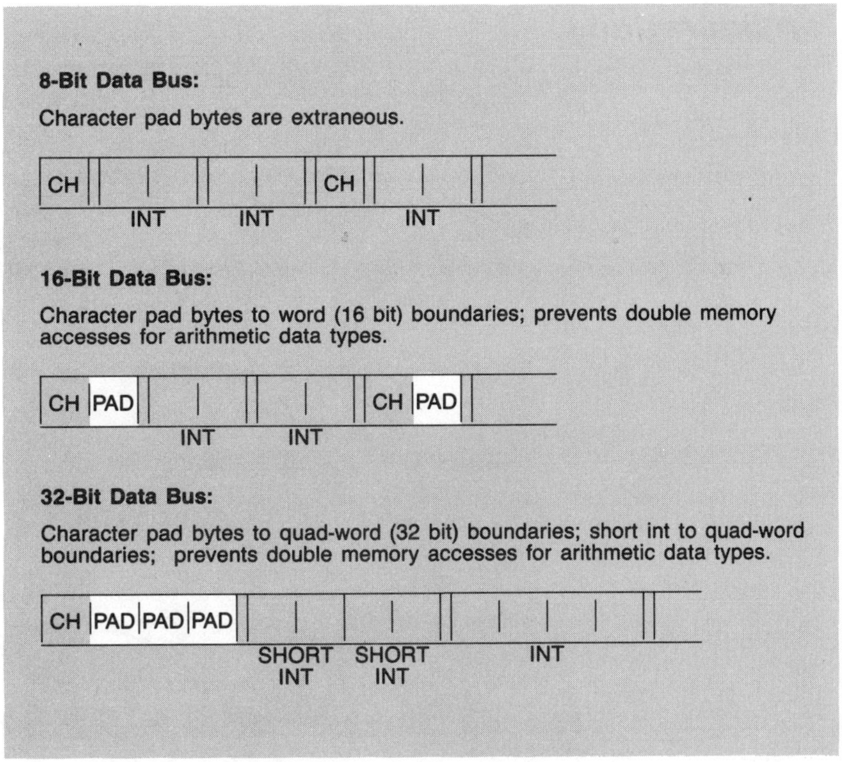

Figure 2.5– *Pad bytes—guidelines of sound practice*

physical size (including the NULL delimiter); however, the length of a string is generally thought of as the count of bytes until the NULL delimiter is encountered. Initialization, assignment, or reassignment of strings does not force all extraneous bytes (after the NULL delimiter) to any specific value. If character strings are to become a part of record structures, care must be taken to control the value assignment of the extraneous bytes; otherwise, subsequent use of the field for key or sorting purposes will create undesireable effects. (The function utcharcb.c is provided in Chapter 5 to control and overcome this problem.)

The effects of using this function on character strings are depicted in Figure 2.6.

Sorting Considerations

It is difficult to separate sorting package features from those of indexed file management products discussed above. We have done so to assist in the process of product evaluation

Static Char	Fname [10]	=	"ROBERT";										
	Fname	=	R	O	B	E	R	T	\0	?	?	?	
CTRL = 1:	Utcharcb (1, Fname, 10);												
	Fname	=	ƀ	ƀ	ƀ	ƀ	ƀ	ƀ	ƀ	ƀ	ƀ	\0	
CTRL = 2:	Utcharcb (2, Fname, 10);												
	Fname	=	R	O	B	E	R	T	\0	ƀ	ƀ	ƀ	
CTRL = 3:	Utcharcb (3, Fname, 10);												
	Fname	=	R	O	B	E	R	T	ƀ	ƀ	ƀ	\0	

Figure 2.6– *Character string padding*

and selection because commercial products are marketed separately for file management and sorting (see Appendix C).

There are many parallels between indexed file and sorting product features. Where we spoke of C data types supported as key field identifiers, we speak of C data types supported as *sort field identifiers.* The binary-type specification for sorting is analogous to that for indexed files. The number of allowable sort field specifications for sorting is analogous to the support of segmented keys for indexed files.

Sort packages also differ from indexed file products in that both fixed and variable length records are supported as well as noncompiler data types such as *packed decimal, zoned decimal,* and other proprietary file structures unique to some broadly used software products such as Btrieve, dBASE III and COBOL.

Obviously, when it comes to sorting, smaller record and sort field sizes directly relate to increased performance. This overall objective can be achieved by combining logical data type fields into record structures using the file and sort design guidelines developed in this book. Clearly, larger record and sort field sizes can only result when inefficient physical representations of common commercial fields of input are utilized or pad bytes are introduced unnecessarily.

Because sorting is such a fundamental component of all system design, the products that have survived and are commercially available are quite flexible and efficient. With sorting packages, sort performance is the crucial evaluation criteria.

The question to consider is how fast and efficiently (in terms of disk and memory space) can the desired sort be performed. Because overall performance is a function of many variables, to get an answer to this question you must often perform a benchmark test that closely simulates the target file for sorting in terms of record size, number of records, number and size of sort fields, and scratch space allocated, among other factors.

The matter of sort field specification similarly emerges as the critical file design issue, beyond the obvious performance and capacity ratings of a given product offering.

Remember that all decisions regarding file design depend upon the features of each vendor's sorting software product. Disregarding this fact can only result in a requirement for more disk scratch space and poorer overall sorting performance.

Structured Data Entry Programming

Now that we understand the inherent limitations of using standard C I/O, and have been introduced to the fundamental concepts of the proposed structured data entry methodology, let's take a look ahead at how easy it will be to write programs using these functions and the more advanced functions that will be presented in the chapters that follow.

We have developed a demonstration program called demo.c that implements the hypothetical employee record structure discussed earlier in this chapter in the section "Overcoming the Limitations." This program, shown in Listing 2.1, provides for the data entry and validation of such an employee record, and highlights the versatility of all seven logical data types implemented in Part 2 of this book.

```
/*
** file    : demo.c
** desc    : Structured Data Entry Methodology Demo
** link    : @demo.lnk,demo,nul,lcs
*/

#include "ldt.h"

main ()
{
        int dvcharyn(), dvdummy();

        static char mssn[]    = "???-??-????";
        static char mlname[]  = "???????????????";
        static char mfname[]  = "??????????";
        static char minit[]   = "?.";
        static char mbirth[]  = "??/??/???? [MM/DD/YYYY]";
        static char mhome[]   = "???/???-????";
        static char mshift[]  = "??:???";
        static char mpay[]    = "$????????? /WK";
        static char mbonus[]  = "?????%";
        static char mask[]    = "??????????????????????????????????";
        static char myn[]     = "?";

        char str[35], destr[35];
        char ynchar, ch;

        int i, erc, lpe, nuexit, maxstr;
        int smlname, smfname;

        struct record { INT  ssn;
                        CHAR lname[15];
                        CHAR fname[10];
                        CHAR init;
                        DATE birth;
                        TELE home;
                        TIME shift;
                        DOLR pay;
                        REAL bonus; } emp_rec;

        smlname = nondel(mlname);
        smfname = nondel(mfname);

        maxstr = sizeof(str)-1;
```

```
/*
** Initialize Video Display
*/

blanksc(1,1,MAX_ROW,MAX_COL);
setcrc(1,1);
putstr("STRUCTURED DATA ENTRY METHODOLOGY DEMO:",LR,"",DISP_F);
setcrc(3,17);
putstr("ENxxxx:",LR,"",DISP_F);
setcrc(3,45);
putstr("DExxxx:",LR,"",DISP_F);
setcrc(3,75);
putstr("xxxx:",LR,"",DISP_F);



/*
** Set System Convention for Error Logging/Screen Printing
** lpe == logprerr function argument: 10 = log/noprint; also
** make STDLOG entry for Start-of-Program Message.
*/

lpe = 10;
logwrite(5,"DEMO",0,"Enter DEMO");

/*
** Primary Data Entry Loop
*/

for (;;)
{
blanksc(4,1,MAX_ROW,MAX_COL);
setcrc(1,1);

/*
** Enter Social Security Number ===============================
*/

movcrc(4,-MAX_COL);
putstr("Enter-SSN      : ",LR,"",DISP_F);

erc = getint(str,maxstr,NO,mssn,LR,"",MAND_F,YES,&nuexit,
            &emp_rec.ssn,PHY_INT4,2,MAND_F,lpe,dvdummy);
if (lderc(erc) == 9) break;

movcrc(0,28);
putint(destr,MAX_INT4,&emp_rec.ssn,PHY_INT4,0,L_JUST,
       LR,mask,DISP_F,lpe);
movcrc(0,30);
putstr("[INT ]",LR,"",DISP_F);

/*
** Enter Last Name ============================================
*/

movcrc(2,-MAX_COL);
putstr("Last-Name      : ",LR,"",DISP_F);

erc = getchar(str,maxstr,NO,mlname,LR,"",MAND_F,NO,
            &nuexit,&emp_rec.lname,smlname,0,MAND_F,lpe,
            dvdummy);
if (lderc(erc) == 9) continue;



movcrc(0,28);
putchar(destr,smlname,&emp_rec.lname,smlname,1,NO_JUST,
       LR,mlname,DISP_F,lpe);
movcrc(0,30);
putstr("[CHAR]",LR,"",DISP_F);
```

```
/*
** Enter First Name ==========================================
*/

movcrc(2,-MAX_COL);
putstr("First-Name    : ",LR,"",DISP_F);

erc = getchar(str,maxstr,NO,mfname,LR,"",MAND_F,NO,
              &nuexit,&emp_rec.fname,smfname,0,MAND_F,lpe,
              dvdummy);
if (lderc(erc) == 9) continue;

movcrc(0,28);
putchar(destr,smfname,&emp_rec.fname,smfname,1,NO_JUST,
        LR,mfname,DISP_F,lpe);
movcrc(0,30);
putstr("[CHAR]",LR,"",DISP_F);

/*
** Enter Middle Initial ======================================
*/

movcrc(2,-MAX_COL);
putstr("Middle-Initial: ",LR,"",DISP_F);

erc = getchar(str,maxstr,NO,minit,LR,"",NMAN_F,NO,
              &nuexit,&emp_rec.init,1,10,NMAN_F,lpe,
              dvdummy);
if (lderc(erc) == 9) continue;

movcrc(0,28);
putchar(destr,1,&emp_rec.init,1,11,NO_JUST,
        LR,myn,DISP_F,lpe);
movcrc(0,30);
putstr("[CHAR]",LR,"",DISP_F);

/*
** Enter Date of Birth =======================================
*/

movcrc(2,-MAX_COL);
putstr("Date-of-Birth : ",LR,"",DISP_F);

erc = getdate(str,MAX_DATE,NO,mbirth,LR,"",MAND_F,NO,
              &nuexit,&emp_rec.birth,PHY_DATE,234,MAND_F,
              lpe,dvdummy);
if (lderc(erc) == 9) continue;
movcrc(0,28);
putdate(destr,MAX_DATE,&emp_rec.birth,PHY_DATE,6741,NO_JUST,
        LR,mask,DISP_F,lpe);
movcrc(0,30);
putstr("[DATE]",LR,"",DISP_F);

/*
** Enter Home Telephone ======================================
*/

movcrc(2,-MAX_COL);
putstr("Home-Telephone: ",LR,"",DISP_F);

erc = gettele(str,MAX_TELE,YES,mhome,LR,DEF_AC,NMAN_F,NO,
              &nuexit,&emp_rec.home,PHY_TELE,0,NMAN_F,lpe,
              dvdummy);
if (lderc(erc) == 9) continue;

movcrc(0,28);
puttele(destr,MAX_TELE,&emp_rec.home,PHY_TELE,0,NO_JUST,
        LR,mask,DISP_F,lpe);
movcrc(0,30);
putstr("[TELE]",LR,"",DISP_F);
```

```
/*
** Enter Shift Start Time ======================================
*/

movcrc(2,-MAX_COL);
putstr("Start-Time    : ",LR,"",DISP_F);

erc = gettime(str,MAX_TIME,YES,mshift,LR,"0530p",MAND_F,NO,
              &nuexit,&emp_rec.shift,PHY_TIME,0,MAND_F,lpe,
              dvdummy);
if (lderc(erc) == 9) continue;

movcrc(0,28);
puttime(destr,MAX_TIME,&emp_rec.shift,PHY_TIME,1,NO_JUST,
        LR,mask,DISP_F,lpe);
movcrc(0,30);
putstr("[TIME]",LR,"",DISP_F);

/*
** Enter Weekly Pay ============================================
*/

movcrc(2,-MAX_COL);
putstr("Weekly-Pay    : ",LR,"",DISP_F);

erc = getdolr(str,MAX_DOLR,NO,mpay,LR,"",MAND_F,NO,
              &nuexit,&emp_rec.pay,PHY_DOLR,2,MAND_F,
              lpe,dvdummy);

if (lderc(erc) == 9) continue;

movcrc(0,28);
putdolr(destr,MAX_DOLR,&emp_rec.pay,PHY_DOLR,22,L_JUST,
        LR,mask,DISP_F,lpe);
movcrc(0,30);
putstr("[DOLR]",LR,"",DISP_F);

/*
** Enter Percent Bonus =========================================
*/

movcrc(2,-MAX_COL);
putstr("Percent-Bonus : ",LR,"",DISP_F);

erc = getreal(str,MAX_REAL,NO,mbonus,LR,"",MAND_F,NO,
              &nuexit,&emp_rec.bonus,PHY_REAL,1,MAND_F,lpe,
              dvdummy);
if (lderc(erc) == 9) continue;

emp_rec.bonus.f4 = emp_rec.bonus.f4 / 100.;

movcrc(0,28);
putreal(destr,MAX_REAL,&emp_rec.bonus,PHY_REAL,14,L_JUST,
        LR,mask,DISP_F,lpe);
movcrc(0,30);
putstr("[REAL]",LR,"",DISP_F);

/*
** Recycle for another RECORD?
*/

setcrc(MAX_ROW-1,-MAX_COL);
putstr("Continue? [Yes/No] or [ESCape]: ",LR,"",DISP_F);

erc = getchar(str,maxstr,NO,myn,LR,"Y",MAND_F,NO,
              &nuexit,&ynchar,1,11,MAND_F,lpe,dvcharyn);

if ((lderc(erc) == 9) || (ynchar == 'N')) break;

}       /* Primary Loop End     */
```

```
        /*
        ** Program Cleanup/Exit
        */

        logwrite(6,"DEMO",0,"End DEMO");
        blanksc(1,1,MAX_ROW,MAX_COL);
        exit(0);
}
```

The record structure used is called the emp_rec and has the following members:

Field Description	Field Name	Logical Data Type
Social-Security-Number	ssn	integer
Last-Name	lname	character
First-Name	fname	character
Middle-Initial	init	character
Date-of-Birth	birth	date
Home-Telephone	home	telephone
Shift-Start-Time	shift	time
Weekly-Pay	pay	dollar
Percent-Bonus	bonus	real

The demo.c program first initializes the display by blanking the video, positioning the cursor, and displaying the heading. This is accomplished with the following source code:

```
.
.
blanksc(1,1,MAX_ROW,MAX_COL);
setcrc(1,1);
putstr("STRUCTURED DATA ENTRY METHODOLOGY DEMO:",
      LR," ",DISP_F);
      .
      .
```

Next, the Social-Security-Number (ssn) field is prompted for with the following code:

```
.
.
movcrc(4,-MAX_COL);
putstr("Enter-SSN            : ",LR," ",DISP_F);
erc = getint(str,maxstr,NO,mssn,LR," ",MAND_F,YES,&nuexit,
             &emp-rec.ssn,PHY_INT4,2,MAND_F,lpe,dvdummy);
if (lderc(erc) = = 9) break;
.
.
```

The single function call to getint performs all of the following activities:

1. It displays mask mssn in reverse video with no initial value under the enxxxx column.
2. It clears the keyboard type ahead buffer.
3. It performs all keyboard and cursor handling activities.
4. It requires that the field be completed (mandatory).
5. It accepts only positive integer values.
6. It encodes, with error control and recovery, the user character input without any upper- lowercase transformation into a long integer field called emp_rec.ssn.

If an alphabetic character is mistakenly entered, error processing begins with an audible beep and an appropriate error message display on the video error message line. Figure 2.7 demonstrates this point.

The message

"Encode Data Type Error ... ERC = 1041"

indicates that the user put an alphabetic character in a numeric field because the encode requirements for logical data type integers have not been met and the data entry attempt has failed. More user friendly messaging and supporting Help screens would typically be implemented in a completed software product to further clarify this message for the user. The user must correct the error with the various editing facilitites provided before proceeding or escape the field to restart the program and begin the entire data entry process over.

After successfully entering the ssn field, the program displays the emp_rec.ssn value under the dexxxx column without hyphenation and indicates the [int5] field logical data type under the xxxx column. Each field processed by the demo.c program is encoded and then decoded to emphasize the ease and flexibility of entering data and formatting output fields using the functions included in this book. If the user inadvertently hits the return key at the First-Name field before entering any characters, the program returns the message shown in Figure 2.8.

Since the First-Name field is mandatory (reverse video confirms this fact for the user), the field cannot be left blank. The user must correct the error before proceeding or escape the field to begin the entire data entry process over. You can see in Figure 2.9 that the Middle-Initial field is underlined, indicating

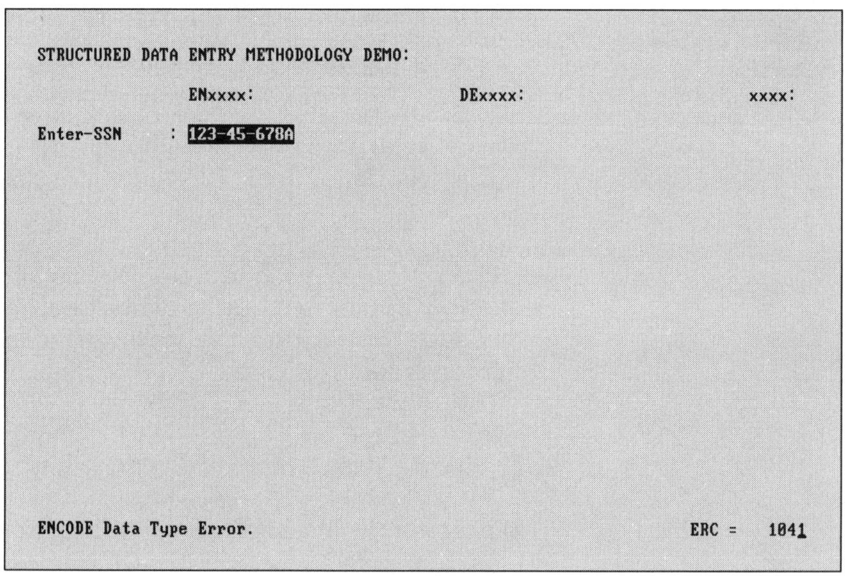

***Figure 2.7**– Encode data type error message*

that it is not mandatory, therefore it may be left blank. To skip it, the user simply hits the return key.

If the user enters an invalid date in the Date-of-Birth field, the error message shown in Figure 2.9 appears at the bottom of the screen.

This message indicates that 02/29/1941 is an error because 1941 was not a leap year. When the correct date entry is input (02/28/1941), it is decoded to read "FRI February 28, 1941" with the following code:

```
.
.
movcrc(0,28);
putdate(destr,MAX_DATE,&emp_rec.birth,PHY_DATE,
        6741,NO_JUST,LR,mask,DISP_F,lpe);
.
.
```

The single function call to putdate transforms the encoded date value emp_rec.birth to the desired date format by specifying the

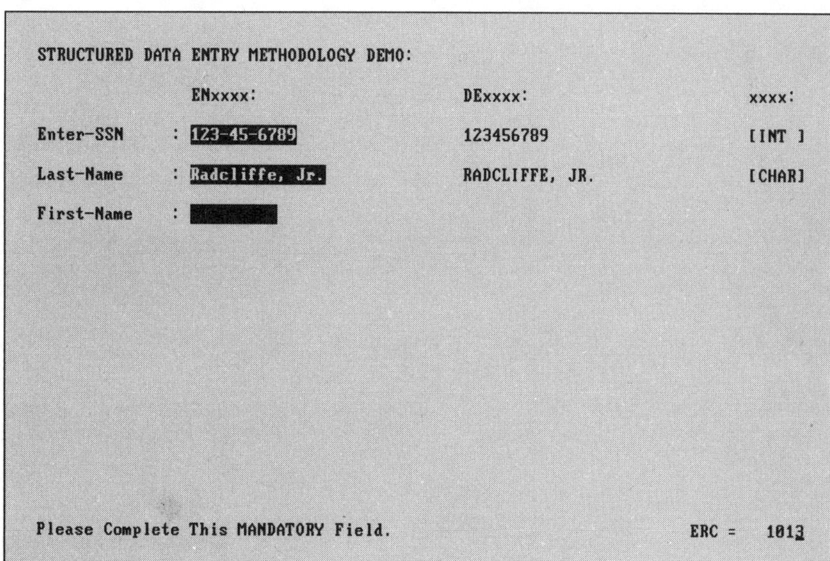

Figure 2.8– *Incompleted mandatory field message*

decode subtype of 6741. The subtype constructs a date description based upon its digit values: 6 = monthname, 7 = DAY dd, 4 = yyyy, and 1 = spaces as delimiters between date field components (the comma is automatically inserted for readability). Putdate also controls the field location, mask used, and video attributes desired for display.

After completing the optional Home-Telephone field, which accepts valid alphabetic telephone exchanges, and the Shift-Start-Time in am/pm format, which is subsequently displayed in military format, data entry continues. For this example, we displayed the Weekly-Pay field with a helpful mask that reinforces it as a dollar field and a weekly salary, not per annum. Then we entered a Percent-Bonus of +8.75%, which, when decoded, becomes a real number equaling 0.0875. These completed fields are shown in Figure 2.10.

Next the program asks whether the user wants to continue. If the user then enters an X, or anything other than Y or N, the data validation error shown in Figure 2.10 results.

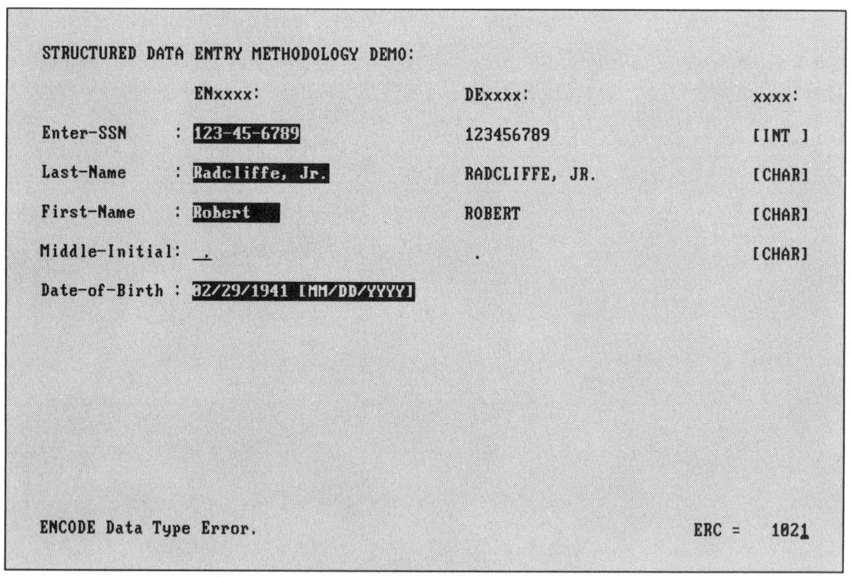

Figure 2.9– *Invalid date field error message*

The following source code handles the processing and validation of this Yes/No response field:

```
.
.
setcrc(MAX_ROW-1,-MAX_COL);
putstr("Continue? [Yes/No] or [ESCape]: ",LR," ",DISP_F);
erc = getchar(str,maxstr,1,NO,myn,LR,"Y",MAND_F,NO,&nuexit,
              &ynchar,1,11,MAND_F,lpe,dvcharyn);
if ((lderc(erc) == 9) || (lderc(erc) == 'N')) break;
.
.
```

The getchar function displays the mask myn with an initial value of Y, processes the field as a single character to variable ynchar, and applies the data validation function dvcharyn.c. Dvcharyn.c detects the error condition if an X is entered, instead of a Y or N. To satisfy this data entry field the user can either choose to continue with another employee record by

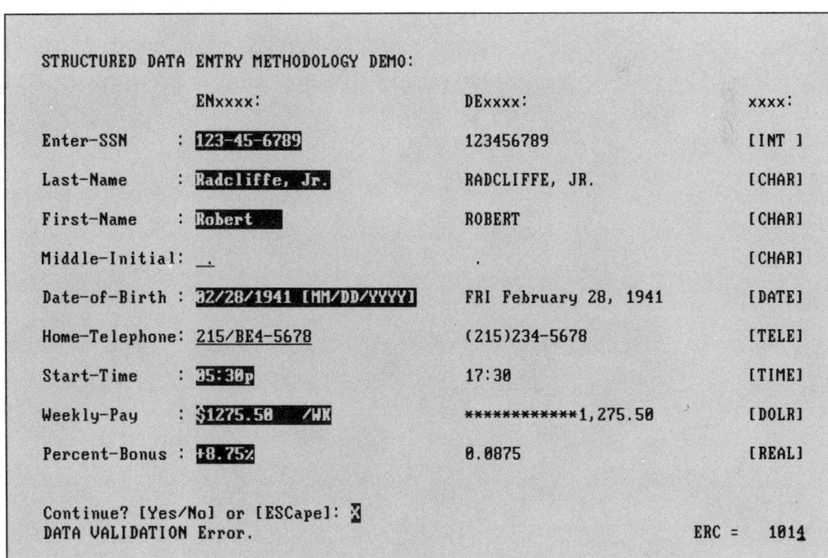

Figure 2.10– *Data entry screen with all fields completed*

entering Y, or end the data entry session by entering N or hitting the Escape key.

You can see how easy it will be to prepare a program once you have learned to use the structured techniques developed in this book. We will now examine further the remaining interface definitions for getstr/fgetstr, putstr/fputstr, getxxxx/fgetxxxx, and putxxxx/fputxxxx. With these concepts, and with the tools provided in Part 2 of this book, it will become clear how to overcome the I/O limitations of the C programming language and the power of this structured methodology will be at your fingertips.

Summary

In this chapter we have examined (from both a native C and logical data type point of view) the impact that data types have upon the three major components of any commercial software system: data entry, file processing, and sorting. The clear advantages of adopting the proposed structured data entry methodology over the alternative use of standard C I/O have been presented. In the following chapters we will further explore the development of this structured methodology and help you understand the additional benefits that will result from its use.

Encoding, Decoding and Validating Data

3

In this chapter we will present the standard interface definitions for the encode, decode, and data validation functions, which are fundamental to our structured data entry methodology. Each interface definition documents a function's type, name, and argument list, and as such only serves as a blueprint or specification. The actual C source code implementations of these functional specifications are unique to each logical data type and can be found in Part 2, Chapters 5 through 11.

Any "xxxx" logical data type implementation that you develop must adhere to these interface specifications if the overall structure of this approach is to be maintained.

Although we have restricted all source code development in this book to the C programming language, these interface definitions can be implemented in other programming languages as well.

This chapter also presents the source code for underlying functions that are supportive and common to all logical data type source code implementations of the standard interfaces presented for encoding, decoding, and validating.

Encode Interface Definition

Syntax

```
int enxxxx (pstrin, maxin, pphys, maxphys, ensubtype, mflag)
```

Explanation

int	Function type
en	Standard encode function prefix
xxxx	Standard logical data type identifier such as:

char: character field
date: date field
dolr: dollar field
int: integer field
real: real (floating point) field
tele: telephone number field
time: time field

pstrin	Pointer to a C character string (array of characters)
maxin	Integer count of the maximum allowable number of characters in pstrin exclusive of the NULL delimiter. Standardized global maximum values (which can be altered) are included in ldt.h (see Appendix G) and are of the form MAX_xxxx

pphys — Pointer to a C data storage type such as:

char
int
long int
float
long float
double

or:

structure of above data types
union of above data types

maxphys — Integer count of the maximum allowable size or string length of pphys in characters or bytes, as appropriate. Standardized global values (which can be altered) are included in ldt.h (see Appendix G) and of the form PHY_xxxx. Maxphys must be large enough to accept the results of the encode of pstrin or truncation will occur and a *Bad Encode Function Argument Error* will result.

ensubtype — Integer encoding subtype specification for conversion control that varies by logical data type (see Part 2).

mflag — Integer mandatory field flag as follows (defined in ldt.h):

0 = FALSE = NO = NMAN_F == non-mandatory field
1 = TRUE = YES = MAND_F == mandatory field

where *mandatory* implies that valid data must be entered (the field may not contain all spaces) and *nonmandatory* implies that the field may be skipped completely.

Assignment of Error Return Codes

1. Successful encode functions return the following status code:

   ```
   erc = ERC_OK;
   ```

   where ERC_OK is defined in ldt.h and is equivalent to zero (0).

2. Encode function errors due to data entry error return an erc computed as follows:

   ```
   erc = ERC_BASE + ENxxxx_E;
   ```

   where ERC_BASE is a base value for all ercs associated with structured data entry assigned in ldt.h. This value can be altered to shift the group of assigned ercs to avoid conflict with existing status and error codes of the operating system and applications software. ENxxxx_E represents the individual error return codes assigned to each logical data type encode function. These individual values are included in ldt.h.

3. An error caused by specifying a bad function argument value returns an erc computed as follows:

   ```
   erc = ERC_BASE + ENxxxx_E + 1;
   ```

4. An error caused by the failure to satisfy the mandatory condition specified returns an erc computed as follows:

   ```
   erc = ERC_BASE + ENxxxx_E + 2;
   ```

Typical Source Code Implementation for LDT Char

```
#include "ldt.h"

char pstrin[..], pphys[..];
int maxin, maxphys, ensubtype, mflag;
int erc;

erc = enchar (pstrin, maxin, pphys, maxphys, ensubtype, mflag);
```

With an ERC_BASE value of 1000 and an ENCHAR_E value of 11, the erc value returned in the example above would be 1011 if the Encode function failed for data entry reasons; 1012 if a bad function argument value was specified; 1013 if the mandatory field specification was not satisfied; and 0 if the function was successful.

Decode Interface Definition

Syntax

int dexxxx (pstrout, maxout, pphys, maxphys, desubtype, jflag)

Explanation

int	Function type
de	Standard decode function prefix
xxxx	Standard logical data type identifier
pstrout	Pointer to a C character string (array of characters)
maxout	Integer count of the maximum allowable number of characters in pstrout exclusive of the NULL delimiter. Standardized global maximum values (which can be altered) are included in ldt.h and are of the form MAX_xxxx. Maxout must be large enough to accept the results of the decode of pphys or truncation will occur and a *Bad Decode Function Argument Error* will result.

pphys	Pointer to a C data storage type
maxphys	Integer count of the maximum allowable size or string length of pphys in characters or bytes, as appropriate. Standardized global values (which can be altered) are included in ldt.h and are of the form PHY_xxxx.
desubtype	Integer decoding subtype specification for conversion control that varies by logical data type
jflag	Integer justification flag as follows (defined in ldt.h):

0 = NO_JUST == No justification
1 = L_JUST == Left-justify output field
2 = C_JUST == Center output field
3 = R_JUST == Right-justify output field

Assignment of Error Return Codes

1. Successful decode functions return the following status code:

   erc = ERC_OK;

   where ERC_OK is defined in ldt.h and is equivalent to zero (0).

2. An error caused by specifying a bad function argument value returns an erc computed as follows:

   erc = ERC_BASE + ENxxxx_E + 5;

   where ERC_BASE and ENxxxx_E have been defined for ENxxxx.

Typical Source Code Implementation for LDT Int

```
#include "ldt.h"

char  pstrout[..];
int   maxout, maxphys, desubtype, jflag;
INT   pphys;
int   erc;

erc = deint (pstrout, maxout, &pphys, maxphys, desubtype, jflag);
```

With an ERC_BASE value of 1000 and an ENCHAR_E value of 11, the erc value returned in the example above would be 1016 if a bad argument specification was made; it would be 0 if the function was successful.

Data Validation Interface Definition

Syntax

```
int dvxxxxyy (pphys, maxphys)
```

Explanation

int	Function type
dv	Standard data validation function prefix
xxxx	Standard logical data type identifier
yy	Sub-identifier of the data validation function for a given logical data type. *Note:* dvdummy is the system-wide, no-op data validation function.

pphys	Pointer to a previously encoded logical data type variable, struct or union.
maxphys	Integer count of the maximum allowable size of pphys in characters or bytes as appropriate. Standardized global values (which can be altered) are included in ldt.h and are of the form PHY_xxxx.

Assignment of Error Return Codes

1. Successful data validation functions return the following status code:

   ```
   erc = ERC_OK;
   ```

   where ERC_OK is defined in ldt.h and is equivalent to zero (0).

2. Unsuccessful data validation functions return an erc computed as follows:

   ```
   erc = ERC_BASE + ENxxxx_E + 3;
   ```

   where ERC_BASE and ENxxxx_E have been defined for ENxxxx.

3. A bad data validation function argument returns an erc computed as follows:

   ```
   erc = ERC_BASE + ENxxxx_E + 4;
   ```

Typical Source Code Implementation for Ldt Char

```
char  pphys[..];
int   maxphys;
int   erc;

erc = dvcharyn (pphys, maxphys);
```

With an ERC_BASE value of 1000 and an ENCHAR_E value of 11, the erc value returned in the example above would be 1014 if the data validation function failed; 1015 if a bad function argument was detected; and 0 if the function was successful.

EV (Encode and Validate) Interface Definition

Syntax

For convenience, the encode and validate interface combines the encode and data validation interfaces and is of the following form:

int evxxxx (pstrin, maxin, pphys, maxphys, ensubtype, mflag, dvxxxxyy)

Refer to Figure 2.1 to see where the evxxxx interface fits into the overall scheme.

Explanation

The ev parameters are identical to the encode parameters defined at the beginning of the chapter, with the following exceptions:

ev	Standard encode and validate function prefix
dv	Standard data validation function prefix
yy	Sub-identifier of this data validation function for a given logical data type. *Note:* dvdummy is the system-wide, no-op data validation function.

Assignment of Error Return Codes

1. Successful encode and validate functions return the following status code:

   ```
   erc = ERC_OK;
   ```

   where ERC_OK is defined in ldt.h and is equivalent to zero (0).

2. Unsuccessful encode and validate functions return an erc that is either

   - erc = unsuccessful result of encode function (see encode interface definition above).
   - erc = unsuccessful result of data validation function (see data validation interface above).

Typical Source Code Implementation for LDT Char

Using the prior example for encode and the system-wide no-op data validation function, a typical implementation would be

```
#include "ldt.h"

char   pstrin[..], pphys[..];
int    maxin, maxphys ensubtype, mflag;
int    erc;
int    dvdummy();

erc = evchar (pstrin, maxin, pphys, maxphys, ensubtype, mflag,
              dvdummy);
```

Within evchar, the function dvdummy would be declared as follows:

```
int (*dvxxxxyy)();
```

and referenced as follows:

```
erc = (*dvxxxxyy)(pphys,maxphys);
```

With an ERC_BASE value of 1000 and an ENCHAR_E value of 11, the erc value returned in the example above would be 1011 if the encode function failed for data entry reasons; 1012 if a bad encode function argument was specified; 1013 if the mandatory field condition was not satisfied; 1014 if the data validation function failed; 1015 if a bad data validation function argument was detected; and 0 if the function was successful.

Summary of Possible EN/DE/DV Error Return Codes

If the erc is not equal to ERC_OK (0), an error condition has been detected by one of the functions described above. The following error conditions can be inferred from the least significant (rightmost) digit of the erc (xxxxd) using the ENxxxx_E values proposed in Appendix G (ldt.h header file) and the formulas used to compute ercs using ERC_BASE and ENxxxx_E:

Digit D	Meaning
1	Encode Data Entry Error
2	Bad Encode Function Argument
3	No Data in Encode Mandatory Field
4	Data Validation Error
5	Bad Data Validation Function Argument
6	Bad Decode Function Argument
7	Reserved for Utxxxxyy Errors
8	Unused
9	Getstr Abnormal User Exit Escape

The source code listing of function lderc.c—which interrogates an erc and returns the least significant digit (D above), and can be used for "switching" purposes—is included in the section that follows.

Common Underlying Support Functions

The following functions are integral to the encode, decode, and validation functions developed for any logical data type. For convenience they have been grouped as follows: data validation, error handling, string processing, and test programs.

Data Validation

Dvdummy.c

Serves as the system-wide no-op data validation function for use with functions calls to evxxxx, getxxxx, and fgetxxxx when no data validation is to be performed, but a data validation function argument must be specified.

```
/* file    : dvdummy.c
** function: int dvdummy (pphys, maxphys)
** desc    : System-wide "no-op" data validation routine
** test pgm:
*/

#include "ldt.h"

        int dvdummy (pphys, maxphys)

        int *pphys, maxphys;
        {

        return(ERC_OK);

        }
```

Error Handling

Lderc.c

Computes least significant digit of an erc.

```
/*
** file    : lderc.c
** function: int lderc(erc);
** desc    : return the last (rightmost) digit of an erc.
** test pgm:
*/

#include "stdio.h"

        int lderc(erc)
        int erc;
        {
        int idig;
```

```
/*
** Always work with absolute value of ERC
** abs() function from "stdio.h"
*/

erc = abs(erc);

idig = erc % 10;

return(idig);
}
```

Logreset.c

Initializes the stdlog error handling and message file discussed in Chapter 13.

```
/* file    : logreset.c
** function: int logreset()
** desc    : reset (empty) the stdlog file
** test pgm: Any qaxxxx.c test program
*/

#include "dos.h"
#include "stdio.h"
#include "iosl.h"
#include "ldt.h"

        int logreset()
        {

        FILE *fp3;

        /*
        ** By reopening file "stdlog" in "w"rite mode
        ** any contents of the file are destroyed. The
        ** subsequent reopening in "a"ppend puts the
        ** "stdlog" file in its original mode.
        */

        fp3 = freopen("stdlog","w",stdlog);
        fp3 = freopen("stdlog","a",stdlog);

        if (fp3 == NULL)
                {
                fprintf(stderr,"Can't reopen STDLOG file\n");
                exit(1);
                }

        return(ERC_OK);

        }
```

- Note the issue of freopen in write mode to clear stdlog, and the subsequent freopen in append mode to allow all subsequent entries written to stdlog to be appended to the end.

- Reference to fp3 is a file pointer to stdlog as assigned in _main and described in the header file stdio.h (see Appendix G). File pointers fp0, fp1, and fp2 are automatically assigned to stdin, stdout, and stderr respectively.

Logwrite.c

Writes a standard record to the stdlog error handling and message file discussed in Chapter 13.

```
/* file    : logwrite.c
** function: int logwrite (mesgtype, pgmid, erc, note)
** desc    : stdlog message writing function
** test pgm: Any qaxxxx.c test program
*/

#include "stdio.h"
#include "ldt.h"

        int logwrite ( mesgtype, pgmid, erc, note)
        int mesgtype, erc;
        char *pgmid, *note;
        {

        char cdate[9], ctime[7], cmesg[9], cpgmid[9], cerc[7];
        DATE sysdate, utdatesi();
        TIME systime, uttimesi();
        int slgth;

        /*
        ** Text vs. Binary Write mode to STDLOG in effect?
        */

        extern int _fmode;

        /*
        ** get SYSDATE
        */

        sysdate = utdatesi();
        deint(cdate,8,&sysdate,PHY_INT4,0,L_JUST);

        /*
        ** get SYSTIME
        */

        systime = uttimesi();
        detime(ctime,6,&systime,PHY_TIME,0,R_JUST);

        /*
        ** setup Message Type
        */

        switch (mesgtype)
        {
                case 1: strcpy(cmesg,"ERROR   ");
                        break;
                case 2: strcpy(cmesg,"WARNING ");
                        break;
                case 3: strcpy(cmesg,"SECURITY");
                        break;
                case 4: strcpy(cmesg,"INSTALL ");
                        break;
```

```
        case 5: strcpy(cmesg,"ENTRY   ");
                break;
        case 6: strcpy(cmesg,"EXIT    ");
                break;
        case 7: strcpy(cmesg,"GENERAL ");
                break;
       default: strcpy(cmesg,"MISC    ");
                break;
}

/*
** setup ERC
*/

deint(cerc,6,&erc,PHY_INT,1,R_JUST);

/*
** setup Program Identifier
*/

slgth = strlen(pgmid);
if (slgth > 8) pgmid[9] = C_NUL;

strcpy(cpgmid, pgmid);

utcharcb(3,cpgmid,9);

/*
** setup for STDLOG entry
*/

fprintf(stdlog,"%s%s%s%s%s%s",
        cdate, ctime, cmesg, cerc, cpgmid, note);

if ( _fmode == 0x00 ) fprintf(stdlog,"\n");
else fprintf(stdlog,"\r\n");

return(ERC_OK);
}
```

- Sysdate is acquired with function utdatesi(). Function deint is used in a stand-alone basis for converting sysdate from internal date format to a character string.
- Systime is acquired with function uttimesi(). Function detime is used on a standalone basis for converting systime from internal time format to a character string.
- The mesgtype function argument designates which message type is written to the stdlog file. These case entries can be easily modified to meet your specific requirements.
- Function deint is used on a standalone basis to convert function argument erc from an integer to a character string.
- Note that if function argument pgmid is greater than the eight characters allocated in the stdlog file structure,

pgmid is truncated. If pgmid is less than eight characters, the trailing character positions up to length 8 are converted to blank characters by the function utcharcb(3,cpgmid,9) to facilitate future sorting for reporting purposes.

- Note how the stdlog entry is written using the standard C I/O function fprintf with function argument file pointer stdlog.
- Note that each record written to stdlog is CR/LF (carriage return/line feed) delimited to facilitate sorting. The external reference extern int _fmode allows logwrite to determine whether text files written using standard I/O are in standard ASCII (_fmode == 0x00) or binary (_fmode != 0x00). Knowing _fmode then controls whether a CR/LF [\r\n] must be emitted or simply a LF [\n]. The default use of standard C I/O sets _fmode == 0x00 and automatically expands a LF [0x0A] to a CR/LF sequence.

Mesende.c

Performs all standard encode/decode dialog for errors and warnings with the user, and all optional error logging and screen printing.

```
/* file     : mesende.c
** function: int mesende(erc, pflag)
** desc     : standard messaging for encode/decode functions.
**          : uses console row MAX_ROW.
**          : "pflag" = 00 : NO LOG Entry; NO Screen Print.
**          :         = 01 : NO LOG Entry; Screen Print.
**          :         = 10 : LOG Entry   ; NO Screen Print.
**          :         = 11 : LOG Entry   ; Screen Print.
** test pgm: Any qaxxxx.x test program
*/

#include "ldt.h"

        int mesende(erc, pflag)
        int erc, pflag;
        {

        int irow, icol, digit2, digit1;
        char str[7], mes[40];

        digit2 = pflag / 10;
        if ( (digit2 < 0) || (digit2 > 1) ) digit2 = 0;
```

```
digit1 = pflag % 10;
if ( (digit1 < 0) || (digit1 > 1) ) digit1 = 0;

getcrc(&irow,&icol);
setcrc(MAX_ROW,1);
blanksc(MAX_ROW,1,MAX_ROW,MAX_COL);

switch (lderc(erc))
{
case 0: setcrc(irow,icol);
        return(ERC_OK);
case 1: strcpy(mes,"ENCODE Data Type Error.");
        break;
case 2: strcpy(mes,"Bad ENCODE Function Argument.");
        break;
case 3: strcpy(mes,"Please Complete This MANDATORY Field.");
        break;
case 4: strcpy(mes,"DATA VALIDATION Error.");
        break;
case 5: strcpy(mes,"Bad DATA VALIDATION Function Argument.");
        break;
case 6: strcpy(mes,"Bad DECODE Function Argument.");
        break;
case 7: strcpy(mes,"ENCODE/DECODE Utility Function Error.");
        break;

default: strcpy(mes,"Invalid/Undefined ERC.");
         break;
}

putstr(mes,LR,"",DISP_F);
deint(str, MAX_INT, &erc, PHY_INT, 0, NO_JUST);
movcrc(0,MAX_COL);
movcrc(0,-11);
putstr("ERC = ",LR,"",DISP_F);
putstr(str,LR,"",DISP_F);

beep(1);
delay(2);
beep(1);

if ( (digit1 == TRUE) && (lderc(erc) != 3) ) pscreen();
else delay(5);

if ( (digit2 == TRUE) && (lderc(erc) != 3) )
     logwrite(1,"EN/DE",erc,"");

blanksc(MAX_ROW,1,MAX_ROW,MAX_COL);
setcrc(irow,icol);

return(ERC_OK);
}
```

- This primary error processing function is designed to use MAX_ROW (= 25) of the video display for messaging. Examples of the use of this function can be found by examining or executing any qaxxxx function in this book.
- It would be preferable in a commercial application system to provide additional video space for error messaging and recovery other than a single video row. It is important to have that allocated space be uniform

throughout a system so the user is conditioned to expect error messaging and recovery to occur visually in the same location.

- If an error condition is detected, automatic screen printing provides a helpful way for users to capture errors for review by software developers. Without automatic screen printing, it is often difficult to capture exactly what was done by the user to cause the error. Additionally, the user can make written comments on the printed screen display for review at a later time.
- Note the use of the "beep" (the audible speaker). It is best to standardize the audible alarm (number of beeps and duration) throughout a system so that users are not confused by an array of different audibles.

String Processing

Cjust.c

Center justifies the text of a character string.

```
/* file    : cjust.c
** function: int cjust(ch,string)
** desc    : center the text in "string" surrounded by "ch"
** test pgm: tjust.c
*/

#include "ldt.h"

        int cjust(ch,s)
        char ch, *s;
        {
        int nlb, ntb, slgth;

        /*
        ** nlb = number leading "ch"
        ** ntb = number trailing "ch"
        ** slgth = string length
        */

        char *bads = s;
        char *sads, *lads;

        /*
        ** *bads = beginning string address
        ** *sads = starting (first non-"ch") address
        ** *lads = last string address
        */
```

```
/*
** right justify string first
*/

rjust(ch,s);

slgth = snlbntb(ch,&nlb,&ntb,s);

if (( slgth == 0 ) || ( nlb <= 1 ) || ( nlb == slgth ))
return(ERC_OK);

/*
** left justify string at starting address
** [s + (nlb/2)] rather than [s]
*/

ljust(ch,s + (nlb/2));

return(ERC_OK);

}
```

- Note that this function can be used to center any character string within bounding characters other than spaces.
- The technique used right justifies the string surrounded by character first, finds the number of leading characters, then left justifies the string to a centering offset from the starting address of string.

Ljust.c

Left justifies the text of a character string.

```
/* file    : ljust.c
** function: int ljust(ch,string)
** desc    : remove left "ch" of the text in "string"
** test pgm: tjust.c
*/

#include "ldt.h"

        int ljust(ch,s)
        char ch, *s;
        {

        int nlb, ntb, slgth;

        /*
        ** nlb = number of leading "ch"
        ** ntb = number trailing "ch"
        ** slgth = string length
        */

        char *bads = s;
        char *sads, *lads;
```

```
/*
** *bads = string beginning address
** *sads = address of first non-"ch" character
** *lads = string last address
*/

slgth = snlbntb(ch,&nlb,&ntb,s);

if (( slgth == 0 ) || ( nlb == 0 ) || ( nlb == slgth))
return(ERC_OK);

/*
** setup address limits for looping
*/

sads = bads + nlb;
lads = bads + slgth - 1;

while ( sads <= lads )
{
*bads = *sads;
bads++;
*sads = C_BLANK;
sads++;
}

return(ERC_OK);

}
```

- Note that this function can be used to left justify any character string within bounding characters other than spaces.

Rjust.c

Right justifies the text of a character string.

```
/* file    : rjust.c
** function: int rjust(ch,string)
** desc    : remove the right "ch" of the text in "string"
** test pgm: tjust.c
*/

#include "ldt.h"

        int rjust(ch,s)
        char ch, *s;
        {
        int nlb, ntb, slgth;

        /*
        ** nlb = number leading "ch"
        ** ntb = number trailing "ch"
        ** slgth = string length
        */

        char *bads, *sads;
        char *lads = s;
```

```
/*
** *bads = beginning string address
** *sads = address of first non-"ch" character
** *lads = last string address
*/

slgth = snlbntb(ch,&nlb,&ntb,s);

if (( slgth == 0 ) || ( ntb == 0 )) return(ERC_OK);

/*
** setup address limits for looping
*/

bads = lads + slgth - 1;
sads = bads - ntb;

while ( sads >= lads )
{
*bads = *sads;
bads--;
*sads = C_BLANK;
sads--;
}

return(ERC_OK);

}
```

- Note that this function can be used to right justify any character string within bounding characters other than spaces.

Snlbntb.c

Gets the length, number of leading characters, and number of trailing characters for a character string.

```
/* file    : snlbntb.c
** function: int snlbntb(ch,&nlb,&ntb,s)
** desc    : calculate the "nlb" number of leading "ch"aracters
**           "ntb" number of trailing "ch" and return the
**           size (length) of "s" string.
** test pgm: tjust.c
*/

#include "ldt.h"

        int snlbntb(ch,nlb,ntb,s)
        int *nlb, *ntb;
        char ch, *s;
        {
        int nlbflag, ntbflag;
        int slgth;
        char *p = s;

        nlbflag = TRUE;
        *nlb = 0;
        ntbflag = TRUE;
        *ntb = 0;
```

```
while ( *p != C_NUL)
{
if ((nlbflag == TRUE) && ( *p == ch ))
(*nlb)++;
else
nlbflag = FALSE;
p++;
}
slgth = (p-s);

if (*nlb == slgth) return(slgth);

p--;

while ( p != s )
{
if ((ntbflag == TRUE) && ( *p == ch ))
(*ntb)++;
else
{       ntbflag = FALSE;
        break;
}
p--;
}
return (slgth);
}
```

Test Programs

Tjust.c

Tests all string justification functions.

```
/*
** file   : tjust.c
** desc   : test program for just.c, cjust.c, ljust.c and rjust.c
** link   : @tjust.lnk,tjust,nul,lcs
*/

#include "ldt.h"

main ()
{
        int strsize;
        static char string[79] = "    SYBEX BOOKS         ";

        strsize = sizeof(string);
        printf("\tDeclared size  : %d\n\n", strsize);

        printf("\tOriginal string: ?%s?\n",string);

        ljust(C_BLANK,string);
        printf("\tLjust    string: ?%s?\n",string);

        rjust(C_BLANK,string);
        printf("\tRjust    string: ?%s?\n",string);

        cjust(C_BLANK,string);
        printf("\tCjust    string: ?%s?\n",string);

        exit(0);
}
```

- Note that the sizeof function returns the size of a string or any data type exactly as declared in the function where it is declared.
- We use *sizeof(string) − 1* to satisfy the function arguments: maxin and maxout.
- Be careful when using sizeof on strings that have been passed as pointers to a function and not explicitly declared within a function. Strings are always passed as pointers. When sizeof is applied to a pointer, a value of 2 is returned if using the s memory model of Lattice C.
- See Figure 3.1 for an example of tjust output.

```
Declared size  : 79

Original string: ?    SYBEX BOOKS          ?
Ljust    string: ?SYBEX BOOKS              ?
Rjust    string: ?               SYBEX BOOKS?
Cjust    string: ?       SYBEX BOOKS       ?
```

Figure 3.1– *Tjust sample output*

Field Data Entry Processing

4

The goal of the structured data entry methodology presented thus far has been to reduce all user dialog to accepting character strings of input and then responding to those strings with prompts, warnings, and error messages—the responses being based on the encode and data validation of the strings.

To fully achieve this goal, this chapter develops the design criteria and source code for the getstr and putstr functions that are used for all direct user interaction throughout this book. By isolating these routines you can promote a high degree of consistency for user dialog, while separating all other application source code from the responsibilities of servicing direct user interaction. This separation would also enable you to replace getstr and putstr with equivalent functions if necessary, while still using the encode, decode, data validation, and evxxxx functions we have presented.

We will first examine the functionality of the getstr routine. Getstr is the first line of defense in error control. Its primary responsibility is to provide the user with a standard way to input a character string, accepting the string only if it satisfies the minimum data entry requirements for the particular field of input. None of getstr's responsibilities should overlap with those of the encode or data validation routines that go on to process the character string of input after it is acquired by getstr.

Keyboard and Codes

Input comes from the keyboard, so our first considerations are the use of the standard IBM keyboard for the implementation of getstr under PC-DOS, the processing of ASCII characters and the PC-DOS extended character set using scan codes.

Keyboard Handling (ASCII and Scan Codes)

The programmer's first task is to decide which keyboard characters and scan codes will be allowable as input to getstr. Since getstr protects against the whim of the user, when an unacceptable keystroke sequence is made it should beep audibly, immediately clear the type-ahead buffer, and recycle for an additional character read.

Getstr is the first filter that reduces the set of possible keystroke combinations from a user to an acceptable subset. This reduced set of keystroke sequences is composed of the set of acceptable ASCII characters, plus the set of allowable getstr control characters, plus the set of PC-DOS system mandatory control characters.

PC-DOS and the IBM Keyboard

This book assumes you are using an IBM PC and PC-DOS environment, although the keyboard-handling concepts developed are readily applicable to other keyboard and operating system environments. Figure 4.1 depicts the standard IBM PC keyboard.

The PC-DOS BIOS interprets approximately 221 uniquely identifiable codes from the IBM standard keyboard, which has only 83 keys. Each key produces a different code when pressed, and additional codes are generated when keys are pressed along with the Shift, Alt, Ctrl, and (in some cases) Num Lock keys. Since there are more keyboard codes than the 128 combinations possible with the standard ASCII character set, and because not all desired key meanings are covered by the ASCII character set definition, an extended range of codes called *scan codes* are utilized. Refer to your PC-DOS Technical Reference Manual ("IBM keyboard," and "Keyboard Encoding and Usage") for additional information about these matters.

Acceptable ASCII Characters

From the possible range of ASCII characters (see Appendix C), it would seem prudent to limit character input to a hexadecimal range of 0x20 through 0x7E. There may exist, in certain instances, strong arguments for eliminating other characters at the getstr level for software interface reasons. For example, you could exclude two characters in the range of 0x20 to 0x7E in order to reserve them to support MailMerge features of certain word processing systems for use as record and field delimiters; thus preventing such data entry characters

Figure 4.1 *– The IBM PC keyboard*

from mistakenly being interpreted as record or field delimiters. For this book however, we will accept all ASCII characters 0x20 through 0x7E.

Allowable Getstr Control Characters

Certain character input by the user performs cursor and field control functions. These include the following from the set of ASCII character hexadecimal values:

0x08 = Backspace (destructive)

0x09 = Forward horizontal tab (field exit)

0x0D = Carriage return (field exit)

0x18 = Cancel (Ctrl-X: clear entire field)

0x1B = Escape (abnormal field exit)

Also included in this category are a series of extended keyboard or scan code decimal values:

15 = Back horizontal tab (field exit)

59 = F1 (help)

60 = F2 (copy screen to printer)

71 = Home (move cursor to first field character)

72 = ↑ (field exit)

73 = Page up (field/screen exit)

75 = ← (move cursor left one character)

77 = → (move cursor right one character)

79 = End (move cursor to last field character)

80 = ↓ (field exit)

81 = Page down (field/screen exit)

83 = Delete (character at cursor position and shift field left)

117 = Ctrl-End (clear field from cursor to EOF)

PC-DOS System Mandatory Control Characters

Certain keystroke sequences must be retained to maintain compatibility with the PC-DOS operating system interrupt handling conventions:

Alt-Ctrl-Del: System reboot (no reset button exists)

Ctrl-NumLock: Keyboard read pause until next keystroke

Ctrl-PrtSc: Toggle Shift-PrtSc

Shift-PrtSc: Screen print

Ctrl-Break: Disabled in _main (see Appendix F)

Video Coordinate System Standards

All the function interface definitions in this book assume a video display coordinate system with the origin at

[row = 1, col = 1] : top-left-corner

and limited at

[row = MAX_ROW, col = MAX_COL]

as defined in ldt.h. All software developed using these interfaces should therefore conform to this convention to avoid problems with cursor control and location.

Because the PC-DOS BIOS considers the video coordinate origin to be at

[row = 0, col = 0] : top-left-corner

we adjust for this in all video functions included in this book.

Video Error Messaging

We have reserved [row = MAX_ROW = 25 : bottom line] for all error message display. In actual practice, it is probably better to allot two or three lines of the video display for error messages and recovery processing. A standard should be established at the start of every software development project. Error messaging and recovery processing should be handled consistently throughout an entire software system so as not to confuse the user.

The mesende.c and mesgsps.c functions determine whether an error message is displayed at MAX_ROW, an error log entry is made to stdlog, or a screen print is automatically generated when a user data entry error is detected. The error logging and screen printing features are optional, but are often advantageous if part of an overall error control and recovery design scheme.

The Mask Concept

The concept of using *masks* is integral to the I/O functions developed for this book. The formulators of this concept had two key objectives in mind:

1. To make the formatting of many commercial fields of input simpler (inserting character separators such as "-", "/", and " ").

2. To minimize transcription errors and eye fatigue when working with such fields visually by breaking large ID numbers into smaller groups of characters (see: Galitz "Human Factors in Office Automation").

A mask is simply a character string that consists of two classes of positions: nondelimiters and delimiters. The question mark character (**?**) is the only nondelimiter character. All other characters are delimiters and have unalterable character positions displayed as part of a field of input or output.

Every user I/O field of input is displayed with a mask and a video display attribute (see ldt.h: V_PSWD, V_MAND, V_NMAN, V_DISP). The mask defines the field width, and controls which character positions the user can enter or modify. The video attributes visually reinforce a systemwide convention of field type (password, mandatory, nonmandatory, display only), and highlight the field width.

Initial values (init) can be specified for display in a mask under ginitflg control: LR = left justified in mask; RL = right justified in mask. The characters of the init value character string are only displayed in mask nondelimiter positions.

When getstr/fgetstr acquires a user field of input from the video display, it does so under the control of gmaskflg which, if FALSE, accepts characters of input only from nondelimiter mask positions; or, if TRUE, accepts characters of input from both delimiter and nondelimiter positions.

The mask is a very powerful and flexible tool. By allowing you to formulate masks with delimiters and nondelimiters, display initial character strings in the mask either left or right justified, and either include or exclude delimiter character positions with the gmaskflg acquisition control, the mask mechanism satisfies a myriad of situations common to many commercial application programs.

In our programs the mask concept is employed for all data acquisition and display functions. Coupled with the powerful LDT encode and decode features, the mask concept makes the structured data entry methodology even more useful.

The overall inadequacies of using standard C I/O become particularly clear when measured against the features and capabilities that comprise the getstr/putstr, encode/decode, and getxxxx/putxxxx functions whose counterparts are the standard C scanf/fscanf/sscanf/printf/fprintf/sprintf and atox functions.

Getstr/Fgetstr Design Considerations

The following list presents the major functional design responsibilities of the getstr function.

1. Cursor control
   a. Beep: user is trying to move outside field width
   b. ⟵ (backspace key): destructive backspace (0x08)
   c. Del: delete character at cursor and shift field left (scan code 83)
   d. Ctrl-End: delete from cursor to end of field (scan code 117)
   e. Ctrl-X: delete entire field and move cursor to first character position (0x18)
   f. Home: moves cursor to first character position of the field (scan code 71)

g. ←/→ (left arrow/right arrow): nondestructive cursor movement (scan codes 75 and 77)

h. End: moves cursor to last character position of field (scan code 79)

i. Ins: not necessary for character insert at cursor

j. [window/row/column] coordinates: optional

2. Keyboard control

a. Acceptable ASCII characters: (0x20 – 0x7E)

b. Commands for exiting a field:

Esc: user abnormal exit (0x1B)

↵: carriage return (0x0D)

↑/↓: up arrow/down arrow (scan codes 72 and 80)

⇆: back tab/forward tab (scan code 15 and 0x09)

c. Commands for exiting a screen or field (for interfacing with screen/window management packages): PgUp (scan code 73) and PgDn (scan code 81)

d. Special Alt, Shift, Ctrl, and NumLock sequences:

Alt-Ctrl-Del: system reboot

Shift-PrtSc: screen print

Ctrl-Break: disabled in main.c

Ctrl NumLock: keyboard read pause

Ctrl-PrtSc: toggle Shift-PrtSc

e. Beep: invalid key or character set value is entered.

f. Echo to console: only data, not control characters

g. Numeric key pad: fully supported.

3. Special features

a. Help: since there is no standard keyboard Help key, the programs in this book support F1 with a standard message that "No help" is available.

b. Copy: driven from F2. Since Shift-PrtSc is interrupt driven by the PC-DOS BIOS, it cannot be disabled.

Use of F2 is better because of the form-feed to top-of-page after the screen copy.

c. Keyboard type-ahead buffer: control over clearing the type-ahead buffer before next keyboard read to prevent queueing of user responses.

4. Field masking

a. Required for all fields of input/output. Specification: **?** is a non-delimiter data entry position; any other mask character is an unmodifiable display delimiter. The string length of the mask becomes the total field width for input.

b. Mask delimiter characters are not affected by character or field deletion/insertion.

c. The overall field is marked by the video attributes of the display mask. If the field is mandatory, the display attribute is reverse video (attr = 0x78); if nonmandatory, the attribute is underline (attr = 0x01); if a password, the attribute is invisible (attr = 0x00).

5. Initial values

a. Set only upon initial display of a field. Not subsequently reset if the field is cleared. May be filled from the left or right according to ginitflg. The initial value does not affect delimiter positions.

Getstr/Fgetstr Pseudocode

1. If a coordinate error, then return

erc = ERC_BASE + GET_E;

If an argument error, then return

erc = ERC_BASE + GET_E + 1;

2. Display mask in reverse video (0x78) if a mandatory field or video underline (0x01) if a nonmandatory field. Show blank character (C_BLANK) for all **?** non-delimiters; all delimiters displayed as specified.

3. Display initial value, if any, according to ginitflg (for example, LR = left justified; RL = right justified). Place init characters only in nondelimiter mask positions.

4. Get a user keystroke:

   a. If EQ 0x00 *scan code* to follow; get another character; qualify scan code; if OK, reflect action; if not OK, beep, clear type-ahead buffer and recycle to get another character.

   b. If NE 0x00 *ASCII character;* qualify character; if OK reflect action; if not OK, beep, clear type-ahead buffer and recycle to get another character.

5. If a user exit is detected in step 4 above:

   a. Construct string from video display for return under gmaskflg control.

   b. If normal exit of field (cr, rtab, ltab, up, dn), return (ERC_OK). Set nuexit accordingly.

   c. If abnormal exit of field (Esc), then return

      erc = ERC_BASE + GET_E + 8;
      Set nuexit = −1.

Getstr/Fgetstr Interface Definition

Alternative forms of the getstr interface have been created to facilitate different application environments. Use getstr for a prompt environment when the window number (win) can be ignored, and the cursor has been properly positioned before the call. Getstr automatically sets up the window, row, and column and calls fgetstr. Screen text can be created using standard C I/O printf or putstr. Text can be intermixed with calls to getstr or fgetstr. Use fgetstr directly for full control of the window, row, and column or when interfacing with screen/window management packages (see Appendix C).

Syntax

int getstr (string, maxstr, gmaskflg, mask, ginitflg, init, ftype, cltab, &nuexit)

or

int fgetstr (win, row, col, string, maxstr, gmaskflg, mask, ginitflg, init, ftype, cltab, &nuexit)

Explanation

int	Integer function type.
win	Integer screen-frame or window number for interfacing with "full screen" software packages (not implemented in this book). Default = 0.
row	Integer field starting row number (assumes 1 = top row). Forced to limit of [1 . . MAX_ROW].
col	Integer field starting column number (assumes 1 = left column). Forced to limit of [1 . . MAX_COL].
string	Pointer to a C character string (array of characters) to get. String is concatenated from the video field display under the control of gmaskflg when the user departs the field. If string is not large enough to receive the mask data, a *Utility Function Error* erc results where **lderc(erc) = 7**

maxstr	Integer count of the maximum allowable number of characters in string exclusive of the NULL delimiter. Must not exceed MAX_CHAR defined in ldt.h (see Appendix G).
gmaskflg	Integer mask field flag as follows:

0 = FALSE = NO == delimiters *do not* become part of string
1 = TRUE = YES == delimiters *do* become part of string

mask	Pointer to a mask character string. The field width is the length of the mask string where the question mark is a nondelimiter character designator. For example:

Social security number	: ???-??-????
Date	: ??/??/????
Telephone number	: ???/???-????
Zip+4	: ?????-????

Since the mask defines the input field width it has enforced size limits:

NULL < mask <= MAX_xxxx

where MAX_xxxx is the maximum field widths specified for each logical data type set in ldt.h.

ginitflg	Integer init field flag as follows:

0 = FALSE = LR == fill mask field with init left justified
1 = TRUE = RL == fill mask field with init right justified

init	Pointer to an initial value character string. If no initial value is desired, init becomes a NULL

string (""). Init characters are placed into nondelimiter positions of the mask only. If the length of init is greater than the number of nondelimiter positions in mask, a *Putstr Argument Error* results.

ftype — Integer field type flag. Mask display utilizes video attributes to delineate the size of the field and connote the type of field.

−1 = PSWD_F == password field
0 = NMAN_F == nonmandatory field
1 = MAND_F == mandatory field
2 = DISP_F == display only field

These flags control mask visual attributes for a field as shown below:

V_PSWD = attr = 0x00 nondisplay
V_NMAN = attr = 0x01 underline
V_MAND = attr = 0x78 reverse video
V_DISP = attr = 0x07 normal display

See putchs.c for details about attr, and see ldt.h for globals shown above.

cltab — Integer clear keyboard type-ahead buffer flag. It can be either 0 or 1, indicating:

0 = NO == *do not* clear keyboard buffer before first read
1 = YES == *do* clear keyboard buffer before first read

nuexit — Returned value exit flag for interfacing with full-screen software packages that indicates the directionality of the user field/screen exit.

−1 = user escape (also covered by erc)
0 = carriage return field exit
1 = up directional field exit
2 = right directional field exit
3 = down directional field exit
4 = left directional field exit
5 = up directional screen exit
6 = down directional screen exit

Assignment of Error Return Codes

1. Successful functions return the following code:

   ```
   erc = ERC_OK;
   ```

   where ERC_OK is defined in ldt.h and is equivalent to zero (0).

2. An error caused by an invalid [win, row, col] value or starting col position which would cause a field to be written out-of-bounds returns the erc

   ```
   erc = ERC_BASE + GET_E;
   ```

   where ERC_BASE is a base value for all ercs associated with structured data entry assigned in ldt.h. This value can be altered to shift the group of assigned ercs to avoid conflict with existing status and error codes of the operating system and applications software. GET_E is the individual error return code assigned to getstr and fgetstr and can be found in ldt.h.

3. An error caused by the specification of an invalid function argument value returns an erc, computed as follows:

   ```
   erc = ERC_BASE + GET_E + 1;
   ```

4. A function error caused by a user escape or abnormal field exit is computed as follows:

   ```
   erc = ERC_BASE + GET_E + 8;
   ```

Getstr.c/Fgetstr.c Source Code and Commentary

The source code for getstr.c and fgetstr.c is shown below.

```
/* file    : getstr.c
** function: int getstr ( string, maxstr, gmaskflg, mask,
**         :              ginitflg, init, ftype, cltab, &nuexit)
** desc    : get "string" under "mask" control, "init" control,
**         : and "ftype" control. "nuexit" return a flag value which
**         : indicates the directionality of the user exit; "nuexit"
**         : is useful for interfacing with "full screen" packages.
**         : "cltab" clear keyboard type-ahead buffer first?
** test pgm: tgetstr.c
*/

#include "ldt.h"

        int getstr (string, maxstr, gmaskflg, mask,
                    ginitflg, init, ftype, cltab, nuexit)

        char *string, *mask, *init;
        int maxstr, gmaskflg, ginitflg, ftype, cltab, *nuexit;

        {
        int erc, win, row, col;

        /*
        ** setup coordinates for call to "fgetstr"
        */

        win = 0;                /* not used in this book */

        getcrc(&row,&col);

        erc = fgetstr(win, row, col, string, maxstr, gmaskflg, mask,
                      ginitflg, init, ftype, cltab, nuexit);

        setcrc(row,col);

        return(erc);

        }
```

```
/* file    : fgetstr.c
** function: int fgetstr ( win,row,col,string,maxstr,gmaskflg,mask,
**         :               ginitflg,init,ftype,cltab,&nuexit )
** desc    : get "string" under "mask" control, "init" control,
**         : and "ftype" control from a field starting at video
**         : position (win, row, col). "nuexit" returns a normal
**         : user exit directionality flag for interfacing with
**         : "full screen" packages.
**         : "cltab" clear keyboard type-ahead buffer first?
** test pgm: tgetstr.c
*/

#include "ldt.h"

        int fgetstr (win, row, col, string, maxstr, gmaskflg, mask,
                     ginitflg, init, ftype, cltab, nuexit)
```

```
int win, row, col;
char *string, *mask, *init;
int maxstr, gmaskflg, ginitflg, ftype, cltab, *nuexit;

{                                   /* start of function */
char getchr(), clrtab();
int erc, gerc;
int slgth, mlgth, sinit, smidx, midx, lmidx, midxsave;
int attr, i, irow, icol, j, jrow, jcol;
int readtype, userexit, nrmlexit;
char ch, sch;

gerc = ERC_BASE + GET_E;

*nuexit = -1;

/*
** validate [win,row,col]
*/

if ( ( row < 1 ) || ( row > MAX_ROW) ) return(gerc);
if ( ( col < 1 ) || ( col > MAX_COL) ) return(gerc);

/*
** validate flags
*/

if ( (maxstr < 1) || (maxstr > MAX_CHAR) ) return(gerc+1);
if ( (gmaskflg < NO) || (gmaskflg > YES)) return(gerc+1);
if ( (ginitflg < LR) || (ginitflg > RL)) return(gerc+1);
if ( (ftype < PSWD_F) || (ftype > MAND_F)) return(gerc+1);
if ( (cltab < NO) || (cltab > YES) ) return(gerc+1);

/*
** Validate "mask"
*/
mlgth = strlen(mask);
if (mlgth < 1) return(gerc+1);

if ( ( col + mlgth - 1 ) > MAX_COL ) return(gerc);

smidx = poschr(mask,C_QUEST,LR); /* starting non-del pos */

if (smidx == 0) return(gerc+1);
else smidx--;

/*
** is "maxstr" big enough?
*/

if ( gmaskflg == YES ) slgth = mlgth;
else slgth = nondel(mask);

if ( maxstr < slgth ) return(gerc+1);

/*
** highlight field on the video for the user;
** put "mask" and "init" value , if any.
*/

setcrc(row,col);

erc = fputstr(win, row, col, init, ginitflg, mask, ftype);

if (erc != ERC_OK)
{
utcharcb(1,string,1);
return(erc);
}
```

```
/*
** cursor already positioned at mask[0]; however,
** position cursor @ leftmost non-delimiter position
*/

midx = smidx;           /* current mask index pos */
movcrc(0,smidx);

lmidx = poschr(mask,C_QUEST,RL) - 1; /* last non-del pos */

/*
** if possible, move cursor to next non-delimiter
** position after partial "init" value if ginitflg = FALSE.
*/

sinit = strlen(init);

if ( (ginitflg == LR) && (sinit != 0) &&

     (sinit < nondel(mask)) )
{
for (i=midx+1; i < strlen(mask); i++)
{
if (mask[i] == C_QUEST) sinit--;
if (sinit == 0)
{
midx = i;
movcrc(0,i-smidx);
break;
}
}
}

/*
** main "fgetstr" user interaction/cursor control loop
*/

userexit = FALSE;
nrmlexit = TRUE;
readtype = cltab;

while ( userexit == FALSE )
{

if (readtype == FALSE) getchr(&ch);
else clrtab(&ch);

readtype = FALSE;

if ( ch == 0x00 )                   /* Scan Codes */
{

getchr(&sch);

switch ( sch )
        {


        case 15: *nuexit = 4;           /* back tab  exit */
                 userexit = TRUE;
                 continue;


        case 59: help();                /* user help */
                 continue;

        case 60: pscreen();             /* screen copy */
                 continue;
```

```
case 71: movcrc(0,smidx-midx);  /* home cursor */
         midx = smidx;
         continue;

case 72: *nuexit = 1;           /* up arrow exit */
         userexit = TRUE;
         continue;

case 73: *nuexit = 5;           /* page-up exit */
         userexit = TRUE;
         continue;

case 75: if (midx > smidx)      /* left arrow */
         {
         for (i=midx-1;i>=smidx;i--)
         {
         if (mask[i] == C_QUEST) break;
         }
         movcrc(0,i-midx);
         midx = i;
         }
         else
         {
         beep(2);
         readtype = TRUE;
         }
         continue;

case 77: if (midx < lmidx)      /* right arrow */
         {
         for (i=midx+1;i<=lmidx;i++)
         {
         if (mask[i] == C_QUEST) break;
         }
         movcrc(0,i-midx);
         midx = i;
         }
         else
         {
         beep(2);
         readtype = TRUE;
         }
         continue;

case 79: movcrc(0,lmidx-midx);  /* move to eof */
         midx = lmidx;
         continue;

case 80: *nuexit = 3;           /* down arrow exit */
         userexit = TRUE;
         continue;

case 81: *nuexit = 6;           /* page-down exit */
         userexit = TRUE;
         continue;

case 83: if (midx < lmidx) /* del ch @cur +left shift */
         {
        midxsave = midx;
        getcrc(&irow,&icol);
        jrow = irow;
        jcol = icol;
        j = midx;

        for (i=midx+1; i<=lmidx; i++)
```

```
                    {
                    if ( (mask[j] == C_QUEST)
                         && (mask[i] == C_QUEST) )
                    {
                    movcrc(0,i-j);
                    getcha(&ch,&attr);
                    setcrc(jrow,jcol);
                    putchr(ch);
                    movcrc(0,i-j);
                    getcrc(&jrow,&jcol);
                    j = i;
                    }
                    }
                    movcrc(0,lmidx-j);
                    putchr(C_BLANK);
                    midx = midxsave;
                    setcrc(irow,icol);
                    }
                    else            /* del ch @cursor only */
                    {
                    putchr(C_BLANK);
                    }
                    continue;

          case 117: getcrc(&irow,&icol);  /* delete to eof */
                     for(i=midx;i<=lmidx;i++)
                     {
                     if (mask[i] == C_QUEST)
                     {
                     putchr(C_BLANK);
                     movcrc(0,1);
                     }
                     else movcrc(0,1);
                     }
                     setcrc(irow,icol);
                     continue;

          default: beep(2);        /* valid scan code but not OK */
                   readtype = TRUE;
                   continue;
          }
}                          /* end Scan Codes */

/*
** start ASCII Codes
*/

if ( (ch >= 0x20) && (ch <= 0x7E) )     /* insert valid char */
{
midxsave = midx;
getcrc(&irow,&icol);

for (i=midx; i<=lmidx; i++)
{
if (mask[i] == C_QUEST)
{
movcrc(0,i-midx);
getcha(&sch,&attr);
putchr(ch);
ch = sch;
midx = i;
}
else
{
movcrc(0,1);
midx++;
}
}
```

```
midx = midxsave;
setcrc(irow,icol);

if (midx < lmidx)
{
for(i=midx+1; i<=lmidx; i++)
{
if (mask[i] == C_QUEST) break;
}
movcrc(0,i-midx);
midx = i;
}
continue;
}

else

if (ch == 0x08)                    /* destructive backspace */
{
if (midx > smidx)
{
for (i=midx-1; i>=smidx; i--)
{
if (mask[i] == C_QUEST) break;
}
movcrc(0,i-midx);
midx = i;
midxsave = midx;
getcrc(&irow,&icol);
jrow = irow;
jcol = icol;

j = midx;
for (i=midx+1; i<mlgth; i++)
{
if ( (mask[j] == C_QUEST) && (mask[i] == C_QUEST) )
{
movcrc(0,i-j);
getcha(&ch,&attr);
setcrc(jrow,jcol);
putchr(ch);
movcrc(0,i-j);
getcrc(&jrow,&jcol);
j = i;
}
}
movcrc(0,lmidx-j);
putchr(C_BLANK);
midx = midxsave;
setcrc(irow,icol);
}
else
{
beep(2);
readtype = TRUE;
}
continue;
}

else

if (ch == 0x09)                    /* fwd tab exit */
{
*nuexit = 2;
userexit = TRUE;
continue;
}
```

```
else

if (ch == 0x0D)                  /* carriage return exit */
{
*nuexit = 0;
userexit = TRUE;
continue;
}

else

if (ch == 0x18)                  /* clear entire field */
{
movcrc(0,smidx-midx);
getcrc(&irow,&icol);
midx = smidx;

for (i=smidx; i <= lmidx; i++)
{
if (mask[i] == C_QUEST)
{
putchr(C_BLANK);
movcrc(0,1);
}
else movcrc(0,1);
}
setcrc(irow,icol);
continue;
}

else

if (ch == 0x1B)                  /* escape - abnormal exit */
{                                /* "nuexit" handled by erc */
*nuexit = -1;
gerc = gerc + 8;
userexit = TRUE;
nrmlexit = FALSE;
continue;
}

else

{
beep(2);               /* Invalid Character Keystroke */
readtype = TRUE;
continue;
}

}       /* end of while */

setcrc(row,col);
if (nrmlexit == FALSE) return(gerc);

/*
** construct "string" from video display
** under "gmaskflg" control
*/

utcharcb(1,string,1);

for (i=0; i < mlgth; i++)
{
getcha(&ch,&attr);
if ( (mask[i] == C_QUEST) || (gmaskflg == TRUE) )
{
inschr(string, maxstr, ch, 0);
}
```

```
movcrc(0,1);
}

setcrc(row,col);

return(ERC_OK);

}                          /* end of function */
```

- Getstr.c simply assigns [win = 0, row, col] cursor coordinates and calls fgetstr.c and upon return from fgetstr.c reassigns the starting cursor position.
- Fgetstr.c is essentially a video cursor control function that allows the user to construct a video image of each field of input with the functionality provided for character input and cursor control. The actual character string of input is simply copied from the video display mask under gmaskflg control when the user initiates a field exit control keystroke (see the last eight statements of fgetstr.c source code).
- The main processing loop for each field of input can only be broken by either a normal user exit keystroke, or an abnormal escape; hence fgetstr.c only returns an erc of ERC_OK (zero) or lderc(erc) = 9 (escape); however, nuexit is always properly set as an argument return value.
- The fgetstr.c argument cltab allows control over the first character read performed by fgetstr.c. If cltab is FALSE (zero), function getchr.c is used; otherwise, function clrtab.c is used. The use of clrtab.c first clears the keyboard type-ahead buffer of any queued keystrokes. This is imperative when performing error recovery to eliminate any erroneous type-ahead characters entered by the user after the error character was detected, or when it is desirable, in a precautionary way (first data entry field of a screen), to clear the type-ahead buffer.
- Note that a deliberate design decision was made to have all valid character input be equivalent to keyboard insert mode. Character input is always an insert at the present cursor location (shifting the existing character string to the right). Truncation of the rightmost character

occurs. Similarly therefore:

a. Destructive backspace moves the character string and cursor (from the present cursor location to EOF) left one character position, effectively deleting the character that was to the left of the initial cursor location. A blank character is inserted at the right-most position.

b. Delete removes the character at the present cursor location by shifting the character string (from the adjacent right position to EOF) left one character position. A blank character is inserted at the right-most position. The cursor location is not changed.

- Note that the bulk of the program logic maintains the proper cursor location and only allows characters of input and control actions to affect nondelimiter field mask positions.

Putstr/Fputstr Pseudocode

1. Validate function arguments, if in error return appropriate erc.
2. If NULL mask, treat string as a text field to be written with the specified field video attribute.
3. Put the string under pmaskflg control:
   a. if LR, left justify the string in mask nondelimiter positions.
   b. if RL, right justify the string in mask nondelimiter positions.
4. Check if mask was too small for string, return erc accordingly.

Putstr/Fputstr Interface Definition

As with getstr, alternate forms of the putstr interface have been created to facilitate different application environments. Also like getstr, putstr should be used for a prompt environment when win can be ignored and it assumes the cursor has been properly positioned before the call. It automatically sets up the window, row, and column and calls fputstr. Screen text can be created using standard printf or putstr. Text can be intermixed with calls to getstr/fgetstr. Use fputstr for full control of window, row, and column when interfacing with screen window management packages (see Appendix C).

Syntax

int putstr (string, pmaskflg, mask, ftype)

or

int fputstr (win, row, col, string, pmaskflg, mask, ftype)

Explanation

All the parameters in putstr are the same as those in getstr with the following exceptions:

string	Pointer to a C character string (array of characters) to put. String characters are placed into mask nondelimiter positions only if a mask is specified; otherwise just as is.
pmaskflg	Integer mask field flag as follows:

0 = FALSE = LR == Fill mask field left to right
1 = TRUE = RL == Fill mask field right to left

mask	A NULL mask can be specified to display a string with ftype video attribute control only—ignoring gmaskflg and displaying string as is: left to right. If the number of mask nondelimiter positions is less than the length of string a *Putstring Argument Error* erc results.

Assignment of Error Return Codes

1. Successful functions return the following code:

   erc = ERC_OK;

   where ERC_OK is defined in ldt.h and is equivalent to zero (0).

2. An error caused by an invalid win, row, or col value or starting col position that falls out-of-bounds will produce the following code:

   erc = ERC_BASE + PUT_E;

   where PUT_E is the individual error return code assigned to putstr and fputstr and can be found in ldt.h.

3. An error caused by the specification of an invalid function argument returns an erc computed as follows:

   erc = ERC_BASE + PUT_E + 1;

Putstr.c/Fputstr.c Source Code and Commentary

The source code for putstr.c and fputstr.c is shown below.

```
/* file    : putstr.c
** function: int putstr (string, pmaskflg, mask, ftype)
** desc    : put "string" under "mask" format control
**         : and "ftype" video control.
** test pgm: any qaxxxx.c program
*/

#include "ldt.h"

        int putstr (string, pmaskflg, mask, ftype)

        char *string, *mask;
        int pmaskflg, ftype;

        {
        int erc, win, row, col;
```

```
/*
** setup coordinates for call to "fputstr"
*/

win = 0;                  /* not used in this book */

getcrc(&row,&col);

erc = fputstr(win, row, col, string, pmaskflg, mask, ftype);

getcrc(&row,&col);

setcrc(row,col);

return(erc);

}
```

```
/* file    : fputstr.c
** function: int fputstr (win,row,col,string,pmaskflg,mask,ftype)
** desc    : put "string" under "mask" format control and "ftype"
**         : video control to a field starting at (win, row, col).
**         : if "mask" = NUL; then put "string" only with "ftype"
**         : video control.
** test pgm: any qaxxxx.c program
*/

#include "ldt.h"

        int fputstr (win, row, col, string, pmaskflg, mask, ftype )

        int win, row, col;
        char *string, *mask;
        int pmaskflg, ftype;
        {
        int erc, perc, mlgth, slgth, i, j, ncol;

        perc = ERC_BASE + PUT_E;

        /*
        ** validate [win,row,col]
        */

        if ( ( row < 1 ) || ( row > MAX_ROW ) ) return(perc);
        if ( ( col < 1 ) || ( col > MAX_COL ) ) return(perc);

        /*
        ** validate flags
        */

        if ( (pmaskflg < LR) || (pmaskflg > RL)) return(perc+1);
        if ( (ftype < PSWD_F) || (ftype > DISP_F) ) return(perc+1);

        /*
        ** validate "mask" - case of NULL "mask"
        */

        mlgth = strlen(mask);
        if (mlgth < 1)
        {
        putmask(string,ftype,FALSE);
        return(ERC_OK);
        }
```

```
if ( poschr(mask,C_QUEST,LR) == 0 ) return(perc+1);

/*
** case of "mask" != NULL
*/

setcrc(row,col);
putmask(mask, ftype, TRUE);

slgth = strlen(string);
if (slgth < 1) return(ERC_OK);

ncol = 1;

if (pmaskflg == RL)
{
utcharrs(string);
utcharrs(mask);
ncol = -1;
movcrc(0, mlgth - 1);
}

/*
** put the "string"
*/

j = 0;
for (i=0; i < mlgth; i++)
{
if ( mask[i] == C_QUEST )
{
if ( j < slgth )
{
putchr(string[j]);
movcrc(0,ncol);
j++;
}
else break;
}
else movcrc(0,ncol);
}

if (pmaskflg == RL)
{
utcharrs(string);
utcharrs(mask);
}

setcrc(row,col);

/*
** was "mask" too small for "string"?
*/

if (j != slgth) erc = perc + 1;
else erc = ERC_OK;

return(erc);
}
```

- Putstr.c simply assigns win, row, col cursor coordinates and calls fputstr.c.
- Note that if the mask is a NULL string, putstr.c assumes that string is text and to be written with the specified

video control; otherwise, putstr.c treats the string as a typical I/O field.

- Note that if pmaskflg = RL, a special technique is used for character display: both the string and mask are reversed, then put, and then reversed again.
- Note that if the output string is not large enough to hold the result of putstr.c, an erc is generated.

Basic LDT Field Processing

Basic LDT field processing refers to the use of the enxxxx, dexxxx, dvxxxxyy, evxxxx, getstr, and putstr functions. We consider the use of the getxxxx and putxxxx interfaces as advanced LDT field processing and will discuss them later in the chapter.

For comparison purposes we have included a source code listing of qacharv1.c which uses basic LDT field processing and performs the identical functions to the qachar.c quality assurance program in Chapter 5, which uses advanced LDT field processing. Qacharv1.c consists of 350 lines of source code, while qachar.c consists of only 150 lines of source code. We feel this example best dramatizes the power and self-documenting nature of using the advance functions getxxxx and putxxxx; however, the basic functions are the building blocks of the advanced techniques, and are often quite useful in and of themselves.

Qacharv1.c Source Code and Commentary

The source code for qacharv1 is shown below.

```
/*
** file   : qacharv1.c
** desc   : Version 1.0 QA test program for LDT CHARacter
** link   : @qacharv1.lnk,qacharv1,nul,lcs
*/

#include "ldt.h"

main ()
{
        int dvcharyn(), dvcharqs(), dvcharqc(), dvdummy();
```

```
static char mtype[] = ">??<";
static char mstr[] = ">??????????????????<";
static char myn[] = ">?<";
static char inity[] = "Y";
static char initn[] = "N";

char str[30], enstr[30], destr[19], dechr[2];
char ynchar, ch;

int erc, etype, lpe, nuexit;
int smtype, smstr, smyn;
int digit2, digit1;

smtype = nondel(mtype);
smstr = nondel(mstr);
smyn = nondel(myn);

blanksc(1,1,MAX_ROW,MAX_COL);
setcrc(1,1);

putstr("CHARacter Quality Assurance Program",LR,"",DISP_F);
setcrc(1,40);
putstr("Reset STDLOG? [Yes/No]: ",LR,"",DISP_F);

utcharcb(1,str,1);
strcat(str,initn);

for (;;)
{

erc = getstr(str,sizeof(str)-1,NO,myn,LR,str,MAND_F,
             YES,&nuexit);
if (erc != ERC_OK)
{
mesgsps(erc,NO);
if(lderc(erc) == 9) break;
}

erc = evchar(str,strlen(str),&ynchar,1,11,MAND_F,dvcharyn);
if (erc != ERC_OK)
{

mesende(erc,NO);
continue;
}
else break;
}

if (lderc(erc) == 9) ynchar = 'N';
if (ynchar == 'Y') logreset();

blanksc(1,40,1,MAX_COL);

setcrc(1,40);
putstr("Write STDLOG? [Yes/No]: ",LR,"",DISP_F);

utcharcb(1,str,1);
strcat(str,inity);

for (;;)
{

erc = getstr(str,sizeof(str)-1,NO,myn,LR,str,MAND_F,
             YES,&nuexit);
if (erc != ERC_OK)
{
mesgsps(erc,NO);
if(lderc(erc) == 9) break;
}
```

```
        erc = evchar(str,strlen(str),&ynchar,1,11,MAND_F,dvcharyn);
        if (erc != ERC_OK)
        {
        mesende(erc,NO);
        continue;
        }
        else break;
        }

        if (lderc(erc) == 9) ynchar = 'N';
        if (ynchar == 'Y') digit2 = 1; else digit2 = 0;;

        blanksc(1,40,1,MAX_COL);

        setcrc(1,40);
        putstr("Print Screen? [Yes/No]: ",LR,"",DISP_F);

        utcharcb(1,str,1);
        strcat(str,inity);

        for (;;)
        {

        erc = getstr(str,sizeof(str)-1,NO,myn,LR,str,MAND_F,
                     YES,&nuexit);
        if (erc != ERC_OK)
        {
        mesgsps(erc,NO);
        if(lderc(erc) == 9) break;
        }

        erc = evchar(str,strlen(str),&ynchar,1,11,MAND_F,dvcharyn);
        if (erc != ERC_OK)
        {
        mesende(erc,NO);
        continue;
        }
        else break;
        }

        if (lderc(erc) == 9) ynchar = 'N';
        if (ynchar == 'Y') digit1 = 1; else digit1 = 0;;

        blanksc(1,40,1,MAX_COL);

        lpe = (digit2 * 10) + digit1;

        if ( (lpe == 10) || (lpe == 11) )
                logwrite(5,"QACHARV1",0,"Begin Testing");

        for (;;)
        {

        blanksc(2,1,MAX_ROW,MAX_COL);
        setcrc(1,1);

/*
** String Testing
*/
        movcrc(2,-MAX_COL);
        putstr("Enter String ENCODE Subtype: ",LR,"",DISP_F);

        utcharcb(1,str,1);
        strcat(str,"0");
```

```
for (;;)
{
erc = getstr(str,sizeof(str)-1,NO,myn,LR,str,
            MAND_F,YES,&nuexit);
if (erc != ERC_OK)
{
mesgsps(erc,lpe);
if (lderc(erc) == 9) break;
}

erc = evint(str,smyn,&etype,PHY_INT,1,MAND_F,dvcharqs);
if (erc != ERC_OK)
{
mesende(erc,lpe);
continue;
}
else break;
}

if (lderc(erc) == 9) break;

movcrc(2,-MAX_COL);
putstr("Enter a String        : ",LR,"",DISP_F);

utcharcb(1,str,1);

for (;;)
{

erc = getstr(str,sizeof(str)-1,NO,mstr,LR,str,
            MAND_F,NO,&nuexit);
if (erc != ERC_OK)
{
mesgsps(erc,lpe);
if (lderc(erc) == 9) break;
continue;
}

erc = evchar(str,smstr,enstr,sizeof(enstr)-1,
            etype,MAND_F,dvdummy);
if (erc != ERC_OK)
{
mesende(erc,lpe);
continue;
}
else break;

}

if (lderc(erc) == 9) continue;


movcrc(2,-MAX_COL);
putstr("ENCODEed String       : ",LR,"",DISP_F);
erc = putstr(enstr,LR,mstr,DISP_F);
if (erc != ERC_OK) mesgsps(erc,NO);

movcrc(2,-MAX_COL);
putstr("DECODEed Subtype [0]: ",LR,"",DISP_F);
erc = dechar(destr,smstr,enstr,strlen(enstr),0,NO_JUST);
if (erc != ERC_OK) mesende(erc,lpe);
erc = putstr(destr,LR,mstr,DISP_F);
if (erc != ERC_OK) mesgsps(erc,lpe);
```

```
		{

		erc = getstr(str,sizeof(str)-1,NO,myn,LR,"Y",
			MAND_F,NO,&nuexit);
		if (erc != ERC_OK)
		{
		mesgsps(erc,lpe);
		if (lderc(erc) == 9) break;
		}

		erc = evchar(str,smyn,&ynchar,1,11,MAND_F,dvcharyn);
		if (erc != ERC_OK)
		{
		mesende(erc,lpe);
		continue;
		}
		else break;

		}

		if (lderc(erc) == 9) break;
		if (ynchar == 'N') break;

		}

		if ( (lpe == 10) || (lpe == 11) )
			logwrite(6,"QACHARV1",0,"End Testing");

		blanksc(1,1,MAX_ROW,MAX_COL);
		exit(0);

		movcrc(1,-MAX_COL);
		putstr("DECODEed Subtype [1]: ",LR,"",DISP_F);
		erc = dechar(destr,smstr,enstr,strlen(enstr),1,NO_JUST);
		if (erc != ERC_OK) mesende(erc,lpe);
		erc = putstr(destr,LR,mstr,DISP_F);
		if (erc != ERC_OK) mesgsps(erc,lpe);

		movcrc(1,-MAX_COL);
		putstr("DECODEed Subtype [2]: ",LR,"",DISP_F);
		erc = dechar(destr,smstr,enstr,strlen(enstr),2,NO_JUST);
		if (erc != ERC_OK) mesende(erc,lpe);
		erc = putstr(destr,LR,mstr,DISP_F);
		if (erc != ERC_OK) mesgsps(erc,lpe);


	/*
	** Character Testing
	*/

		movcrc(3,-MAX_COL);
		putstr("Enter Character ENCODE Subtype: ",LR,"",DISP_F);

		utcharcb(1,str,1);
		strcat(str,"10");

		for (;;)
		{

		erc = getstr(str,sizeof(str)-1,NO,mtype,LR,str,
			MAND_F,NO,&nuexit);
		if (erc != ERC_OK)
		{
		mesgsps(erc,lpe);
		if (lderc(erc) == 9) break;
		}

		erc = evint(str,smtype,&etype,PHY_INT,1,MAND_F,dvcharqc);
		if (erc != ERC_OK)
```

```
{
mesende(erc,lpe);
continue;
}
else break;
}

if (lderc(erc) == 9) continue;

movcrc(2,-MAX_COL);
putstr("Enter a Character    : ",LR,"",DISP_F);

utcharcb(1,str,1);

for (;;)
{

erc = getstr(str,sizeof(str)-1,NO,myn,LR,str,
          MAND_F,NO,&nuexit);
if (erc != ERC_OK)
{
mesgsps(erc,lpe);
if (lderc(erc) == 9) break;
continue;
}

erc = evchar(str,smyn,&ch,1,etype,MAND_F,dvdummy);
if (erc != ERC_OK)
{
mesende(erc,lpe);
continue;
}
else break;

}

if (lderc(erc) == 9) continue;

movcrc(2,-MAX_COL);
putstr("ENCODEed Character   : ",LR,"",DISP_F);
utcharcs(1,&ch,dechr);
erc = putstr(dechr,LR,myn,DISP_F);
if (erc != ERC_OK) mesgsps(erc,lpe);

movcrc(2,-MAX_COL);
putstr("DECODEed Subtype [10]: ",LR,"",DISP_F);
erc = dechar(dechr,smyn,&ch,1,10,NO_JUST);
if (erc != ERC_OK) mesende(erc,lpe);
erc = putstr(dechr,LR,myn,DISP_F);
if (erc != ERC_OK) mesgsps(erc,lpe);

movcrc(1,-MAX_COL);
putstr("DECODEed Subtype [11]: ",LR,"",DISP_F);
erc = dechar(dechr,smyn,&ch,1,11,NO_JUST);
if (erc != ERC_OK) mesende(erc,lpe);
erc = putstr(dechr,LR,myn,DISP_F);
if (erc != ERC_OK) mesgsps(erc,lpe);

movcrc(1,-MAX_COL);
putstr("DECODEed Subtype [12]: ",LR,"",DISP_F);
erc = dechar(dechr,smyn,&ch,1,12,NO_JUST);
if (erc != ERC_OK) mesende(erc,lpe);
erc = putstr(dechr,LR,myn,DISP_F);
if (erc != ERC_OK) mesgsps(erc,lpe);

setcrc(MAX_ROW - 1,-MAX_COL);
putstr("Continue? [Yes/No] or [ESCape]: ",LR,"",DISP_F);

for (;;)
```

1. All dvxxxxyy functions to be used as function arguments *must* be declared explicitly in the calling program.

2. All masks are declared with outermost field delimiters so that the field limits can always be known regardless of the type of field (video attributes) chosen for display.

3. All initial values are declared to make their revision easy, if necessary.

4. Both destr[19] and dechr[2] match the nondelimiter size of masks mstr[] and myn[] respectively. It is necessary that the size of a displayed string not exceed the corresponding number of mask nondelimiter positions, if a mask is used for display purposes.

5. The user is first queried for responses to the following questions which can be answered only Yes or No:

   ```
   Reset stdlog?  [Yes/No]:
   Write stdlog?  [Yes/No]:
   Print screen?  [Yes/No]:
   ```

   Variable lpe is calculated from these responses and effectively becomes the standard function argument logprerr.

6. Anywhere in the source code where

   ```
   if (lderc(erc == 9)
   ```

   appears, an equivalent statement

   ```
   if (nuexit == -1)
   ```

   can be specified instead.

7. Note that because there were only three possible choices for both ensubtype and desubtype, qacharv1.c simply generates decode [0, 1, and 2] for strings and decode [10, 11, and 12] for characters.

8. Note that hitting the Escape key recycles the program unless performed at

   Enter string encode subtype:

   or

   Continue? [Yes/No] or [ESCape]:

   where it will exit the program. Hitting Ctrl-Break has no effect because Ctrl-Break has been turned-off in function _main.

Advanced LDT Field Processing

Once you have learned the basic LDT functions you are ready to take advantage of the power and flexibility of the more advanced functions, getxxxx and putxxxx.

Getxxxx/Fgetxxxx Interface Definitions

The getxxxx interface is useful in performing the combined duties of getstr and evxxxx. The xxxx corresponds to a LDT identifier described in Chapter 3. By combining the getstr and evxxxx standard interfaces, getxxxx performs the useful function of looping until the user either satisfies the requirements for data entry for a field or presses Escape. Use of these functions also promotes source code development that is noticeably self-documenting. (Refer to Figure 2.1.)

Alternative forms of the getxxxx interface have been created to facilitate different application environments. Use getxxxx for a prompt environment when "win" can be ignored. Getxxxx assumes the cursor has been properly positioned before the call. It automatically sets up the window, row, and column and calls fgetxxxx. Screen text can be created using standard printf or putstr. Text can be intermixed with calls to getxxxx. Use fgetxxxx for full control of window, row, and column when interfacing with screen/window management packages (see Appendix C).

Syntax

```
int getxxxx (string, maxstr, gmaskflg, mask, ginitflg, init, ftype, cltab,
             &nuexit, pphys, maxphys, ensubtype, mflag, logprerr,
             dvxxxxyy)
```

or

```
int fgetxxxx (win, row, col, string, maxstr, gmaskflg, mask, ginitflg, init,
              ftype, cltab, &nuexit, pphys, maxphys, ensubtype, mflag,
              logprerr, dvxxxxyy)
```

Explanation

The parameters for getxxxx are the same as those for getstr, encode, and validation with the following exceptions:

logprerr	Integer flag to control stdlog error logging and screen printing if an error condition is detected:

00 = no stdlog entry; no screen print
01 = no stdlog entry; screen print
10 = stdlog entry; no screen print
11 = stdlog entry; screen print

Assignment of Error Return Codes

1. Successful functions return a status code:

   ```
   erc = ERC_OK;
   ```

   where ERC_OK is 0 as defined in ldt.h.

2. Unsuccessful functions produce an error return code which is either

   a. erc = unsuccessful result of getstr function. (See getstr interface definition above.)

   b. erc = unsuccessful result of encode function. (See encode interface definition, Chapter 3.)

c. erc = unsuccessful result of data validation function. (See data validation interface definition, Chapter 3.)

Putxxxx/Fputxxxx Interface Definitions

The putxxxx interface combines the functions of decode and putstr. The use of putxxxx eliminates redundant calls to dexxxx before each putstr when displaying LDT encoded data. Use of these functions also promotes self-documenting source code. (Refer to Figure 2.1.)

Alternative forms of the putxxxx interface facilitate different application environments. Use putxxxx for a prompt environment when win can be ignored. Putxxxx assumes the cursor has been properly positioned before the call. It automatically sets up the window, row, and column and calls fputxxxx. Screen text can be created using standard printf of putstr. Text can be intermixed with calls to putxxxx. Use fputxxxx for full control of window, row, and column when interfacing with screen/window management packages.

Syntax

```
int putxxxx (pstrout, maxout, pphys, maxphys, desubtype, jflag,
             pmaskflg, mask, ftype, logprerr)
```

or

```
int fputxxxx (win, row, col, pstrout, maxout, pphys, maxphys, desub-
             type, jflag, pmaskflg, mask, ftype, logprerr)
```

Explanation

Putxxxx has a few new parameters that have not been covered yet in this chapter:

pstrout	Pointer to a C character string (array of characters) to put.
maxout	Integer count of the maximum allowable number of characters in pstrout exclusive of the NULL delimiter.

Assignment of Error Return Codes

1. Successful functions return a status code

   ```
   erc = ERC_OK;
   ```

   where ERC_OK is 0 as defined in ldt.h.

2. Unsuccessful functions return an error return code which is either

   a. erc = unsuccessful result of decode function. (See decode interface definition, Chapter 3.)

   b. erc = unsuccessful result of putstr function. (See putstr interface definition above.)

Video Scratch Pad Technique

So far, all of the underlying interface definitions of the structured data entry methodology have been presented as shown in Figure 2.1:

enxxxx	encode a field
dexxxx	decode a field
dvxxxxyy	validate a field
getstr/fgetstr	get a character string
putstr/fputstr	put a character string
getxxxx/fgetxxxx	get, encode and validate a field
putxxxx/fputxxxx	decode and put a field

A careful look at the interface definitions reveals that the power of masks can only be accessed when used in conjunction with the actual display of a mask to the video followed by a subsequent field get or put function.

When you want to use decode functions in a stand-alone manner, and yet take advantage of the formatting flexibility of masks, you must use the *video scratch pad technique,* another advanced LDT field processing method.

By way of example, let's consider the case of outputting a social security number (SSN) in the format nnn-nn-nnn. If the SSN is stored as a long integer, the use of deint would not output the desired hyphens to a printer or disk file. By using an unused portion of the video display as a scratch pad, we could use putint on the SSN with the following mask and invisible password field type:

```
#include "ldt.h"
static char mssn[] = "???-??-????";
long int ssn;
char string[10], charssn[12];
erc = putint (string, 9, &ssn, PHY_INT4, 0, L_JUST, LR, mssn,
              PSWD_F, 0);
```

Then we could issue a call to getmstr to retrieve charssn formatted to include the hyphens as desired:

```
erc = getmstr (charssn, 11, YES, mssn);
```

The getmstr.c function then lies at the heart of the video scratch pad technique and functionally extends the standalone use of the decode functions.

Getmstr.c Source Code and Commentary

```
/*
** file    : getmstr.c
** function: int getmstr ( string, maxstr, gmaskflg, mask )
** desc    : get "string" under "mask" control.
** test pgm:
*/

#include "ldt.h"

        int getmstr (string, maxstr, gmaskflg, mask)

        char *string, *mask;
        int maxstr, gmaskflg;

        {
        int i, erc, row, col, attr;
        char ch;

        getcrc(&row,&col);

        utcharcb(1,string,1);

        for (i=0; i < strlen(mask); i++)
        {
        getcha(&ch,&attr);
```

```
if( (mask[i] == C_QUEST) || (gmaskflg == TRUE) )
{
erc = inschr(string,maxstr,ch,0);
if (erc != ERC_OK) break;
}
movcrc(0,1);
}

setcrc(row,col);

return(erc);

}
```

- This function retrieves a character string from the video display under control of gmaskflg and mask.
- Independent of getstr.c and fgetstr.c and in combination with the PSWD_F (invisible display) and decode functions, putstr can be used to "scratch pad" display to the video and then retrieve the result. Getmstr.c can enhance the stand-alone use of dexxxx.c functions by formatting data that is normally not provided by desubtype.

Summary of Possible Error Return Codes

If the erc is not equal to ERC_OK, an error condition has been detected by one of the functions described above. The following error conditions can be inferred from the least significant (rightmost) digit of the erc (xxxxD) using the GET_E, PUT_E and ENxxxx_E values proposed in Appendix G (ldt.h header file) and the formulas used to compute ercs using ERC_BASE and ENxxxx_E:

Digit D	Meaning
1	Bad getstr win, row, or col coordinates
2	Bad getstr argument
3	Reserved for full screen mandatory field message
4	Reserved for full screen user Escape

5	Bad putstr win, row, or col coordinates
6	Bad putstr function argument
7	Reserved for supporting getstr and putstr utility functions
8	Unused
9	Getstr abnormal user exit (Esc)

Refer to Chapter 3 for function lderc.c that is used to interrogate an erc and return the rightmost (least significant) digit (D) for program switching purposes.

Common Underlying Support Functions

There are six groups of functions: error handling, keyboard handling, video handling, printer handling, string processing, and test programs.

Error Handling

Beep.c

Makes speaker audible for n (1/10th) seconds.

```
/* file    : beep.c
** function: int beep(n)
** desc    : make the speaker port audible for n * (1/10th) seconds
** test pgm: tbeep.c
*/

#include "dos.h"
#include "ldt.h"

        int beep(n)
        int n;
        {

        /*
        ** Use Lattice C port I/O functions
        ** outp (port, mask) and inp (port, mask)
        ** to toggle speaker (BEL_PORT) ON/OFF
        */

        outp (BEL_PORT, inp(BEL_PORT) | 0x03);
        delay(n);
        outp (BEL_PORT, inp(BEL_PORT) & 0xFC);

        return(ERC_OK);

        }
```

- This function creates a step function to make the speaker audible by turning on the speaker, delaying, then turning off the speaker.
- The various constants are defined in dos.h and ldt.h.

Delay.c

Invokes a delay of n (1/10th) seconds.

```
/* file    : delay.c
** function: int delay(n)
** desc    : make a time delay for n * (1/10th) seconds
** test pgm: tbeep.c
*/

#include "dos.h"
#include "ldt.h"

        int delay(n)
        int n;
        {
        long int i,j;

        j = (long)DEL_ITER * (long)n;
        for (i=0; i < j; i++);

        return(ERC_OK);

        }

/*
**      Calibrate delay() for your computer by running "tbeep.c"
**      and adjusting "DEL_ITER" in "dos.h" so that 5 seconds
**      elapse when running "tbeep.c"
*/
```

- This function is chip dependent. The delay is achieved by performing a null statement for-loop DEL_ITER times. (DEL_ITER is defined in dos.h).
- Use test program tbeep.c to calibrate (by trial and error) the delay function to a five-second test, thereby balancing DEL_ITER cycles with 1/10th of a second.

Help.c

Dummy help function (F1).

```
/* file    : help.c
** function: int help()
** desc    : dummy "user HELP" function.
** test pgm: tgetstr.c
*/
```

```
#include "ldt.h"

        int help()
        {
        int irow, icol;

        getcrc(&irow,&icol);
        setcrc(MAX_ROW,1);
        blanksc(MAX_ROW,1,MAX_ROW,MAX_COL);
        putstr("Sorry, NO HELP is supported!",LR,"",DISP_F);
        beep(1);
        delay(2);
        beep(1);
        delay(5);
        blanksc(MAX_ROW,1,MAX_ROW,MAX_COL);
        setcrc(irow,icol);

        return(ERC_OK);
        }
```

- This function is strictly a dummy used to highlight the importance of standardizing upon a keyboard key F1 location for a system-wide help feature.
- On the IBM PC keyboard, we have elected to reserve F1 for help, F2 for copy, and Esc for cancel/escape because they are adjacent and their upper keyboard location makes them less likely to be struck by accident.

Mesgsps.c

Getstr/putstr standard user error messaging.

```
/* file    : mesgsps.c
** function: int mesgsps(erc, pflag)
** desc    : messaging for Getstr/Putstr functions.
**         : "pflag" = 00 : NO LOG Entry; NO Screen Print.
**         :         = 01 : NO LOG Entry; Screen Print.
**         :         = 10 : LOG Entry   ; NO Screen Print.
**         :         = 11 : LOG Entry   ; Screen Print.
** test pgm: Any qaxxxx.c program
*/

#include "ldt.h"

        int mesgsps(erc, pflag)
        int erc, pflag;
        {

        int irow, icol, digit2, digit1, terc, tercf;
        char str[7], mes[40];

        digit2 = pflag / 10;
        if ( (digit2 < 0) || (digit2 > 1) ) digit2 = 0;

        digit1 = pflag % 10;
        if ( (digit1 < 0) || (digit1 > 1) ) digit1 = 0;
```

```
getcrc(&irow,&icol);
setcrc(MAX_ROW,1);
blanksc(MAX_ROW,1,MAX_ROW,MAX_COL);

switch (lderc(erc))
{
case 0:  setcrc(irow,icol);
         return(ERC_OK);
case 1:  strcpy(mes,"Bad GETSTRing Coordinates.");
         break;
case 2:  strcpy(mes,"Bad GETSTRing Function Argument.");
         break;
case 3:  strcpy(mes,"Please Complete ALL Mandatory Fields.");
         break;
case 4:  strcpy(mes,"User ESCaped Screen.");
         break;
case 5:  strcpy(mes,"Bad PUTSTRing Coordinates.");
         break;
case 6:  strcpy(mes,"Bad PUTSTRing Function Argument.");
         break;
case 7:  strcpy(mes,"GETSTR/PUTSTR Utility Function Error.");
         break;
case 9:  strcpy(mes,"User ESCaped Field.");
         break;

default: strcpy(mes,"Invalid/Undefined ERC.");
                break;
}

putstr(mes,LR,"",DISP_F);
deint(str, MAX_INT, &erc, PHY_INT, 0, NO_JUST);
movcrc(0,MAX_COL);
movcrc(0,-11);
putstr("ERC = ",LR,"",DISP_F);
putstr(str,LR,"",DISP_F);

beep(1);
delay(2);
beep(1);

terc = lderc(erc);
tercf = TRUE;
if ( (terc == 9) || (terc == 3) || (terc == 4) )
     tercf = FALSE;

if ( (digit1 == TRUE) && (tercf == TRUE) ) pscreen();
else delay(5);

if ( (digit2 == TRUE) && (tercf == TRUE) )
     logwrite(1,"GS/PS",erc,"");

blanksc(MAX_ROW,1,MAX_ROW,MAX_COL);
setcrc(irow,icol);

return(ERC_OK);
}
```

- This is the principal error messaging, logging, and automatic screen printing function for all getstr/putstr function calls.
- Note that this function assumes that the custom _main program in Appendix F has been linked into the application program, for stdlog is actually assigned there and subsequently defined for used in stdio.h.

- This function assumes the full use of video display row = MAX_ROW (=25) for messaging purposes.
- This function assumes the error numbering scheme described in this book is supported by all functions that yield a meaningful least significant digit for switching purposes.

Uprompt.c

Prompt for user runtime controls.

```
/*
** file    : uprompt.c
** function: int uprompt ( &lpe )
** desc    : Global user prompts for Reset STDLOG?;
**         : Write STDLOG?; and Print Screen?
** test pgm: Any QAxxxx Test Program.
*/

#include "ldt.h"

        int uprompt(lpe)
        int *lpe;

        {
        int dvcharyn();

        static char myn[] = "?";
        char str[2];
        char ynchar, ch;
        int erc, nuexit;
        int digit2, digit1;

        setcrc(1,40);
        putstr("Reset STDLOG? [Yes/No]: ",LR,"",DISP_F);

        erc = getchar(str,sizeof(str)-1,NO,myn,LR,"N",MAND_F,YES,
                      &nuexit,&ynchar,1,11,MAND_F,NO,dvcharyn);

        if (lderc(erc) == 9) ynchar = 'N';
        if (ynchar == 'Y') logreset();
        blanksc(1,40,1,MAX_COL);

        setcrc(1,40);
        putstr("Write STDLOG? [Yes/No]: ",LR,"",DISP_F);

        erc = getchar(str,sizeof(str)-1,NO,myn,LR,"Y",MAND_F,NO,
                      &nuexit,&ynchar,1,11,MAND_F,NO,dvcharyn);

        if (lderc(erc) == 9) ynchar = 'N';
        if (ynchar == 'Y') digit2 = 1; else digit2 = 0;
        blanksc(1,40,1,MAX_COL);

        setcrc(1,40);
        putstr("Print Screen? [Yes/No]: ",LR,"",DISP_F);

        erc = getchar(str,sizeof(str)-1,NO,myn,LR,"N",MAND_F,NO,
                      &nuexit,&ynchar,1,11,MAND_F,NO,dvcharyn);

        if (lderc(erc) == 9) ynchar = 'N';
        if (ynchar == 'Y') digit1 = 1; else digit1 = 0;
        blanksc(1,40,1,MAX_COL);
```

```
*lpe = (digit2 * 10) + digit1;

return(ERC_OK);
}
```

- This function handles all user runtime control data entry used by all qaxxxx test programs and others.
- Note that function argument lpe is a calculated returned value used by functions mesende.c and mesgsps.c for control purposes.

Keyboard Handling

Clrtab.c

Clears the type-ahead buffer.

```
/* file    : clrtab.c
** function: char clrtab(&kbdch)
** desc    : clear the standard keyboard type-ahead buffer
**         : and perform same as "getchr.c". Return "char"
**         : by function and value.
*/

#include "dos.h"

        char clrtab(kbchr)
        char *kbchr;
        {

        union REGS ir, or;

        ir.h.ah = DOS_CTAB;
        ir.h.al = DOS_GKBC;

        int86 (INT_DOS, &ir, &or);

        *kbchr = or.h.al;

        return(or.h.al);

        }
```

- This function both clears the keyboard type-ahead buffer, and performs a keyboard read equivalent to getchr.c.

Getchr.c

Reads a character.

```
/* file    : getchr.c
** function: char getchr(&kbdch)
** desc    : get a character from the keyboard; no echo, no checks.
**         : Return "char" by function and value.
*/

#include "dos.h"

        char getchr(kbchr)
        char *kbchr;
        {

        union REGS ir, or;

        ir.h.ah = DOS_GKBC;

        int86 (INT_DOS, &ir, &or);

        *kbchr = or.h.al;

        return(or.h.al);

        }
```

- This function performs a BIOS keyboard character read, which waits for a valid keystroke, does not echo to the console, and does not check for Ctrl-Break or Ctrl-PrtSc.
- The character read is returned both as a function return value and a function argument.

Video Handling

Blanksc.c

Blanks some or all of the display.

```
/* file    : blanksc.c
** function: int blanksc (tlrow,tlcol,brrow,brcol)
** desc    : blank the concole screen;
**         : from top left [row,col] to bottom right [row,col]
**         : assumes user [tlrow,tlcol] = [1,1]
**         : assumes user [brrow,brcol] = [MAX_ROW,MAX_COL]
**         ; present cursor position is not altered by "blanksc"
** test pgm: tcursor.c
*/
```

```
#include "ldt.h"
#include "dos.h"

        int blanksc (tlrow,tlcol,brrow,brcol)
        int tlrow, tlcol, brrow, brcol;
        {

        union REGS ir, or;

        ir.h.ah = VID_SCUP;

        ir.h.al = 0;

        if (tlrow < 1) tlrow = 1;
        if (tlrow > MAX_ROW) tlrow = MAX_ROW;

        if (tlcol < 1) tlcol = 1;
        if (tlcol > MAX_COL) tlcol = MAX_COL;

        if (brrow < 1) brrow = 1;
        if (brrow > MAX_ROW) brrow = MAX_ROW;

        if (brcol < 1) brcol = 1;
        if (brcol > MAX_COL) brcol = MAX_COL;


        ir.h.ch = tlrow - 1;
        ir.h.cl = tlcol - 1;

        ir.h.dh = brrow - 1;
        ir.h.dl = brcol - 1;

        ir.h.bh = V_DISP;

        int86 (INT_VID, &ir, &or);

        return(ERC_OK);

        }
```

- Note that by convention in this book, all source code uses a video coordinate system with origin [1,1 : top left]; while the BIOS video interrupt expects an origin of [0,0 : top left].
- Each row and column coordinate is forced to fall within defined screen limits for [1,1] to [MAX_ROW, MAX_COL].
- This function may be used to blank any portion of the video display that can be defined by a pair of [top left] and [bottom right] coordinates.

Getcrc.c

Gets (row,col) coordinates at cursor position.

```
/* file    : getcrc.c
** function: int getcrc (&row, &col))
** desc    : get the cursor and return location (row, col)
**         : call assumes a (1, 1) origin at upper/left corner
** test pgm: tcursor.c
*/
```

```
#include "dos.h"
#include "ldt.h"

        int getcrc (row, col)
        int *row, *col;
        {

        union REGS ir, or;

        ir.h.ah = VID_GETC;
        ir.h.bh = 0;

        int86 (INT_VID, &ir, &or);

        *row = or.h.dh + 1;
        *col = or.h.dl + 1;

        return(ERC_OK);

        }
```

- This function returns the row and column coordinates at the present cursor location in DOS [0,0] origin form which are adjusted by +1 to conform to our software standard of origin [1,1].

Getcha.c

Gets character and attribute at cursor.

```
/* file    : getcha.c
** function: int getcha ( &char, &attr )
** desc    : get/return the character and attribute
**         : at the present cursor location.
** test pgm: tcursor.c
*/

#include "dos.h"
#include "ldt.h"

        int getcha (ch, attr)
        char *ch, *attr;
        {

        union REGS ir, or;

        ir.h.ah = VID_GETA;
        ir.h.bh = 0;

        int86 (INT_VID, &ir, &or);

        *ch = or.h.al;
        *attr = or.h.ah;

        return(ERC_OK);

        }
```

- This function assumes the present location of the cursor and returns the character and video attribute.

- Because the character and attribute are separate entities for each screen location, passwords may be read and written with a video attribute of 0x00 which simply prevents display to the video.

Movcrc.c

Moves cursor relative to present position.

```
/* file    : movcrc.c
** function: int movcrc (rowdif, coldif)
** desc    : move the cursor from current cursor location
**         : +/-rowdif, +/-coldif. Limited by overall range
**         : of [1,1] to [MAX_ROW,MAX_COL]
** test pgm: tmovcrc.c
*/

#include "ldt.h"
#include "dos.h"

        int movcrc (rowdif, coldif)
        int rowdif, coldif;
        {

        /*
        ** for [rowdif, coldif]:
        **   + == [down,right]
        **   - == [up, left]
        */

        int row, col;
        union REGS ir, or;

        getcrc(&row,&col);

        row = row + rowdif;
        if (row < 1 ) row = 1;
        if (row > MAX_ROW) row = MAX_ROW;

        col = col + coldif;
        if (col < 1) col = 1;
        if (col > MAX_COL) col = MAX_COL;

        ir.h.ah = VID_SETC;
        ir.h.bh = 0;
        ir.h.dh = row - 1;
        ir.h.dl = col - 1;

        int86 (INT_VID, &ir, &or);

        return(ERC_OK);

        }
```

- This relative move assumes the present cursor location and moves the cursor relative to that location.
- The function maintains the move within the video display limits from [1,1] to [MAX_ROW,MAX_COL].

Putchr.c

Writes a character.

```
/* file    : putchr.c
** function: int putchr (chr)
** desc    : write a character to the console; doesn't alter
**         : existing video attribute or cursor location.
*/

#include "dos.h"
#include "ldt.h"

        int putchr (chr)
        char chr;
        {

        union REGS ir, or;

        ir.h.ah = VID_WRCO;

        ir.h.bh = 0;
        ir.x.cx = 1;
        ir.h.al = chr;

        int86 (INT_VID, &ir, &or);

        return(ERC_OK);

        }
```

- This function puts a chr to the video display at the present cursor location without altering the existing video attribute for that location. The cursor is *not* automatically advanced.

Putchs.c

Writes character(s) with attribute control.

```
/* file    : putchs.c
** function: int putchs (chr, attr, cnt)
** desc    : put  "cnt" "chr" characters to the video
**         : with "attr" control. Doesn't alter cursor location.
** test pgm: tmovcrc.c
*/

#include "dos.h"
#include "ldt.h"

        int putchs (chr, attr, cnt)
        char chr, attr;
        int cnt;
```

```
{

/*
** "chr"  = character to be written.
** "cnt"  = count of characters to be written.
** "attr" = character attribute as follows:
**
**      BIT:    DESC:
**
**      7       Blink Control [ 0=off; 1= on]
**      6       Background Red-gun
**      5       Background Green-gun
**      4       Background Blue-gun
**      3       Intensity Control [ 0=low; 1=high]
**      2       Foreground Red-gun
**      1       Foreground Green-gun
**      0       Foreground Blue-gun
**
**      BACK RGB:       FORE RGB:       EFFECT:
**
**           000             000        Non-Display
**           000             001        UnderLine
**           000             111        White/Black Background
**           111             000        Reverse Video
**
** Example: 0x07 = 0000 0111 Normal Display!
**
*/

union REGS ir, or;

ir.h.ah = VID_WRCA;

ir.h.bh = 0;
ir.x.cx = cnt;
ir.h.al = chr;
ir.h.bl = attr;

int86 (INT_VID, &ir, &or);
return(ERC_OK);
}
```

- Unlike putchr.c, this function puts chr to the video display at the present cursor location, altering the video attribute, and optionally putting more than just one chr at a time. The cursor is *not* automatically advanced.

Putmask.c

Puts mask to console.

```
/* file    : putmask.c
** function: int putmask (mask, ftype, qflag)
** desc    : write a field "mask" to the Console under "ftype"
**         : video control:
**         :   -1 = password field      = no display 0x00
**         :    0 = non-mandatory field = underline  0x01
**         :    1 = mandatory field     = rev video  0x78
**         :    2 = display only field  = normal b/w 0x07
**         : "qflag": 0 = FALSE == do not transform mask.
**         :          1 = TRUE  == transform mask.
** test pgm: tgetstr.c
*/
```

```
#include "ldt.h"

        int putmask (mask, ftype, qflag)

        char *mask;
        int ftype, qflag;
        {

        char kbchr, attr, sattr;
        int i, mlgth, row, col;

        switch (ftype)
        {
                case -1: attr = V_PSWD;
                         break;
                case 0: attr = V_NMAN;
                        break;
                case 1: attr = V_MAND;
                        break;
                case 2: attr = V_DISP;
                        break;
                default: attr = V_DISP;
                         break;
        }

        if ( (qflag < 0 ) || (qflag > 1) ) qflag = 0;

        mlgth = strlen(mask);

        getcrc(&row,&col);

        sattr = attr;

        for (i=0; i < mlgth; i++)
        {

        attr = sattr;
        kbchr = mask[i];

        if ( (kbchr != C_QUEST) && (ftype == -1)) attr = V_DISP;

        if (qflag == 1)
        {
                if (kbchr == C_QUEST) kbchr = C_BLANK;
        }

        putchs(kbchr, attr, 1);

        movcrc(0,1);

        }

        if( qflag == 0 ) return(ERC_OK);

        setcrc(row,col);

        return(ERC_OK);

        }
```

- The qflag function argument allows putmask.c to be used to display both mask strings and nonmask strings so that video attribute control can be exerted for text as well as I/O fields.

- Note that when qflag = 0, text, and not a mask, is assumed, and the cursor position remains at the last character displayed; otherwise it is reset to the starting character position.
- Note that when ftype is pswd, delimiter characters are displayed. This allows masks containing character delimiters to have the delimited characters visible, because password fields have a video attribute of 0x00 = nondisplay.

Setcrc.c

Sets cursor at (row,col) coordinates.

```
/* file    : setcrc.c
** function: int setcrc (row, col)
** desc    : set the cursor at location (row, col)
**         : call assumes a (1, 1) origin at upper/left corner
** test pgm: tcursor.c
*/

#include "dos.h"
#include "ldt.h"

        int setcrc (row, col)
        int row, col;
        {

        union REGS ir, or;

        if (row < 1) row = 1;
        if (row > MAX_ROW) row = MAX_ROW;

        if (col < 1) col = 1;
        if (col > MAX_COL) col = MAX_COL;


        ir.h.ah = VID_SETC;
        ir.h.bh = 0;
        ir.h.dh = row - 1;
        ir.h.dl = col - 1;

        int86 (INT_VID, &ir, &or);

        return(ERC_OK);

        }
```

- This function call assumes a software standard video display origin of [1,1]. The subsequent call to the BIOS adjusts the argument by −1.

Printer Handling

Pscreen.c

Prints the screen (F2).

```
/* file    : pscreen.c
** function: int pscreen ()
** desc    : print screen + form feed
** test pgm: tinsdel.c
*/

#include "dos.h"
#include "ldt.h"

        int pscreen ()
        {

        char ch;
        union REGS ir, or;

        /*
        ** initiate "Shift-PrtSc"
        */

        int86 (INT_PSC, &ir, &or);

        /*
        ** Add a Form Feed - to top-of-page
        */

        ch = C_FF;
        pstdprn(ch);

        return(ERC_OK);

        }
```

- This function performs a Shift-PrtSc followed by a form feed to the printer to reset the top-of-page.

Pstdprn.c

Prints a character.

```
/* file    : pstdprn.c
** function: int pstsprn (ch)
** desc    : put character "ch" to the standard printer device.
** test pgm: tinsdel.c
*/

#include "dos.h"
#include "ldt.h"

        int pstdprn (ch)
        char ch;
        {

        union REGS ir, or;
```

```
ir.h.ah = DOS_PPRN;
ir.h.dl = ch;

int86(INT_DOS, &ir, &or);

return(ERC_OK);

}
```

- This function allows any character to be sent to the standard printer port.

String Processing

Delchr.c

Deletes a character.

```
/* file    : delchr.c
** function: int delchr (string, loc)
** desc    : delete a character at "loc" in "string".
**         : the first "loc" position of "string" is [1];
**         : if "loc" = [0] given then the last character
**         : of "string" is deleted.
** test pgm: tinsdel.c
*/

#include "ldt.h"

        int delchr(string, loc)
        char *string;
        int loc;
        {
        int strlen();
        int slgth, erc;

        char *bads = string;
        char *dads, *lads;

        /*
        ** *bads = beginning string address
        ** *dads = address of delete string position
        ** *lads = address of last character in "string"
        */

        erc = ERC_BASE + PUT_E + 2;

        slgth = strlen(string);

        if (slgth == 0) return(erc);

        if (loc == 0) loc = slgth;
        if ( (loc < 1) || ( loc > slgth) ) return(erc);

        /*
        ** setup address limits for looping
        */

        dads = bads + loc - 1;
        lads = bads + slgth - 1;
```

```
while ( dads <= lads )
{
*dads = *(dads + 1);
dads++;
}

return(ERC_OK);

}
```

- Note that string positions are origined at [1] not [0] for this function.
- Note that, by design, a loc = [0] indicates that the last string loc is to be deleted. This convention eliminates the need to call strlen(string) before delchr(string,loc) in the calling program to get the last string loc.

Inschr.c

Inserts a character.

```
/* file    : inschr.c
** function: int inschr(string, size, chr, loc)
** desc    : insert "chr" at "loc" in "string" of (declared
**         : length-1) "size"; the first "loc" position of
**         : "string" is [1]; if "loc" = [0] given, then
**         : "chr" is inserted at last "string" position.
** test pgm: tinsdel.c
*/


#include "ldt.h"


        int inschr(string, size, chr, loc)
        char *string, chr;
        int size, loc;
        {
        int slgth, erc;
        char *bads = string;
        char *iads, *lads;

        /*
        ** *bads = beginning string address
        ** *iads = (ads + 1) of insert "loc"
        ** *lads = address of "string NUL
        */

        erc = ERC_BASE + PUT_E + 2;

        /*
        ** check that a character can be added to string
        */

        slgth = strlen(string);
        if ( (slgth + 1) > size ) return(erc);

        if (loc == 0) loc = slgth + 1;
        if ( (loc < 1) || ( loc > (slgth + 1) ) ) return(erc);
```

```
/*
** setup address limits for looping
*/

iads = bads + loc;
lads = bads + slgth;

*(lads + 1) = C_NUL;

while ( lads >= iads )
{
*lads = *(lads - 1);
lads--;
}

*lads = chr;
return(ERC_OK);
}
```

- Note that string positions are origined at [1] not [0] for this function.
- Note that by design a loc = [0] indicates that chr is to be inserted in the last loc of string. This convention eliminates the need to call strlen(string) before inschr(string,loc) in the calling program to get the last string loc.

Nondel.c

Computes number of mask nondelimiter positions.

```
/* file    : nondel.c
** function: int nondel ( mask )
** desc    : return the count of non-delimiters in "mask"
** test pgm: qaint.c
*/

#include "ldt.h"

        int nondel ( mask )

        char *mask;
        {

        int slgth, i, cnt;

        slgth = strlen(mask);

        cnt = 0;

        for (i=0; i < slgth; i++)
        {

        if (mask[i] == C_QUEST) cnt++;

        }

        return(cnt);

        }
```

- Under the convention that question marks are nondelimiters in mask definitions, this function returns the number of nondelimited positions in a mask.

Poschr.c

Gets the first or last occurrence of a character.

```
/* file    : poschr.c
** function: int poschr (string, chr, fl)
** desc    : return location ( origin 1 ) of "chr"
**         : in "string". if "fl" = 0 return first
**         : occurrence; if "fl" = 1 return last
**         : occurrence; Return (0) if not present.
** test pgm: tinsdel.c
*/

#include "ldt.h"

        int poschr(string, chr, fl)
        char *string, chr;
        int fl;
        {

        int slgth, loc;
        char *bads = string;
        char *lads, *cads;

        /*
        ** *bads = address of first string position
        ** *cads = current address
        ** *lads = address of last string position
        */

        if ( (fl < LR) || (fl > RL) ) fl = LR;

        slgth = strlen(string);

        loc = 0;

        if (slgth == 0) return(loc);

        /*
        ** setup address limits for looping
        */

        cads = bads;
        lads = bads + slgth - 1;

        while ( cads <= lads )
        {
        if (*cads == chr)
        {
        loc = (cads - bads) + 1;
        if ( fl == LR ) break;
        }
        cads++;
        }

        return(loc);
        }
```

- This function returns [0] if no occurrence of chr is found in string.
- Location of the first = LR or last = RL chr is controlled by fl.

Utcharcb.c

Creates various forms of a blank string. See Chapter 5 D.2.0 for source code.

Utcharrs.c

Reverses a string. See Chapter 5 D.6.0 for source code.

Test Programs

Tbeep.c

Tests beep.c.

```
/*
** file    : tbeep.c
** desc    : test program for beep.c and delay.c
** link    : @tbeep.lnk,tbeep,nul,lcs
*/

main ()
{
        int i;

        /*
        ** The total elapsed time from first through last
        ** beep in this test should be 5 seconds. If not,
        ** alter DEL_ITER in "dos.h" accordingly
        */

        for (i=0; i < 5; i++)
        {
        beep(5);
        delay(5);
        }

        exit(0);
}
```

- Use this function to calibrate the DEL_ITER value in ldt.h for your microprocessor so that indeed the delay.c function argument is in 1/10ths of a second.

Tgetstr.c

Tests getstr/fgetstr.

```
/*
** file    : tgetstr.c
** desc    : test program for GETSTRing & PUTSTRing (Password Field)
** link    : @tgetstr.lnk,tgetstr,tgetstr,nul,lcs
*/

#include "ldt.h"

main ()
{
        int erc;
        static char mask1[] = "???-??-????";
        static char mask2[] = "*???-??-????*";
        static char mpswd[] = ":>????????<:";
        static char init[] = "13638";

        char ssn1[12], ssn2[14], pswd[14];
        int nuexit;

        blanksc(1,1,MAX_ROW,MAX_COL);

        setcrc(5,5);
        printf("Enter SSN: ");

        erc = getstr( ssn1, sizeof(ssn1)-1, NO, mask1,
                      LR, init, MAND_F, YES, &nuexit);

        if ( erc != 0)
        {       setcrc(25,1);
                printf("erc = %5d  nuexit = %d", erc, nuexit);
        } else
        {       setcrc(5,35);
                printf("str = %s  nuexit = %d", ssn1, nuexit);
        }

        setcrc(10,5);
        printf("Enter SSN: ");

        erc = getstr( ssn2, sizeof(ssn2)-1, YES, mask2,
                      RL, init, NMAN_F, NO, &nuexit);

        if ( erc != 0)
        {       setcrc(25,1);
                printf("erc = %5d  nuexit = %d", erc, nuexit);
        } else
        {       setcrc(10,35);
                printf("str = %s  nuexit = %d", ssn2, nuexit);
        }
```

```
        setcrc(15,5);
        printf("Enter Password: ");
        erc = getstr( pswd, sizeof(pswd)-1, NO, mpswd,
                      LR, "", PSWD_F, NO, &nuexit);

        if ( erc != 0)
        {       setcrc(25,1);
                printf("erc = %5d  nuexit = %d", erc, nuexit);
        } else
        {       setcrc(15,35);
                printf("str = %s  nuexit = %d", pswd, nuexit);
        }

        exit(0);
}
```

- Note that this program fully demonstrates the features of masks, the ginitflg function argument, and how pswd type fields naturally fit into the overall structured data entry scheme.

Part Two: Logical Data Types

While Part 1 of this book describes *what* structured data entry is and *why* it is useful, Part 2 demonstrates *how* to implement this methodology. Chapters 5–11 provide comprehensive looks into seven logical data types (xxxx) that are common to many application programming environments:

Chapter 5: Characters (char)
Chapter 6: Dates (date)
Chapter 7: Dollars (dolr)
Chapter 8: Integers (int)
Chapter 9: Reals (real)
Chapter 10: Telephone Numbers (tele)
Chapter 11: Times (time)

Each of these chapters has the same format. Once you have worked with a chapter about one logical data type, it will be easy to reference and study the material presented for another LDT.

There are six major headings in each chapter:

A.0.0 Encode function development (enxxxx.c, evxxxx.c, getxxxx.c)
B.0.0 Decode function development (dexxxx.c, putxxxx.c)
C.0.0 Data validation function development (dvxxxxyy.c)
D.0.0 Utility function development (utxxxxyy.c)
E.0.0 Application tips and reminders
F.0.0 Testing and quality assurance (qaxxxx.c)

There is a heading and subheading indentifying scheme that is common to these chapters, as you can see from the outline that follows. We hope this will speed your access to the reference material presented.

A.0.0 Encode Function Development (enxxxx.c)
- A.1.0 Enxxxx.c Specifications
  - A.1.1 Design Objectives
  - A.1.2 Field Size
  - A.1.3 Physical Format
  - A.1.4 Character Set Restrictions

A.1.5 Subtype Definition
A.1.6 Other Format Controls
A.1.7 Editing
A.1.8 Default Values
A.1.9 Error Codes
A.2.0 Enxxxx.c Source Code and Commentary
A.3.0 Encode and Validate (evxxxx.c) Source Code and Commentary
A.4.0 Advanced Encode Field Processing
A.4.1 Getxxxx.c/Fgetxxxx.c Error Codes
A.4.2 Getxxxx.c and Fgetxxxx.c Source Code and Commentary
A.4.3 Associated Mask Utilization Techniques

B.0.0 Decode Function Development (dexxxx.c)
B.1.0 Dexxxx.c Specifications
B.1.1 Design Objectives
B.1.2 Subtype Definition
B.1.3 Default Values
B.1.4 Error Codes
B.2.0 Dexxxx.c Source Code and Commentary
B.3.0 Advanced Decode Field Processing
B.3.1 Putxxxx.c/Fputxxxx.c Error Codes
B.3.2 Putxxxx.c and Fputxxxx.c Source Code and Commentary
B.3.3 Associated Mask Utilization Techniques

C.0.0 Data Validation Function Development (dvxxxxyy.c)
C.1.0 Dvxxxxyy.c Standard Error Codes
C.2.0 Dvxxxxyy.c Function Specification
C.2.1 Dvxxxxyy.c Design Objectives
C.2.2 Dvxxxxyy.c Source Code and Commentary

•

•

•

C.*n*.0 More Dvxxxxyy.c Function Specifications
C.*n*.1 Dvxxxxyy.c Design Objectives
C.*n*.2 Dvxxxxyy.c Source Code and Commentary

D.0.0 Utility Function Development (utxxxxyy.c)
  D.1.0 Utxxxxyy.c Standard Error Codes
  D.2.0 Utxxxxyy.c Function Specification
    D.2.1 Utxxxxyy.c Design Objectives
    D.2.2 Utxxxxyy.c Source Code and Commentary
    •
    •
    •
  D.*n*.0 More Utxxxxyy.c Function Specifications
    D.*n*.1 Utxxxxyy.c Design Objectives
    D.*n*.2 Utxxxxyy.c Source Code and Commentary

E.0.0 LDTxxxx Application Tips and Reminders
  E.1.0 Helpful Notes
  E.2.0 Special Uses
    •
    •
    •
  E.*n*.0 More Utxxxxyy.c Function Specifications
    E.*n*.1 Utxxxxyy.c Design Objectives
    E.*n*.2 Utxxxxyy.c Source Code and Commentary

F.0.0 Testing and Quality Assurance (qaxxxx.c)
  F.1.0 Qaxxxx.c Specifications
    F.1.1 Qaxxxx.c Design Objectives
    F.1.2 Qaxxxx.c Error Codes
  F.2.0 Qaxxxx.c Source Code and Commentary

Chapter 12 follows, with guidelines for modifying these logical data types and creating your own logical data types. Chapter 13 discusses techniques for handling error control and recovery, and completes Part 2.

Characters

5

This chapter covers the I/O of both individual character fields and character string fields. Individual characters are simple ASCII representations, while character strings terminate with a NULL character according to the standard C convention. The storage format for logical data type char is specified by the following statement in ldt.h:

```
typedef char CHAR;
```

Both kinds of character fields are used as data fields in disk record structures and as key fields (indices) when interfacing with file management and sorting software packages as described in Chapter 2.

Each interface definition described in Part 1 of this book is implemented for the character logical data type (xxxx = char). The encode and decode functions we have developed support the upper- and lowercase transformation of both input and output by simply specifying an appropriate ensubtype or desubtype argument value. Several useful data validation functions are provided that support alphanumeric data entry fields, true/false/yes/no logical fields, and modulus 10 and 11 check digit validation. Also, function dvcharan.c demonstrates how dvxxxx-yy.c function calls can be cascaded, while dvcharlg.c shows how pphys values can be modified.

We have provided utility functions that facilitate the handling and manipulation of character strings: blanking, comparison, conversion to and from single characters, justification, reversal, and stripping. There are additional utility functions that extend the use of character strings for check digit computation, name formatting, radix transformations, and soundex codes.

Finally, we have included a testing and quality assurance program (qachar.c) that allows you to examine and test most of the functions developed in this chapter.

The following chapter index lists the char source code that you will find in this chapter.

Standard Interface Source Code

A.2.0	Enchar.c:	Encode LDT char
A.3.0	Evchar.c:	Encode and validate LDT char
A.4.0	Getchar.c/ Fgetchar.c:	Combined getstr.c and evchar.c
B.2.0	Dechar.c:	Decode LDT char
B.3.0	Putchar.c/ Fputchar.c:	Combined dechar.c and putstr.c

Data Validation (dvcharyy.c) Functions

C.2.0	Dvcharan.c:	Checks u/c alpha, numeric and special characters.
C.3.0	Dvcharlg.c:	Checks logical field (**T**/**F**).
C.4.0	Dvcharqc.c:	Checks for *character* ensubtype only.
C.5.0	Dvcharqs.c:	Checks for *string* ensubtype only.
C.6.0	Dvcharsc.c:	Checks for special characters only.
C.7.0	Dvcharyn.c:	Checks for **Y**es/**N**o response.
C.8.0	Dvchar10.c:	Validates modulus 10 check digit.
C.9.0	Dvchar11.c:	Validates modulus 11 check digit.

Utility (utcharyy.c) Functions

D.2.0	Utcharcb.c:	Creates various forms of a blank string.
D.3.0	Utcharcm.c:	Compares strings.
D.4.0	Utcharcs.c:	Converts character and string.
D.5.0	Utcharjs.c:	Justifies a string.
D.6.0	Utcharrs.c:	Reverses a string.
D.7.0	Utcharsb.c:	Strips lead/trail characters from a string.
E.3.0	Utcharmd.c:	Computes modulus 10/11 check digits.
E.4.0	Utcharna.c:	Displays various name formats.
E.5.0	Utcharrx.c:	Converts radix.
E.6.0	Utcharsx.c:	Computes a soundex code.

Quality Assurance Programs

F.2.0	Qachar.c:	Standard quality assurance test program.

A.0.0 Encode Function Development (enchar.c)

A.1.0 Enchar.c Specifications

A.1.1 Design Objectives

This function allows the user to input both single characters and character strings without the side-effects of white space characters while limiting the user's working character set and providing optional control over conversion to upper- and lowercase.

A.1.2 Field Size (maxin)

The maximum field width of a character is 1, while character strings can range from 1 to MAX_CHAR = 80. Note that the MAX_CHAR value for strings excludes the NULL string delimiter. Strings, when defined, must have one additional character position for the NULL delimiter beyond the desired field width observed by the user.

A.1.3 **Physical Format (maxphys)**

The C programming language dictates the choice of native C data types for the logical data type char. Individual characters are ASCII equivalents, and character strings are consecutive characters that are NULL terminated. Maxphys for characters must always be set to 1. Maxphys for strings has the default value of PHY_CHAR = 80. Note that the PHY_CHAR value for strings does not include the NULL string delimiter. As with MAX_CHAR, strings must have one additional character position beyond the desired field width to account for the NULL delimiter.

A.1.4 **Character Set Restrictions**

According to the design of getstr.c and fgetstr.c, the enchar.c function only "sees" ASCII 0x20 through 0x7E. (Refer to Appendix E for a complete definition of the ASCII character set.) If it is necessary to further restrict the allowable set of input characters, write a dvcharyy function (see C.2.0 Dvcharan.c).

A.1.5 **Subtype Definition (ensubtype)**

0	Accepts string exactly as input.
1	Converts string input to uppercase.
2	Converts string input to lowercase.
10	Accepts character exactly as input.
11	Converts character input to uppercase.
12	Converts character input to lowercase.

A.1.6 **Other Format Controls**

N/A

A.1.7 Editing

N/A

A.1.8 Default Values

character = 0x20 = SPACE
string = 0x00 = NULL character string

A.1.9 Error Codes

Based upon the ERC_BASE (1000) and ENCHAR_E (11) values defined in the ldt.h header file, the following ercs are possible:

1011	Encode Data Entry Error By User
1012	Bad Encode Function Argument
1013	Encode Mandatory Field Not Satisfied

A.2.0 Enchar.c Source Code and Commentary

```
/* file    : enchar.c
** function: int enchar (pstrin, maxin, pphys, maxphys,
**         :                  ensubtype, mflag)
** desc    : Encode a logical data type char
** test pgm: qachar.c
*/

#include "ctype.h"
#include "ldt.h"

        int enchar (pstrin, maxin, pphys, maxphys, ensubtype, mflag)

        char *pstrin;
        CHAR *pphys;
        int maxin, maxphys, ensubtype, mflag;
        {

        int erc, eerc, i, j, slgth;
        char *ps = pstrin;
        char *pp = pphys;
```

```
/*
** Table of valid ENCODE subtypes:
**     0 = normal string
**     1 = to upper case string
**     2 = to lower case string
**    10 = normal character
**    11 = to upper case character
**    12 = to lower case character
*/

/*
** Validate the function arguments:
*/

erc = ERC_BASE + ENCHAR_E + 1;

/*
** validate "maxin"
*/

if (( maxin < 1 ) || ( maxin > MAX_CHAR )) return (erc);

/*
** validate "maxphys"
*/

if (( maxphys < 1 ) || ( maxphys > PHY_CHAR )) return (erc);

/*
** validate "mflag" for TRUE/FALSE
*/


if (( mflag < FALSE ) || ( mflag > TRUE ))
        return (erc);

/*
** validate "ensubtype", mandatory field,
** and set "default" values
*/

eerc = dvcharqs(&ensubtype,PHY_INT);
if ( eerc != ERC_OK )
{
eerc = dvcharqc(&ensubtype,PHY_INT);
if ( eerc != ERC_OK ) return(eerc);
}

switch ( ensubtype )
{
case 0:
case 1:
case 2: utcharcb(1,pphys,1);
        slgth = strlen( pstrin );
        break;
case 10:
case 11:
case 12: if ( maxphys != 1 ) return (erc);
         *(pphys) = C_BLANK;
         slgth = 1;
         break;
default: return (erc);
}
```

```
/*
** Mandatory Field satisfied?
*/

if ( mflag == TRUE)
{

j = 0;
for (i=0; i < slgth; i++)
{
if (pstrin[i] == C_BLANK) j++;
}
if (j == slgth) return(erc+1);

}

/*
** is "pphys" large enough?
*/

if (slgth > maxphys) return(erc);


/*
** ensubtype processing
*/

for ( i=0; i < slgth; i++ )
{
switch ( ensubtype )
{
        case  0:
        case 10: *pp = *ps;
                 pp++;
                 ps++;
                 break;
        case  1:
        case 11: *pp = toupper(*ps);
                 pp++;
                 ps++;
                 break;
        case  2:
        case 12: *pp = tolower(*ps);
                 pp++;
                 ps++;
                 break;
}
}

/*
** Append NUL character if a String.
*/

switch ( ensubtype )
{
        case 0:
        case 1:
        case 2: *pp = *ps;
                break;
       default: break;
}
return (ERC_OK);
}
```

- The switch (ensubtype) statement both validates the allowable ensubtype argument value and assigns default values of blank (0x20) to character and NULL (0x00) to string.
- For the char LDT, if pstrin contains all blank characters (0x20), it will not satisfy the mandatory mflag field requirement for either character or string.
- An erc will be generated if the string length of pstrin is greater than the maxphys string length of pphys.
- Note that all characters are copied from pstrin to pphys using address arithmetic. If a string rather than a character ensubtype is specified, a NULL character is appended.

A.3.0 Encode and Validate (evchar.c) Source Code and Commentary

```
/*
** file    : evchar.c
** function: int evchar( pstrin, maxin, pphys, maxphys,
**         :          ensubtype, mflag, dvcharyy );
** desc    : combined encode/data validation for char
** test pgm: qachar.c
*/

#include "ldt.h"

        int evchar( pstrin, maxin, pphys, maxphys,
                    ensubtype, mflag, dvcharyy )

        char *pstrin;
        CHAR *pphys;
        int maxin, maxphys, ensubtype, mflag, (*dvcharyy)();

        {

        int erc;

        erc = enchar(pstrin, maxin, pphys, maxphys, ensubtype, mflag);

        if (erc != ERC_OK) return(erc);

        else

        erc = (*dvcharyy)(pphys,maxphys);

        return(erc);

        }
```

- Note the technique used to pass and utilize the dvcharyy function:

  int . . . . (*dvcharyy)( )

  and

  erc = (*dvcharyy)(pphys,maxphys)

- Note that evchar.c will return both encode or data validation error return codes as appropriate.

A.4.0 **Advanced Encode Field Processing**

A.4.1 **Getchar.c and Fgetchar.c Error Codes**

Based upon the ERC_BASE (1000) and GET_E (1) values defined in the ldt.h header file, the following ercs are possible:

1001	Bad Getstr (win,row,col) Coordinate
1002	Bad Getstr Function Argument
1007	Supporting Getstr Utility Function Error
1009	Getstr Abnormal User Exit Escape

A.4.2 **Getchar.c and Fgetchar.c Source Code and Commentary**

```
/*
** file    : getchar.c
** function: int getchar( string, maxstr, gmaskflg, mask, ginitflg, init,
**         :          ftype, cltab, &nuexit, pphys, maxphys,
**         :          ensubtype, mflag, prnerr, dvcharyy );
** desc    : combined getstr and evchar
** test pgm: qachar.c
*/
```

```
#include "ldt.h"

        int getchar( string, maxstr, gmaskflg, mask, ginitflg, init,
                     ftype, cltab, nuexit, pphys, maxphys,
                     ensubtype, mflag, prnerr, dvcharyy )

        char *string, *mask, *init;
        CHAR *pphys;
        int maxstr, gmaskflg, ginitflg, ftype, cltab, *nuexit;
        int maxphys, ensubtype, mflag, prnerr, (*dvcharyy)();

        {

        int erc, win, row, col;

        win = 0;

        getcrc(&row,&col);

        erc = fgetchar(win, row, col,
                       string, maxstr, gmaskflg, mask, ginitflg, init,
                       ftype, cltab, nuexit, pphys, maxphys,
                       ensubtype, mflag, prnerr, dvcharyy);

        return(erc);
        }
```

```
/*
** file    : fgetchar.c
** function: int fgetchar( win, row, col,
**         :             string, maxstr, gmaskflg, mask, ginitflg, init,
**         :             ftype, cltab, &nuexit, pphys, maxphys,
**         :             ensubtype, mflag, prnerr, dvcharyy );
** desc    : combined getstr and evchar
** test pgm: qachar.c
*/

#include "ldt.h"

        int fgetchar( win, row, col,
                      string, maxstr, gmaskflg, mask, ginitflg, init,
                      ftype, cltab, nuexit, pphys, maxphys,
                      ensubtype, mflag, prnerr, dvcharyy )

        char *string, *mask, *init;
        CHAR *pphys;
        int win, row, col;
        int maxstr, gmaskflg, ginitflg, ftype, cltab, *nuexit;
        int maxphys, ensubtype, mflag, prnerr, (*dvcharyy)();

        {
        int erc;

        utcharcb(1,string,1);
        strcat(string, init);

        for (;;)
        {

        erc = fgetstr(win, row, col,
                      string, maxstr, gmaskflg, mask, ginitflg, string,
                      ftype, cltab, nuexit);

        if (erc != ERC_OK)
        {
        mesgsps(erc, prnerr);
        if (lderc(erc) == 9) break;
        }
```

```
erc = evchar(string, strlen(string), pphys, maxphys,
          ensubtype, mflag, dvcharyy);

if (erc != ERC_OK)
{
mesende(erc, prnerr);
cltab = YES;
continue;
}
else break;
}
return(erc);
}
```

- Getchar.c simply assigns the win coordinate (not used in this book) to zero, the row and col coordinates to the current cursor position, and then calls fgetchar.c.
- Getchar.c simply returns the error return code supplied by fgetchar.c.
- Note how init is copied to "string," and "string" is subsequently passed as an argument to fgetstr.c in place of the init argument. This technique allows a user to continue to see the string for which an error is detected.
- Remember that the erc returned from fgetstr.c can only be ERC_OK or a User Escape (lderc(erc) = 9 or nuexit = −1).
- All error processing (stdlog error logging, screen printing, video error message display) is handled by mesgsps.c and mesende.c.
- When an error is detected by evchar.c, the fgetstr.c function argument cltab is set to YES. This effectively instructs fgetstr.c to clear the keyboard type-ahead buffer, thus eliminating any queued keystrokes from erroneously being processed.

A.4.3 ***Associated Mask Utilization Techniques***

Based upon the function argument gmaskflg, mask delimiter characters are either included (YES) or excluded (NO) from the acquired input string. This makes it easy to introduce character separators that reduce the eye fatigue that can occur when entering lengthy ID numbers. Separators also allow you to add check digits to ID numbers without typing a hyphen. For example:

ID number with check digit: "??????-?"

For certain LDTs included in this book, it might appear the effects of ensubtype format control overlap with what can be accomplished using the gmaskflg associated with getstr.c/fgetstr.c. It is important to remember that enchar.c can be utilized independently of the getstr.c/fgetstr.c and getchar.c/fgetchar.c functions so that some functional redundancy is required to expand the independent use of the enxxxx.c interface definitions.

B.0.0 Decode Function Development (dechar.c)

B.1.0 Dechar.c Specifications

B.1.1 Design Objectives

This function transforms a single character or character string to another character string with formatting control over upper-lowercase transformation and justification.

B.1.2 Subtype Definition (desubtype)

0	Output string exactly as encoded
1	Output string in uppercase
2	Output string in lowercase
10	Output character exactly as encoded
11	Output character in uppercase
12	Output character in lowercase

Note: Since pstrout is always a string, if pphys is a character, it is output as a string.

B.1.3 ***Default Values***

character = 0x20 = SPACE
string = 0x00 = NULL character string

B.1.4 ***Error Codes***

Based upon the ERC_BASE (1000) and ENCHAR_E (11) values defined in ldt.h, the following erc is possible:

1016	Bad Decode Function Argument

B.2.0 **Dechar.c Source Code and Commentary**

```
/* file    : dechar.c
** function: int dechar ( pstrout, maxout, pphys, maxphys,
**         :                desubtype, jflag )
** desc    : decode a logical data type char
** test pgm: qachar.c
*/

#include "ctype.h"
#include "ldt.h"

        int dechar (pstrout, maxout, pphys, maxphys, desubtype, jflag)

        char *pstrout;
        CHAR *pphys;
        int maxout, maxphys, desubtype, jflag;
        {

        int erc, derc, i, slgth;
        char *ps = pstrout;
        char *pp = pphys;

        /*
        ** Table of valid DECODE subtypes:
        **     0 = normal string
        **     1 = to upper case string
        **     2 = to lower case
        **    10 = normal character
        **    11 = to upper case character
        **    12 = to lower case character
        */

        /*
        ** Validate the function arguments:
        */

        erc = ERC_BASE + ENCHAR_E + 5;
```

```
/*
** validate "maxout"
*/

if (( maxout < 1 ) || ( maxout > MAX_CHAR )) return (erc);

/*
** validate "maxphys"
*/

if (( maxphys < 1 ) || ( maxphys > PHY_CHAR )) return (erc);

/*
** validate "desubtype" and set "default" values
*/

derc = dvcharqs(&desubtype,PHY_INT);
if ( derc != ERC_OK )
{
derc = dvcharqc(&desubtype,PHY_INT);
if ( derc != ERC_OK ) return(derc);
}

switch ( desubtype )
{
case 0:
case 1:
case 2: slgth = strlen( pphys );
        utcharcb(1,pstrout,1);
        break;
case 10:
case 11:
case 12: if ( maxphys != 1 ) return (erc);
         slgth = 1;
         *(pstrout) = C_BLANK;
         *(pstrout+1) = C_NUL;
         break;
default: return (erc);
}

/*
** validate "jflag" for (NO_JUST, L_JUST, C_JUST, R_JUST)
*/

if (( jflag < NO_JUST) || ( jflag > R_JUST ))
        return (erc);

/*
** check that "pstrout" is large enough
*/

if (slgth > maxout) return(erc);

/*
** desubtype processing
*/

for ( i=0; i < slgth; i++ )
{
switch ( desubtype )
{
        case  0:
        case 10: *ps = *pp;
                 pp++;
                 ps++;
                 break;
        case  1:
        case 11: *ps = toupper(*pp);
                 pp++;
                 ps++;
                 break;
```

```
        case  2:
        case 12: *ps = tolower(*pp);
                 pp++;
                 ps++;
                 break;
    }
    }

    /*
    ** append NUL character to pstrout
    */

    *ps = C_NUL;

    /*
    ** Justify output string
    */

    utcharcb(3,pstrout,maxout+1);

    utcharjs(jflag, pstrout);

    return (ERC_OK);
    }
```

- The switch (desubtype) statement both validates the allowable desubtype argument value and assigns the default value blank (0x20) to character and NULL (0x00) to string.
- An erc is generated if the string length of pphys is greater than the maxout string length of pstrout.
- Note that all characters are copied from pphys to pstrout using address arithmetic. A NULL (0x00) character is always appended whether desubtype is of type character or string.
- String justification occurs within the total string field width maxout because of the function call to utcharcb (3,pstrout,maxout + 1).

B.3.0 Advanced Decode Field Processing

B.3.1 Putchar.c and Fputchar.c Error Codes

Based upon the ERC_BASE (1000) and PUT_E (5) values defined in ldt.h, the following ercs are possible:

1005	Bad Putstr (win,row,col) Coordinate
1007	Supporting Putstr Utility Function Error

B.3.2 Putchar.c and Fputchar.c Source Code and Commentary

```
/*
** file    : putchar.c
** function: int putchar( pstrout, maxout, pphys, maxphys,
                          desubtype, jflag,
                          pmaskflg, mask, ftype, prnerr)
** desc    : combined dechar and putstr
** test pgm: qachar.c
*/

#include "ldt.h"

        int putchar( pstrout, maxout, pphys, maxphys,
                     desubtype, jflag,
                     pmaskflg, mask, ftype, prnerr)

        char *pstrout, *mask;
        CHAR *pphys;
        int maxout, maxphys, desubtype, jflag;
        int pmaskflg, ftype, prnerr;

        {

        int erc, win, row, col;

        win = 0;

        getcrc(&row,&col);

        erc = fputchar (win, row, col,
                        pstrout, maxout, pphys, maxphys,
                        desubtype, jflag,
                        pmaskflg, mask, ftype, prnerr);

        return(erc);
        }
```

```
/*
** file    : fputchar.c
** function: int fputchar( win, row, col,
**         :               pstrout, maxout, pphys, maxphys,
**         :               desubtype, jflag,
**         :               pmaskflg, mask, ftype, prnerr)
** desc    : combined dechar and putstr
** test pgm: qachar.c
*/

#include "ldt.h"

        int fputchar ( win, row, col,
                       pstrout, maxout, pphys, maxphys,
                       desubtype, jflag,
                       pmaskflg, mask, ftype, prnerr)

        char *pstrout, *mask;
        CHAR *pphys;
        int win, row, col;
        int maxout, maxphys, desubtype, jflag;
        int pmaskflg, ftype, prnerr;
```

```
{
int erc;
erc = dechar (pstrout, maxout, pphys, maxphys,
              desubtype, jflag);
if (erc != ERC_OK) mesende(erc, prnerr);
erc = fputstr (win, row, col,
               pstrout, pmaskflg, mask, ftype);
if (erc != ERC_OK) mesgsps(erc, prnerr);
return(ERC_OK);
}
```

- Putchar.c simply assigns the win coordinate (not used in this book) to zero, the current cursor row and col coordinates, and subsequently calls fputchar.c.
- Putchar.c simply returns the error return code supplied by fputchar.c. Fputchar.c always returns an erc of ERC_OK. Any errors detected are displayed, and logged or printed, but because they are strictly code-dependent and no user correction is possible, processing continues.
- All error processing (stdlog error logging, screen printing, video error message display) is handled by mesende.c and mesgsps.c.

B.3.3 ***Associated Mask Utilization Techniques***

- In an analogous manner, putstr.c/fputstr.c and putchar.c/fputchar.c can be used to output a decoded string to a mask field with or without delimiters. Again it may appear that the effects of desubtype format control overlap with what can be accomplished with putstr.c/fputstr.c. It is important to remember that dechar.c can be used independently of the putstr.c/fputstr.c and putchar.c/fputchar.c functions so that some functional redundancy is required to expand the independent use of the dexxxx.c interface definitions.
- The getmstr.c function allows the video display to be used as a scratch pad (see Chapter 4) and functionally

extends the standalone utility of each dexxxx.c function. Since the power of masks is only useful with video display, getmstr.c retrieves the putxxxx.c string from the video display with mask formatting to enhance the variety of decoded formats that can be created with using dexxxx.c functions in a standalone manner.

C.0.0 Data Validation Function Development (dvcharyy.c)

C.1.0 Dvcharyy.c Standard Error Codes

Based upon the ERC_BASE (1000) and ENCHAR_E (11) values defined in ldt.h, all dvcharyy.c functions report the following ercs:

1014	Data Validation Error
1015	Bad Data Validation Function Argument

C.2.0 Dvcharan.c Function Specification

C.2.1 Dvcharan.c Design Objectives

This function is specifically designed to validate a string for use as an ID number field with a modulus check digit scheme. It requires that a character string of input be further limited from the character set permitted by fgetstr.c. Pphys is allowed to consist only of numeric characters, uppercase alpha characters, or one of the following special character delimiters: blank ( ), ampersand (&), hyphen (-), or slash (/). Dvcharan.c, therefore, checks for the presence of illegal characters.

It also exemplifies how one dvxxxxyy.c function can cascade its validation by calling another dvxxxxyy.c function. In this case dvcharsc.c is called to check for the remaining valid special characters, hence the name dvcharsc.c.

Note that dvcharsc.c is still fully useable with characters as a standalone dvxxxxyy.c function.

C.2.2 *Dvcharan.c Source Code and Commentary*

```
/* file    : dvcharan.c
** function: int dvcharan ( pphys, maxphys )
** desc    : Validate string "pphys" for use as an ID number
**         : 1) check that a digit, or
**         : 2) check that only upper case alphabetic, or
**         : 3) check that one of ' ', '&', '-', '/'.
**         : Example of a dvxxxxyy function calling
**         : another dvxxxxyy for data validation
** test pgm: tucharmd.c
*/

#include "ctype.h"
#include "ldt.h"

        int dvcharan ( pphys, maxphys )

        CHAR *pphys;
        int maxphys;
        {

        int erc;
        char ch, slgth, i;

        erc = ERC_BASE + ENCHAR_E + 3;

        if ( (maxphys < 0) || (maxphys > PHY_CHAR) )
        return(erc+1);

        slgth = strlen(pphys);
        if (slgth == 0) return(ERC_OK);

        erc = ERC_OK;

        for (i=0; i < slgth; i++)
        {
        ch = *(pphys+i);

        if ( isdigit(ch) != 0 ) continue;
        if ( (isalpha(ch) != 0) && (isupper(ch) != 0) ) continue;

        erc = dvcharsc(&ch,1);

        if (erc != ERC_OK) break;
        }

        return(erc);
        }
```

- Note the use of CHAR *pphys. The uppercase CHAR is a typedef from ldt.h, which is

  typedef char CHAR;

The use of the CHAR typedef then is equivalent to specifying char.

- Note how each character of the pphys string is interrogated for validity. The continue statement is utilized to stop validation once a criterion is satisfied.
- Note how dvcharsc.c is used to validate a character as one of the allowable special characters.
- Note that dvcharan.c always returns the erc from dvcharsc.c since it is the last validation to be accepted or rejected.

C.3.0 Dvcharlg.c Function Specification

C.3.1 Dvcharlg.c Design Objectives

This function is specifically designed to validate a character for use as a logical field encoded as FALSE (F) or TRUE (T). It therefore validates that pphys consists of only the following characters:

FALSE = F,f,N,n = F
TRUE = T,t,Y,y = T

It also exemplifies how a dvxxxxyy.c function can be used to transform input to standard internal terminology, because pphys is passed as a pointer for all LDTs. In this case all valid FALSE characters are transformed to F and TRUE characters to T.

C.3.2 Dvcharlg.c Source Code and Commentary

```
/* file    : dvcharlg.c
** function: int dvcharlg ( &pphys, maxphys )
** desc    : Data validation for a logical field of input.
**         : Checks for [T,t,F,f,Y,y,N,n].
**         : Transforms [T,t,Y,y] = [T] = TRUE; [F,f,N,n] = [N].
** test pgm: (none)
*/

#include "ctype.h"
#include "ldt.h"

        int dvcharlg ( pphys, maxphys )
```

```
CHAR *pphys;
int maxphys;
{

int erc;
char lgchar;

erc = ERC_BASE + ENCHAR_E + 3;

if (maxphys != 1) return(erc+1);

lgchar = toupper(*pphys);

switch (lgchar)
{
        case 'F':
        case 'N': *pphys = 'F';
                  return(ERC_OK);

        case 'T':
        case 'Y': *pphys = 'T';
                  return(ERC_OK);

        default: return(erc);
}

}
```

- Note the use of CHAR *pphys. Again, the uppercase CHAR is a typedef from the ldt.h header file and is equivalent to specifying char. (See C.2.2.)
- Note how the pphys character is interrogated for validity and transformed if valid to either F or T by the switch statement; otherwise dvcharlg.c returns erc.

C.4.0 Dvcharqc.c Function Specification

C.4.1 Dvcharqc.c Design Objectives

This function validates that an acceptable ensubtype and desubtype argument value has been specified for the char LDT. Note that only codes for *character* types are acceptable.

C.4.2 Dvcharqc.c Source Code and Commentary

```
/* file    : dvcharqc.c
** function: int dvcharqc ( &pphys, maxphys )
** desc    : Data validation for char; valid encode subtypes
**         : for "characters" only!
** test pgm: qachar.c
*/

#include "ldt.h"
```

```
int dvcharqc ( pphys, maxphys )

INT *pphys;
int maxphys;
{
int erc, pi2;

erc = ERC_BASE + ENINT_E + 3;

if (maxphys != PHY_INT) return(erc+1);

pi2 = (*pphys).i2;

if (( pi2 < 10 ) || ( pi2 > 12))
return (erc);

else return(ERC_OK);

}
```

- Note the use of INT *pphys. The uppercase INT is a typedef from ldt.h:

  typedef union { int i2; long int i4; } INT;

  The use of the INT typedef allows either int or long int arguments to be passed to dvcharqc.c. By design only int types are acceptable to dvcharqc.c.

- Note that all ensubtype arguments are of type integer, therefore maxphys must equal PHY_INT specified in ldt.h.

- Because of the use of typedef INT discussed above, the value of pphys is retrieved by the statement:

  pi2 = (*pphys).i2;

C.5.0 Dvcharqs.c Function Specification

C.5.1 Dvcharqs.c Design Objectives

This function validates that an acceptable ensubtype and desubtype argument value has been specified for the char LDT. Note that only codes for *string* types are acceptable.

C.5.2 Dvcharqs.c Source Code and Commentary

```
/* file    : dvcharqs.c
** function: int dvcharqs ( &pphys, maxphys )
** desc    : Data validation for char; valid encode subtypes
**         : for "strings" only!
** test pgm: qachar.c
*/
```

```
#include "ldt.h"

        int dvcharqs ( pphys, maxphys )

        INT *pphys;
        int maxphys;
        {
        int erc, pi2;

        erc = ERC_BASE + ENINT_E + 3;

        if (maxphys != PHY_INT) return(erc+1);

        pi2 = (*pphys).i2;

        if (( pi2 < 0 ) || ( pi2 > 2))
        return (erc);

        else return(ERC_OK);

        }
```

- See comments in section C.4.2 above.

C.6.0 Dvcharsc.c Function Specification

C.6.1 Dvcharsc.c Design Objectives

This function validates that a character consists only of the following special characters:

blank ( )	0x20
ampersand (&)	0x26
hyphen (-)	0x2D
slash (/)	0x2F

hence the function name dvchar*sc*.c. For this function, pphys is expected to be a character, not a character string.

C.6.2 Dvcharsc.c Source Code and Commentary

```
/* file    : dvcharsc.c
** function: int dvcharsc ( &pphys, maxphys )
** desc    : Data validation for char; validate for an ID number.
**         : check that character "pphys" one of ' ', '&', '-', '/'.
** test pgm: tucharmd.c
*/

#include "ldt.h"

        int dvcharsc ( pphys, maxphys )
```

```
CHAR *pphys;
int maxphys;
{

int erc;
char ch;

erc = ERC_BASE + ENCHAR_E + 3;

if ( maxphys != 1 ) return (erc+1);

ch = *(pphys);

if ( (ch == C_BLANK) || (ch == C_DASH) || (ch == C_AMPER) ||
     (ch == C_SLASH) ) return(ERC_OK);

else return(erc);

}
```

- Note again the use of the uppercase CHAR *pphys.
- Note how maxphys must be 1 when pphys is a single character.

C.7.0 **Dvcharyn.c Function Specification**

C.7.1 **Dvcharyn.c Design Objectives**

This function validates that a **Y**es or **N**o character is passed as pphys. In this case dvcharyn.c anticipates a character, not a string, to be passed as pphys.

C.7.2 **Dvcharyn.c Source Code and Commentary**

```
/* file    : dvcharyn.c
** function: int dvcharyn ( &pphys, maxphys )
** desc    : Data validation for char; check for
**         : 'Y'es/'N'o response
** test pgm: any qaxxxx.c program
*/

#include "ctype.h"
#include "ldt.h"

        int dvcharyn ( pphys, maxphys )

        CHAR *pphys;
        int maxphys;
        {

        int erc;
        char ynchar;

        erc = ERC_BASE + ENCHAR_E + 3;

        if (maxphys != 1) return(erc+1);
```

```
ynchar = toupper(*pphys);

if( (ynchar == 'Y') || (ynchar == 'N') ) return(ERC_OK);
else return(erc);

}
```

- Note the use of CHAR *pphys. (See C.2.2.)
- Note that pphys is expected to be a character therefore maxphys must equal 1.
- Because of the use of typedef CHAR discussed above, the value of pphys is retrieved by the statement

  ynchar = toupper (*pphys);

  which forces ynchar to uppercase alpha. The macro toupper is located in the ctype.h header file in Appendix G.

C.8.0 Dvchar10.c Function Specification

C.8.1 Dvchar10.c Design Objectives

This function is designed to work in conjunction with utcharmd.c. Dvchar10.c validates that the modulus 10 check digit appended to the pphys string is correct (ERC_OK) or incorrect (erc). Refer to Appendix J for detailed discussion of the modulus 10 check digit.

C.8.2 Dvchar10.c Source Code and Commentary

```
/* file    : dvchar10.c
** function: int dvchar10 ( pphys, maxphys )
** desc    : Data validation for char; modulus 10 check digit
** test pgm: tucharmd.c
*/

#include "ldt.h"

        int dvchar10 ( pphys, maxphys )
        CHAR *pphys;
        int maxphys;

        {
        char ch;
        int erc, i, good, slgth, rem;
        long int wgt, sum;

        erc = ERC_BASE + ENCHAR_E + 3;

        if ( (maxphys < 0) || (maxphys > PHY_CHAR) ) return(erc+1);
```

```
slgth = strlen(pphys);
if (slgth == 0) return (erc);

wgt = 2;
sum = pphys[slgth-1] - C_ZERO;

for (i= (slgth - 2); i >= 0; i--)
{
good = FALSE;
ch = pphys[i];

if ( dvcharsc(&ch,1) == 0 ) continue;

if ( (ch >= C_A) && (ch <= C_Z)) good = TRUE;
if ( (ch >= C_ZERO) && (ch <= C_NINE)) good = TRUE;

if ( good == FALSE ) return (erc);

sum = sum + (long)ch * wgt;

if ( wgt == (long)1 ) wgt = 2;
else wgt = 1;
}

if (sum == (long)0) return(erc);

rem = sum % (long)10;

if (rem == 0) return (ERC_OK);
else
return (erc);
}
```

- Note the use of CHAR *pphys. (See C.2.2.)
- Note that pphys is expected to be a character string, and typically maxphys must be the string length of pphys, but not to exceed PHY_CHAR from ldt.h.
- It is assumed that the last character position in pphys contains the modulus 10 check digit (0–9). Each character of pphys is validated, and the validation procedure described in Appendix J is performed to either validate or reject pphys based upon the check digit.

C.9.0 ***Dvchar11.c Function Specification***

C.9.1 ***Dvchar11.c Design Objectives***

This function is designed to work in conjunction with utcharmd.c. Dvchar11.c validates that the modulus 11 check digit appended to the pphys string is correct (ERC_OK) or incorrect (erc). Refer to Appendix J for detailed discussion of the modulus 11 check digit.

C.9.2 Dvchar11.c Source Code and Commentary

```
/* file    : dvchar11.c
** function: int dvchar11 ( pphys, maxphys )
** desc    : Data validation for char; modulus 11 check digit
** test pgm: tucharmd.c
*/

#include "ldt.h"

        int dvchar11 ( pphys, maxphys )
        CHAR *pphys;
        int maxphys;
        {

        char ch;
        int erc, i, good, slgth, rem;
        long int wgt, sum;

        erc = ERC_BASE + ENCHAR_E + 3;

        if ( (maxphys < 0) || (maxphys > PHY_CHAR) ) return(erc+1);

        slgth = strlen(pphys);
        if (slgth == 0) return (erc);

        wgt = 2;
        sum = pphys[slgth-1] - C_A;
        if (sum > 8) sum = sum - (long)1;

        for (i= (slgth - 2); i >= 0; i--)
        {
        good = FALSE;
        ch = pphys[i];

        if ( dvcharsc(&ch,1) == 0 ) continue;

        if ( (ch >= C_A) && (ch <= C_Z)) good = TRUE;
        if ( (ch >= C_ZERO) && (ch <= C_NINE)) good = TRUE;

        if ( good == FALSE ) return (erc);

        sum = sum + (long)ch * wgt;

        wgt = wgt + (long)1;
        }

        if (sum == (long)0) return(erc);

        rem = sum % (long)11;

        if (rem == 0) return (ERC_OK);
        else
        return (erc);
        }
```

- Note the use of CHAR *pphys. See C.2.2.
- Note that pphys is expected to be a character string, and typically maxphys must be the string length of pphys, but not exceed PHY_CHAR.

- It is assumed that the last character position in pphys contains the modulus 11 check digit (A–L, no I). Each character of pphys is validated, and the validation procedure described in Appendix J is performed to either validate or reject pphys based upon the check digit.

D.0.0 Utility Function Development (utcharyy.c)

D.1.0 Utcharyy.c Standard Error Codes

Based upon the ERC_BASE (1000) and ENCHAR_E (11) values in ldt.h, all utcharyy.c functions report the same erc as follows:

1017	Utility Function Error

D.2.0 Utcharcb.c Specifications

D.2.1 Utcharcb.c Design Objectives

This function is widely used throughout this book to implement the character string padding shown in Figure 2.6. A string definition in the C programming language does not initialize memory with a NULL string; therefore we use utcharcb.c to perform this job. This function gives the software developer total logical control over strings when concatenating, justifying, using strings in record structures, and so on.

D.2.2 Utcharcb.c Source Code and Commentary

```
/* file    : utcharcb.c
** function: int utcharcb ( ctrl, string, plgth )
** desc    : create blanks for "string" as follows:
**         : where "plgth" is the declared or
**         : desired physical "string" length.
**         : "plgth" > 0 only.
**         :    ctrl = 1: string of length "plgth"
**         :    ctrl = 2: from "\0" to "plgth"
**         :    ctrl = 3: move "\0" to "plgth" padding blanks.
** test pgm: tucharcb.c
*/
```

```
#include "ldt.h"

        int utcharcb ( ctrl, string, plgth )

        char *string;
        int ctrl, plgth;
        {

        int erc, slgth;
        char *bads = string;
        char *sads, *lads;

        erc = ERC_BASE + ENCHAR_E + 6;

        /*
        ** validate "ctrl"
        */

        if (( ctrl < 1 ) || ( ctrl > 3 )) return ( erc );

        slgth = strlen(string);

        if (plgth < 1) return(erc);

        switch ( ctrl )
        {
                case 1: sads = bads;
                        lads = bads + plgth - 1;
                        while ( sads < lads )
                        {
                        *sads = C_BLANK;
                        sads++;
                        }
                        *sads = C_NUL;
                        break;

                case 2: if (slgth >= plgth - 1 ) break;
                        sads = bads + slgth + 1;
                        lads = bads + plgth - 1;
                        while ( sads <= lads )
                        {
                        *sads = C_BLANK;
                        sads++;
                        }
                        break;

                case 3: if (slgth >= plgth - 1) break;
                        sads = bads + slgth;
                        lads = bads + plgth - 1;
                        while ( sads < lads )
                        {
                        *sads = C_BLANK;
                        sads++;
                        }
                        *sads = C_NUL;
                        break;
        }
        return(ERC_OK);
        }
```

- The effects of the ctrl function argument are described in Figure 2.6.

- The plgth function argument is the declared string size. For example,

```
char string[23];
```

plgth would be 23. Plgth then locates the NULL character position of a string. Similarly plgth must be greater than 0.

- Note the use of address arithmetic for the implementation of ctrl functions 1, 2, and 3.

D.3.0 Utcharcm.c Specifications

D.3.1 Utcharcm.c Design Objectives

This function compares two strings while allowing control over the results that upper- and lowercase and string length have on the comparison. The function returns the difference between the last characters or bytes (str2[i] − str1[i]). If they are equal under the chosen ctrl value, a 0 difference is returned; otherwise the function returns either a $+n$ *or* $-n$ value. Four ctrl values control the basis of the string comparison:

- Ctrl = 1. Results in a literal string comparison; each character of the two strings is compared until one string is exhausted. The trailing NULL (0x00) is considered a character of each string, and treated as such.
- Ctrl = 2. Same as ctrl = 1, except that any upper- or lowercase differences are ignored when computing byte differences.
- Ctrl = 3. Same as ctrl = 1, except that the comparison is controlled up to strlen(str2); i.e., the NULL delimiter of str2 is not treated as a part of str2.
- Ctrl = 4. Same as ctrl = 2, except that the comparison is controlled up to strlen(str2).

Note that ctrl = 3 or 4 is useful for prefix comparisons of strings. This technique is used in function endate.c for checking day and month names.

D.3.2 ***Utcharcm.c Source Code and Commentary***

```
/* file    : utcharcm.c
** function: int utcharcm ( ctrl, str1, str2 )
** desc    : compare "str2" to "str1"
**         :    ctrl = 1: literal compare of "str2" to "str1"
**         :    ctrl = 2: compare "str2" to "str1" w/o U/l case.
**         :    ctrl = 3: as "ctrl=1" for length of "str2"
**         :    ctrl = 4: as "ctrl=2" for length of "str2"
**         : returned values:
**         :    0  = equal
**         :    -n = "str2" < "str1"; last byte diff value.
**         :    +n = "str2" > "str1"; last byte diff value
** test pgm: tucharcm.c
*/

#include "stdio.h"
#include "ldt.h"
#include "ctype.h"

        int utcharcm ( ctrl, str1, str2 )
        char *str1, *str2;
        int ctrl;
        {
        int lstr1, lstr2, lmin, lim, flag2, i, dbyte;

        /*
        ** validate "ctrl"
        */

        if (( ctrl < 1 ) || ( ctrl > 4 )) ctrl = 1;

        /*
        ** establish "loop" limits
        */

        lstr1 = strlen(str1);
        lstr2 = strlen(str2);
        lmin = min(lstr1,lstr2);
        flag2 = TRUE;
        if (lmin != lstr2) flag2 = FALSE;

        switch (ctrl)
        {
                case 1:
                case 2: lim = lmin + 1;
                        break;
                case 3:
                case 4: if ( flag2 == FALSE ) lim = lmin + 1;
                        else lim = lmin;
                        break;
        }


        {
        switch ( ctrl )
        {
                case 1:
                case 3: dbyte = str2[i] - str1[i];
                        break;

                case 2:
                case 4: dbyte = toupper(str2[i]) - toupper(str1[i]);
                        break;
        }
        if (dbyte != 0) return(dbyte);
        }

        return(dbyte);
        }
```

- The loop limits are set based upon the relative lengths of str1 and str2 and the choice of ctrl. Once set, the variable, lim, controls the outcome of the string comparison.
- Note that the string comparison is terminated at the first byte inequality when processed left to right. If, for some reason, a string comparison must be evaluated right to left, use function utcharrs.c to reverse both str1 and str2 before calling utcharcm.c.

D.4.0 **Utcharcs.c Specifications**

D.4.1 ***Utcharcs.c Design Objectives***

This function converts character to string and vice-versa. It can be used in lieu of enchar.c and dechar.c. and is often useful when a function argument type of character or string must be satisfied.

D.4.2 ***Utcharcs.c Source Code and Commentary***

```
/* file    : utcharcs.c
** function: int utcharcs ( ctrl, &ch, string )
** desc    : if ctrl = 1 = TRUE : convert "ch" to "string"
**         : if ctrl = 0 = FALSE: convert first character
**         :                      of "string" to "ch".
** test pgm: qachar.c
*/

#include "ldt.h"

        int utcharcs (ctrl, ch, string)
        char *ch, *string;
        int ctrl;
        {

        /*
        ** if ctrl = TRUE ch ==> string; else string ==> ch
        */

        if (ctrl == TRUE)
        {
        *(string) = *ch;
        *(string+1) = C_NUL;
        return(ERC_OK);
        }

        else
        {
        *ch = *(string);
        return(ERC_OK);
        }
        }
```

- If converting from string to character, only the first character of the string is used. No transformations are made on any characters as provided for by enchar.c and dechar.c.

D.5.0 Utcharjs.c Specifications

D.5.1 Utcharjs.c Design Objectives

This function is used by dexxxx.c functions that provide mandatory string justification. The standard NO_JUST, C_JUST, L_JUST, and R_JUST are handled. If a bad jflag argument is provided, NO_JUST is assumed.

D.5.2 Utcharjs.c Source Code and Commentary

```
/* file    : utcharjs.c
** function: int utcharjs ( jflag, string )
** desc    : justify "string" according to "jflag"
**         : where "jflag" = NO_JUST, C_JUST, L_LUST, or R_JUST
** test pgm: tucharjs.c
*/

#include "ldt.h"

        int utcharjs (jflag,string)

        char *string;
        int jflag;
        {

        /*
        ** Justify string
        */

        switch (jflag)
        {
                case NO_JUST: break;

                case L_JUST:  ljust(C_BLANK,string);
                              break;

                case R_JUST:  rjust(C_BLANK,string);
                              break;

                case C_JUST:  cjust(C_BLANK,string);
                              break;

                   default:   break;
        }
        return (ERC_OK);
        }
```

- The source code for the underlying component functions cjust.c, ljust.c, and rjust.c are covered in Chapter 3.

D.6.0 Utcharrs.c Specifications

D.6.1 Utcharrs.c Design Objectives

This function, reverses the characters of a string in place. It is used, for example, by the fputstr.c function which must fill a mask with an init character string from right to left (RL).

D.6.2 Utcharrs.c Source Code and Commentary

```
/* file    : utcharrs.c
** function: int utcharrs ( string )
** desc    : reverse the characters in "string".
** test pgm: tucharjs.c
*/

#include "stdio.h"
#include "ldt.h"

        int utcharrs (string)
        char *string;

        {
        char swap;
        char *bads = string;
        char *sads, *lads;
        int slgth, nlb, ntb, mb, i;

        /*
        ** Reverse string
        */

        slgth = snlbntb(C_BLANK,&nlb, &ntb, string);

        if ( (slgth - nlb - ntb) < 1 ) return(ERC_OK);

        mb = min( nlb, ntb );

        sads = bads + mb;
        lads = bads + slgth - mb - 1;

        mb = ((lads - sads) + 1) / 2;

        for (i=0; i < mb; i++)
        {
        swap = *sads;
        *sads = *lads;
        *lads = swap;
        sads++;
        lads--;
        }
        return (ERC_OK);
        }
```

- Note that no excessive "character swaps" are made when leading and trailing blank (0x20) characters are involved. The variable, mb, accounts for this situation.

D.7.0 Utcharsb.c Specifications

D.7.1 Utcharsb.c Design Objectives

This function is used extensively throughout the book by enxxxx.c functions. It strips leading, trailing, or leading and trailing characters from a string under control of function argument ctrl. If a bad ctrl value is passed, no action is taken.

D.7.2 Utcharsb.c Source Code and Commentary

```
/* file    : utcharsb.c
** function: int utcharsb ( ctrl, string, ch )
** desc    : strip "ch" from "string" as follows:
**         :    ctrl = 1: strip leading "ch"
**         :    ctrl = 2: strip trailing "ch"
**         :    ctrl = 3: strip both leading & trailing "ch"
** test pgm: tucharsb.c
*/

#include "ldt.h"

        int utcharsb ( ctrl, string, ch )

        char *string, ch;
        int ctrl;
        {

        int erc, nlb, ntb, slgth;
        char *bads = string;
        char *lads;

        slgth = snlbntb( ch, &nlb, &ntb, string );
        if ( slgth == 0 ) return (ERC_OK);

        switch ( ctrl )
        {
                case 1: ljust(ch,string);
                        lads = bads + slgth - nlb;
                        *lads = C_NUL;
                        break;
                case 2: lads = bads + slgth - ntb;
                        *lads = C_NUL;
                        break;
                case 3: ljust(ch,string);
                        lads = bads + slgth - nlb - ntb;
                        *lads = C_NUL;
                        break;

                default:break;
        }
        return(ERC_OK);
        }
```

- Note that ctrl = 1 is *not* equivalent to left justification of a string, because when stripping characters, additional blanks cannot be added to the end of the string.

- Note that ctrl = 2 is *not* equivalent to right justification of a string, because when stripping characters, additional blanks cannot be added to the beginning of a string.

E.0.0 LDT Char Application Tips and Reminders

E.1.0 Helpful Notes

Using the standard interface function definitions for the char logical data type might seem somewhat more complicated than for the other LDTs included in this book. This is because C passes all strings as pointers, string lengths in C are delimited by a trailing NULL character, and because single characters must be passed as "&character" to satisfy the standard interface definitions.

Let's highlight some helpful reminders about using the functions included in this chapter.

- **Enchar.c and evchar.c:** The maxin function argument should be the sizeof(pstrin) − 1. Maxin is the declared pstrin (size − 1) so as not to include the NULL delimiting character. For a character ensubtype, pphys should be the &character and maxphys should be 1; for a string ensubtype, pphys should be a string and maxphys should be sizeof(pphys) − 1.
- **Getchar.c and fgetchar.c:** The maxstr function argument should be the sizeof(string) − 1. Cltab only controls the very first character read operation performed. Nuexit is a returned value and therefore must be passed as &nuexit.
- **Dechar.c, putchar.c, and fputchar.c:** The maxout function argument should be the sizeof(pstrin) − 1. Maxout is the declared pstrout (size − 1) so as not to include the NULL delimiting character. Maxout must be large enough to receive the decoded pphys or an erc will

result. For a character desubtype, pphys should be the &character and maxphys should be 1; for a string desubtype, pphys should be a string and maxphys should be sizeof(pphys) – 1 so as not to include the trailing NULL delimiter.

- **Dvcharyy.c:** When these functions are used as function arguments they must be explicitly declared in the calling program.
- **General:** Initialize all strings before using them with utcharcb.c (see D.2.0).

E.2.0 Special Uses

The char logical data type obviously can be utilized to represent many commonly encountered commercial fields of data. Insights into the special use of this LDT are highlighted by the dvcharyy.c and special utcharyy.c functions for handling the following:

- **Check digits:** Both modulus 10 and 11 check digits are fully explored for alphanumeric strings. See functions dvchar10.c, dvchar11.c, and utcharmd.c (C.8.2, C.9.2, E.3.2)
- **ID numbers:** Alphanumeric strings are covered by the functions dvcharan.c and dvcharsc.c (C.2.2, C.6.2).
- **Logicals:** These are fields that are one character or byte long and record a FALSE or TRUE indicator flag. They are one-byte characters, not two-byte integers. See function dvcharlg.c (C.3.2).
- **Names:** The formatting of names (first, middle, last) is covered by function utcharna.c (E.4.2).
- **Radix conversions:** The utcharrx.c function is provided to perform base2 through base16 number system conversions (E.5.2).
- **Soundex codes:** The soundex "sounds-like" coding system is implemented by the function utcharsx.c as a possible database element to facilitate data retrieval on a "sounds-like" basis (E.6.2).

- **Zip codes:** United States standard zip and zip + 4 codes are numeric by design and are covered by the LDT int; however, overseas postal schemes (Canada, Britain, etc.) utilize alphanumeric zip coding schemes. The LDT char can be used in system design to accommodate these schemes.

E.3.0 Utcharmd.c Specifications

E.3.1 Utcharmd.c Design Objectives

This function is designed to compute a modulus 10 (0–9) or modulus 11 (A–L no I) check digit ckdig based upon ctrl for a character string consisting only of numeric, uppercase alpha, or one of the allowable delimiting characters.

A ckdig character of blank (0x20) is returned if an error condition is encountered.

E.3.2 Utcharmd.c Source Code and Commentary

```
/* file    : utcharmd.c
** function: int utcharmd ( ctrl, string, &ckdig )
** desc    : compute "ckdig" from "string" under "ctrl"
**         :    ctrl = 10: Modulus 10 check digit ['0' => '9']
**         :    ctrl = 11: Modulus 11 check digit ['A' => 'L']
**         :                                       no 'I' used
** test pgm: tucharmd.c
*/

#include "ldt.h"

        int utcharmd ( ctrl, string, ckdig )
        char *string, *ckdig;
        int ctrl;

        {
        char ch;
        int erc, i, good;
        int slgth, rem;
        long int wgt, sum, nten;

        *ckdig = C_BLANK;

        erc = ERC_BASE + ENCHAR_E + 6;

        /*
        ** validate "ctrl"
        */

        if (( ctrl < 10 ) || ( ctrl > 11 )) return ( erc );
```

```
slgth = strlen(string);
if ( slgth == 0 ) return (ERC_OK);

wgt = 2;
sum = 0;

for ( i = (slgth - 1); i >= 0; i--)
{
good = FALSE;
ch = string[i];

if ( dvcharsc(&ch,1) == 0 ) continue;

if ( (ch >= C_A) && (ch <= C_Z)) good = TRUE;
if ( (ch >= C_ZERO) && (ch <= C_NINE)) good = TRUE;

if ( good == FALSE ) return (erc);

sum = sum + (long)ch * wgt;

switch (ctrl)
{
        case 10: if (wgt == (long)1) wgt = 2;
                 else wgt = 1;
                 break;

        case 11: wgt = wgt + (long)1;
                 break;
}
}

if (sum == (long)0) return(erc);

switch (ctrl)
{
        case 10: nten = ((sum + (long)10)/(long)10) * (long)10;
                 rem = nten - sum;
                 if (rem == 10) rem = 0;
                 *ckdig = C_ZERO + rem;
                 break;

        case 11: rem = sum % (long)11;
                 if (rem != 0) rem = 11 - rem;
                 if (rem < 8) *ckdig = C_A + rem;
                 else *ckdig = 'J' + rem - 8;
                 break;

}

return(ERC_OK);

}
```

- Note that for a modulus 10, ckdig can only be character 0–9.
- Note that for a modulus 11, ckdig can only be a character A–L; no I is used to avoid confusion with lowercase l or the numeral 1.

E.4.0 Utcharna.c Specifications

E.4.1 Utcharna.c Design Objectives

This function is designed to provide a variety of output name formats given a firstn (first name string), mi (middle initial or middle name string), and lastn (last name string).

This function is designed to return a character pointer so that definition of a string to contain the formatted output name is not necessary as a function argument. Missing elements (i.e., firstn, mi, or lastn) are formatted on output to appear as an underline character (0x5F).

E.4.2 Utcharna.c Source Code and Commentary

```
/* file     : utcharna.c
** function: char *utcharna (ctrl, firstn, mi, lastn)
** desc     : return a pointer to name field requested by "ctrl":
**          : ctrl = 1: "firstn mi. lastn"
**          : ctrl = 2: "lastn, firstn mi."
**          : ctrl = 3: "firstninit. mi. lastn"
**          : ctrl = 4: "lastn, firstninit. mi."
**          : ctrl = 5: "firstn lastn"
**          : ctrl = 6: "lastn, firstn"
**          : ctrl = 7: "firstninit. lastn"
**          : ctrl = 8: "last, firstninit."
** test pgm: tucharna.c
*/

#include "ldt.h"
#include "ctype.h"

        char *utcharna (ctrl, firstn, mi, lastn)
        int ctrl;
        char *firstn, *mi, *lastn;
        {

        static char *name[40];

        char first[15], last [25];
        char fi, firstinit[3], minit[3];
        int sname, sminit;

        sname = sizeof(name) - 1;
        utcharcb(1,name,1);
        utcharcb(2,name,sizeof(name));

        if ( (ctrl < 1) || (ctrl > 8) ) ctrl = 1;

        strcpy(first, firstn);
        strcpy(last, lastn);

        *(first) = toupper(first[0]);
        utcharsb(3,first,C_BLANK);
        *(mi) = toupper(mi[0]);
        *(last) = toupper(last[0]);
        utcharsb(3,last,C_BLANK);
```

```
fi = first[0];
if (strlen(first) == 0)
{
fi = C_UL;
inschr(first, sizeof(first)-1, fi, 1);
}
utcharcs(1, &fi, firstinit);
inschr(firstinit, sizeof(firstinit)-1, C_PERIOD, 0);

if (*(mi) == C_SPACE) utcharcb(1,minit,1);
else
{
utcharcs(1, mi, minit);
inschr(minit, sizeof(minit)-1, C_PERIOD, 0);
}

sminit = strlen(minit);

*(last) = toupper(last[0]);
if (strlen(last) == 0) inschr(last, sizeof(last)-1, C_UL, 1);


switch (ctrl)

{


        case 1: strcat(name, first);
                inschr(name, sname, C_SPACE, 0);
                strcat(name, minit);
                if (sminit != 0) inschr(name,sname,C_SPACE,0);
                strcat(name, last);
                break;

        case 2: strcat(name, last);
                inschr(name, sname, C_COMMA, 0);
                inschr(name, sname, C_SPACE, 0);
                strcat(name, first);
                if (sminit != 0) inschr(name,sname,C_SPACE,0);
                strcat(name, minit);
                break;

        case 3: strcat(name, firstinit);
                inschr(name, sname, C_SPACE, 0);
                strcat(name, minit);
                if (sminit != 0) inschr(name,sname,C_SPACE,0);
                strcat(name, last);
                break;

        case 4: strcat(name, last);
                inschr(name, sname, C_COMMA, 0);
                inschr(name, sname, C_SPACE, 0);
                strcat(name, firstinit);
                if (sminit != 0) inschr(name,sname,C_SPACE,0);
                strcat(name, minit);
                break;

        case 5: strcat(name, first);
                inschr(name, sname, C_SPACE, 0);
                strcat(name, last);
                break;

        case 6: strcat(name, last);
                inschr(name, sname, C_COMMA, 0);
                inschr(name, sname, C_SPACE, 0);
                strcat(name, first);
                break;
```

```
        case 7: strcat(name, firstinit);
                inschr(name, sname, C_SPACE, 0);
                strcat(name, last);
                break;

        case 8: strcat(name, last);
                inschr(name, sname, C_COMMA, 0);
                inschr(name, sname, C_SPACE, 0);
                strcat(name, firstinit);
                break;
}

return(name);

}
```

- Note the overall handling of this function as a character pointer.

  char *utcharna(. . . . .);
  static char *name[40];

- Note that if the use of inschr(name, sname, etc.) tries to expand name beyond sname in length, inschr simply truncates name at that point.

- The insertion of underline characters where name elements are missing is intended to highlight the missing element so that it can be corrected; otherwise, misleading names could be generated.

E.5.0 Utcharrx.c Specifications

E.5.1 Utcharrx.c Design Objectives

This function allows conversions between number systems of base (radix) 2 through 16, which is essential for a complete understanding of the fundamental C data types of char, int, long int, float, and double. It allows not only whole numbers, but also fractions to be converted easily.

E.5.2 Utcharrx.c Source Code and Commentary

```
/* file    : utcharrx.c
** function: char *utcharrx ( rin, str, rout )
** desc    : convert whole number "str" of radix "rin" to
**         : a string pointed to by *utcharrx of radix "rout"
**         :    rin/rout limited to [2 => 16]
**         :    digits are [0 => 9; A => F]
**         : "str" format: wwwww.fffff [whole.fraction]
**         : largest www.fff is [32].[52]
** test pgm: tucharrx.c
*/
```

```
#include "ldt.h"
#include "ctype.h"

        char *utcharrx ( rin, str, rout)
        char *str;
        int rin, rout;
        {

        static char *rxconv[86];
        static char digits[] = { '0', '1', '2', '3', '4', '5',
                                 '6', '7', '8', '9',
                                 'A', 'B', 'C', 'D', 'E', 'F'};
        char whole[32], fraction[52];
        int erc, i, j, pos;
        int slgth, digfl, digvalue, rem;
        long int wgt, value;
        char ch;
        double dvalue, dwgt;

        utcharcb(1, rxconv, 1);

        slgth = strlen(str);
        if (slgth == 0) return(rxconv);

        if ( (rin < 2) || (rin > 16) ) rin = 16;
        if ( (rout < 2) || ( rout > 16 ) ) rout = 16;

        /*
        ** get whole & fraction portions of "str"
        */

        utcharcb(1,whole,1);
        utcharcb(1,fraction,1);

        pos = poschr(str, C_PERIOD, 0);
        if (pos == 0) strcpy(whole,str);
        else
        {
        for (i=0; i < (pos - 1); i++)
        {
        inschr(whole,sizeof(whole)-1,str[i],0);
        }
        for (i = pos; i < slgth; i++)
        {
        inschr(fraction,sizeof(fraction)-1,str[i],0);
        }
        }

        /*
        ** process "whole" portion of "str"
        */

        slgth = strlen(whole);

        value = 0;
        wgt = 1;

        for (i = (slgth - 1); i >=0; i--)
        {
        digfl = FALSE;
        for (j=0; j < rin; j++)
        {
        whole[i] = toupper(whole[i]);
        if (whole[i] == digits[j])
        {
        digfl = TRUE;
        break;
        }
        }
```

```
if (digfl == FALSE) return(rxconv);
digvalue = whole[i] - C_ZERO;
if (whole[i] > C_NINE) digvalue = whole[i] - C_A + 10;

value = value + (long)digvalue * wgt;
wgt = wgt * (long)rin;
}

if (value == (long)0)
{
inschr(rxconv, sizeof(rxconv)-1, digits[0], 1);
}

while ( value > 0)
{
rem = value % (long)rout;
ch = digits[rem];
inschr(rxconv, sizeof(rxconv)-1, ch, 1);
value = value / (long)rout;
}

/*
** insert separating '.' for "whole"."fraction"
*/

inschr(rxconv,sizeof(rxconv)-1,C_PERIOD,0);

/*
** process "fraction" portion of "str"
*/

slgth = strlen(fraction);

dvalue = 0;
dwgt = (double)1.0 / (double)rin;

for (i=0; i < slgth; i++)
{
digfl = FALSE;
for (j=0; j < rin; j++)
{
fraction[i] = toupper(fraction[i]);
if (fraction[i] == digits[j])
{
digfl = TRUE;
break;
}
}
if (digfl == FALSE) return(rxconv);
digvalue = fraction[i] - C_ZERO;
if (fraction[i] > C_NINE) digvalue = fraction[i] - C_A + 10;

dvalue = dvalue + (double)digvalue * dwgt;
dwgt = dwgt / (double)rin;
}

if (dvalue == (double)0.0)
{
inschr(rxconv, sizeof(rxconv)-1, digits[0], 0);
return(rxconv);
}

for (i=0; i < 52; i++)
```

```
{
dvalue = dvalue * (double)rout;
rem = dvalue;
ch = digits[rem];
inschr(rxconv, sizeof(rxconv)-1, ch, 0);
dvalue = dvalue - (double)rem;
if (dvalue <= 0.0000000000000001) break;
}

return(rxconv);
}
```

- Because utcharrx.c uses the data type double, some rounding error is introduced, but as you will see, it is quite acceptable and, for the most part, obvious.
- Function utcharrx.c is of type character pointer, returning a pointer to an expanded radix conversion string.

E.6.0 ***Utcharsx.c Specifications***

E.6.1 ***Utcharsx.c Design Objectives***

Given the extensive use of names in commercial application programs and the emphasis upon database oriented systems and query languages, this function provides an alternative method of retrieving names by incorporating the soundex "sounds-like" code.

If a four-character data element is introduced into a database consisting of the corresponding soundex code, retrievals can be made for a user, based upon "sounds-like" spelling of a name, when the exact spelling is not known. This function has been implemented according to the description provided by the government publication credited after the utcharsx.c source code listing.

E.6.2 ***Utcharsx.c Source Code and Commentary***

```
/* file    : utcharsx.c
** function: int utcharsx ( lname, scode )
** desc    : compute the four-char soundex scode from surname lname
** test pgm: tucharsx.c
*/
```

```
#include "ldt.h"
#include "ctype.h"

        int utcharsx (lname, scode)
        char *lname, *scode;
        {

        char sname[30];
        char *bads = lname;
        char *sads, *lads, ch, lch, sch;
        int erc, slgth, i;

        erc = ERC_BASE + ENCHAR_E + 6;

        /*
        ** STEP #1:
        **
        ** copy "lname" to "sname":
        **      accepting only alphabetic characters;
        **      forcing all remaining letters to upper case;
        **      eliminating all blank characters;
        */

        utcharcb(1,scode,1);
        utcharcb(1,sname,1);

        slgth = strlen(lname);
        if (slgth == 0) return(ERC_OK);

        lads = bads + slgth - 1;
        sads = bads;

        while ( sads <= lads )
        {
        ch = toupper(*sads);
        sads++;

        if (isalpha(ch) == FALSE) continue;

        switch (ch)
        {
                case ' ': break;

                default: inschr(sname, sizeof(sname)-1, ch, 0);
                         break;
        }
        }


        /*
        ** STEP #2:
        **
        **      eliminate adjacent remaining like characters;
        */


        slgth = strlen(sname);
        if (slgth == 0) return(ERC_OK);

        for (i=1; i < slgth; i++)
        {
        if (sname[i] == sname[i-1])
        {
        delchr(sname,i);
        slgth = slgth - 1;
        i--;
        }
        }
```

```
/*
** STEP #3:
**
** Construct soundex code;
** eliminating characters: A,E,I,O,U,W,Y,H
** eliminate adjacent like soundex codes;
** fill trailing unused code positions with zeroes;
** always keep the 1st character of last name.
*/

slgth = strlen(sname);
if (slgth == 0) return(ERC_OK);

for (i=0; i < slgth; i++)
{
ch = sname[i];
switch (ch)
{
        case 'A':
        case 'E':
        case 'I':
        case 'O':
        case 'U':
        case 'W':
        case 'Y':
        case 'H': sch = '*';
                  break;

        case 'B':
        case 'P':
        case 'F':
        case 'V': sch = '1';
                  break;

        case 'C':
        case 'S':
        case 'K':
        case 'G':
        case 'J':
        case 'Q':
        case 'X':
        case 'Z': sch = '2';
                  break;

        case 'D':
        case 'T': sch = '3';
                  break;

        case 'L': sch = '4';
                  break;

        case 'M':
        case 'N': sch = '5';
                  break;

        case 'R': sch = '6';
                  break;

        default: return(erc);
}

if ( i == 0 )
{
lch = sname[0];
inschr(scode, 4, lch, 0);
lch = sch;
continue;
}
```

```
        if (sch == '*')
        {
        lch = sch;
        continue;
        }

        if (sch == lch) continue;

        lch = sch;
        inschr(scode, 4, sch, 0);
        }

        for (i=1; i <= 3; i++) inschr(scode, 4, '0', 0);

        return (ERC_OK);
        }

/*
** Reference:
** National Archives & Record Service:
** "Getting Started Beginning Your Genealogical Research"
*/
```

- Computing the proper soundex code is a bit trickier than it first appears. The rules for construction as described in the publication must be studied carefully.

F.0.0 *Testing and Quality Assurance (qachar.c)*

F.1.0 *Qachar.c Specifications*

F.1.1 *Qachar.c Design Objectives*

The design objectives of each qaxxxx.c function are the same: to provide an independent, comprehensive method of testing the various standard interfaces defined in Part 1 of this book. Qachar.c is unique to the char logical data type, but is in keeping with all other qaxxxx.c routines.

Qachar.c utilizes enchar.c, evchar.c, getchar.c, fgetchar.c, dechar.c, putchar.c, and fputchar.c, as well as dvcharyy.c, utcharyy.c, and supporting functions as indicated in the linker automatic response file, qachar.lnk, listed in Appendix I.

Qachar.c provides runtime control over the resetting of stdlog, making stdlog entries, and screen printing upon error detection, as well as the interactive testing of each allowable ensubtype and desubtype value.

Each qaxxxx.c program is not only an excellent example of LDT testing, but also demonstrates techniques for the use of the various standard interfaces portrayed in this book. A close examination of qachar.c will reveal a powerful program of only 145 statements.

F.1.2 Qachar.c Error Codes

Qaxxxx.c functions do not have any reserved ercs of their own; rather, they simply report the ercs detected during processing by the underlying standard interface functions.

All ercs detected for LDT char, however, are governed by the following ldt.h header file values:

ERC_BASE	1000
GET_E	1
PUT_E	5
ENCHAR_E	11

F.2.0 Qachar.c Source Code and Commentary

```
/*
** file   : qachar.c
** desc   : quality assurance test program for LDT CHARacter
** link   : @qachar.lnk,qachar,nul,lcs
*/

#include "ldt.h"

main ()
{
        int dvcharyn(), dvcharqs(), dvcharqc(), dvdummy();

        static char mtype[] = ">??<";
        static char mstr[] = ">??????????????????<";
        static char myn[] = ">?<";

        static char inits[] = "0";
        static char initc[] = "10";
        static char inity[] = "Y";
        static char initn[] = "N";

        char str[30], enstr[30], destr[19], dechr[2];
        char ynchar, ch;

        int erc, etype, lpe, nuexit;
        int smstr, smyn;

        smstr = nondel(mstr);
        smyn = nondel(myn);

        blanksc(1,1,MAX_ROW,MAX_COL);
        setcrc(1,1);
        putstr("CHARacter Quality Assurance Program",LR,"",DISP_F);
```

```
        /*
        ** Prompt for User Runtime Controls
        */

        uprompt (&lpe);

        if ( (lpe == 10) || (lpe == 11) )
                logwrite(5,"QACHAR",0,"Begin Testing");

        for (;;)
        {

        blanksc(2,1,MAX_ROW,MAX_COL);
        setcrc(1,1);

/*
** String Testing
*/
        movcrc(2,-MAX_COL);
        putstr("Enter String ENCODE Subtype: ",LR,"",DISP_F);

        erc = getint(str,sizeof(str)-1,NO,myn,LR,inits,MAND_F,YES,
                     &nuexit,&etype,PHY_INT,1,MAND_F,lpe,dvcharqs);

        if (lderc(erc) == 9) break;

        movcrc(2,-MAX_COL);
        putstr("Enter a String        : ",LR,"",DISP_F);


        erc = getchar(str,sizeof(str)-1,NO,mstr,LR,"",MAND_F,NO,&nuexit,
                      enstr,sizeof(enstr)-1,etype,MAND_F,lpe,dvdummy);

        if (lderc(erc) == 9) continue;

        movcrc(2,-MAX_COL);
        putstr("ENCODEed String       : ",LR,"",DISP_F);
        putstr(enstr,LR,mstr,DISP_F);

        movcrc(2,-MAX_COL);
        putstr("DECODEed Subtype [0]: ",LR,"",DISP_F);
        putchar(destr,smstr,enstr,strlen(enstr),0,NO_JUST,
                LR,mstr,DISP_F,lpe);

        movcrc(1,-MAX_COL);
        putstr("DECODEed Subtype [1]: ",LR,"",DISP_F);
        putchar(destr,smstr,enstr,strlen(enstr),1,NO_JUST,
                LR,mstr,DISP_F,lpe);

        movcrc(1,-MAX_COL);
        putstr("DECODEed Subtype [2]: ",LR,"",DISP_F);
        putchar(destr,smstr,enstr,strlen(enstr),2,NO_JUST,
                LR,mstr,DISP_F,lpe);

/*
** Character Testing
*/

        movcrc(3,-MAX_COL);
        putstr("Enter Character ENCODE Subtype: ",LR,"",DISP_F);

        erc = getint(str,sizeof(str)-1,NO,mtype,LR,initc,MAND_F,NO,
                     &nuexit,&etype,PHY_INT,1,MAND_F,lpe,dvcharqc);

        if (lderc(erc) == 9) continue;

        movcrc(2,-MAX_COL);
        putstr("Enter a Character     : ",LR,"",DISP_F);
```

```
    erc = getchar(str,sizeof(str)-1,NO,myn,LR,"",MAND_F,NO,
                &nuexit,&ch,1,etype,MAND_F,lpe,dvdummy);

    movcrc(2,-MAX_COL);
    putstr("ENCODEed Character    : ",LR,"",DISP_F);
    utcharcs(1,&ch,str);
    putstr(str,LR,myn,DISP_F);

    movcrc(2,-MAX_COL);
    putstr("DECODEed Subtype [10]: ",LR,"",DISP_F);
    putchar(dechr,smyn,&ch,1,10,NO_JUST,
            LR,myn,DISP_F,lpe);

    movcrc(1,-MAX_COL);
    putstr("DECODEed Subtype [11]: ",LR,"",DISP_F);
    putchar(dechr,smyn,&ch,1,11,NO_JUST,
            LR,myn,DISP_F,lpe);

    movcrc(1,-MAX_COL);
    putstr("DECODEed Subtype [12]: ",LR,"",DISP_F);
    putchar(dechr,smyn,&ch,1,12,NO_JUST,
            LR,myn,DISP_F,lpe);


    setcrc(MAX_ROW - 1,-MAX_COL);
    putstr("Continue? [Yes/No] or [ESCape]: ",LR,"",DISP_F);

    erc = getchar(str,sizeof(str)-1,NO,myn,LR,inity,MAND_F,NO,
                &nuexit,&ynchar,1,11,MAND_F,lpe,dvcharyn);

    if (lderc(erc) == 9) break;
    if (ynchar == 'N') break;

    }

    if ( (lpe == 10) || (lpe == 11) )
            logwrite(6,"QACHAR",0,"End Testing");

    blanksc(1,1,MAX_ROW,MAX_COL);
    exit(0);
}
```

- All dvxxxxyy.c functions to be used as function arguments *must* be declared explicitly in the calling program.
- All masks are declared with outermost field delimiters so that the field limits can always be known, regardless of the type of field and hence video attribute chosen for display.
- All initial values are declared to make their revision easy should it become necessary.
- Both destr[19] and dechr[2] match the nondelimiter size of masks mstr[ ] and myn[ ] respectively. The size of a displayed string must not exceed the corresponding number of mask nondelimiter positions, if a mask is used for display purposes.

- Variable lpe is calculated by uprompt.c from runtime user responses and effectively becomes the standard function argument logprerr. (See Chapter 13 for more information.)

- Anywhere in the source code where

  ```
  if (lderc(erc) = = 9)
  ```

  appears, an equivalent statement

  ```
  if (nuexit = = -1)
  ```

  could have been specified.

- Note that because there were only three possible choices for both ensubtype and desubtype, qachar.c simply generates decode [0,1, and 2] for strings and decode [10,11, and 12] for characters. Other qaxxxx.c programs handle this differently.

- Note that hitting the Escape key recycles the program unless performed at

  "Enter String ENCODE Subtype:"

  or

  "Continue? [Yes/No] or [Escape]:"

  where it exits the program. Hitting Ctrl-Break has no effect in qaxxxx.c programs because Ctrl-Break has been turned off in function _main (see Appendix H).

- Note sample output in Figure 5.1.

```
CHARacter Quality Assurance Program

Enter String ENCODE Subtype: >0<

Enter a String       : >R.A. RAdcliffe    <

ENCODEed String      : >R.A. RAdcliffe    <

DECODEed Subtype [0]: >R.A. RAdcliffe    <
DECODEed Subtype [1]: >R.A. RADCLIFFE    <
DECODEed Subtype [2]: >r.a. radcliffe    <


Enter Character ENCODE Subtype: >10<

Enter a Character     : >r<

ENCODEed Character    : >r<

DECODEed Subtype [10]: >r<
DECODEed Subtype [11]: >R<
DECODEed Subtype [12]: >r<

Continue? [Yes/No] or [ESCape]: >Y<
```

Figure 5.1– Qachar.c Sample Output

Dates

6

This chapter covers the I/O of date fields that are encoded to and decoded from a storage format as specified by the following statement in ldt.h:

typedef long int DATE;

All date fields are stored as long int values in the form yyyymmdd. For example, February 28, 1986 is stored as the integer value 19860228. Date fields are probably the most common data element found in the disk record structures of commercial applications. They are often used as key fields (indices) when interfacing with file management and sorting software packages as described in Chapter 2.

Each interface definition described in Part 1 of this book is implemented for the date logical data type (xxxx = date). The endate.c function accepts all dedate.c formats and, by the specification of the ensubtype function argument, controls the date sequence (format) that is anticipated. The ensubtype argument is an integer of up to three digits chosen from the numbers one to four (with the meanings below) in the order you want for your date input format:

1 = yy (two digit year)
2 = mm (month number, optional three character abbreviation mmm, or full monthname)
3 = dd (day number, optional three character abbreviation ddd, or full dayname)
4 = yyyy (four digit year)

If fewer than three digits are specified for an ensubtype argument value, the missing component(s) are taken from the current system date and added to those input by the user. To input February 28, 1986 for example, using the ensubtype argument of 231, enter one of the following:

022886 or 02 28 86 or 02-28-86 or 02/28/86

The dedate.c function generates date output character representations under the format control of a desubtype argument value and the justification control of the jflag argument. The desubtype argument is an integer of up to four digits. The last digit is mandatory and selects a delimiter character to separate the date components (0 = none, 1 = blank, 2 = hyphen, 3 = slash, and 4 = period). The delimiter digit is preceded by up to three digits chosen from the following eight values, in the order you want for your output format:

1 = yy
2 = mm
3 = dd
4 = yyyy
5 = mmm
6 = monthname
7 = ddd + DD
8 = dayname + dd

(Note that mmm and ddd are standard three-character alphabetical abbreviations for the month and the day of the week.)

Only those components specified by the digits chosen are decoded and there is no defaulting of missing components as there is for endate.c. 790 different date formats can be generated with desubtype. For our example above, a desubtype argument of 6841 would yield the following string:

Friday February 28, 1986

The date data validation functions check the allowable encode and decode subtype values discussed above, and function dvdategs.c makes sure that a date is greater than or equal to the current system date.

A complete set of utility functions is provided to perform conversions between the four internal working formats used for dates: PC-DOS system (s), internal (i), julian (j), and gregorian (g). Additional utility functions calculate age in years, months, and days, next day (given a signed offset value), and the number of days between dates.

Finally, a testing and quality assurance program (qadate.c) is provided that allows you to examine and test interactively most of the functions developed in this chapter.

The following chapter index highlights the source code that is provided.

Standard Interface Source Code

A.2.0	Endate.c:	Encode LDT date
A.3.0	Evdate.c:	Encode and validate LDT date
A.4.0	Getdate.c/ Fgetdate.c:	Combined getstr.c and evdate.c
B.2.0	Dedate.c:	Decode LDT date
B.3.0	Putdate.c/ Fputdate.c:	Combined dedate.c and putstr.c

Data Validation Functions (dvdateyy.c)

C.2.0	Dvdatede.c:	Checks for allowable desubtypes.
C.3.0	Dvdateen.c:	Checks for allowable ensubtypes.
C.4.0	Dvdategs.c:	Checks if date is greater than or equal to current sysdate.

Utility Functions (utdateyy.c)

D.2.0	Utdatedm.c:	Computes number of days in a month.
D.3.0	Utdatedw.c:	Computes day-of-week number
D.4.0	Utdatejy.c:	Computes day number of same year from julian (j) format.
D.5.0	Utdately.c:	Computes leap year adjustment for February.
D.6.0	Utdatedd.c:	Gets a standard three-character day name.
D.7.0	Utdatedn.c:	Gets a standard full day name.
D.8.0	Utdatemm.c:	Gets a standard three-character month name.
D.9.0	Utdatemy.c:	Gets a standard full month name.
D.10.0	Utdategi.c:	Converts from gregorian (g) to internal (i) format.
D.11.0	Utdategj.c:	Converts from gregorian (g) to julian (j) format.
D.12.0	Utdateig.c:	Converts internal (i) to gregorian (g) format.
D.13.0	Utdateij.c:	Converts from internal (i) to julian (j) format.
D.14.0	Utdatejg.c:	Converts from julian (j) to gregorian (g) format.
D.15.0	Utdateji.c:	Converts from julian (j) to internal (i) format.
D.16.0	Utdatesg.c:	Converts sysdates to gregorian (g) format.
D.17.0	Utdatesi.c:	Converts sysdates to internal (i) format.
D.18.0	Utdatesj.c:	Converts sysdates to julian (j) format.
D.19.0	Utdatega.c:	Computes age from gregorian (g) birth date.
D.20.0	Utdateia.c:	Computes age from internal (i) birth date.
D.21.0	Utdateja.c:	Computes age from julian (j) birth date.
D.22.0	Utdategd.c:	Computes delta days from gregorian (g) dates.

D.23.0	Utdateid.c:	Computes delta days from internal (i) dates.
D.24.0	Utdatejd.c:	Computes delta days from julian (j) dates.
D.25.0	Utdateng.c:	Computes next gregorian (g) day, given offset.
D.26.0	Utdateni.c:	Computes next internal (i) day, given offset.
D.27.0	Utdatenj.c:	Computes next julian (j) day, given offset.

Quality Assurance Programs

F.2.0	Qadate.c:	Standard quality assurance test program

A.0.0 Encode Function Development (endate.c)

A.1.0 Endate.c Specifications

A.1.1 Design Objectives

Endate.c is a comprehensive date processing function that can accurately handle date text made up of combinations of the following components:

yy: Two-digit year within current century
mm: Standard month number (01 = Jan . . . 12 = Dec)
dd: Day-of-month number (1 . . . 31)
yyyy: Full four-digit year
mmm: Standard three-character month (Jan . . . Dec)
month: Full standard monthname (January . . .)
ddd: Standard three-character day (Sun . . . Sat)
day: Full standard dayname (Sunday . . .)

The date components can be delimited consistently by one of the following characters:

'' (No delimiting character)
' ' (Space or blank character)
'-' (Dash, minus, or hyphen character)
'/' (Slash character)
'.' (Period character)

If any components are missing, endate.c defaults to the corresponding component from the current system date (sysdate).

Internally all dates are represented as C data type long int and are consistently in the yyyymmdd form, rather than in an absolute julian form common to many popular microcomputer software products today.

The range of allowable dates is controllable by the user-specified YYYY_MIN and YYYY_MAX constants defined in the ldt.h header file. Mathematically, dates are correct for the range yyyy/mm/dd (0001/01/01 through 9999/12/31).

A full set of utdateyy.c functions are provided for converting dates between the four standard formats, determining age using sysdate, figuring the next day given an offset, and figuring the number of days between dates.

A.1.2 ***Field Size (maxin)***

Because of the numerous combinations of date formats possible, you should establish standard formats for each particular application system and select a corresponding MAX_DATE field width. In ldt.h we have set MAX_DATE equal to 30.

We also have established a minimum acceptable date of 1885/01/01 with YYYY_MIN = 1885; and a maximum acceptable date of 2020/12/31 with YYYY_MAX = 2020.

A.1.3 ***Physical Format (maxphys)***

The choice of an appropriate C data type for the internal storage format for dates merits some discussion. Many existing commercial systems only utilize a two-digit year structure. This will be a problem when the year 2000 comes around! Needless to say, it seems imperative that date fields should store a complete yyyy designation.

Many existing systems also utilize alphanumerics to store dates in a variety of character sequences, which poses sorting problems and consumes excessive disk storage space. Perhaps in the days of mainframes, disk storage space seemed limitless; however, with microcomputers, disk space is still a premium item, at least for now.

Current microcomputer-based products (dBASE III, Lotus 1–2–3 and their derivatives) utilize an integer julian format. Unfortunately, without the knowledge of the specific algorithm used, file compatibility is difficult to ensure.

For these reasons and because of the advent of query languages and report writers, we have assumed the following standard internal storage format for dates:

```
typedef long int DATE;
```

The date January 31, 1986, for example would be represented, internally, as the integer number 19860131. The corresponding PHY_DATE value = 4 is fixed in ldt.h to reflect the physical size of a long int. It is easy to see that this integer number can easily be broken into its date components of year, month, and day by using simple integer division or modulus arithmetic. No knowledge of any algorithms for conversion to or from an absolute julian format is necessary.

By using this date field format it is possible to directly access relational or flat data files with a query language or report writer. This way, the files do not have to be loaded into another software file format to reformat them from a proprietary absolute julian form. This also eliminates the need to double the disk file storage requirement!

The date LDT (and all others in this book) have been designed with this space-saving philosophy in mind. Our objective is to create compact yet recognizable internal storage formats for data elements that do not require knowledge of complex algorithms, thus allowing data elements to be transmitted as part of an interface to another software product or computer system for additional processing.

In the coming age of "true" distributed processing, the need to transmit data elements will become the norm and not the exception as it largely is today.

A.1.4 ***Character Set Restrictions***

By design of the getstr.c/fgetstr.c function, the endate.c function only "sees" ASCII 0x20 through 0x7E. (Refer to Appendix E for a complete definition of the ASCII character set.) The complete range of character input is accepted for date fields; however, endate processing imposes additional restrictions based upon the date ensubtype format chosen and the corresponding edit checks that then apply. (See A.1.6 and A.1.7 below.)

A.1.5 ***Subtype Definition (ensubtype)***

The date ensubtype is a single integer value constructed from the selection and ordering of one to three digits from the list below:

1 = yy
2 = mm (optional mmm or monthname)
3 = dd (optional ddd or dayname)
4 = yyyy

If fewer than three digits are specified, the current system date (sysdate) is used to default the missing components. The redundant use of components is not allowed.

If a ddd or dayname is present it must be the first component of the input string; it is not a substitute for dd, which must be provided and is simply stripped, not interpreted in any manner. When either mmm, monthname, ddd, or dayname are entered, they may be of any combination of upper- or lowercase characters.

Delimiters can be used to separate date components, but they must be consistent. Mixed use of delimiters is not allowed. Delimiting characters can separate some or all of the component elements.

The different ensubtype values specify which date components are input, and in which order they appear:

123	yymmdd sequence
423	yyyymmdd sequence
3	dd only, defaulting yyyymm from sysdate
23	mmdd, defaulting yyyy from sysdate

A.1.6 Other Format Controls

Only one comma is accepted per date field. It is transformed to a space before date encode processing.

Delimiting characters must be used consistently, and can separate some or all of the date components.

Nondelimited date components must be padded to satisfy the size requirements of the specification. For example, mmdd can be represented in the following three ways: 01/01, 1/1, and 0101. But it can't be represented as 011, 101, or 11.

A.1.7 Editing

The component elements of every encoded date field are edited as follows:

```
YYYY_MIN  <= yyyy  <= YYYY_MAX
1         <= mm    <= 12
1         <= dd    <= utdatedm(year,mm)
```

A.1.8 Default Values

Upon initial entry to the endate.c function, the date field is initialized to YYYY_MIN/01/01. Date elements are defaulted to corresponding sysdate components if not specified as part of the ensubtype chosen; if dd is defaulted from sysdate and is in error for the given yyyymm, then utdatedm(yyyy,mm) is used.

A.1.9 Error Codes

Based upon the ERC_BASE (1000) and ENDATE_E (21) values defined in ldt.h, the following ercs are possible:

1021	Encode Data Entry Error by User
1022	Bad Encode Function Argument
1023	Encode Mandatory Field not Satisfied

A.2.0 Endate.c Source Code and Commentary

```
/* file     : endate.c
** function: int endate ( pstrin, maxin, pphys, maxphys,
**          :                ensubtype, mflag )
** desc     : encode a logical data type date
** test pgm: qadate.c
*/

#include "ctype.h"
#include "ldt.h"

        int endate (pstrin, maxin, pphys, maxphys, ensubtype, mflag)

        char *pstrin;
        DATE *pphys;
        int maxin, maxphys, ensubtype, mflag;
        {

        int erc, eerc, i, j, k, slgth;
        int year, month, day, ymd, century, ddef;
        int floc, lloc, hloc, ploc, sloc, hcnt, pcnt, scnt;
        char str[30], scr[30];
        char *dn, *dd, *my, *mm;
        DATE utdategi();
        char *utdatedn(), *utdatedd(), *utdatemy(), *utdatemm();

        /*
        ** ENCODE internal (i) format == YYYYMMDD == Long INT
        **
        ** Table of valid ENCODE subtypes:
        **
        ** NOTE: "ensubtype"  indicates undelimited size
        **       & sequence of expected input!
        **
        ** Elements: YY = 1; MM = 2; DD = 3; YYYY = 4;
        **
        ** Rules: A valid ensubtype integer value consists
        **        of from 1 to 3 digits in any order of elements
        **        [YY,MM,DD,YYYY] above. If less than
        **        3-digits specified, SYSDATE is used to
        **        provide the missing elements. Duplicates
        **        not allowed! If a "ddd" or "dayname" is
        **        present (must be first), it is just stripped
        **        and not validated against the DD. Mixed delimiter
        **        types are not acceptable.
        **
        ** Examples:
        **
        **       123 = YYMMDD sequence.
        **       423 = YYYYMMDD sequence.
        **       3   = DD only defaulting YYMM.
        **       23  = MMDD defaulting YY.
        **
        */


        /*
        ** Validate the function arguments:
        */

        erc = ERC_BASE + ENDATE_E + 1;  /* set to bad arg err */

        if (( maxin < 1 ) || ( maxin > MAX_DATE)) return (erc);
```

```
if (maxphys != PHY_DATE) return(erc);

eerc = dvdateen(&ensubtype,PHY_INT);
if (eerc != ERC_OK) return(eerc);

/*
** set "default" values
*/

utdatesg(&year,&month,&day);
ddef = TRUE;

century = (year/100) * 100;

*pphys = utdategi(YYYY_MIN,1,1);

if (( mflag < NO ) || ( mflag > YES ))
        return (erc);

/*
** Validate mandatory field requirement
** OK to check before any other pre-processing
*/

slgth = strlen( pstrin );
if (( mflag ) && ( slgth < 1 ))
        return(erc + 1);

erc = erc - 1;          /* set to ENCODE Error */

/*
** ENCODE PROCESSING
*/

strcpy(str, pstrin);

/*
** strip leading/trailing blanks if any
*/

utcharsb(3,str,C_BLANK);

slgth = strlen(str);
if(slgth < 1) return(erc+2);



if ( (hcnt > 0) && ( (pcnt > 0) || (scnt > 0) ) ) return(erc);
if ( (pcnt > 0) && ( (hcnt > 0) || (scnt > 0) ) ) return(erc);
if ( (scnt > 0) && ( (pcnt > 0) || (hcnt > 0) ) ) return(erc);

utcharsb(1,str,C_BLANK);
slgth = strlen(str);
if(slgth < 1) return(erc);


/*
** check for optional leading "day name"; validate & strip
** if not "dayname" may be "monthname" depending upon
** "ensubtype"
*/

if ( isalpha(str[0]) != 0 )     /* is 1st char alpha? */
{
strcpy(scr,str);
floc = poschr(scr,C_BLANK,LR);
if (floc != 0) scr[floc-1] = C_NUL;
```

```
for (i=0; i < 7; i++)
{

dd = utdatedd(i);
dn = utdatedn(i);

if ( (utcharcm(4,scr,dd) == 0) ||
     (utcharcm(4,scr,dn) == 0) )
{
if ( utcharcm(4,scr,dd) == 0 ) floc = strlen(dd);
if ( utcharcm(4,scr,dn) == 0 ) floc = strlen(dn);
for (i=0; i < floc; i++)
{
delchr(str,1);
}
utcharsb(1,str,C_BLANK);
slgth = strlen(str);
if (slgth < 1) return(erc);
break;
}
}
}                /* end of alpha, if any */

/*
** PROCESS ENSUBTYPE
*/

for (i=3; i>0; i--)
{

switch (i)
{

/*
** allow only 1-comma & transform to space.
*/

floc = poschr(str,C_COMMA,LR);
if ( floc != 0 )
{
lloc = poschr(str,C_COMMA,RL);
if (floc != lloc) return(erc);
delchr(str,floc);
inschr(str,999,C_BLANK,floc);
utcharsb(1,str,C_BLANK);
slgth = strlen(str);
if (slgth < 1) return(erc);
}

/*
** transform any [-], [/] or [.] to space!
*/

hcnt = 0;
pcnt = 0;
scnt = 0;

for (;;)
{
hloc = poschr(str,C_HYPHEN,LR);
ploc = poschr(str,C_PERIOD,LR);
sloc = poschr(str,C_SLASH,LR);
if (hloc != 0)
{
hcnt++;
delchr(str,hloc);
inschr(str,999,C_BLANK,hloc);
}
```

```
if (ploc != 0)
{
pcnt++;
delchr(str,ploc);
inschr(str,999,C_BLANK,ploc);
}
if (sloc != 0)
{
scnt++;
delchr(str,sloc);
inschr(str,999,C_BLANK,sloc);
}
if ( (hloc == 0) && (ploc == 0) && (sloc == 0) ) break;
}

        case 3: ymd = ensubtype / 100;
                if (ymd == 0) continue;
                break;
        case 2: ymd = (ensubtype % 100) / 10;
                if (ymd == 0) continue;
                break;
        case 1: ymd = ensubtype % 10;
                break;
}

/*
** GET "DAY" ( DD )
**
** get 1 or 2 digits + delimiter if any & strip from "str"
** "ddd" or "dayname" already stripped if existed.
*/

if ( ymd == 3 )
{

ddef = FALSE;

if (slgth < 1) return(erc);

floc = poschr(str,C_BLANK,LR);

if (floc == 1) return(erc);

if ( (floc == 0) || (floc > 3) )        /* non-delim case */
{
if (slgth < 2) return(erc);
if ( (isdigit(str[0]) == 0) ||
     (isdigit(str[1]) == 0) ) return(erc);

utilfn(2,&day,str,&slgth);

}                                      /* end non-delim case */
else                                   /* delim case 1 or 2 */
{
if (isdigit(str[0]) == 0) return(erc);
if ( (floc == 3) && (isdigit(str[1]) != 0) )
{

utilfn(2,&day,str,&slgth);

}
else
if (floc == 2)
{

utilfn(1,&day,str,&slgth);

}
```

```
else return(erc);

}                                      /* delim case 1 or 2    */
continue;
}                                      /* end DAY      */


/*
** GET "MONTH" ( MM; or "mmm"; or "monthname" )
*/

if ( ymd == 2 )
{

/*
** check for "month name"; validate & strip
*/

if (slgth < 1) return(erc);

if ( isalpha(str[0]) != 0 )
{
strcpy(scr,str);
floc = poschr(scr,C_BLANK,LR);

if (floc != 0) scr[floc-1] = C_NUL;

for (j=1; j < 13; j++)
{

mm = utdatemm(j);
my = utdatemy(j);

if ( (utcharcm(4,scr,mm) == 0) ||
     (utcharcm(4,scr,my) == 0) )
{
month = j;

if ( utcharcm(4,scr,mm) == 0 ) floc = strlen(mm);
if ( utcharcm(4,scr,my) == 0 ) floc = strlen(my);

for (k=0; k < floc; k++)
{
delchr(str,1);
}


utcharsb(1,str,C_BLANK);
slgth = strlen(str);
break;
}
}
if (j == 13) return(erc);
else continue;
}                              /* end alpha month, if any      */

else
{


/*
** get 2-dig month strip from string + delimiter if any!
*/

floc = poschr(str,C_BLANK,LR);

if (floc == 1) return(erc);
```

```
if ( (floc == 0) || (floc > 3) )        /* non-del case */
{
if (slgth < 2) return(erc);
if ( (isdigit(str[0]) == 0) ||
     (isdigit(str[1]) == 0) ) return(erc);

utilfn(2,&month,str,&slgth);

}
else                          /* delim case 1 or 2 */
{
if (isdigit(str[0]) == 0) return(erc);
if ( (floc == 3) && (isdigit(str[1]) != 0) )
{

utilfn(2,&month,str,&slgth);

}
else
if (floc == 2)
{

utilfn(1,&month,str,&slgth);

}
else return(erc);

}                /* delim case 1 or 2 */

}                /* end else alpha */
continue;
}                /* end MONTH    */


/*
** GET "YEAR" ( YY or YYYY )
*/

if  (ymd == 1)
{

if (slgth < 1) return(erc);

floc = poschr(str,C_BLANK,LR);

if (floc == 1) return(erc);

if ( (floc == 0) || (floc > 3) )        /* non-delim case */
{
if (slgth < 2) return(erc);
if ( (isdigit(str[0]) == 0) ||
     (isdigit(str[1]) == 0) ) return(erc);

utilfn(2,&year,str,&slgth);
year = year + century;

}                                /* end non-delim case */
else                             /* delim case 2 only */
{
if (floc != 3) return(erc);
if ( (isdigit(str[0]) == 0) || (isdigit(str[1]) == 0) )
     return(erc);

utilfn(2,&year,str,&slgth);
year = year + century;

}                         /* end delim case 2 only */
continue;
}                /* end if (year == 1)   */
```

```
if  (ymd == 4)
{

if (slgth < 1) return(erc);

floc = poschr(str,C_BLANK,LR);

if (floc == 1) return(erc);

if ( (floc == 0) || (floc > 5) )          /* non-delim case */
{
if (slgth < 4) return(erc);
if ( (isdigit(str[0]) == 0) ||
     (isdigit(str[1]) == 0) ||
     (isdigit(str[2]) == 0) ||
     (isdigit(str[3]) == 0) ) return(erc);

utilfn(4,&year,str,&slgth);

}                                    /* end non-delim case */
else                                 /* delim case 4 only */
{
if (floc != 5) return(erc);
if ( (isdigit(str[0]) == 0) ||
     (isdigit(str[1]) == 0) ||
     (isdigit(str[2]) == 0) ||
     (isdigit(str[3]) == 0) ) return(erc);

utilfn(4,&year,str,&slgth);

}                                    /* end delim case 4 only */
continue;
}                /* end if (year == 4)   */

}                /* end for loop [3,2,1] */


if (slgth != 0) return(erc);         /* extraneous data remains */

/*
** validate [year,month,day]
*/

if ( (year < YYYY_MIN) || (year > YYYY_MAX) ) return(erc);

if ( (month < 1) || (month > 12) ) return(erc);

if (day < 1) return(erc);

if ( (ddef == FALSE) && (day > utdatedm(year,month)) )
     return(erc);

if ( (ddef == TRUE) && (day > utdatedm(year,month)) )
     day = utdatedm(year,month);

*pphys = utdategi(year,month,day);

return (ERC_OK);

}

int utilfn (iter, var, str, slgth)
int iter, *var, *slgth;
char *str;
{

int i;
```

```
switch (iter)
{
        case 1: *var = (str[0] - C_ZERO);
                break;
        case 2: *var = ((str[0] - C_ZERO) * 10) +
                        (str[1] - C_ZERO);
                break;
        case 4: *var = ((str[0] - C_ZERO) * 1000) +
                        ((str[1] - C_ZERO) * 100) +
                        ((str[2] - C_ZERO) * 10) +
                        (str[3] - C_ZERO);
                break;
        default: *var = 0;
                 return(ERC_BASE+ENDATE_E);
}

for (i=0;i < iter; i++)
{
delchr(str,1);
}

utcharsb(1,str,C_BLANK);

*slgth = strlen(str);

return(ERC_OK);

}
```

- Note that pphys is declared to be of type DATE. Uppercase DATE is a typedef from ldt.h. DATE is therefore equivalent to long int.

- For the date LDT, if pstrin contains all blank characters, it will not satisfy the mandatory mflag field requirement.

- Note the consistent use of utcharsb.c to strip extraneous blank characters from pstrin (same as str).

- Note the use of the string compare function utcharcm.c to check for ddd or dayname. Option 4 is used to check str up to the string length of both dd and dn. Both are simply stripped, not interpreted, supporting the overall encode/decode philosophy that an encode function should accept all output from its corresponding decode function.

- The main process ensubtype loop processes ymd from left to right (i.e., digit3 → digit2 → digit1).

- Function utilfn (utility function) is a local function defined for endate.c to perform repetitive logical steps found throughout the processing of day, month, and year.

- Month and mmm processing parallels that for ddd and dayname, except for the fact that both month and mmm are actually interpreted, not simply stripped.

- Year processing is complicated by the acceptability of both two-character or four-character numerals, with or without intervening delimiters.

- Each component of a date field (year, month, day) is validated as previously explained. If a day is defaulted, and is in error for the given month (for example, if sysdate = 1985/12/31 and you entered month = 09, then day 31 is invalid for month 09. In this case, utdatedm(1985,09) would assign the defaulted day value of 30.)

A.3.0 Evdate.c Source Code and Commentary

The source code and commentary for function evdate.c parallels evchar.c (Chapter 5, A.3.0). To create function evdate.c, simply copy evchar.c and edit as follows:

- Change all occurrences of char to date and CHAR to DATE except for the following statement:

```
char *pstrin;
```

- Update the commented function description.

The completed source code is available on disk.

A.4.0 *Advanced Encode Field Processing*

A.4.1 *Getdate.c and Fgetdate.c Error Codes*

See Chapter 5, A.4.1.

A.4.2 *Getdate.c and Fgetdate.c Source Code and Commentary*

The source code and commentary for getdate.c parallels that of getchar.c (Chapter 5, A.4.0). To create function getdate.c, copy getchar.c and edit it as follows:

- Change all occurrences of char to date and CHAR to DATE except for the statement

```
char *string, *mask, *init;
```

Similarly, fgetdate.c parallels fgetchar.c (also Chapter 5, A.4.0). To create fgetdate.c, copy fgetchar.c and edit as follows:

- Change all occurrences of char to date and CHAR to DATE except for statements

```
char *string, *mask, *init;
utcharcb(1,string,1);
```

The complete source code is available on disk.

A.4.3 *Associated Mask Utilization Techniques*

Based upon the function argument gmaskflg, mask delimiter characters are either included (YES) or excluded (NO) from the acquired input string. Each facilitates the introduction or elimination of date field separators, for example:

```
Date field: "??/??/??"
```

It might appear that the ensubtype format control effects overlap with the effects of using the gmaskflg associated with getstr.c/fgetstr.c. It is important to remember that endate.c can be utilized independently of the getstr.c/fgetstr.c and getdate.c/

fgetdate.c functions so that some functional redundancy is required to expand the independent use of the enxxxx.c interface definitions developed in this book.

B.0.0 Decode Function Development (dedate.c)

B.1.0 Dedate.c Specifications

B.1.1 Design Objectives

This function provides a comprehensive date processing function that can display standard internal dates in any combination of the following components:

yy	Two-digit year within current century
mm	Standard month number (01 = JAN . . . 12 = DEC)
dd	Day of month number (1 . . . 31)
yyyy	Full four-digit year
mmm	Standard three-character month (JAN . . . DEC)
month	Full standard monthname (January . . .)
ddd	Standard three-character day (SUN . . . SAT)
day	Full standard dayname (Sunday . . .)

The combinations of components in turn can be delimited by one of the following characters:

'' : No delimiting character
' ': Space or blank character
'-': Dash, minus or hyphen character
'/': Slash character
'.': Period character

Internally all dates are represented as C data type long int and are of the consistent form yyyymmdd, rather than in absolute julian form.

B.1.2 Subtype Definition (desubtype)

The date desubtype is a single integer value constructed from the selection and ordering of one to three digits from the list below:

1 = yy
2 = mm
3 = dd
4 = yyyy
5 = mmm
6 = monthname
7 = ddd + dd
8 = dayname + dd

and one additional required digit that specifies the delimiting character to be used:

0 = no delimiting character
1 = ' ' (space)
2 = '-' (dash, hyphen, minus)
3 = '/' (slash)
4 = '.' (period)

Only those date components specified by desubtype are formatted to become the pstrout. The redundant use of components is not allowed.

If a ddd or dayname is specified, it is always the first (left-most) in pstrout, and dd is also always displayed. Monthname, mmm, dayname, and ddd are always displayed in standard format as controlled by functions utdatemy.c and utdatedn.c.

The delimiter chosen is used to separate all date components.

The chosen desubtype value specifies which date components appear on output, and in which order:

681	Dayname monthname dd
4233	yyyy/mm/dd
1230	yymmdd
6841	Dayname monthname dd, yyyy

In the last example above, a comma is automatically introduced to conform with standard display conventions for dates of the form: month day, year.

B.1.3 ***Default Values***

No default is assumed by dedate.c. The output character string pstrout is simply set to a NULL string before processing begins.

B.1.4 ***Error Codes***

Based upon the ERC_BASE (1000) and ENDATE_E (21) values defined in ldt.h, the following erc is possible:

1026	Bad Decode Function Argument

B.2.0 ***Dedate.c Source Code and Commentary***

```
/* file    : dedate.c
** function: int dedate ( pstrout, maxout, pphys, maxphys,
**         :               desubtype, jflag )
** desc    : decode a logical data type date.
** test pgm: qadate.c
*/

#include "ctype.h"
#include "ldt.h"

        int dedate (pstrout, maxout, pphys, maxphys, desubtype, jflag)
```

```
char *pstrout;
DATE *pphys;
int maxout, maxphys, desubtype, jflag;
{

int erc, derc, i, slgth, rem, dpos, pos, size;
int digit1, digit2, digit3, digit4, sn, ln;
int year, month, day, dow;
char str [30], *ps, *pl;
char *utdatemy(), *utdatemm(), *utdatedn(), *utdatedd();


/*
** Table of valid DECODE subtypes:
**
** NOTE: "desubtype" indicates undelimited size
**       & sequence of expected output!
**
** Elements:    YY = 1; YYYY = 4;
**              MM = 2; mmm = 5; monthname = 6;
**              DD = 3; ddd+DD = 7; dayname+DD = 8;
**
**              F(ormat) for Delimiter:
**               0 = no delimiters;
**               1 = 'space' delimiter;
**               2 = '-' delimiter;
**               3 = '/' delimiter.
**               4 = '.' delimiter.
**
** RULES: A valid desubtype integer value consists of from
**        2 to 4 digits. The units digit must always be
**        a "F(ormat)" value. At least one of the Year/
**        Month/Day format elements  must be specified.
**        No duplicate values are allowed!
**        If "ddd" or "dayname" are specified, "ddd" or
**        "dayname" always precede the remaining date
**        with DD. See example below. A comma will be
**        introduced on output for readability when
**        [F]ormat = 0 = space.
**
** Examples:
**
**      681  = dayname monthname DD
**      4233 = YYYY/MM/DD
**      1230 = YYMMDD
**      6741 = ddd monthname DD, YYYY
**
*/


/*
** Validate the function arguments:
*/

erc = ERC_BASE + ENDATE_E + 5;

if (( maxout < 1 ) || ( maxout > MAX_DATE)) return (erc);

if (maxphys != PHY_DATE) return(erc);

derc = dvdatede(&desubtype,PHY_INT);
if (derc != ERC_OK) return(derc);

utcharcb(1,pstrout,1);
utcharcb(1,str,1);

if (( jflag < NO_JUST) || ( jflag > R_JUST ))
       return (erc);
```

```
/*
** get desubtype digits
*/

digit4 = desubtype / 1000;
digit3 = (desubtype % 1000) / 100;
digit2 = (desubtype % 100) / 10;
digit1 = desubtype % 10;


/*
** convert from internal format to gregorian
*/

utdateig(*pphys,&year,&month,&day);


/*
** desubtype processing
*/

/*
** put "day" or "dayname" ?
*/


sn = FALSE;
ln= FALSE;

if ( (digit4 == 7) || (digit3 == 7) ||
     (digit2 == 7) ) sn = TRUE;

if ( (digit4 == 8) || (digit3 == 8) ||
     (digit2 == 8) ) ln = TRUE;

dow = utdatedw(year,month,day);

if (sn == TRUE) ps = utdatedd(dow);
if (ln == TRUE) ps = utdatedn(dow);

if ( (sn == TRUE) || (ln == TRUE) )
{
strcat(str,ps);
putdelim(digit1,str);
}


if (digit4 != 0)
{
swdigit(digit4,str,year,month,day);
putdelim(digit1,str);
}

if (digit3 != 0)
{
swdigit(digit3,str,year,month,day);

/*
** comma?
*/

if ( ( (digit4 >= 5) && (digit4 <= 6) ) &&
     ( (digit3 == 3) || (digit3 == 7) || (digit3 == 8) )
     && (digit1 == 1) ) inschr(str,999,C_COMMA,0);

putdelim(digit1,str);
}
```

```
if (digit2 != 0)
{
swdigit(digit2,str,year,month,day);
}

/*
** check if "pstrout" big enough?
*/

utcharcb(3,str,maxout+1);
slgth = strlen(str);
if (slgth > maxout) return(erc);
else strcpy(pstrout,str);

/*
** Justify output string
*/

utcharjs(jflag, pstrout);

return (ERC_OK);

}                                /* end DECODE DATE */

int swdigit(digit,str,year,month,day)
int digit, year, month, day;
char *str;
{

switch (digit)
{
        case 1:
        case 4: putyear(digit,str,year);
                break;
        case 2:
        case 5:
        case 6: putmonth(digit,str,month);
                break;
        case 3:
        case 7:
        case 8: putday(digit,str,day);
                break;
}
}

int putyear(digit,str,year)
int digit, year;
char *str;
{

char digit4, digit3, digit2, digit1;

digit4 = C_ZERO + (year / 1000);
digit3 = C_ZERO + ((year % 1000) / 100);
digit2 = C_ZERO + ((year % 100) / 10);
digit1 = C_ZERO + (year % 10);
if (digit == 4)
{
inschr(str,999,digit4,0);
inschr(str,999,digit3,0);
}

inschr(str,999,digit2,0);
inschr(str,999,digit1,0);

}
```

```
int putmonth(digit,str,month)
int digit, month;
char *str;
{

char *my, *mm;
char digit2, digit1;

if (digit == 2)
{
digit2 = C_ZERO + (month /10);
digit1 = C_ZERO + (month % 10);

inschr(str,999,digit2,0);
inschr(str,999,digit1,0);
}

if (digit == 5)
{
mm = utdatemm(month);
strcat(str,mm);
}

if (digit == 6)
{
my = utdatemy(month);
strcat(str,my);
}

}


int putday(digit,str,day)
int digit, day;
char *str;
{

char digit2, digit1;
digit2 = C_ZERO + (day / 10);
digit1 = C_ZERO + (day % 10);

inschr(str,999,digit2,0);
inschr(str,999,digit1,0);

}


int putdelim(digit,str)
int digit;
char *str;
{

switch (digit)
{
        case 0: break;
        case 1: inschr(str,999,C_BLANK,0);
                break;
        case 2: inschr(str,999,C_HYPHEN,0);
                break;
        case 3: inschr(str,999,C_SLASH,0);
                break;
        case 4: inschr(str,999,C_PERIOD,0);
                break;
}
}
```

- In contrast to the endate.c function, dedate.c is quite simple, since it actively formats a previously encoded date field, whereas endate.c must passively respond to the whims of a users correct or incorrect data entry.

- All decisions are made concerning the left to right output processing of each date field based upon digit4, digit3, digit2, and digit1.

- The local functions to dedate.c (swdigit, putyear, putmonth, putday, and putdelim) structure dedate.c processing.

- A discretionary comma is inserted only for certain desubtype values to more closely conform to business letter standards (of the form month day, year).

- An erc is generated if the string length of str is greater than the maxout string length of pstrout.

- String justification occurs within the total string field width maxout because of the function call to utcharcb (3,str,maxout+1).

- Local function swdigit translates any desubtype digit into a corresponding function call to its correct corresponding year, month, day.

- Local function putyear puts either a two-character or four-character year to str.

- Local function putmonth puts either a two-character month, mmm, or monthname to str.

- Local function putday always puts a two-character day to str.

- Local function putdelim consistently puts the chosen delimiter to str.

B.3.0 Advanced Decode Field Processing

B.3.1 Putdate.c and Fputdate.c Error Codes

See Chapter 5, B.3.1.

B.3.2 Putdate.c and Fputdate.c Source Code and Commentary

The source code and commentary for putdate.c and fputdate.c parallels that of putchar.c and fputchar.c (Chapter 5, B.3.0). To create putdate.c or fputdate.c, copy its corresponding file and edit as follows:

- Change all occurrences of char to date and CHAR to DATE except for the statement

```
char *pstrout, *mask;
```

The complete source code is available on disk.

B.3.3 Associated Mask Utilization Techniques

In an analogous manner, putstr.c/fputstr.c and putdate.c/fputdate.c can be used to output a decoded string to a mask field with or without delimiters. For example,

```
Date Field: "??/??/??"
```

Use of the getmstr.c function allows use of the video display as a scratch pad (see Chapter 4) and functionally extends the stand-alone utility of each dexxxx.c. Since the power of masks is only pertinent with video display, getmstr.c retrieves the putxxxx.c string from the video display with mask formatting to enhance the variety of decoded formats that may be created when using dexxxx.c functions in a stand-alone manner.

C.0.0 Data Validation Function Development (dvdateyy.c)

C.1.0 Dvdateyy.c Standard Error Codes

Based upon the ERC_BASE (1000) and ENDATE_E (21) values defined in ldt.h, all dvdateyy.c functions report the same ercs:

1024	Data Validation Error
1025	Bad Data Validation Function Argument

C.2.0 Dvdatede.c Function Specification

C.2.1 Dvdatede.c Design Objectives

This function simply validates that an acceptable desubtype argument value has been specified for the date LDT.

C.2.2 Dvdatede.c Source Code and Commentary

```
/* file    : dvdatede.c
** function: int dvdatede ( pphys, maxphys )
** desc    : data validation for date: valid decode subtypes
** test pgm: tdedate.c
*/

#include "ldt.h"

        int dvdatede ( pphys, maxphys )

        INT *pphys;
        int maxphys;
        {

        int erc, val, notfirst, i;
        int digit, digit1, digit2, digit3, digit4;

        erc = ERC_BASE + ENINT_E + 3;

        if (maxphys != PHY_INT) return(erc+1);
```

```
val = (*pphys).i2;

if ( ( val < 10 ) || ( val > 8644) ) return (erc);

notfirst = FALSE;

for (i=4; i > 0; i--)
{

switch (i)
{
        case 4: digit4 = val / 1000;
                if ( digit4 != 0 ) notfirst = TRUE;
                else
                {
                digit4 = -4;
                break;
                }
                if ( (digit4 < 1) || (digit4 > 8) )
                return(erc);
                break;

        case 3: digit3 = (val % 1000) / 100;
                if ( (notfirst == TRUE) &&
                     (digit3 == 0) ) return(erc);
                if (digit3 != 0) notfirst = TRUE;
                else
                {
                digit3 = -3;
                break;
                }
                if ( (digit3 < 1) || ( digit3 > 8) )
                return(erc);
                break;

        case 2: digit2 = (val % 100) / 10;
                if ( (digit2 < 1) || ( digit2 > 8) )
                return(erc);
                break;

        case 1: digit1 = val % 10;
                if ( (digit1 < 0) || (digit1 > 4) )
                return(erc);
                break;
}

}

for (i=4; i > 1; i--)
{
if (i == 4) digit = digit4;
if (i == 3) digit = digit3;
if (i == 2) digit = digit2;

switch (digit)
{
        case 1:
        case 4: digit = 1;
                break;
        case 2:
        case 5:
        case 6: digit = 2;
                break;
        case 3:
        case 7:
        case 8: digit = 3;
                break;
}
```

```
if (i == 4) digit4 = digit;
if (i == 3) digit3 = digit;
if (i == 2) digit2 = digit;

}

if ( (digit4 != digit3) && (digit4 != digit2) &&
     (digit3 != digit2) ) return(ERC_OK);
else
return(erc);

}
```

- Note the use of INT *pphys. The uppercase INT is a typedef from ldt.h which is

  typedef union {int i2; long int i4;} INT;

  The use of the INT typedef allows either int or long int arguments to be passed to dvdatede.c. By design, only int types are acceptable to dvdatede.c.

- Note how the desubtype is retrieved:

  val = (*pphys).i2;

- Note that the present overall limit on acceptable values for desubtype is from 10 through 8644.
- Since desubtype can be made up of two to four digits, considerable editing of each digit must be performed.
- Digits of the same date component type are grouped to determine whether or not duplicates have been specified. For example: 1 = yy and 4 = yyyy are of the same date component type "year."

C.3.0 ***Dvdateen.c Function Specification***

C.3.1 ***Dvdateen.c Design Objectives***

This function simply validates that an acceptable ensubtype argument value has been specified for the date LDT.

C.3.2 **Dvdateen.c Source Code and Commentary**

```
/* file    : dvdateen.c
** function: int dvdateen ( pphys, maxphys )
** desc    : data validation for date: valid encode subtypes
** test pgm: tendate.c
*/

#include "ldt.h"

        int dvdateen ( pphys, maxphys )

        INT *pphys;
        int maxphys;
        {
        int erc, val, notfirst, i;
        int digit1, digit2, digit3;

        erc = ERC_BASE + ENINT_E + 3;

        if (maxphys != PHY_INT) return(erc+1);

        val = (*pphys).i2;

        if ( ( val < 1 ) || ( val > 432) ) return (erc);

        notfirst = FALSE;

        for (i=3; i > 0; i--)
        {

        switch (i)
        {
                case 3: digit3 = val / 100;
                        if ( digit3 != 0 ) notfirst = TRUE;
                        else
                        {
                        digit3 = -3;
                        break;
                        }
                        if ( (digit3 < 1) || ( digit3 > 4 ) )
                        return(erc);
                        break;

                case 2: digit2 = (val % 100) / 10;
                        if ( (notfirst == TRUE) &&
                             (digit2 == 0) ) return(erc);
                        if (digit2 != 0 ) notfirst = TRUE;
                        else
                        {
                        digit2 = -2;
                        break;
                        }
                        if ( (digit2 < 1) || ( digit2 > 4) )
                        return(erc);
                        break;

                case 1: digit1 = val % 10;
                        if ( (digit1 < 1) || (digit1 > 4) )
                        return(erc);
                        break;

        }

        }
```

```
if (digit1 == 4) digit1 = 1;
if (digit2 == 4) digit2 = 1;
if (digit3 == 4) digit3 = 1;

if ( (digit3 != digit2) && ( digit3 != digit1) &&
     (digit2 != digit1) ) return(ERC_OK);
else return(erc);

}
```

- Note the use of INT *pphys. See C.2.2 commentary for explanation.
- Note that the present overall limit on acceptable values for ensubtype is from 1 through 432.
- Since ensubtype can be made up of one to three digits, considerable editing of each digit must be performed.
- Digits of "like" date component type are also grouped to determine whether or not duplicates have been specified.

C.4.0 Dvdategs.c Function Specification

C.4.1 Dvdategs.c Design Objectives

This function tests that the pphys date is greater than or equal to the current sysdate.

C.4.2 Dvdategs.c Source Code and Commentary

```
/* file    : dvdategs.c
** function: int dvdategs ( pphys, maxphys )
** desc    : data validation for date; is "*pphys" >= SYSDATE?
** test pgm: (none)
*/

#include "ldt.h"

        int dvdategs ( pphys, maxphys )

        DATE *pphys;
        int maxphys;
        {

        DATE utdatesi();
        int erc;

        erc = ERC_BASE + ENDATE_E + 3;

        if (maxphys != PHY_DATE) return(erc+1);
```

```
if (*pphys >= utdatesi()) return (ERC_OK);
else
return(erc);
}
```

- Note the use of DATE *pphys. DATE is a typedef from ldt.h, which is:

  typedef long int DATE;

  The use of the date typedef requires only long int arguments to be passed to dvdategs.c.
- Because of the use of typedef DATE discussed above, the value of pphys is retrieved by the expression *pphys.

D.0.0 Utility Function Development (utdateyy.c)

Each y in the utdateyy.c naming convention, while not completely standardized, represents one of the following four date storage formats:

s: operating system format
i: standard internal format
j: absolute julian format
g: gregorian format

The first y indicates the format you are converting from, and the second y indicates the format you are converting to, for example:

utdatesi: operating system to internal conversion
utdateij: internal to julian conversion
utdatejg: julian to gregorian conversion
utdategi: gregorian to internal conversion

This naming convention will help you to immediately distinguish most utdateyy.c functions. We have conformed to the standard DOS file naming convention of xxxxxxxx.xxx: eight-character names with a three-character suffix. Conformance to that standard ensures that all file names appear in directory listings without truncation, but forces us to assume a two-character yy suffix given the file naming standards we have adopted for our logical data type methodology.

D.1.0 **Utdateyy.c Standard Error Codes**

Based upon the ERC_BASE (1000) and ENDATE_E (21) values defined in ldt.h, utdateyy.c functions of type int report the following erc:

1027	Utility Function Error

D.2.0 **Utdatedm.c Specifications**

D.2.1 **Utdatedm.c Design Objectives**

This function calculates the number of days in a month for any given yyyy (including the February leap year correction) and mm.

D.2.2 **Utdatedm.c Source Code and Commentary**

```
/* file    : utdatedm.c
** function: int utdatedm (year, month)
** desc    : days in month for "yyyy/mm":
**         : 1 = January . . . 12 = December.
** test pgm: tutdate.c
*/

        int utdatedm (year, month)
        int year, month;
        {

        int days;
        switch (month)
        {
                case 1:
                case 3:
                case 5:
                case 7:
                case 8:
                case 10:
                case 12: days = 31;
                         break;
```

```
        case 4:
        case 6:
        case 9:
        case 11: days = 30;
                 break;

        case 2: days = 28 + utdately(year);
                break;

        default: days = 0;
                 break;
}
return(days);
}
```

- The switch statement handles each month and checks to see if an invalid month number is provided.
- Function utdately.c handles the leap year calculation.

D.3.0 *Utdatedw.c Specifications*

D.3.1 *Utdatedw.c Design Objectives*

This function represents the implementation of an algorithm sometimes referred to as "Zeller's Day of Week" discussed at length in the reference cited at the end of the code. Essentially, given any (yyyy,mm,dd), it calculates a weekday number (0 = Sunday, 1 = Monday, etc.).

D.3.2 *Utdatedw.c Source Code and Commentary*

```
/* file    : utdatedw.c
** function: int utdatedw (year, month, day)
** desc    : day of week number: 0 = SUN, 1 = MON . . . 6 = SAT.
**         : arguments ( yyyy, mm, dd )
** test pgm: tcalendr.c
*/

        int utdatedw (year, month, day)
        int year, month, day;
        {
        int dow, y, m, c, dy;

        if (month > 2)
        {
        m = month - 2;
        y = year;
        }
        else
        {
        m = month + 10;
        y = year - 1;
        }
```

```
        c = y / 100;
        dy = y - (100 * c);

        dow = ((13 * m - 1) / 5) + day + dy + (dy / 4)
              + (c / 4) - c - c + 77;

        dow = dow - 7 * (dow / 7);

        return(dow);
        }

/*
**      Reference:
**      Uspensky & Heaslet. "Elementary Number Theory".
**      Appendix A: Calendar Problems.
*/
```

- Note that the function argument year is of the form yyyy, not yy.
- Refer to the reference cited for algorithm details.

D.4.0 *Utdatejy.c Specifications*

D.4.1 *Utdatejy.c Design Objectives*

Given an absolute julian date (n-days from origin), this function computes the relative julian day number in the same year.

D.4.2 *Utdatejy.c Source Code and Commentary*

```
/* file    : utdatejy.c
** function: int utdatejy (jdate)
** desc    : convert absolute julian date "jdate" to
**         : day number of this year.
** test pgm: tutdate.c
*/

#include "ldt.h"

        int utdatejy (jdate)
        DATE jdate;
        {

        DATE utdatejd(), utdategj();
        int utdatejg();
        int year, month, day, days;
        DATE fjdate;

        utdatejg(jdate, &year, &month, &day);

        fjdate = utdategj (year, 1, 1);

        days = (int) utdatejd (jdate, fjdate);

        return (days);
        }
```

- This function demonstrates the difference between absolute julian and relative julian dates.
- Note that this function returns an integer day number in the corresponding year.
- Note the use of the int cast on the date returned value of the function utdatejd.c.

D.5.0 Utdately.c Specifications

D.5.1 Utdately.c Design Objectives

Computes the February leap year correction given any year (yyyy).

D.5.2 Utdately.c Source Code and Commentary

```
/* file    : utdately.c
** function: int utdately (year)
** desc    : day increment for February in a leap year
** test pgm: tutdate.c
*/

        int utdately (year)
        int year;
        {

        int leap;

        leap = 0;
        if ((year % 4) == 0) leap = 1;
        if ((year % 100) == 0) leap = 0;
        if ((year % 400) == 0) leap = 1;

        return (leap);
        }

/*
**      Reference:
**      Uspensky & Heaslet. "Elementary Number Theory".
**      Appendix A: Calendar Problems.
*/
```

- Note that a value of 0 or 1 is always returned by this function.
- Refer to the reference citation for a detailed discussion of the leap year correction.

D.6.0 Utdatedd.c Specifications

D.6.1 Utdatedd.c Design Objectives

This function returns a character pointer to a standard three-character abbreviation for a weekday name.

Given a weekday number (0 = Sunday, 1 = Monday, etc.), a pointer is returned to a standard uppercase weekday name (SUN, MON, etc.).

D.6.2 Utdatedd.c Source Code and Commentary

```
/* file    : utdatedd.c
** function: char *utdatedd (dow)
** desc    : return a pointer to day name of "dow"
**         : where "dow" is 0 = SUN . . . 6 = SAT
**         : in three-character form MMM.
** test pgm: tcalendr.c
*/

#include "ctype.h"

        char *utdatedd(dow)
        int dow;
        {

        char *utdatedn();
        static char *ddd = "   ";
        char *day;
        int i;

        day = utdatedn(dow);
        for (i=0; i < 3; i++)
        {
        *(ddd+i) = toupper(day[i]);
        }
        return (ddd);
        }
```

- When using this function, the calling program must explicitly declare this function to be

  char *utdatedd();

- Note how function utdatedn.c is used to get the standard day names and force the first three characters to uppercase using the macro toupper from the ctype.h header file.

- Note the use of address arithmetic to assign the character values to ddd:

  ***(ddd + i) = toupper(day[i]);**

- Note how the

  return (ddd);

  returns a pointer to ddd by virtue of the definition of ddd as char *ddd.

D.7.0 Utdatedn.c Specifications

D.7.1 Utdatedn.c Design Objectives

Given a weekday number (0 = Sunday, 1 = Monday, etc.), this function returns a character pointer to the corresponding standard weekday name.

D.7.2 Utdatedn.c Source Code and Commentary

```
/* file    : utdatedn.c
** function: char *utdatedn (dow)
** desc    : return a pointer to day name of "dow"
**         : where "dow" is 0 = Sunday . . 6 = Saturday
** test pgm: tcalendr.c
*/

        char *utdatedn(dow)
        int dow;
        {

        static char *name[] = {
                "Sunday","Monday","Tuesday","Wednesday",
                "Thursday","Friday","Saturday","Illegal" };

        if ((dow < 0) || (dow > 6)) return(name[7]);
        else
        return(name[dow]);
        }
```

- Note how the character pointer array *name[] is specified and initialized with the array elements.
- If an invalid weekday number is specified, the message "Illegal" is returned.
- When using this function, it must explicitly be declared as: char *utdatedn();.

D.8.0 Utdatemm.c Specifications

D.8.1 Utdatemm.c Design Objectives

This function returns a character pointer to a standard three-character abbreviation for a month name. Given a month number (1 = January, 2 = February, etc.), a pointer is returned to a standard uppercase month name (JAN, FEB, etc.).

D.8.2 Utdatemm.c Source Code and Commentary

```
/* file    : utdatemm.c
** function: char *utdatemm (month)
** desc    : return a pointer to month name of "month" n
**         : where "month" is 1 = JAN . . . 12 = DEC
**         : in three-character form MMM.
** test pgm: tcalendr.c
*/

#include "ctype.h"

        char *utdatemm(month)
        int month;
        {

        char *utdatemy();
        static char *mmm = "   ";
        char *mon;
        int i;

        mon = utdatemy(month);
        for (i=0; i < 3; i++)
        {
        *(mmm+i) = toupper(mon[i]);
        }
        return (mmm);
        }
```

- When using this function, the calling program must explicitly declare this function to be:

  char *utdatemm();

- Note how function utdatemy.c is used to get the standard month names and force the first three characters to uppercase using the macro toupper from the ctype.h header file.

- Note the use of address arithmetic to assign the character values to mmm:

  ***(mmm + i) = toupper(mon[i]);**

- Note how the return (mmm) returns a pointer to mmm by virtue of the definition of mmm as char *mmm.

D.9.0 Utdatemy.c Specifications

D.9.1 Utdatemy.c Design Objectives

Given a month number, this function returns a character pointer to the standard month name.

D.9.2 Utdatemy.c Source Code and Commentary

```
/* file    : utdatemy.c
** function: char *utdatemy (month)
** desc    : return a pointer to month name of "month" n
**         : where "month" is 1 = January . . 12 = December
** test pgm: tcalendr.c
*/

        char *utdatemy(month)
        int month;
        {

        static char *name[] = {
                "Illegal","January","February","March",
                "April","May","June","July","August",
                "September","October","November",
                "December"  };

        if ((month < 1) || (month > 12 )) return(name[0]);
        else
        return(name[month]);
        }
```

- Note how the character pointer array *name[ ] is specified and initialized with the array elements.
- If an invalid month number is specified, the message "Illegal" is returned.
- When using this function, it must be explicitly declared as

  char *utdatemy( );

D.10.0 Utdategi.c Specifications

D.10.1 Utdategi.c Design Objectives

This function converts a date in gregorian (yyyy, mm, dd) to standard internal (yyyymmdd) format.

D.10.2 Utdategi.c Source Code and Commentary

```
/* file    : utdategi.c
** function: date utdategi (year, month, day)
** desc    : convert (year, month, day) to
**         : LDT encoded date format ( yyyymmdd = Long int )
** test pgm: tutdate.c
*/

#include "ldt.h"

        DATE utdategi(year, month, day)
        int year, month, day;
        {

        DATE idate;

        if (year < 1) year = 1;

        idate = ( (DATE)year * (DATE)10000 ) +
                ( (DATE)month * (DATE)100 ) + (DATE)day;

        return (idate);
        }
```

- Note that utdategi.c is of type DATE, the typedef equivalent of long int from the ldt.h header file.
- The function argument year is of the form yyyy and must be greater than zero. Valid function arguments range from 0001/01/01 through 9999/12/31.
- Note the use of the typedef DATE as a cast in the C language. When uncertain about the rules of precedence in the evaluation of expressions, be explicit!

D.11.0 Utdategj.c Specifications

D.11.1 Utdategj.c Design Objectives

This function converts a date in gregorian format (yyyy, mm, dd) to absolute julian format (n-days from origin).

D.11.2 Utdategj.c Source Code and Commentary

```
/* file    : utdategj.c
** function: date utdategj (year, month, day)
** desc    : convert gregorian ( year, month, day ) to
**         : julian format.
** test pgm: tutdate.c
*/
```

```
#include "ldt.h"

        DATE utdategj (year, month, day)
        int year, month, day;
        {

        DATE y, m, d, c, cy, jdate;

        d = day;

        if (year < 1) year = 1;

        y = year;

        if ( month > 2 ) m = month - 3;
        else
        {
        m = month + 9;
        y = year - 1;
        }

        c = y / 100;
        cy = y - 100 * c;

        jdate = (146097 * c) / 4 + (1461 * cy) / 4 +
                (153 * m + 2) / 5 + d + 1721119;

        return (jdate);
        }

/*      Reprinted by permission of ACM. Collected
**      Algorithms of the ACM. Algorithm #199.
**      Robert B. Tantzen.  New York: ACM, 1980.
*/
```

- This code represents an implementation of ACM algorithm #199. It has been tested and is mathematically sound from 0001/01/01 through 9999/12/31.
- Note that this function is of type DATE.

D.12.0 Utdateig.c Specifications

D.12.1 Utdateig.c Design Objectives

This function converts a date in standard internal format (yyyymmdd) to gregorian format (yyyy, mm, dd).

D.12.2 Utdateig.c Source Code and Commentary

```
/* file    : utdateig.c
** function: int utdateig (idate, &year, &month, &day)
** desc    : convert internal LDT date format (idate) to
**         : gregorian ( year, month, day )
** test pgm: tutdate.c
*/
```

```
#include "ldt.h"

        int utdateig (idate, year, month, day)
        int *year, *month, *day;
        DATE idate;
        {

        DATE y, md, m, d;

        y = idate / (DATE)10000;
        md = idate % (DATE)10000;
        m = md / (DATE)100;
        d = md % (DATE)100;

        *year  = (int)y;
        *month = (int)m;
        *day   = (int)d;

        return (ERC_OK);
        }
```

- Note the year, month, and day function arguments are returned values and must be passed as the address of (&).
- Note the use of the casts DATE and int. When in doubt about precedence criteria for evaluation of expressions, be explicit!

D.13.0 ***Utdateij.c Specifications***

D.13.1 ***Utdateij.c Design Objectives***

This function converts a date in standard internal format (yyyymmdd) to absolute julian format (n-days from origin).

D.13.2 ***Utdateij.c Source Code and Commentary***

```
/* file    : utdateij.c
** function: date utdateij (idate)
** desc    : convert idate internal LDT date format
**         : to julian date
** test pgm: tutdate.c
*/

#include "ldt.h"

        DATE utdateij (idate)
        DATE idate;
        {

        DATE utdategj();
        DATE jdate;
        int year, month, day, md;
```

```
year = idate / (DATE)10000;
md = idate % (DATE)10000;
month = md / 100;
day = md % 100;

jdate = utdategj(year, month, day);

return (jdate);
}
```

- Note that this function is of type DATE, not int.
- Note the use of the cast DATE, a typedef equivalent of long int found in ldt.h.

D.14.0 Utdatejg.c Specifications

D.14.1 Utdatejg.c Design Objectives

This function converts a date in absolute julian format (n-days from origin) to gregorian format (yyyy, mm, dd).

D.14.2 Utdatejg.c Source Code and Commentary

```
/* file    : utdatejg.c
** function: int utdatejg (jdate, &year, &month, &day)
** desc    : convert julian date (jdate) to
**         : gregorian ( year, month, day )
** test pgm: tutdate.c
*/

#include "ldt.h"

    int utdatejg (jdate, year, month, day)
    int *year, *month, *day;
    DATE jdate;
    {

    DATE j, y, m, d;

    j = jdate - 1721119;
    y = (4 * j - 1) / 146097;
    j = 4 * j - 1 - 146097 * y;
    d = j / 4;
    j = (4 * d + 3) / 1461;
    d = 4 * d + 3 - 1461 * j;
    d = (d + 4) / 4;
    m = (5 * d - 3) / 153;
    d = 5 * d - 3 - 153 * m;
    d = ( d + 5) / 5;
    y = 100 * y + j;

    if ( m < 10 ) m = m + 3;
    else
    {
    m = m - 9;
    y = y + 1;
    }
```

```
        *year = (int) y;
        *month = (int) m;
        *day = (int) d;

        return (ERC_OK);
        }

/*      Reprinted by permission of ACM. Collected
**      Algorithms of the ACM. Algorithm #199.
**      Robert B. Tantzen.  New York: ACM, 1980.
*/
```

- This code represents an implementation of ACM algorithm #199. It has been tested and is mathematically sound from 0001/01/01 through 9999/12/31.
- The function arguments, year, month, and day, are returned values, and hence must be passed as address of (&).

D.15.0 ***Utdateji.c Specifications***

D.15.1 ***Utdateji.c Design Objectives***

This function converts a date in absolute julian format (n-days from origin) to standard internal format (yyyymmdd).

D.15.2 ***Utdateji.c Source Code and Commentary***

```
/* file    : utdateji.c
** function: date utdateji (jdate)
** desc    : convert julian date "jdate" to
**         : internal LDT encoded date format ( yyyymmdd = Long int)
** test pgm: tutdate.c
*/

#include "ldt.h"

        DATE utdateji (jdate)
        DATE jdate;
        {

        DATE utdategi();
        int year, month, day;
        DATE idate;

        utdatejg(jdate, &year, &month, &day);

        idate = utdategi(year, month, day);

        return (idate);
        }
```

- This function is of type DATE, not int.
- Note the use of functions utdatejg.c and utdategi.c.

D.16.0 Utdatesg.c Specifications

D.16.1 Utdatesg.c Design Objectives

This function gets the current system date (sysdate) and converts it into gregorian date format (yyyy, mm, dd).

D.16.2 Utdatesg.c Source Code and Commentary

```
/*
** file    : utdatesg.c
** function: int utdatesg(&year, &month, &day)
** desc    : convert the DOS system date to
**         : gregorian format.
** test pgm: tutdate.c
*/

#include "dos.h"
#include "ldt.h"

        int utdatesg(year, month, day)
        int *year, *month, *day;
        {

        union REGS ir, or;
        int yy, mm, dd;

        ir.h.ah = DOS_DATE;
        int86(INT_DOS,&ir,&or);
        yy = or.x.cx;
        mm = or.h.dh;
        dd = or.h.dl;

        *year = yy;
        *month = mm;
        *day = dd;

        return(ERC_OK);
        }
```

- For a complete explanation of the technique used in this function, refer to Appendix D.
- The function arguments year, month, and day are returned values, and hence must be passed as the address of (&).

D.17.0 Utdatesi.c Specifications

D.17.1 Utdatesi.c Design Objectives

This function gets the current system date (sysdate) and converts it into standard internal date format (yyyymmdd).

D.17.2 Utdatesi.c Source Code and Commentary

```
/*
** file    : utdatesi.c
** function: date utdatesi()
** desc    : convert the DOS system date to
**         : LDT encoded date format ( yyyymmdd = Long int )
** test pgm: tutdate.c
*/

#include "dos.h"
#include "ldt.h"

        DATE utdatesi()
        {

        DATE utdategi();
        int year, month, day;
        DATE idate;

        utdatesg(&year, &month, &day);

        idate = utdategi(year, month, day);

        return(idate);
        }
```

- This function is of type DATE, not int.
- Function utdatesg.c is called and followed by function call utdategi.c to yield the internal format of the system date.

D.18.0 Utdatesj.c Specifications

D.18.1 Utdatesj.c Design Objectives

This function gets the current system date (sysdate) and converts it into absolute julian date format (n-days from origin).

D.18.2 Utdatesj.c Source Code Commentary

```
/*
** file    : utdatesj.c
** function: date utdatesj()
** desc    : convert the DOS system date to
**         : julian format
** test pgm: tutdate.c
*/

#include "dos.h"
#include "ldt.h"
```

```
DATE utdatesj()
{

DATE utdategj();
int year, month, day;
DATE jdate;

utdatesg(&year, &month, &day);

jdate = utdategj(year, month, day);

return(jdate);
}
```

- This function is of type DATE, not int.
- Function utdatesg.c is called, followed by function call utdategj.c to yield the julian format of the system date.

D.19.0 ***Utdatega.c Specifications***

D.19.1 ***Utdatega.c Design Objectives***

Given a birth date in gregorian format (yyyy, mm, dd), this function computes the age based upon the current system date (sysdate) in years, months, and days.

D.19.2 ***Utdatega.c Source Code and Commentary***

```
/* file    : utdatega.c
** function: int utdatega (byy, bmm, bdd, &ayy, &amm, &add)
** desc    : from gregorian birth date (byymmdd)
**         : compute age (ayymmdd)
** test pgm: tutdate.c
*/

#include "ldt.h"

        int utdatega (byy, bmm, bdd, ayy, amm, add)
        int byy, bmm, bdd, *ayy, *amm, *add;
        {

        DATE utdategj(),utdatesj(),utdatejd(),utdatenj();
        DATE jhdate, jldate, jdays, jzero;

        jhdate = utdatesj();
        jldate = utdategj(byy, bmm, bdd);

        jdays = utdatejd(jhdate, jldate);
        jzero = utdategj(1,1,1);
        jdays = utdatenj(jdays,jzero);

        utdatejg(jdays, ayy, amm, add);

        *ayy = *ayy - 1;
        *amm = *amm - 1;
        *add = *add - 1;

        return (ERC_OK);
        }
```

- Note how several functions are declared as type DATE. Uppercase DATE is a typedef from ldt.h. DATE is therefore equivalent to long int. C requires that all functions not of type int be explicitly declared whenever they are used. Failure to do so causes the function to try to return a long int as an int (garbage!).
- The function arguments ayy, amm, and add are passed as

  address of (&)

  because they are returned values.
- The computation of an age in integral units of years, months and days is trickier than it may seem. Jhdate (julian high date) is the sysdate. Jldate (julian low date) is the birth date. Jdays is the number of days between birth date and sysdate. So far simple, right? Next we set jzero to the lowest valid date that can be converted by the function utdatejg.c. Then we add jdays to jzero giving a new jdays offset from jzero. We then call utdatejg.c to convert jdays to ayy, amm, add, lastly subtracting the effects of jzero which could not be zero (0, 0, 0) but rather one (1, 1, 1). It works!

D.20.0 ***Utdateia.c Specifications***

D.20.1 ***Utdateia.c Design Objectives***

Given a birth date in standard internal format (yyyymmdd), this function computes the age based upon the current system date (sysdate) in years, months, and days.

D.20.2 ***Utdateia.c Source Code and Commentary***

```
/* file    : utdateia.c
** function: int utdateia (bidate, &ayy, &amm, &add)
** desc    : compute age (ayymmdd) from birth date in
**         : internal LDT encoded date format
** test pgm: tutdate.c
*/
```

```
#include "ldt.h"

        int utdateia (bidate, ayy, amm, add)
        int *ayy, *amm, *add;
        DATE bidate;
        {

        DATE utdatesj(),utdateij(),utdatejd(),utdatenj();
        DATE utdategj();
        DATE hjdate, ljdate, jdays, jzero;

        hjdate = utdatesj();
        ljdate = utdateij(bidate);
        jdays = utdatejd(hjdate, ljdate);
        jzero = utdategj(1,1,1);
        jdays = utdatenj(jdays,jzero);

        utdatejg(jdays, ayy, amm, add);

        *ayy = *ayy - 1;
        *amm = *amm - 1;
        *add = *add - 1;

        return (ERC_OK);
        }
```

- For a complete description of the technique, refer to Section D.19.2 for function utdatega.c.

D.21.0 **Utdateja.c Specifications**

D.21.1 **Utdateja.c Design Objectives**

Given a birth date in absolute julian format (n-days from origin), this function computes the age based upon the current system date (sysdate) in years, months, and days.

D.21.2 **Utdateja.c Source Code and Commentary**

```
/* file    : utdateja.c
** function: int utdateja (bjdate, &ayy, &amm, &add)
** desc    : compute age (ayymmdd) from birth date
**         : bjdate in julian format
** test pgm: tutdate.c
*/

#include "ldt.h"

        int utdateja (bjdate, ayy, amm, add)
        int *ayy, *amm, *add;
        DATE bjdate;
        {

        DATE utdatesj(),utdatejd(),utdatenj();
        DATE utdategj();
        DATE hjdate, jdays, jzero;
```

```
hjdate = utdatesj();
jdays = utdatejd(hjdate, bjdate);
jzero = utdategj(1,1,1);
jdays = utdatenj(jdays,jzero);

utdatejg(jdays, ayy, amm, add);

*ayy = *ayy - 1;
*amm = *amm - 1;
*add = *add - 1;

return (ERC_OK);
}
```

- For a complete description of the technique, refer to section D.19.2 for function utdatega.c.

D.22.0 ***Utdategd.c Specifications***

D.22.1 ***Utdategd.c Design Objectives***

Given two gregorian dates (yyyy1, mm1, dd1), and (yyyy2, mm2, dd2), this function computes the number of days between them. It conforms to the convention that (dd1 – dd1) = 1.

D.22.2 ***Utdategd.c Source Code and Commentary***

```
/* file    : utdategd.c
** function: date utdategd (hyy, hmm, hdd, lyy, lmm, ldd)
** desc    : compute the number of day difference (hyymmdd - lyymmdd)
**         : between gregorian formats.
** test pgm: tutdate.c
*/

#include "ldt.h"

        DATE utdategd (hyy, hmm, hdd, lyy, lmm, ldd)
        int hyy, hmm, hdd, lyy, lmm, ldd;
        {

        DATE utdategj(), utdatejd(), hjdate, ljdate, days;

        hjdate = utdategj(hyy, hmm, hdd);
        ljdate = utdategj(lyy, lmm, ldd);

        days = utdatejd(hjdate, ljdate);

        return (days);
        }
```

- Both function argument gregorian dates are converted to absolute julian form, and then are passed to utdatejd.c which returns the number of days difference in DATE not int format. DATE is a typedef for long int.

D.23.0 Utdateid.c Specifications

D.23.1 Utdateid.c Design Objectives

Given two internal dates (yyyymmdd1) and (yyyymmdd2), this function computes the number of days between them. It conforms to the convention that (dd1 – dd1) = 1.

D.23.2 Utdateid.c Source Code and Commentary

```
/* file    : utdateid.c
** function: date utdateid (hidate, lidate)
** desc    : compute the number of day difference (hidate - lidate)
**         : between internal LDT encoded date format
** test pgm: tutdate.c
*/

#include "ldt.h"

        DATE utdateid (hidate, lidate)
        DATE hidate, lidate;
        {

        DATE utdateij(), utdatejd();
        DATE jhi, jli, days;

        jhi = utdateij (hidate);
        jli = utdateij (lidate);

        days = utdatejd(jhi, jli);

        return (days);
        }
```

- Both function argument internal dates are converted to absolute julian form, then simply passed to utdatejd.c which returns the number of days difference in DATE, not int, format. DATE is a typedef for long int.

D.24.0 Utdatejd.c Specifications

D.24.1 Utdatejd.c Design Objectives

Given two absolute julian dates, this function computes the number of days between them. It conforms to the convention that (dd1 – dd1) = 1.

D.24.2 Utdatejd.c Source Code and Commentary

```
/* file    : utdatejd.c
** function: date utdatejd (hjdate, ljdate)
** desc    : compute the number of day difference (hjdate - ljdate)
**         : between julian formats.
** test pgm: tutdate.c
*/

#include "ldt.h"
#include "stdio.h"

        DATE utdatejd (hjdate, ljdate)
        DATE hjdate, ljdate;
        {

        DATE days;

        days = max(hjdate,ljdate)  - min(hjdate,ljdate) + 1;

        return (days);
        }
```

- Note that this function is of type DATE, not int.
- Note the use of the macros min and max found in header file stdio.h. The computed days are always positive numbers. The abs macro could have been used to achieve the same result.

D.25.0 Utdateng.c Specifications

D.25.1 Utdateng.c Design Objectives

Given a gregorian formatted date (yyyy, mm, dd) and an offset value (+/− ndays), this function computes the resulting gregorian date (nyyyy, nmm, ndd).

D.25.2 Utdateng.c Source Code and Commentary

```
/* file    : utdateng.c
** function: int utdateng (yy, mm, dd, ndays, &nyy, &nmm, &ndd)
** desc    : shift "yy, mm, dd" by "+/- ndays" yielding
**         : "nyy, nmm, ndd". Note that "ndays" is a long int!
** test pgm: tutdate.c
*/

#include "ldt.h"

        int utdateng (yy, mm, dd, ndays, nyy, nmm, ndd)
        int yy, mm, dd, *nyy, *nmm, *ndd;
```

```
DATE ndays;
{

DATE utdategj(), utdatenj();
DATE jdate;

jdate = utdategj(yy, mm, dd);

jdate = utdatenj(jdate, ndays);

utdatejg(jdate, nyy, nmm, ndd);

return (ERC_OK);
}
```

- The approach is to convert the base gregorian date to absolute julian format, add the offset (+/− ndays), then convert the resulting absolute julian date to gregorian format again.
- The function arguments nyyy, nmm, and ndd are returned values and hence must be passed as the address of (&).

D.26.0 **Utdateni.c Specifications**

D.26.1 **Utdateni.c Design Objectives**

Given a standard internal formatted date (idate) and an offset value (+/− ndays), this function computes the resulting internal date (function return value).

D.26.2 **Utdateni.c Source Code and Commentary**

```
/* file    : utdateni.c
** function: date utdateni (idate, ndays)
** desc    : shift "idate" by "+/- ndays".
** test pgm: tutdate.c
*/

#include "ldt.h"

        DATE utdateni (idate, ndays)
        DATE idate, ndays;
        {

        DATE utdateij(), utdatenj(), utdateji();
        DATE nidate, jdate;
```

```
jdate = utdateij(idate);
jdate = utdatenj(jdate, ndays);
nidate = utdateji(jdate);

return (nidate);
}
```

- This function is of the type DATE, not int.
- The approach is to convert the base internal date to absolute julian format, add the offset (+/− ndays), then convert the resulting absolute julian date to internal format again.

D.27.0 Utdatenj.c Specifications

D.27.1 Utdatenj.c Design Objectives

Given an absolute julian formatted date (jdate) and an offset value (+/− ndays), this function computes the resulting julian date (returned function value).

D.27.2 Utdatenj.c Source Code and Commentary

```
/* file    : utdatenj.c
** function: date utdatenj (jdate, ndays)
** desc    : shift "jdate" by "+/- ndays".
** test pgm: tutdate.c
*/

#include "ldt.h"

        DATE utdatenj (jdate, ndays)
        DATE jdate, ndays;
        {

        DATE njdate;

        njdate = jdate + ndays;

        return (njdate);
        }
```

- This function is of the type DATE, not int.
- Since jdate is already in absolute julian format, simply add the offset value (+/− ndays) to yield the answer and return the value.

E.0.0 LDT Date Application Tips and Reminders

E.1.0 Helpful Notes

Using the standard interface function definitions for the date logical data type is somewhat less complicated than for LDT char. This is because the pphys argument is always passed as an "address of" (&pphys) since pphys is of type DATE (typedef synonymous with long int).

Let's highlight some helpful reminders about using the functions included in this chapter.

- **Endate.c and evdate.c:** The maxin function argument should be the sizeof(pstrin) – 1. Maxin is the declared pstrin (size – 1) and doesn't include the NULL delimiting character. Maxphys in all instances should be PHY_DATE.
- **Getdate.c and fgetdate.c:** The maxstr function argument should be the sizeof(string) – 1. Cltab only controls the very first character read operation performed. Nuexit is a returned value and therefore must be passed as &nuexit.
- **Dedate.c, putdate.c, and fputdate.c:** The maxout function argument should be the sizeof(pstrin) – 1. Maxout is the declared pstrout (size – 1) as not to include the NULL delimiting character. Maxout must be large enough to receive the decoded pphys or an erc will result. In all instances maxphys should be PHY_DATE.
- **Dvdateyy.c:** When these functions are used as function arguments they must be declared explicitly in the calling program.
- **Utdateyy.c:** Be careful to declare explicitly the types of the functions being referenced. Many utdateyy.c functions are *not* of type integer.
- **General:** Initialize all strings before using them.

E.2.0 Special Uses

We will not present any additional special uses for LDT date.

F.0.0 Testing and Quality Assurance (qadate.c)

F.1.0 Qadate.c Specification

F.1.1 Qadate.c Design Objectives

Qadate.c is unique to the date logical data type, but is in keeping with all other qaxxxx.c routines. Qadate.c utilizes endate.c, evdate.c, getdate.c, fgetdate.c, dedate.c, putdate.c, and fputdate.c as well as dvdateyy.c, utdateyy.c and supporting functions as indicated in the linker automatic response file qadate.lnk (see Appendix L).

Qadate.c provides runtime control over the resetting of stdlog, making stdlog entries, screen printing upon error detection, and testing all encode and decode subtypes values.

Each qaxxxx.c function is an excellent example of not only LDT testing, but also techniques for the use of the various standard interfaces portrayed in this book. A close examination of qadate.c reveals a powerful program of about 100 statements.

F.1.2 Qadate.c Error Codes

Qaxxxx.c functions do not have any reserved ercs of their own; rather, they simply report the ercs detected during processing by the underlying standard interface functions.

All ercs detected for LDT date, however, are governed by the ldt.h header file values in effect for

ERC_BASE	1000
GET_E	1
PUT_E	5
ENDATE_E	21

F.2.0 Qadate.c Source Code and Commentary

```
/*
** file   : qadate.c
** desc   : quality assurance test program for LDT DATE
** link   : @qadate.lnk,qadate,nul,lcs
*/

#include "ldt.h"

main ()
{
        int dvcharyn(), dvdateen(), dvdatede(), dvdummy();
        int erc;

        static char mtype[] = ">????<";
        static char mstr[] = ">??????????????????????????????<";
        static char myn[] = ">?<";

        static char initen[] = "231";
        static char initde[] = "2343";
        static char inity[] = "Y";
        static char initn[] = "N";

        char str[35], destr[31], ynchar;
        int entype, detype, nuexit,lpe;
        DATE dval;
        int smstr;

        smstr = nondel(mstr);

        blanksc(1,1,MAX_ROW,MAX_COL);
        setcrc(1,1);
        putstr("DATE Quality Assurance Program",LR,"",DISP_F);

        /*
        ** Prompt for User Runtime Controls
        */

        uprompt(&lpe);

        if ( (lpe == 10) || (lpe == 11) )
                logwrite(5,"QADATE",0,"Begin Testing");

        for (;;)
        {

        blanksc(2,1,MAX_ROW,MAX_COL);
        setcrc(1,1);

        movcrc(2,-MAX_COL);
        putstr("Enter ENCODE Subtype  : ",LR,"",DISP_F);

        erc = getint(str,sizeof(str)-1,NO,mtype,LR,initen,MAND_F,YES,
                     &nuexit,&entype,PHY_INT,1,MAND_F,lpe,dvdateen);

        if (lderc(erc) == 9) break;

        movcrc(2,-MAX_COL);
        putstr("Enter DATE String     : ",LR,"",DISP_F);

        erc = getdate(str,sizeof(str)-1,NO,mstr,LR,"",MAND_F,NO,
                  &nuexit,&dval,PHY_DATE,entype,MAND_F,lpe,dvdummy);

        if (lderc(erc) == 9) continue;
```

```
            movcrc(2,-MAX_COL);
            putstr("ENCODEed Internal DATE: ",LR,"",DISP_F);
            putint(destr,MAX_INT4,&dval,PHY_INT4,0,L_JUST,
                   LR,mstr,MAND_F,lpe);

            movcrc(2,-MAX_COL);
            putstr("Enter DECODE Subtype   : ",LR,"",DISP_F);

            erc = getint(str,sizeof(str)-1,NO,mtype,LR,initde,MAND_F,NO,
                         &nuexit,&detype,PHY_INT,1,MAND_F,lpe,dvdatede);

            if (lderc(erc) == 9) continue;

            movcrc(2,-MAX_COL);
            putstr("DECODEed DATE          : ",LR,"",DISP_F);
            putdate(destr,smstr,&dval,PHY_DATE,detype,L_JUST,
                    LR,mstr,MAND_F,lpe);

            setcrc(24,1);
            putstr("Continue? [Yes/No] or [ESCape]: ",LR,"",DISP_F);

            erc = getchar(str,sizeof(str)-1,NO,myn,LR,inity,MAND_F,NO,
                          &nuexit,&ynchar,1,11,MAND_F,lpe,dvcharyn);

            if (lderc(erc) == 9) break;
            if (ynchar == 'N') break;
            }

            if ( (lpe == 10) || (lpe == 11) )
                    logwrite(6,"QADATE",0,"End Testing");

            blanksc(1,1,MAX_ROW,MAX_COL);
            exit(0);
}
```

- All dvxxxxyy.c functions to be used as function arguments must explicitly be declared in the calling program.
- All masks are declared with outermost field delimiters so that the field limits may always be known regardless of the type of field and hence video attribute chosen for display.
- All init values are declared to make any necessary revision easy.
- Destr[31] matches the nondelimiter size of the date field mask mstr[]. The size of a displayed string must not exceed the corresponding number of mask nondelimiter positions, if a mask is used for display purposes.

- Variable lpe is calculated by uprompt.c from runtime user responses and effectively becomes the standard function argument logprerr. (See Chapter 13.)

- Anywhere in the source code where

  if (lderc(erc) = = 9)

  appears, an equivalent statement

  if (nuexit = = −1)

  could have been specified.

- Note that because there are hundreds of possible ensubtype and desubtype values, qadate.c differs from qachar.c (Chapter 5, F.2.0) in that only one ensubtype and desubtype pair can be tested at a time.

- Note that hitting the Escape key recycles the program unless performed at

  Enter ENCODE Subtype:

  or

  Continue? [Yes/No] or [ESCape]:

  where it exits the program. Hitting Ctrl-Break will have no effect in qaxxxx.c functions because Ctrl-Break has been turned off in function _main (see Appendix F).

- Four additional test programs are available on disk: tdedate.c, tendate.c, tcalendr.c, and tutdate.c.

- Note sample output for qadate.c in Figure 6.1.

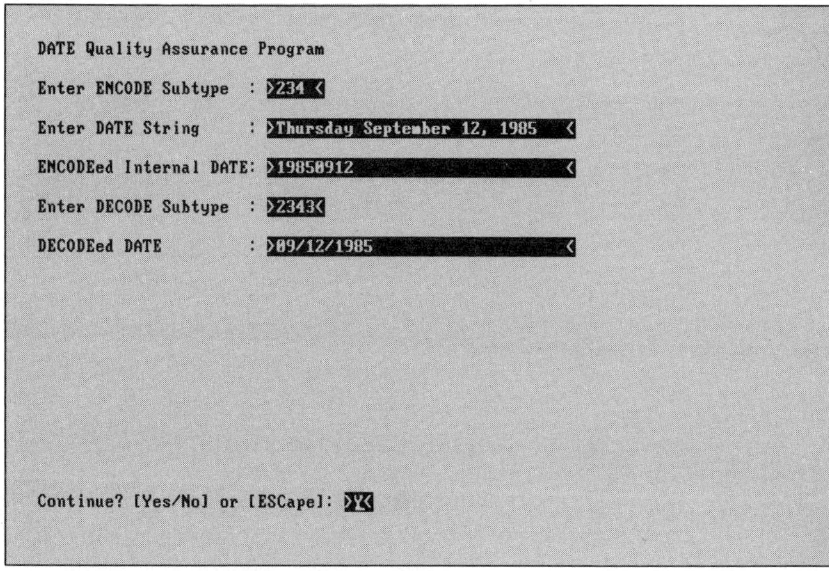

Figure 6.1– *Qadate.c sample output.*

Dollars

7

This chapter covers the I/O of dollar fields that are encoded to and decoded from a storage format as specified by the following statement in header file ldt.h:

```
typedef long int DOLR;
```

Every dollar field is therefore internally represented as a long integer (four bytes) in whole cents. The dollar amount $12.75, for example, is stored as the integer value 1275. Dollar fields are commonly used in disk record structures, and as sort fields when interfacing to sorting software products.

This dolr logical data type represents a faster and more compact dollar storage format than either a floating point double representation (eight bytes) or commercially available decimal arithmetic utility functions (ten bytes). Although limited to a range of values on the 8088/86/186 class of microprocessor

(+/− $21,474,836.47), extended allowable value ranges can be achieved with the advent of the 80286/386 and companion 80287/387 NPX.

Each interface definition described in Part 1 of this book is implemented for the dollar logical data type (xxxx = dolr). The endolr.c function provided accepts all dedolr.c formats and, with the specification of the ensubtype function argument, controls which combination of negative, zero, and positive values are acceptable. The dedolr.c function generates dollar character representations under format control with the specification of a desired desubtype argument value. The data validation functions validate the allowable encode and decode subtype values.

This chapter presents utility functions that simplify the addition, subtraction, multiplication, and division of dollar fields and provide for overflow checking. Additional utility functions are included that extend the formatting options available with the dedolr.c function for check-writing purposes.

Finally, a testing and quality assurance program (qadolr.c) allows you to interactively examine and test most of the functions developed in this chapter.

The following chapter index lists all the source code that you will find in this chapter.

Standard Interface Source Code

A.2.0	Endolr.c:	Encode LDT dolr
A.3.0	Evdolr.c:	Encode and validate LDT dolr
A.4.0	Getdolr.c/ Fgetdolr.c:	Combined getstr.c and evdolr.c
B.2.0	Dedolr.c:	Decode LDT dolr
B.3.0	Putdolr.c/ Fputdolr.c:	Combined dedolr.c and putstr.c

Data Validation (dvdolryy.c) Functions

C.2.0	Dvdolrde.c:	Checks for allowable desubtypes.
C.3.0	Dvdolren.c:	Checks for allowable ensubtypes.

Utility (utdolryy.c) Functions

D.2.0	Utdolrad.c:	Adds dolr fields.
D.3.0	Utdolrdv.c:	Divides dolr fields.

D.4.0	Utdateml.c:	Multiplies dolr fields.
D.5.0	Utdatesb.c:	Subtracts dolr fields.
E.3.0	Utdolrcw.c:	Check-writing function (dolr to text description).
E.4.0	Utdolrda.c:	Supporting dollar amount function for utdolrcw.c.

Testing and Quality Assurance Program

F.2.0	Qadolr.c:	Standard quality assurance test program.

A.0.0 **Encode Function Development (endolr.c)**

A.1.0 **Endolr.c Specifications**

A.1.1 **Design Objectives**

The dolr logical data type provides an alternative method of handling dollar fields in a C commercial programming environment, different from the handling provided in a typical COBOL, Lotus 1–2–3, or dBASE III application.

In a COBOL programming environment, *packed decimal* fields are typically specified for dollar fields; analogous decimal arithmetic software packages are commercially available for C (see Appendix C).

On the other hand, a number of popular software products (dBASE III, Lotus 1–2–3, and their derivatives) utilize standard IEEE formatted floating point numbers for dollar representation (conforming to the C language "double"), because they tend to be used for financial planning and do not provide the precise cents accuracy provided by COBOL for pure accounting applications.

Dolr is a compact, fast alternative for use with dollar fields, if its allowable value range is deemed acceptable for a given application environment. Since dolr fields are represented as C data type long int, and because all dolr fields are stored in whole cents, the allowable range of a dollar field using LDT dolr is between −$21,474,836.47 and +$21,474,836.47.

If this constraint is acceptable, dolr will serve you well. Cent accuracy is assured and overflow checking is provided. A full discussion of the tradeoffs between data storage formats is provided in section A.1.3 below.

A.1.2 ***Field Size (maxin)***

For the dolr LDT we have set the MAX_DOLR field width to 20 (see ldt.h), which accommodates the largest possible dolr decode value with formatting, e.g.:

(**$21,474,836.47CR)

A.1.3 ***Physical Format (maxphys)***

As indicated in Section A.1.1, we are using dolr as an alternative to the decimal arithmetic approach. Clearly, dolr could be modified to encode to and decode from decimal arithmetic functions, but we have chosen to portray a more compact and faster dollar field alternative for use in a C programming environment. The use of long int dictates that MAXPHYS must equal 4 (PHY_DOLR), the size in bytes of a long int.

Consider the storage requirement and relative speed of dollar fields represented by the three common storage formats listed in Table 7.1.

	Long int	Double	Decimal
Size bytes:	4	8	10
Relative speed:	1x	*5x	*2x

* Estimated, based on the timings derived from comparable test programs that added 1000 consecutive numbers for each data storage type shown.

Table *7.1–Alternative dollar field storage and performance*

If the range-of-value restriction of the proposed LDT dolr is acceptable for use with your application, the LDT is clearly advantageous.

A.1.4 Character Set Restrictions

By design of the getstr.c/fgetstr.c functions, the endolr function only "sees" ASCII 0x20 through 0x7E. (Refer to Appendix E for a complete definition of the ASCII character set.) For dolr fields of input this complete range of character input is restricted further. Endolr.c processing imposes additional edit checks. See sections A.1.6 and A.1.7 below.

A.1.5 Subtype Definition (ensubtype)

The ensubtype parameter provides immediate data entry editing for negative, zero, and positive dollar values as follows:

0	Any negative, zero, or positive dollar value
1	Only zero or positive dollar values
2	Only positive dollar values
3	Only negative or zero dollar values
4	Only negative dollar values

Although this editing can be satisfied by data validation functions, such editing is so common that it is better if the ensubtype function argument takes care of this level of editing and leaves reasonability checks of dollar fields up to custom data validation functions.

A.1.6 Other Format Controls

The syntax of an acceptable dolr field is as follows:

```
[b..b] [ ( ]  [*..*] [-] [$]   [ddd,..ddd][.][dd]  [-] [ ) ] [b..b]
              [b..b]           [b.......b]         [CR]
                                                   [DR]
                                                   [RV]
                                                   [b..b]
```

where

[ ]	indicates optional
b	is a blank or space character (0x20)
–	is an optional sign placement; only a leading or trailing one may be specified, not both.
d	is a digit only (0 through 9)

From the above dolr field syntax the following format checks are made by endolr.c to assure data integrity:

- At least one d (digit) must be specified to satisfy the mandatory field requirement, if specified.
- Outermost paired parentheses signify negative and cannot be specified in addition to a minus sign (–).
- All leading asterisks are simply stripped, not interpreted in any manner.
- Only one leading or trailing minus sign can be specified, and it cannot be specified together with the use of paired parentheses.
- If a credit, debit, or reversal is present, it is stripped and is not interpreted in any manner.
- Only one dollar sign, positioned as shown above can be specified. It, too, is stripped.
- Only one decimal point, positioned as shown above, can be specified. It is stripped, but designates the boundary between whole dollars and cents. Dollar fields may be specified as shown below:

Input	**Equivalent**
1	$1.00
1.	$1.00
1.2	$1.20
1.23	$1.23
.1	$0.10
.12	$0.12

- If delimiting commas are specified, they must delineate the thousands place. If they are incorrectly placed, an erc is generated; otherwise, commas are simply stripped.
- All characters remaining after the above syntax checking must be ds (digits); otherwise an erc is generated.
- No plus sign is permitted.

A.1.7 ***Editing***

As described in A.1.5, dollar field sign detection has been attributed to the ensubtype parameter.

Overflow checking ensures that all dolr fields remain within the allowable range (−$21,474,836.47 through +$21,474,836.47).

If exceeded, the following erc is generated:

erc = ERC_BASE + ENDOLR_E

A.1.8 ***Default Values***

Upon initial entry to the endolr.c function, the dolr field is initialized to zero.

A.1.9 ***Error Codes***

Based upon the ERC_BASE (1000) and ENDOLR_E (31) values defined in ldt.h the following ercs are possible:

1031	Encode Data Entry Error By User
1032	Bad Encode Function Argument
1033	Encode Mandatory Field Not Satisfied

A.2.0 ***Endolr.c Source Code and Commentary***

```
/* file    : endolr.c
** function: int endolr ( pstrin, maxin, pphys, maxphys,
**         :              ensubtype, mflag )
** desc    : Encode a logical data type dolr.
** test pgm: qadolr.c
*/

#include "ctype.h"
#include "ldt.h"
```

```
int endolr (pstrin, maxin, pphys, maxphys, ensubtype, mflag)

char *pstrin;
DOLR *pphys;
int maxin, maxphys, ensubtype, mflag;
{

static double maxdolr = 2147483647.0;
double dval, wgt;
int erc, eerc, i, slgth, digit, first, loc;
char str[30], sign;

/*
** Table of valid ENCODE subtypes:
**     0 = any dollar
**     1 = 0/+ dollar only
**     2 = + dollar only
**     3 = 0/- dollar only
**     4 = - dollar only
*/

/*
** Allowable Syntax of Dollar Entry Fields: []optional
**
**     [(][*...*][-][$][ddd,...ddd][.][dd][- ]    [)]
**        [b...b]       [b...b]            [CR]
**                                         [DR]
**                                         [RV]
**                                         [b...b]
*/

/*
** Validate the function arguments:
*/

erc = ERC_BASE + ENDOLR_E + 1;

if (( maxin < 1 ) || ( maxin > MAX_DOLR )) return (erc);

if (maxphys != PHY_DOLR) return(erc);

if (( mflag < NO ) || ( mflag > YES )) return (erc);

/*
** validate "ensubtype" and set "default" values
*/

eerc = dvdolren(&ensubtype,PHY_INT);
if(eerc != ERC_OK) return(eerc);

*pphys = (DOLR)0;

/*
** Validate mandatory field requirement
** OK to check before any other preprocessing
*/

slgth = strlen( pstrin );
if (( mflag ) && ( slgth < 1 )) return (erc+1);

erc = erc - 1;

/*
** encode processing
*/

strcpy(str, pstrin);
sign = C_BLANK;
```

```
/*
** strip leading/trailing blanks, if any
*/

utcharsb(3,str,C_BLANK);
slgth = strlen(str);
if(slgth < 1) return(erc+2);

/*
** strip "negative" paired parentheses " ( ... )", if any
*/

if ( (str[0] == C_LPAR) && (str[slgth-1] == C_RPAR) )
{
sign = C_MINUS;
delchr(str,1);
delchr(str,0);
utcharsb(3,str,C_BLANK);
slgth = strlen(str);
if (slgth < 1) return(erc+2);
}

/*
** strip leading "asterisks", if any.
*/

utcharsb(1,str,C_AST);
slgth = strlen(str);
if (slgth < 1) return(erc+2);

/*
** strip leading/trailing '-', if any
*/

if ( (str[0] == C_MINUS) || (str[slgth-1] == C_MINUS))
{
if (sign == C_MINUS) return(erc);
if ( (str[0] == C_MINUS) && (str[slgth-1] == C_MINUS) )
     return(erc);
sign = C_MINUS;
if (str[0] == C_MINUS) delchr(str,1);
else delchr(str,0);
slgth = strlen(str);
if (slgth < 1) return(erc+2);
}

/*
** strip trailing "CR","DR" or "RV"
*/

if ( isalpha(str[slgth-1]) != 0 )
{
if ( toupper(str[slgth-1]) == 'R' )
{
if ( (toupper(str[slgth-2]) == 'C') ||
     (toupper(str[slgth-2]) == 'D') )
{
delchr(str,0);
delchr(str,0);
}
}
else
if ( toupper(str[slgth-1]) == 'V' )
{
if ( toupper(str[slgth-2]) == 'R' )
{
delchr(str,0);
delchr(str,0);
}
}
```

```
else return(erc);
}

slgth = strlen(str);
if (slgth < 1) return(erc+2);

/*
** strip leading "$" sign, only one, if any.
*/

if ( str[0] == C_DSIGN )
{
delchr(str,1);
utcharsb(1,str,C_BLANK);
slgth = strlen(str);
if (slgth < 1) return(erc+2);
}

/*
** find '.' if any
*/

loc = poschr(str,C_PERIOD,LR);
if (loc == 0)
{
loc = slgth;
}
else
{
delchr(str,loc);
loc = loc - 1;
slgth = strlen(str);
if (slgth < 1) return(erc+2);
}

/*
** check number of "cents" positions
*/

if ( loc == slgth )
{
inschr(str,999,C_ZERO,0);
inschr(str,999,C_ZERO,0);
}
else
if ( loc == (slgth - 1) )
{
inschr(str,999,C_ZERO,0);
}
else
if ( loc < (slgth - 2) ) return(erc);

slgth = strlen(str);

/*
** check for delimiting comma's if any
*/

first = TRUE;
for (i=loc-4; i > 0; i=i-4)
{
if (first == TRUE)
{
if ( str[i] != C_COMMA ) break;
else
{
first = FALSE;
delchr(str,i+1);
}
}
```

```
else
{
if (str[i] != C_COMMA) return(erc);
else
{
delchr(str,i+1);
}
}
}

slgth = strlen(str);


/*
** check that all digits remain!
*/

for ( i=0; i < slgth; i++ )
{
if ( isdigit(str[i]) == 0 ) return(erc);
}

switch ( ensubtype )
{
        case 0: break;
        case 1:
        case 2: if (sign == C_MINUS) return(erc);
                break;
        case 3: break;
        case 4: if (sign != C_MINUS) return(erc);
                break;

}


wgt = 1.0;
dval = 0.0;

for ( i= (slgth - 1); i >=0; i--)
{
digit = str[i] - C_ZERO;
dval = dval + wgt * (double)digit;
wgt = wgt * (double)10.0;
}

if (dval > maxdolr) return(erc);

if ( sign == C_MINUS ) dval = -dval;

switch (ensubtype)
{

        case 0: break;
        case 1: if (dval < 0.0) return(erc);
                break;
        case 2: if (dval <= 0.0) return(erc);
                break;
        case 3: if (dval > 0.0) return(erc);
                break;
        case 4: if (dval >= 0.0) return(erc);
                break;
}

*pphys = (DOLR)dval;

return (ERC_OK);

}
```

- Note that pphys is declared to be type DOLR. Uppercase DOLR is a typedef from the ldt.h header file. DOLR is therefore equivalent to long int.
- For the dolr LDT, if pstrin does not contain at least one d (digit), it will not satisfy the mandatory mflag field requirement.
- Note the consistent use of utcharsb.c to strip extraneous blank characters and leading asterisks from pstrin (same as str).
- Note that variables of type double are used to accumulate the value of each dollar field. This is acceptable because we are accumulating only a whole number of cents for the dollar field, and 15 significant digits can be accumulated without any loss of significance. The LDT dolr long int supports only up to ten significant digits. The valid range for dolr is checked against variable maxdolr.

A.3.0 Encode and Validate Source Code and Commentary (evdolr.c)

The source code and commentary for function evdolr.c parallels evchar.c (Chapter 5, A.3.0). To create function evdolr.c, simply copy file evchar.c and edit as follows:

- Change all occurrences of char to dolr and CHAR to DOLR except for the statement:

```
char *pstrin;
```

- Update the commented function description.

The complete source code is available on disk.

A.4.0 Advanced Encode Field Processing

A.4.1 Getdolr.c and Fgetdolr.c Error Codes

See Chapter 5, A.4.1.

A.4.2 *Getdolr.c and Fgetdolr.c Source Code and Commentary*

The source code and commentary for function getdolr.c parallels getchar.c (Chapter 5, A.4.0). To create function getdolr.c, simply copy file getchar.c and edit as follows:

- Change all occurrences of char to dolr and CHAR to DOLR except for the statement

```
char *string, *mask, *init;
```

The source code and commentary for function fgetdolr.c also parallels fgetchar.c (Chapter 5, A.4.0). To create function fgetdolr.c, copy fgetchar.c and edit it as follows:

- Change all occurrences of char to dolr and CHAR to DOLR except for the statements

```
char *string, *mask, *init;
utcharcb(1,string,1);
```

The complete source code is available on disk.

A.4.3 *Associated Mask Utilization Techniques*

Based upon the function argument gmaskflg, mask delimiter characters may be included (YES) in the acquired input string. This facilitates the introduction of common dollar field identifiers such as the dollar sign and decimal point:

Dollar Field: "$??.??"

For certain LDTs included in this book, it might seem that the ensubtype format control effects overlap with the results of the gmaskflg associated with getstr.c/fgetstr.c. It is important to remember that endolr.c can be utilized independently of the getstr.c/fgetstr.c and getdolr.c/fgetdolr.c functions so that some functional redundancy is required to expand the independent use of the enxxxx.c interface definitions developed in this book.

B.0.0 Decode Function Development (dedolr.c)

B.1.0 Dedolr.c Specifications

B.1.1 Design Objectives

This function provides a dolr processing function that can display dollar fields stored in standard long int format (125075 = $1,250.75) in a variety of commonly needed commercial display formats. Each output format in turn becomes a format that is acceptable to its corresponding endolr.c function.

B.1.2 Subtype Definition (desubtype)

The dolr desubtype is a single integer value consisting of two digits (d2d1). The following are acceptable digit values for d2, which handles negative values:

1 = negative handled by outermost parentheses (..).
2 = negative handled by leading minus sign.
3 = negative handled by trailing minus sign.
4 = credit handled by CR; if negative by (..CR).
5 = debit handled by DR; if negative by (..DR).
6 = reversal handled by RV; if negative by (..RV).

Digit d1 controls the other formatting options:

0 = [d..d].dd
1 = [ddd,..].dd
2 = [*..*][N][ddd,..].dd
3 = [N][$][ddd,..].dd
4 = [*..*][N][$][ddd,..].dd

([N] denotes the position of a leading minus sign if one is specified by d2 above.)

A series of valid desubtype specifications with examples for the dolr variable containing −123456, an overall field width of

12, and right justification are listed below:

```
10:    (1234.56)
11:   (1,234.56)
12: (**1,234.56)
13:  ($1,234.56)
14: (*$1,234.56)
```

B.1.3 **Default Values**

No default is assumed for dedolr.c. The output character string pstrout is simply set to a NULL string before processing begins.

B.1.4 **Error Codes**

Based upon the ERC_BASE (1000) and ENDOLR_E (31) values defined in ldt.h the following erc is possible:

1036	Bad Decode Function Argument

B.2.0 **Dedolr.c Source Code and Commentary**

```
/* file    : dedolr.c
** function: int dedolr ( pstrout, maxout, pphys, maxphys,
**         :              desubtype, jflag )
** desc    : decode a logical data type dollar.
** test pgm: qadolr.c
*/

#include "ctype.h"
#include "ldt.h"

        int dedolr (pstrout, maxout, pphys, maxphys, desubtype, jflag)

        char *pstrout;
        DOLR *pphys;
        int maxout, maxphys, desubtype, jflag;

        {
        int erc, derc, i, slgth, rem, pos, cnt, pflag;
        int digit2, digit1;
        long int value;
        char str[30], digit, ch, sign;
```

```
/*
** Table of valid DECODE subtypes: [digit2|digit1]
**
** where:
**
**      digit2:
**
**      1 = negative handled by outermost "(..)" parentheses.
**      2 = negative handled by leading "-" sign.
**      3 = negative handled by trailing "-" sign.
**      4 = CREDIT handled by trailing "CR"; if neg (..CR).
**      5 = DEBIT handled by trailing "DR"; if neg (..DR).
**      6 = REVERSAL handled by trailing "RV"; if neg (..RV).
**
**      digit1: "N" denotes leading [-] sign position, if any.
**
**      0 = [ddd][.]dd
**      1 = [ddd,][.]dd
**      2 = [***][N][ddd,][.]dd
**      3 = [N][$][ddd,][.]dd
**      4 = [***][N][$][ddd,][.]dd
**
*/

/*
** Validate the function arguments:
*/

erc = ERC_BASE + ENDOLR_E + 5;

if (( maxout < 1 ) || ( maxout > MAX_DOLR)) return (erc);
if (maxphys != PHY_DOLR) return(erc);
if (( jflag < NO_JUST) || ( jflag > R_JUST )) return (erc);

/*
** validate "desubtype" and set "default" values
*/

utcharcb(1,pstrout,1);
utcharcb(1,str,1);

derc = dvdolrde(&desubtype,PHY_INT);
if (derc != ERC_OK) return(derc);

/*
** desubtype processing
*/

value = *pphys;

digit2 = desubtype / 10;
digit1 = desubtype % 10;

sign = C_BLANK;
if (value < (DOLR)0)
{
sign = C_MINUS;
value = -value;
}

if (value == (DOLR)0)
{
strcpy(str,"0.00");
sign = C_BLANK;
}
```

```
/*
** put dollar with/without commas
*/

pos = 0;
while ( value > (DOLR)0)
{
pos++;
rem = value % (DOLR)10;
digit = rem + C_ZERO;

if (digit1 > 0)
{
if ( (pos == 6) || (pos == 9) ) inschr(str,999,C_COMMA,1);
}

inschr(str,999,digit,1);
if (pos == 2) inschr(str,999,C_PERIOD,1);


value = value / (long)10;
}

slgth = strlen(str);
cnt = 4 - slgth;
if (cnt > 0)
{
switch (cnt)
{
        case 3: inschr(str,999,C_ZERO,1);
        case 2: inschr(str,999,C_PERIOD,1);
        case 1: inschr(str,999,C_ZERO,1);
                break;
}
}

/*
** put dollar sign, if any
*/

if ( (digit1 == 3) || (digit1 == 4) ) inschr(str,999,C_DSIGN,1);

/*
** put "-" sign if any
*/

if ( sign == C_MINUS)
{
if (digit2 == 2) inschr(str,999,C_MINUS,1);
if (digit2 == 3) inschr(str,999,C_MINUS,0);
}

/*
** put trailing "CR", "DR" or "RV", if any.
*/

if (digit2 == 4) strcat(str,"CR");
if (digit2 == 5) strcat(str,"DR");
if (digit2 == 6) strcat(str,"RV");

/*
** put (....), if any.
*/

pflag = FALSE;
```

```
if (sign == C_MINUS)
{
if ( (digit2 == 1) || (digit2 == 4) || (digit2 == 5) ||
     (digit2 == 6) )
{
pflag = TRUE;

inschr(str,999,C_LPAR,1);
inschr(str,999,C_RPAR,0);
}
}

/*
** add leading "asterisks" if any
*/

if ( (digit1 == 2) || (digit1 == 4) )
{
slgth = strlen(str);
if (slgth < maxout)
{
cnt = maxout - slgth;
for (i=0; i < cnt; i++)
{
if (pflag == TRUE) inschr(str,999,C_AST,2);
else inschr(str,999,C_AST,1);
}
}
}

/*
** check if pstrout big enough?
*/

utcharcb(3,str,maxout+1);
slgth = strlen(str);
if (slgth > maxout) return(erc);
else strcpy(pstrout,str);

/*
** Justify output string
*/

utcharjs(jflag, pstrout);

return (ERC_OK);

}
```

- Based upon digit2 and digit1, all decisions are made concerning the left to right processing of each dolr field.
- Note the use of the inschr.c function argument loc when constructing str. Use of 0 implies a character insert at the *last* str position; use of 1 implies a character insert at the *first* str position.
- Note that asterisks are padded to str size maxout, if chosen as an output format.

- String justification occurs within the total string field width maxout because of the function call to

```
utcharcb (3,str,maxout + 1)
```

- An erc is generated if the string length of str is greater than the maxout string length of pstrout.

B.3.0 Advanced Decode Field Processing

B.3.1 Putdolr.c and Fputdolr.c Error Codes

See Chapter 5, B.3.1.

B.3.2 Putdolr.c and Fputdolr.c Source Code and Commentary

The source code and commentary for putdolr.c and fputdolr.c parallels putchar.c and fputchar.c (Chapter 5, B.3.0). To create either of these functions, copy its parallel function and edit it as follows:

- Change all occurrences of char to dolr and CHAR to DOLR except for the statement

```
char *pstrout, *mask;
```

The complete source code is available on disk.

B.3.4 Associated Mask Utilization Techniques

- In an analogous manner, putstr.c/fputstr.c and putdolr.c/ fputdolr.c can be utilized to output a decoded string to a mask field with or without delimiters:

  Dollar Field: "$?????"

  Again the desubtype format control effects might seem to overlap with the putstr.c/fputstr.c functions. It is important to remember that dedolr.c can be utilized independently of the putstr.c/fputstr.c and putdolr.c/ fputdolr.c functions so that some functional redundancy is required to expand the independent use of the dexxxx.c interface definitions developed in this book.

- Use of the getmstr.c function allows use of the video display as a scratch pad (see Chapter 4) and functionally extends the standalone utility of each dexxxx.c. Since the power of masks is only pertinent to video display, getmstr.c retrieves the putxxxx.c string from the video display with mask formatting to enhance the variety of decoded formats that may be created when using dexxxx.c functions in a standalone manner.

C.0.0 Data Validation Function Development (dvdolryy.c)

C.1.0 Dvdolryy.c Standard Error Codes

Based upon the ERC_BASE (1000) and ENDOLR_E (31) values defined in the ldt.h header file, all dvdolryy.c functions report the following ercs:

1034	Data Validation Error
1035	Bad Data Validation Function Argument

C.2.0 Dvdolrde.c Function Specification

C.2.1 Dvdolrde.c Design Objectives

This function simply validates that an acceptable desubtype argument value has been specified for the dolr LDT.

C.2.2 Dvdolrde.c Source Code and Commentary

```
/* file    : dvdolrde.c
** function: int dvdolrde ( pphys, maxphys )
** desc    : data validation for dollar: valid decode subtypes
** test pgm: tdedolr.c
*/

#include "ldt.h"

        int dvdolrde ( pphys, maxphys )

        INT *pphys;
        int maxphys;
        {

        int erc, val;
        int digit1, digit2;

        erc = ERC_BASE + ENINT_E + 3;

        if (maxphys != PHY_INT) return(erc+1);

        val = (*pphys).i2;

        digit2 = val / 10;

        if ( (digit2 < 1) || (digit2 > 6) ) return(erc);

        digit1 = val % 10;

        if ( (digit1 < 0) || (digit1 > 4) ) return(erc);

        return(ERC_OK);

        }
```

- Note the use of INT *pphys. The uppercase INT is a typedef from ldt.h which is:

  typedef union {int i2; long int i4;} INT;

  The use of the INT typedef allows either int or long int arguments to be passed to dvdolrde.c. By design only int types are acceptable to dvdolrde.c.

- Note how desubtype is retrieved:

  val = (*pphys).i2;

- Note how each digit component (d2d1) of val is validated.

C.3.0 Dvdolren.c Function Specification

C.3.1 Dvdolren.c Design Objectives

This function simply validates that an acceptable ensubtype argument value has been specified for the dolr LDT.

C.3.2 Dvdolren.c Source Code and Commentary

```
/* file    : dvdolren.c
** function: int dvdolren ( pphys, maxphys )
** desc    : data validation for dollar; valid encode subtype
** test pgm: tdedolr.c
*/

#include "ldt.h"

        int dvdolren ( pphys, maxphys )

        INT *pphys;
        int maxphys;
        {
        int erc, val;

        erc = ERC_BASE + ENINT_E + 3;

        if (maxphys != PHY_INT) return(erc+1);

        val = (*pphys).i2;

        if ( (val < 0) || (val > 4) ) return (erc);

        else return(ERC_OK);

        }
```

- Note the use of INT *pphys (see C.2.2 commentary).

D.0.0 Utility Function Development (utdolryy.c)

D.1.0 Utdolryy.c Standard Error Codes

Based upon the ERC_BASE (1000) and ENDOLR_E (31) values defined in ldt.h, all utdolryy.c functions report the same erc as follows:

1037	Utility Function Error

D.2.0 Utdolrad.c Specifications

D.2.1 Utdolrad.c Design Objectives

This function adds two dolr variables. Dol1 plus addol2 equals eqdol3. If an overflow is detected (outside allowable +/−2147483647) a utility function erc value is returned by function utdolrad.c.

D.2.2 Utdolrad.c Source Code and Commentary

```
/* file    : utdolrad.c
** function: int utdolrad (doll, addol2, &eqdol3)
** desc    : to "doll" add "addol2" giving "eqdol3"
**         : if overflow: set "erc" and "eqdol3" = 0;
** test pgm: tudolrma.c
*/

#include "ldt.h"

        int utdolrad ( doll, addol2, eqdol3 )
        DOLR doll, addol2, *eqdol3;
        {

        int sl, s2, s3, erc;

        sl = TRUE;
        if ( doll < (DOLR)0 ) sl = FALSE;

        s2 = TRUE;
        if ( addol2 < (DOLR)0 ) s2 = FALSE;

        *eqdol3 = doll + addol2;
        erc = ERC_OK;

        if ( sl == s2 )
        {
        s3 = TRUE;
        if ( *eqdol3 < (DOLR)0 ) s3 = FALSE;
        if ( s3 != sl )
        {
        erc = ERC_BASE + ENDOLR_E + 6;
        *eqdol3 = (DOLR)0;
        }
        }

        return(erc);

        }
```

- Note the declaration of dol1, addol2, and *eqdol3 as type DOLR, a typedef for long int. Note that eqdol3 is a returned value.
- Overflow is sensed by an eqdol3 sign change. Integer overflow causes a change of sign.

- If an error is detected, eqdol3 is set to zero.
- Note the use of the DOLR cast. Any simple typedef (i.e. not a structure or union) can be used as a cast.

D.3.0 Utdolrdv.c Specifications

D.3.1 Utdolrdv.c Design Objectives

This function divides a dolr variable by a factor. Dol1 divided by dvfact equals eqdol3. Dvfact is any allowable value of type double. If an overflow is detected (outside allowable +/−2147483647) a utility function erc value is returned by function utdolrdv.c.

D.3.2 Utdolrdv.c Source Code and Commentary

```
/* file    : utdolrdv.c
** function: int utdolrdv (doll, dvfact, &eqdol3)
** desc    : divide "doll" by "dvfact" giving "eqdol3"
**         : rounding to cents automatic.
**         : if overflow: set "erc" and "eqdol3" = 0;
** test pgm: tudolrma.c
*/

#include "ldt.h"

        int utdolrdv ( doll, dvfact, eqdol3 )
        DOLR doll, *eqdol3;
        double dvfact;
        {

        static double maxdolr = 2147483647.0;
        double dollar, round;
        int sign, erc;

        round = 0.5;

        dollar = (double)doll / dvfact;

        sign = TRUE;
        if ( dollar < (double)0.0 )
        {
        sign = FALSE;
        dollar = -dollar;
        }

        dollar = dollar + round;

        *eqdol3 = (DOLR)dollar;

        if ( sign == FALSE ) *eqdol3 = -*eqdol3;

        erc = ERC_OK;
```

```
if ( dollar > maxdolr )
{
erc = ERC_BASE + ENDOLR_E + 6;
*eqdol3 = (DOLR)0;
}

return(erc);

}
```

- Note the declaration of dol1 and *eqdol3 as type DOLR, a typedef for long int. Eqdol3 is a returned value. Dvfact is of type double.
- Overflow is detected by comparing the double result of the divide operation against double value maxdolr. Rounding of the result is handled by 0.5 and adjustment of the absolute value of the result to properly reflect the sign of eqdol3.
- If an error is detected, eqdol3 is set to zero.

D.4.0 ***Utdolrml.c Specifications***

D.4.1 ***Utdolrml.c Design Objectives***

This function multiplies a dolr variable by a factor. Dol1 multiplied by mlfact equals eqdol3. Mlfact is any allowable value of type double. If an overflow is detected (outside allowable +/−2147483647) a utility function erc value is returned by function utdolrml.c.

D.4.2 ***Utdolrml.c Source Code and Commentary***

```
/* file    : utdolrml.c
** function: int utdolrml (doll, mlfact, &eqdol3)
** desc    : multiply "doll" by "mlfact" giving "eqdol3"
**         : rounding to cents automatic.
**         : if overflow: set "erc" and "eqdol3" = 0;
** test pgm: tudolrma.c

*/

#include "ldt.h"

        int utdolrml ( doll, mlfact, eqdol3 )
        DOLR doll, *eqdol3;
        double mlfact;
```

```
{

static double maxdolr = 2147483647.0;
double dollar, round;
int sign, erc;

round = 0.5;

dollar = (double)dol1 * mlfact;

sign = TRUE;
if ( dollar < (double)0.0 )
{
sign = FALSE;
dollar = -dollar;
}

dollar = dollar + round;

*eqdol3 = (DOLR)dollar;

if ( sign == FALSE ) *eqdol3 = -*eqdol3;

erc = ERC_OK;

if ( dollar > maxdolr )
{
erc = ERC_BASE + ENDOLR_E + 6;
*eqdol3 = (DOLR)0;
}

return(erc);

}
```

- Note the declaration of dol1 and *eqdol3 as type DOLR, a typedef for long int. Eqdol3 is a returned value. Mlfact is of type double.
- Overflow is detected by comparing the double result of the multiply operation against double value maxdolr. Rounding of the result is handled by 0.5 and adjustment of the absolute value of the result to properly reflect the sign of eqdol3.
- If an error is detected, eqdol3 is set to zero.

D.5.0 ***Utdolrsb.c Specifications***

D.5.1 ***Utdolrsb.c Design Objectives***

This function subtracts two dolr variables. Dol1 minus sbdol2 equals eqdol3. If an overflow is detected (outside allowable +/−2147483647) a utility function erc value is returned by function utdolrsb.c.

D.5.2 *Utdolrsb.c Source Code and Commentary*

```
/* file    : utdolrsb.c
** function: int utdolrsb (dol1, sbdol2, &eqdol3)
** desc    : to "dol1" subtract "sbdol2" giving "eqdol3"
**         : if overflow: set "erc" and "eqdol3" = 0;
** test pgm: tudolrma.c
*/

#include "ldt.h"

        int utdolrsb ( dol1, sbdol2, eqdol3 )
        DOLR dol1, sbdol2, *eqdol3;
        {

        int s1, s2, s3, erc;

        s1 = TRUE;
        if ( dol1 < (DOLR)0 ) s1 = FALSE;

        s2 = TRUE;
        if ( sbdol2 < (DOLR)0 ) s2 = FALSE;

        *eqdol3 = dol1 - sbdol2;
        erc = ERC_OK;

        if ( s1 != s2 )
        {
        s3 = TRUE;
        if ( *eqdol3 < (DOLR)0 ) s3 = FALSE;
        if ( s3 != s1 )
        {
        erc = ERC_BASE + ENDOLR_E + 6;
        *eqdol3 = (DOLR)0;
        }
        }

        return(erc);

        }
```

- Note the declaration of dol1, sbdol2, and eqdol3 as type DOLR, a typedef for long int.
- Overflow is sensed by detecting a sign change by eqdol3. Integer overflow causes a change of sign.
- If an error is detected, eqdol3 is set to zero.

E.0.0 *LDT Dolr Application Tips and Reminders*

E.1.0 *Helpful Notes*

Using the standard interface function definitions for the dolr (dollar) logical data type is somewhat less complicated than for

LDT char. This is because the pphys argument is always passed as an "address of" (&pphys) because pphys is of type dolr (typedef synonymous with long int).

Let's highlight some points to keep in mind when using the functions included in this chapter.

1. **Endolr.c and evdolr.c**: The maxin function argument should be the sizeof(pstrin) – 1. Maxin is the declared pstrin (size – 1) and does not include the NULL delimiting character. In all instances, maxphys should be PHY_DOLR.
2. **Getdolr.c and fgetdolr.c:** The maxstr function argument should be the sizeof(string) – 1. Cltab only controls the very first character read operation performed. Nuexit is a returned value and therefore must be passed as &nuexit.
3. **Dedolr.c, putdolr.c, and fputdolr.c**: The maxout function argument should be the sizeof(pstrin) – 1. Maxout is the declared pstrout (size – 1) and does not include the NULL delimiting character. "Maxout" must be large enough to receive the decoded pphys or an erc will result. In all instances, maxphys should be PHY_DOLR.
4. **Dvdolryy.c**: When these functions are used as function arguments they must be explicitly declared in the calling program.
5. **General**: Initialize all strings before using them.

E.2.0 Special Uses

We will not present any alternative uses of LDT dolr.

E.3.0 Utdolrcw.c Specifications

E.3.1 Utdolrcw.c Design Objectives

This check-writer function works with LDT dolr variables. It converts the numeric value of a dolr field into a descriptive text string in standard check-writing format.

E.3.2 Utdolrcw.c Source Code and Commentary

```
/* file    : utdolrcw.c
** function: char *utdolrcw (ctrl, dolrcent);
** desc    : return a pointer to string "spelldolr" which spells
**         : out the "dolrcent" amount;
**         : return "**void**" if "dolramt" <= $1.00
**         : or >= $1,000,000.00;
**         : "ctrl" = 0: cents as "dollars and xx cents"
**         : "crtl" = 1: cents as "and xx/100 dollars"
** test pgm: tudolrcw.c
*/
#include "ldt.h"

        char *utdolrcw ( ctrl, dolrcent )
        DOLR dolrcent;
        int ctrl;
        {
        static char *spelldolr[85];
        DOLR dolramt;
        int i, cents, digit;
        char chcent, scents[3];

        cents = dolrcent % (DOLR)100;
        dolramt = dolrcent / (DOLR)100;
        utcharcb(1, spelldolr, 1);

        if ( (dolramt < (DOLR)1) || ( dolramt >= (DOLR)1000000) )
        {
        for (i=0; i < 5; i++)
        {
        strcat(spelldolr, "**VOID**");
        }
        return(spelldolr);
        }

        utdolrda( dolramt, spelldolr );

        utcharcb(1, scents, 1);

        digit = cents / 10;
        chcent = digit + '0';
        inschr(scents, 3, chcent, 1);

        digit = cents % 10;
        chcent = digit + '0';
        inschr(scents, 3, chcent, 0);
        /*
        ** append "crtl" cent amount
        */

        if (ctrl == 0)


        {
        strcat(spelldolr, " dollars and ");
        strcat(spelldolr, scents);
        strcat(spelldolr, " cents");
        }
        else
        {
        strcat(spelldolr, " and ");
        strcat(spelldolr, scents);
        strcat(spelldolr, "/100 dollars");
        }
        return(spelldolr);

        }
```

- When using this function it must be explicitly declared as char *utdolrcw();.
- Note that utdolrcw.c returns a character pointer to the static char *spelldolr[85] array.
- If a dollar amount less than $1.00 or greater than $999,999.99 is specified, the spelldolr array is set equal to **VOID****VOID****VOID** in an attempt to prevent very small or large checks from being processed.
- Nearly all of the work of this function is performed by a call to function utdolrda.c (described in E.4.0).
- Function utdolrcw.c only appends the proper cents amount based upon the function argument ctrl value specified.
- Note how the function return value is specified as return(spelldolr), since spelldolr has been specified as char *spelldolr[85].

E.4.0 ***Utdolrda.c Specifications***

E.4.1 ***Utdolrda.c Design Objectives***

This function is a perfect example of a recursive function in the C programming language. Utdolrda.c expands the dollar amount portion of a dolr dolramt variable, and places the expanded text in spelldolr, which is declared by utdolrcw.c.

E.4.2 ***Utdolrda.c Source Code and Commentary***

(Adapted by permission from Osborne/McGraw-Hill, *Some Common PASCAL Programs* (Berkeley: Osborne/McGraw-Hill, 1982), pp. 201-204.)

```
/* file     : utdolrda.c
** function: int utdolrda (dolramt, spelldolr)
** desc     : return a string "spelldolr" which spells
**          : out the "dolramt"; return "**void**" if
**          : "dolramt" < $1.00 or >= $1,000,000.00;
** test pgm: tudolrcw.c
*/

#include "ldt.h"
```

```
int utdolrda ( dolramt, spelldolr )
DOLR dolramt;
char *spelldolr;
{

if ( (dolramt >= (DOLR)10000) || ( dolramt >= (DOLR)1000) &&
     ( (dolramt % (DOLR)1000) / (DOLR)100  ) == (DOLR)0)
{
utdolrda( dolramt/(DOLR)1000, spelldolr );
strcat(spelldolr, " thousand ");
utdolrda( dolramt % (DOLR)1000, spelldolr);
}

else

if ( dolramt >= (DOLR)100)
{
utdolrda( dolramt / (DOLR)100, spelldolr );
strcat(spelldolr, " hundred ");
utdolrda( dolramt % (DOLR)100, spelldolr );
}

else

if ( dolramt >= (DOLR)20 )
{
switch ( (int)dolramt / 10 )
{
        case 2: strcat(spelldolr, "twenty");
                break;
        case 3: strcat(spelldolr, "thirty");
                break;
        case 4: strcat(spelldolr, "forty");
                break;
        case 5: strcat(spelldolr, "fifty");
                break;
        case 6: strcat(spelldolr, "sixty");
                break;
        case 7: strcat(spelldolr, "seventy");
                break;
        case 8: strcat(spelldolr, "eighty");
                break;
        case 9: strcat(spelldolr, "ninety");


                break;

        default: break;
}
if ( (dolramt % (DOLR)10) != (DOLR)0)
{
inschr( spelldolr, 85, '-', 0);
utdolrda( dolramt % (DOLR)10, spelldolr);
}
}

else

if ( (dolramt == (DOLR)14) || (dolramt == (DOLR)16)
        || (dolramt == (DOLR)17) || (dolramt == (DOLR)18)
        || (dolramt == (DOLR)19) )
{
utdolrda( dolramt % (DOLR)10, spelldolr );
strcat(spelldolr, "teen");
}
```

```
else

if (dolramt >= (DOLR)10)
{
switch ( (int)dolramt)
{
        case 10: strcat(spelldolr, "ten");
                 break;
        case 11: strcat(spelldolr, "eleven");
                 break;
        case 12: strcat(spelldolr, "twelve");
                 break;
        case 13: strcat(spelldolr, "thirteen");
                 break;
        case 15: strcat(spelldolr, "fifteen");
                 break;

        default: break;
}
}

else

if ( dolramt > (DOLR)0)
{
switch ( (int)dolramt )
{
        case 1: strcat(spelldolr, "one");
                break;
        case 2: strcat(spelldolr, "two");
                break;
        case 3: strcat(spelldolr, "three");
                break;
        case 4: strcat(spelldolr, "four");
                break;
        case 5: strcat(spelldolr, "five");
                break;
        case 6: strcat(spelldolr, "six");
                break;
        case 7: strcat(spelldolr, "seven");
                break;
        case 8: strcat(spelldolr, "eight");
                break;
        case 9: strcat(spelldolr, "nine");
                break;

        default: break;
}
}

return(ERC_OK);

}


/*
** Reference:
** "Some Common PASCAL Programs". Osborne/Mc-Graw-Hill. p. 201
*/
```

- Note the use of the *cast* DOLR. When in doubt about the order of precedence, specify a cast to force a variable to be the desired type. Be very careful in C when intermixing ints and long ints!

- The initial If statement is there to accomodate the fact that this function is recursively called.

- Note that case statement values within switch statements are of type int.

- Recursive functions can be a problem to debug because, if in error, they often generate a *stack overflow* message that terminates processing. Be extremely careful about the scope of declared variables.

F.0.0 ***Testing and Quality Assurance (qadolr.c)***

F.1.0 ***Qadolr.c Specification***

F.1.1 ***Qadolr.c Design Objectives***

The qadolr.c test function utilizes endolr.c, evdolr.c, getdolr.c, fgetdolr.c, dedolr.c, putdolr.c, and fputdolr.c as well as dvdolryy.c, utdolryy.c and supporting functions listed for the linker automatic response file, qadolr.lnk, in Appendix L.

Qadolr.c provides runtime control over the resetting of stdlog, the making of stdlog entries, and screen printing upon error detection, as well as the interactive testing of all endolr.c and dedolr.c subtypes.

Each qaxxxx.c function is not only an excellent example of LDT testing, but also a technique for the use of the various standard interfaces portrayed in this book. A close examination of qadolr.c will reveal a powerful program of only 100 statements.

F.1.2 ***Qadolr.c Error Codes***

Because qaxxxx.c functions have no reserved ercs of their own, they simply report the ercs detected during processing by the underlying standard interface functions. All ercs detected for

LDT dolr are governed by the following ldt.h values:

ERC_BASE	1000
GET_E	1
PUT_E	5
ENDOLR_E	31

F.2.0 Qadolr.c Source Code and Commentary

```
/*
** file    : qadolr.c
** desc    : quality assurance test program for LDT DOLR
** link    : @qadolr.lnk,qadolr,nul,lcs
*/

#include "ldt.h"

main ()
{
        int dvcharyn(), dvdolren(), dvdolrde(), dvdummy();
        int erc;

        static char mtype[] = ">??<";
        static char mstr[]  = ">???????????????<";
        static char myn[]   = ">?<";

        static char initen[] = "0";
        static char initde[] = "24";
        static char inity[] = "Y";
        static char initn[] = "N";

        char str[30], destr[30], ynchar;
        int entype, detype, nuexit, lpe;
        DOLR dval;
        int smstr;

        smstr = nondel(mstr);

        blanksc(1,1,MAX_ROW,MAX_COL);
        setcrc(1,1);
        putstr("DOLR Quality Assurance Program",LR,"",DISP_F);

        /*
        ** Prompt for User Runtime Controls
        */

        uprompt(&lpe);

        if ( (lpe == 10) || (lpe == 11) )
                logwrite(5,"QADOLR",0,"Begin Testing");

        for (;;)
        {

        blanksc(2,1,MAX_ROW,MAX_COL);
        setcrc(1,1);

        movcrc(2,-MAX_COL);
        putstr("Enter ENCODE Subtype  : ",LR,"",DISP_F);
```

```
        erc = getint(str,sizeof(str)-1,NO,myn,LR,initen,MAND_F,YES,
                     &nuexit,&entype,PHY_INT,1,MAND_F,lpe,dvdolren);

        if (lderc(erc) == 9) break;

        movcrc(2,-MAX_COL);
        putstr("Enter DOLLAR String    : ",LR,"",DISP_F);

        erc = getdolr(str,sizeof(str)-1,NO,mstr,LR,"",MAND_F,NO,
                &nuexit,&dval,PHY_DOLR,entype,MAND_F,lpe,dvdummy);

        if (lderc(erc) == 9) continue;

        movcrc(2,-MAX_COL);
        putstr("ENCODEed Internal DOLR: ",LR,"",DISP_F);
        putint(destr,MAX_INT4,&dval,PHY_INT4,0,L_JUST,
               LR,mstr,MAND_F,lpe);

        movcrc(2,-MAX_COL);
        putstr("Enter DECODE Subtype   : ",LR,"",DISP_F);

        erc = getint(str,sizeof(str)-1,NO,mtype,LR,initde,MAND_F,NO,
                &nuexit,&detype,PHY_INT,1,MAND_F,lpe,dvdolrde);

        if (lderc(erc) == 9) continue;

        movcrc(2,-MAX_COL);
        putstr("DECODEed DOLLAR        : ",LR,"",DISP_F);
        putdolr(destr,smstr,&dval,PHY_DOLR,detype,R_JUST,
                LR,mstr,MAND_F,lpe);

        setcrc(24,1);
        putstr("Continue? [Yes/No] or [ESCape]: ",LR,"",DISP_F);

        erc = getchar(str,sizeof(str)-1,NO,myn,LR,inity,MAND_F,NO,
                &nuexit,&ynchar,1,11,MAND_F,lpe,dvcharyn);

        if (lderc(erc) == 9) break;
        if (ynchar == 'N') break;

        }

        if ( (lpe == 10) || (lpe == 11) )
                logwrite(6,"QADOLR",0,"End Testing");

        blanksc(1,1,MAX_ROW,MAX_COL);
        exit(0);
}
```

- All dvxxxxyy.c functions to be used as function arguments *must* be declared explicitly in the calling program.

- All masks are declared with outermost field delimiters so that the field limit is always known regardless of the type of field and hence video attribute chosen for display.

- All initial values are declared, making any necessary revision easy.

- In this case destr[30] exceeds the nondelimiter size of mask mstr[ ]. The size of a displayed string must not exceed the corresponding number of mask nondelimiter positions if a mask is used for display purposes.
- Variable lpe is calculated by uprompt.c from runtime user responses and effectively becomes the standard function argument logprerr.
- Anywhere in the source code where

  ```
  if (lderc(erc) = = 9)
  ```

  appears, an equivalent statement

  ```
  if ( nuexit = = -1 )
  ```

  can be specified instead.
- Note that because there were many possible choices for ensubtype and desubtype, qadolr.c only allows one ensubtype and desubtype pair to be tested at a time.
- Note that hitting the Escape key recycles the program unless it is performed at

  "Enter ENCODE Subtype:"

  or

  "Continue? [Yes/No] or [ESCape]:"

  where it exits the program. Hitting Ctrl-Break has no effect on qaxxxx.c functions because Ctrl-Break has been turned off in function _main. (See Appendix F.)
- An additional test program, tdedolr.c, is available on disk. It is intended to drive the complete range of valid desubtypes for both a negative and positive dolr amount (+/− $123,456.78). This value is repeatedly encoded and decoded and printed to test the validity of the dvdolrde.c, endolr.c, and dedolr.c functions.
- Figure 7.1 shows sample output of the qadolr.c program.

```
DOLR Quality Assurance Program

Enter ENCODE Subtype  : >0<

Enter DOLLAR String   : >$123,456.78     <

ENCODEed Internal DOLR: >12345678        <

Enter DECODE Subtype  : >24<

DECODEed DOLLAR       : >****$123,456.78<




Continue? [Yes/No] or [ESCape]: >Y<
```

Figure 7.1– Qadolr.c sample output

Integers

8

This chapter covers the I/O of integer fields that are encoded to and decoded from a storage format as specified by the following statement in header file ldt.h:

```
typedef union {int i2; long int i4;} INT;
```

Integer fields can therefore be represented as either an int (two bytes) or a long int (four bytes). The maxphys function argument value (either 2 or 4) controls the choice of storage format. Integer fields are commonly used as ID numbers, as arithmetic fields in disk record structures, and as key fields (indices) when interfacing with file management and sorting software packages.

Each interface definition described in Part 1 of this book is implemented for the integer logical data type (xxxx = int). The enint.c function provided accepts all deint.c formats and, with the specification of the ensubtype function argument, controls which combination of negative, zero, and positive values are acceptable. The deint.c function generates integer character representations under format control with the specification of a desired desubtype argument value. Data validation functions are provided for the verification of long int variables appended with either modulus 10 or 11 check digits.

The included utility function (utintmd.c) calculates modulus 10 and 11 check digit values for appendage to long int type ID number fields.

Finally, a testing and quality assurance program (qaint.c) is provided, which allows you to interactively examine and test most of the functions developed in this chapter.

The following chapter index lists the source code you will find in this chapter.

Standard Interface Source Code

A.2.0	Enint.c:	Encode LDT integer
A.3.0	Evint.c:	Encode and validate LDT integer
A.4.0	Getint.c/ Fgetint.c:	Combined getstr.c and evint.c
B.2.0	Deint.c:	Decode LDT integer
B.3.0	Putint.c/ Fputint.c:	Combined deint.c and putstr.c

Data Validation Functions (dvintyy.c)

C.2.0	Dvintde.c:	Checks for allowable desubtypes
C.3.0	Dvinten.c:	Checks for allowable ensubtypes
C.4.0	Dvint10.c:	Validates modulus 10 check digit
C.5.0	Dvint11.c:	Validates modulus 11 check digit

Utility Functions (utintyy.c)

E.3.0	Utintmd.c:	Computes modulus 10 and 11 check digits

Quality Assurance Programs

F.2.0	Qaint.c:	Standard quality assurance test program

A.0.0 Encode Function Development (enint.c)

A.1.0 Enint.c Specifications

A.1.1 Design Objectives

The integer LDT supports the C native data types int and long int while overcoming the C I/O shortcomings for integer data types.

Because of the following union typedef specification for LDT integer:

```
union {int i2; long int i4;} INT;
```

either int i2 or long int i4 can be addressed as follows:

```
     int: val = (*pphys).i2;
long int: val = (*pphys).i4;
```

The valid ranges of integers are enforced as follows:

$$-32767 <= \text{int} <= +32767$$
$$-2147483647 <= \text{long int} <= +2147483647$$

Our methodology improves on standard C I/O, by generating an erc if an overflow is detected.

A.1.2 Field Size (maxin)

The maximum field size for the int i2 portion of the union specification is MAX_INT = 6. This allows room for the maximum value of 32767 and a plus or minus sign. Similarly, for the long int i4 portion, a maximum field size of MAX_INT4 = 11 allows room for the maximum value of 2147483647 and a plus or minus sign.

A.1.3 Physical Format (maxphys)

The C programming language dictates the choice of native C data types for LDT int. Short int and int are equivalent to 16-bit integers, while long and long int are equivalent to 32-bit integers.

Because of the union typedef construction, maxphys can only be either PHY_INT = 2 for int i2 or PHY_INT4 = 4 for long int i4. The use of any other value for maxphys generates an erc.

A.1.4 Character Set Restrictions

By design of the getstr.c/fgetstr.c function, the enint.c function only "sees" ASCII 0x20 through 0x7E.

For int fields of input this complete range of input will be accepted; however, enint.c processing imposes additional edit checks. See sections A.1.6 and A.1.7 below.

A.1.5 Subtype Definition (ensubtype)

The ensubtype parameter provides for immediate data entry editing for negative, zero, and positive integer values according to the following list:

0	Any negative, zero, or positive integer value
1	Only zero or positive integer values
2	Only positive integer values
3	Only negative or zero integer values
4	Only negative integer values

Although you can edit for negative, zero, and positive values with the data validation functions, such editing is so common that it is more efficient for the ensubtype function argument to take care of field sign detection and leave reasonability checks of integer fields up to custom data validation functions.

A.1.6 Other Format Control

Int fields can only consist of numeric digits (n), and no embedded spaces, commas, decimals, or other ASCII characters.

Leading asterisks or blanks and trailing blanks are accepted, but simply stripped and not interpreted in any manner.

The location of a minus sign, if present, is anticipated as follows:

```
[-]nnnnn
[-][0..0]nnn
[*..*][-]nnn
```

A plus sign is permitted in place of a minus sign.

A.1.7 Editing

As described in section A.1.5, above, integer field sign detection has been attributed to the ensubtype parameter.

We have provided overflow checking to ensure that all int fields remain within the allowable ranges noted above. If the ranges are exceeded, the following erc is generated:

```
erc = ERC_BASE + ENINT_E
```

A.1.8 Default Values

Upon initial entry to the enint.c function, the appropriate int value, either (*pphys).i2 or (*pphys).i4 as dictated by the maxphys argument value, is initialized to zero.

A.1.9 Error Codes

Based upon the ERC_BASE (1000) and ENINT_E (41) values defined in ldt.h, the following ercs are possible:

1041	Encode Data Entry Error by User
1042	Bad Encode Function Argument
1043	Encode Mandatory Field Not Satisfied

A.2.0 Enint.c Source Code and Commentary

```
/* file    : enint.c
** function: int enint ( pstrin, maxin, pphys, maxphys,
**         :              ensubtype, mflag )
** desc    : encode a logical data type int
**         : if "maxphys" = 2 == int; = 4 == Long int;
** test pgm: qaint.c
*/

#include "ctype.h"
#include "ldt.h"

        int enint (pstrin, maxin, pphys, maxphys, ensubtype, mflag)

        char *pstrin;
        INT *pphys;
        int maxin, maxphys, ensubtype, mflag;
        {

        static double maxi2 = 32767.0;
        static double maxi4 = 2147483647.0;
        double dval, wgt;
        int erc, eerc, size, i, slgth, digit;
        char str[20], sign;

        /*
        ** Table of valid ENCODE subtypes:
        **    0 = any integer
        **    1 = 0/+ integer only
        **    2 = + integer only
        **    3 = 0/- integer only
        **    4 = - integer only
        */

        /*
        ** Note: whether "pphys" is INT (I2) or
        ** Long INT (I4) is controlled by "maxphys"
        **    2 = I2
        **    4 = I4
        **    otherwise, ENINT argument error
        */


        /*
        ** Validate the function arguments:
        */

        erc = ERC_BASE + ENINT_E + 1;

        /*
        ** validate "maxphys"
        */


        if (maxphys == 2) size = MAX_INT;
        else
        if (maxphys == 4) size = MAX_INT4;
        else
        return(erc);

        if (( maxin < 1 ) || ( maxin > size )) return (erc);
```

```
/*
** validate "ensubtype" and set "default" values
*/

eerc = dvinten(&ensubtype,PHY_INT);
if (eerc != ERC_OK) return(eerc);

if ( maxphys == 2) (*pphys).i2 = 0;
else (*pphys).i4 = (long)0;

/*
** validate "mflag" for TRUE/FALSE
*/

if (( mflag < NO ) || ( mflag > YES ))
        return (erc);

/*
** Validate mandatory field requirement
** OK to check before any other pre-processing
*/

slgth = strlen( pstrin );
if (( mflag ) && ( slgth < 1 ))
        return(erc + 1);

erc = erc - 1;

/*
** encode processing
*/

strcpy(str, pstrin);

/*
** strip leading blanks and "asterisk" if any
*/

sign = C_BLANK;
utcharsb(3,str,C_BLANK);
utcharsb(1,str,C_AST);
slgth = strlen(str);
if(slgth < 1) return(erc+2);

if ( (str[0] == C_PLUS) || (str[0] == C_MINUS))
{
sign = str[0];
delchr(str,1);
slgth = strlen(str);
if (slgth < 1) return(erc+2);
}

for ( i=0; i < slgth; i++ )
{
if ( isdigit(str[i]) == 0 ) return(erc);
}

switch ( ensubtype )
{
        case 0: break;
        case 1:
        case 2: if (sign == C_MINUS) return(erc);
                break;
        case 3: break;
        case 4: if (sign != C_MINUS) return(erc);
                break;

}
```

```
wgt = 1.0;
dval = 0.0;

for ( i= (slgth - 1); i >=0; i--)
{
digit = str[i] - C_ZERO;
dval = dval + wgt * (double)digit;
wgt = wgt * (double)10.0;
}

if ( (maxphys == 2) && (dval > maxi2) ) return(erc);
if ( (maxphys == 4) && (dval > maxi4) ) return(erc);

if ( sign == C_MINUS ) dval = -dval;

switch (ensubtype)
{
        case 0: break;
        case 1: if (dval < 0.0) return(erc);
                break;
        case 2: if (dval <= 0.0) return(erc);
                break;
        case 3: if (dval > 0.0) return(erc);
                break;
        case 4: if (dval >= 0.0) return(erc);
                break;
}

if (maxphys == 2) (*pphys).i2 = (int)dval;
else (*pphys).i4 = (long)dval;

return (ERC_OK);

}
```

- Note that pphys is declared to be of type INT. Uppercase INT is a typedef from the ldt.h header file. INT supports both int and long int by virtue of its union specification. Maxphys dictates whether int or long int is intended: if maxphys equals 2 then int is intended; if maxphys equals 4 then long int is intended. Any other maxphys value generates an erc.

- If pstrin contains all blank characters or asterisks, it will not satisfy the mandatory mflag field requirement.

- Note the use of utcharsb.c to strip leading and trailing blanks and leading asterisks.

- Note that variables of type double are used to accumulate the value of each int field. This is OK because we are accumulating only a whole number without fractions, and 15 significant digits can be accumulated without any loss of significance. LDT int only requires a maximum of ten significant digits. Each int is checked against either maxi2 or maxi4 as appropriate.

A.3.0 Encode and Validate Source Code and Commentary (evint.c)

The source code and commentary for evint.c parallels evchar.c (Chapter 5, A.3.0). To create function evint.c, copy evchar.c and change it in the following ways:

- Change all occurrences of char to int and CHAR to INT except for the statement

```
char *pstrin;
```

- Update the commented function description.

The complete source code is available on disk.

A.4.0 Advanced Encode Field Processing

A.4.1 Getint.c and Fgetint.c Error Codes

See Chapter 5, A.4.1.

A.4.2 Getint.c and Fgetint.c Source Code and Commentary

The source code and commentary for getint.c parallels that of getchar.c (Chapter 5, A.4.0). To create function getint.c, copy getchar.c and edit as follows:

- Change all occurrences of char to int and CHAR to INT except for the statement

```
char *string, *mask, *init;
```

The source code and commentary for function fgetint.c parallels fgetchar.c (Chapter 5, A.4.0). To create function fgetint.c, copy file fgetchar.c and edit as follows:

- Change all occurrences of char to int and CHAR to INT except for the following statements:

```
char *string, *mask, *init;
utcharcb(1,string,1);
```

The complete source code is available on disk.

A.4.3 Associated Mask Utilization Techniques

- Based upon the function argument gmaskflg, mask delimiter characters can be excluded (NO) from the acquired input string. Introducing character delimiters helps reduce eye fatigue when entering lengthy ID numbers and eliminates the need for them to be keyed by the user. For example:

  ID number with Modulus II check digits: "???-??-??-??"

Remember that enint.c can be utilized independently of the getstr.c/fgetstr.c and getint.c/fgetint.c functions and some functional redundancy is required to expand the independent use of the enxxxx.c interface definitions.

B.0.0 Decode Function Development (Deint.c)

B.1.0 Deint.c Specifications

B.1.1 Design Objectives

This function provides an integer processing function that can display integer fields stored in either int or long int format in a variety of commonly needed commercial display formats. Each output format in turn becomes a format acceptable to its corresponding enint.c function.

B.1.2 Subtype Definition (desubtype)

0	Normal format [–]nnnnn
1	Leading zeros [–][0..0]nnn
2	Leading asterisks [*..*][–]nnn

B.1.3 Default Values

No default is assumed for deint.c. The output character string pstrout is simply set to a NULL string before processing begins.

B.1.4 Error Codes

Based upon the ERC_BASE (1000) and ENINT_E (41) values defined in ldt.h, the following erc is possible:

1046	Bad Decode Function Argument

B.2.0 Deint.c Source Code and Commentary

```
/* file    : deint.c
** function: int deint ( pstrout, maxout, pphys, maxphys,
**         :                desubtype, jflag )
** desc    : decode a logical data type int
** test pgm: qaint.c
*/

#include "ctype.h"
#include "ldt.h"

        int deint (pstrout, maxout, pphys, maxphys, desubtype, jflag)

        char *pstrout;
        INT *pphys;
        int maxout, maxphys, desubtype, jflag;
        {

        int erc, derc, i, slgth, rem, dpos, pos, size;
        long int value;
        char str[15], digit, ch, sign;

        /*
        ** Table of valid DECODE subtypes:
        **     0 = normal [-]nnnn
        **     1 = leading zeroes [-]000nnnn
        **     2 = leading asterisk ***[-]nnn
        */

        /*
        ** Validate the function arguments:
        */

        erc = ERC_BASE + ENINT_E + 5;
```

```
/*
** validate "maxphys"
*/

if (maxphys == 2) size = MAX_INT;
else
if (maxphys == 4) size = MAX_INT4;
else
return(erc);

/*
** validate "maxout"
*/

if (( maxout < 1 ) || ( maxout > size )) return (erc);

/*
** validate "desubtype" and set "default" values
*/

utcharcb(1,pstrout,1);
utcharcb(1,str,1);

derc = dvintde(&desubtype,PHY_INT);
if (derc != ERC_OK) return(derc);

/*
** validate "jflag" for (NO_JUST, L_JUST, C_JUST, R_JUST)
*/

if (( jflag < NO_JUST) || ( jflag > R_JUST ))
        return (erc);

/*
** desubtype processing
*/

if (maxphys == 2) value = (*pphys).i2;
else value = (*pphys).i4;

sign = C_BLANK;
if (value < (long)0)
{
sign = C_MINUS;
value = -value;
}

while ( value > (long)0)
{
rem = value % (long)10;
digit = rem + C_ZERO;

inschr(str,999,digit,1);

value = value / (long)10;
}

if (strlen(str) == 0)
{
inschr(str,999,C_ZERO,1);
sign = C_BLANK;
}

if (sign == C_MINUS)
{
inschr(str,999,C_MINUS,1);
}
```

```
pos = 1;
switch (desubtype)
{
        case 0: ch = C_BLANK;
                break;
        case 1: ch = '0';
                if (sign == C_MINUS) pos = 2;
                break;
        case 2: ch = C_AST;
                break;
}

dpos = maxout - strlen(str);

for (i=0; i < dpos; i++)
{
inschr(str,999,ch,pos);
}

/*
** check if "pstrout" big enough
*/

utcharcb(3,str,maxout+1);
slgth = strlen(str);
if (slgth > maxout) return(erc);
else strcpy(pstrout,str);

/*
** Justify output string
*/

utcharjs(jflag, pstrout);

return (ERC_OK);

}
```

- Note the use of div and mod functions to convert value into a character equivalent representation where

  digit = rem + C_ZERO;

  Digit then becomes an ASCII character value between 0 (0x30) and 9 (0x39).

- Note how leading blanks, zeros, or asterisks are padded to the maximum str length (maxout) using a loop structure and the function inschr.c.
- String justification occurs within the total string field width (maxout) because of the following function call:

  utcharcb (3,str,maxout + 1)

- An erc is generated if the string length of pphys is greater than the maxout string length of pstrout.

B.3.0 Advanced Decode Field Processing

B.3.1 Putint.c and Fputint.c Error Codes

See Chapter 5, B.3.1.

B.3.2 Putint.c and Fputint.c Source Code and Commentary

The source and commentary for putint.c and fputint.c parallels putchar.c and fputchar.c (Chapter 5, B.3.0). To create either function, copy its corresponding file and edit as follows:

- Change all occurrences of char to int and CHAR to INT except for the statement

```
char *pstrout, *mask;
```

The complete source code is available on disk.

B.3.3 Associated Mask Utilization Techniques

- In an analogous manner, putint.c and fputint.c can be used like putstr.c and fputstr.c to output a decoded string to a mask field with or without delimiters. However, it is important to remember that deint.c can be utilized independently of the putstr.c/fputstr.c and putint.c/fputint.c functions so that some functional redundancy is required to expand the independent use of the dexxxx.c interface definitions.

- The getmstr.c function allows the video display to be used as a scratch pad (see Chapter 4) and functionally extends the stand-alone utility of each dexxxx.c. Since the power of masks is only useful with video display, getmstr.c retrieves the putxxxx.c string from the video display with mask formatting to enhance the variety of decoded formats that can be created when using dexxxx.c functions in a standalone manner.

C.0.0 Data Validation Function Development (dvintyy.c)

C.1.0 Dvintyy.c Standard Error Codes

Based upon the ERC_BASE (1000) and ENINT_E (41) values defined in ldt.h, all dvintyy.c functions report the same ercs:

1044	Data Validation Error
1045	Bad Data Validation Function Argument

C.2.0 Dvintde.c Function Specification

C.2.1 Dvintde.c Design Objectives

This function validates that an acceptable desubtype argument value has been specified for the int LDT.

C.2.2 Dvintde.c Source Code and Commentary

```
/* file    : dvintde.c
** function: int dvintde ( pphys, maxphys )
** desc    : data validation for int; valid decode subtypes
** test pgm: qaint.c
*/

#include "ldt.h"

        int dvintde ( pphys, maxphys )

        INT *pphys;
        int maxphys;
        {
        int erc, val;

        erc = ERC_BASE + ENINT_E + 3;

        if (maxphys != PHY_INT) return(erc+1);

        val = (*pphys).i2;

        if (( val < 0 ) || ( val > 2)) return (erc);

        else return(ERC_OK);

        }
```

- Note the use of INT *pphys. The uppercase INT is a typedef from ldt.h, which is

  typedef union {int i2; long int i4;} INT;

  The use of the INT typedef allows either int or long int arguments to be passed to dvintde.c. By design only int types are acceptable to dvintde.c.

- Note how desubtype is retrieved:

  val = (*pphys).i2;

C.3.0 Dvinten.c Function Specification

C.3.1 Dvinten.c Design Objectives

This function simply validates that an acceptable ensubtype argument value has been specified for the int LDT.

C.3.2 Dvinten.c Source Code and Commentary

```
/* file     : dvinten.c
** function: int dvinten ( pphys, maxphys )
** desc     : data validation for int; valid encode subtype
** test pgm: qaint.c
*/

#include "ldt.h"

        int dvinten ( pphys, maxphys )

        INT *pphys;
        int maxphys;
        {
        int erc, val;

        erc = ERC_BASE + ENINT_E + 3;

        if (maxphys != PHY_INT) return(erc+1);

        val = (*pphys).i2;

        if (( val < 0 ) || ( val > 4)) return (erc);

        else return(ERC_OK);

        }
```

- Note the use of INT *pphys. See C.2.2 commentary for the explanation.

C.4.0 Dvint10.c Function Specification

C.4.1 Dvint10.c Design Objectives

This function is designed to work in conjunction with utintmd.c which calculates a modulus 10 check digit (0 through 9) for a long int pphys. Dvint10.c validates that the modulus 10 check digit appended to the pphys integer is correct (ERC_OK) or incorrect (erc). Refer to Appendix J for a detailed discussion of the modulus 10 check digit. Only long int is used with check digits because the advantages of using check digits for numbers of less than five digits (int) are marginal.

C.4.2 Dvint10.c Source Code and Commentary

```
/* file    : dvint10.c
** function: int dvint10 ( pphys, maxphys )
** desc    : data validation for int; modulus 10 check digit
** test pgm: tuintmd.c
*/

#include "ldt.h"


        int dvint10 ( pphys, maxphys )
        INT *pphys;
        int maxphys;

        {
        int erc, dig, rem;
        long int idnum, wgt, sum;

        erc = ERC_BASE + ENINT_E + 3;

        if (maxphys != PHY_INT4) return(erc+1);

        idnum = (*pphys).i4;

        if (idnum == (long)0) return (erc);

        wgt = 2;
        sum = idnum % (long)10;

        idnum = idnum / (long)10;

        while ( idnum > (long)0)
        {
        dig = idnum % (long)10;

        sum = sum + (long)dig * wgt;

        if ( wgt == (long)1 ) wgt = 2;
        else wgt = 1;

        idnum = idnum / (long)10;
        }
```

```
if (sum == (long)0) return(erc);

rem = sum % (long)10;

if (rem == 0) return (ERC_OK);
else
return (erc);
}
```

- Note that pphys must be of type long int as controlled by the required maxphys value of PHY_INT4. This reinforces the fact that check digits would only be of marginal value for use with int, which has less than five digits.
- Note how pphys is retrieved:

  idnum = (*pphys).i4;

- It is assumed that the least significant (rightmost) digit of pphys contains the modulus 10 check digit (0 through 9). The validation procedure described in Appendix J is performed to either validate or reject pphys based upon the check digit.

C.5.0 Dvint11.c Function Specification

C.5.1 Dvint11.c Design Objectives

This function is designed to work in conjunction with utintmd.c which calculates the modulus 11 check digits (00 through 10) for a long int pphys. Dvint11.c validates that the modulus 11 check digits appended to the pphys integer are correct (ERC_OK) or incorrect (erc). Again, refer to Appendix J for detailed discussion of the modulus 11 check digit.

C.5.2 Dvint11.c Source Code and Commentary

```
/* file    : dvint11.c
** function: int dvint11 ( pphys, maxphys )
** desc    : data validation for int; modulus 11 check digit
** test pgm: tuintmd.c
*/

#include "ldt.h"
```

```
int dvintll ( pphys, maxphys )
INT *pphys;
int maxphys;
{

int erc, dig, rem;
long int idnum, wgt, sum;

erc = ERC_BASE + ENINT_E + 3;

if (maxphys != PHY_INT4) return(erc+1);

idnum = (*pphys).i4;

if (idnum == (long)0) return (erc);

wgt = 2;
sum = idnum % (long)100;

idnum = idnum / (long)100;

while ( idnum > (long)0)
{
dig = idnum % (long)10;

sum = sum + (long)dig * wgt;

wgt = wgt + (long)1;

idnum = idnum / (long)10;
}

if (sum == (long)0) return(erc);

rem = sum % (long)11;

if (rem == 0) return (ERC_OK);
else
return (erc);
}
```

- Note that pphys must be of type long int as controlled by the required maxphys value of PHY_INT4.
- Note how pphys is retrieved:

  idnum = (*pphys).i4;

- It is assumed that the two least significant (rightmost) digits of pphys contain the modulus 11 check digits (00 through 10). The validation procedure described in Appendix J is performed to either validate or reject pphys based upon the check digits.

D.0.0 Utility Function Development (utintyy.c)

D.1.0 Utintyy.c Standard Error Codes

Based upon the ERC_BASE (1000) and ENINT_E (41) values defined in ldt.h, all utintyy.c functions report the same erc:

1047	Utility Function Error

D.2.0 Utint Function Specifications

N/A

E.0.0 LDT Int Application Tips and Reminders

E.1.0 Helpful Notes

Using the standard interface function definitions for the int LDT is less complicated than using char LDT because the pphys argument is always passed as an address of &pphys. This is because pphys is of type INT (typedef synonymous with union {int i2; long int i4;}). Below you'll find some helpful hints to keep in mind when using the functions included in this chapter.

- **Enint.c and evint.c:** The maxin function argument should be the sizeof(pstrin) – 1. Maxin is the declared pstrin (size – 1) and does not include the NULL delimiting character. Maxphys should only be PHY_INT or 2 for type int or PHY_INT4 or 4 for type long int.
- **Getint.c and fgetint.c:** The maxstr function argument should be the sizeof(string) – 1. Cltab only controls the

very first character read operation performed. Nuexit is a returned value and therefore must be passed as &nuexit.

- **Deint.c, Putint.c, and Fputint.c:** The maxout function argument should be the sizeof(pstrin) − 1. Maxout is the declared pstrout (size − 1) not including the NULL delimiting character. Maxout must be large enough to receive the decoded pphys or an erc will result. Maxphys should only be PHY_INT or 2 for type int or PHY _INT4 or 4 for type long int.
- **Dvintyy.c:** When these functions are used as function arguments they must be declared explicitly in the calling program.
- **General:** Initialize all strings before using them.

E.2.0 ***Special Uses***

You can use the int LDT to represent other commonly encountered commercial fields of data. The dvintyy.c and special utintyy.c functions in this chapter supply special ways of handling check digits and ID numbers (see C.2.0–C.5.0 and E.3.0).

E.3.0 ***Utintmd.c Specifications***

E.3.1 ***Utintmd.c Design Objectives***

This function is designed to compute a modulus 10 check digit ckdig (0 through 9) or modulus 11 check digit ckdig (00 through 10) based upon ctrl for a long int idnum. If an error condition is detected, the function utintmd.c returns an erc, and idnum is set to zero.

E.3.2 ***Utintmd.c Source Code and Commentary***

```
/* file    : utintmd.c
** function: int utintmd ( ctrl, idnum, &ckdig )
** desc    : compute "ckdig" from "idnum" under "ctrl"
**         :    ctrl = 10: modulus 10 check digit [0 => 9]
**         :    ctrl = 11: modulus 11 check digit [00 => 10]
** test pgm: tuintmd.c
*/
```

```
#include "ldt.h"

        int utintmd ( ctrl, idnum, ckdig )
        long int idnum;
        int ctrl, *ckdig;

        {
        int erc, dig, rem;
        long int wgt, sum, nten;

        *ckdig = 0;

        erc = ERC_BASE + ENINT_E + 6;

        /*
        ** validate "ctrl"
        */

        if (( ctrl < 10 ) || ( ctrl > 11 )) return ( erc );

        if ( idnum == (long)0 ) return (ERC_OK);

        wgt = 2;
        sum = 0;

        while ( idnum > (long)0)
        {
        dig = idnum % 10;

        sum = sum + (long)dig * wgt;

        switch (ctrl)
        {
                case 10: if (wgt == (long)1) wgt = 2;
                         else wgt = 1;
                         break;

                case 11: wgt = wgt + (long)1;
                         break;
        }

        idnum = idnum / (long)10;

        }


        if (sum == (long)0) return(erc);

        switch (ctrl)
        {
                case 10: nten = ( (sum + (long)10)/(long)10 ) * (long)10;
                         rem = nten - sum;
                         if (rem == 10) rem = 0;
                         break;

                case 11: rem = sum % (long)11;
                         if (rem != 0) rem = 11 - rem;
                         break;

        }

        *ckdig = rem;

        return(ERC_OK);

        }
```

- Note that for a modulus 10 check digit, the integer ckdig can only be 0 through 9.

- Note that for a modulus 11 check digit, the integer ckdig can only be 0 through 10. The calling program must always append the equivalent of two digits (00 through 10) to properly construct an integer ID number with modulus 11 check digits.

F.0.0 Testing and Quality Assurance (qaint.c)

F.1.0 Qaint.c Specification

F.1.1 Qaint.c Design Objectives

Qaint.c is unique to the int logical data type, but has the same testing objectives as all the other qaxxxx.c routines. Qaint.c utilizes enint.c, evint.c, getint.c, fgetint.c, deint.c, putint.c, and fputint.c as well as dvintyy.c, utintyy.c and supporting functions as indicated in the linker automatic response file, qaint.lnk (see Appendix L).

Qaint.c provides runtime control over the resetting of stdlog, making stdlog entries, screen printing upon error detection, and testing all encode and decode subtypes.

Each qaxxxx.c function is an excellent example not only of LDT testing, but also of the various standard interfaces portrayed in this book. A close examination of qaint.c reveals a powerful program of about 125 statements.

F.1.2 Qaint.c Error Codes

Qaxxxx.c functions do not have any reserved ercs of their own; they simply report the ercs detected during processing by the underlying standard interface functions.

All ercs detected for LDT int, however, are governed by the following ldt.h header file values:

ERC_BASE	1000
GET_E	1
PUT_E	5
ENINT_E	41

F.2.0 Qaint.c Source Code and Commentary

```
/*
** file    : qaint.c
** desc    : quality assurance test program for LDT int
** link    : @qaint.lnk,qaint,nul,lcs
*/

#include "ldt.h"

main ()
{
        int dvcharyn(), dvinten(), dvdummy();
        int erc;

        static char mtype[] = ">?<";
        static char mstr2[] = ">??????<";
        static char mstr4[] = ">???????????<";
        static char initi[] = "0";
        static char inity[] = "Y";
        static char initn[] = "N";

        char str[15], destr[15], ynchar;
        int etype, nuexit, smstr2, smstr4;
        int lpe;
        INT *ival;

        smstr2 = nondel(mstr2);
        smstr4 = nondel(mstr4);

        blanksc(1,1,MAX_ROW,MAX_COL);
        setcrc(1,1);
        putstr("INTeger Quality Assurance Program",LR,"",DISP_F);

        /*
        ** Prompt for User Runtime Controls
        */

        uprompt(&lpe);

        if ( (lpe == 10) || (lpe == 11) )
                logwrite(5,"QAINT",0,"Begin Testing");

        for (;;)
        {

        blanksc(2,1,MAX_ROW,MAX_COL);
        setcrc(1,1);
```

```
/*
** INTEGER 2 TESTING
*/
        movcrc(2,-MAX_COL);
        putstr("Enter ENCODE Subtype: ",LR,"",DISP_F);
        erc = getint(str,sizeof(str)-1,NO,mtype,LR,initi,MAND_F,YES,
                     &nuexit,&etype,PHY_INT,1,MAND_F,lpe,dvinten);

        if (lderc(erc) == 9) break;

        movcrc(2,-MAX_COL);
        putstr("Enter INT[2] String : ",LR,"",DISP_F);

        erc = getint(str,sizeof(str)-1,NO,mstr2,LR,"",MAND_F,NO,
                     &nuexit,ival,PHY_INT,etype,MAND_F,lpe,dvdummy);

        if (lderc(erc) == 9) continue;

        movcrc(2,-MAX_COL);
        putstr("DECODEed Subtype [0]: ",LR,"",DISP_F);
        putint(destr,smstr2,ival,PHY_INT,0,NO_JUST,
               LR,mstr2,MAND_F,lpe);

        movcrc(2,-MAX_COL);
        putstr("DECODEed Subtype [1]: ",LR,"",DISP_F);
        putint(destr,smstr2,ival,PHY_INT,1,NO_JUST,
               LR,mstr2,MAND_F,lpe);

        movcrc(2,-MAX_COL);
        putstr("DECODEed Subtype [2]: ",LR,"",DISP_F);
        putint(destr,smstr2,ival,PHY_INT,2,NO_JUST,
               LR,mstr2,MAND_F,lpe);
/*
** INTEGER 4 TESTING
*/
        movcrc(4,-MAX_COL);
        putstr("Enter INT[4] String : ",LR,"",DISP_F);

        erc = getint(str,sizeof(str)-1,NO,mstr4,LR,"",MAND_F,NO,
                     &nuexit,ival,PHY_INT4,etype,MAND_F,lpe,dvdummy);

        if (lderc(erc) == 9) continue;

        movcrc(2,-MAX_COL);
        putstr("DECODEed Subtype [0]: ",LR,"",DISP_F);
        putint(destr,smstr4,ival,PHY_INT4,0,NO_JUST,
               LR,mstr4,MAND_F,lpe);

        movcrc(2,-MAX_COL);
        putstr("DECODEed Subtype [1]: ",LR,"",DISP_F);
        putint(destr,smstr4,ival,PHY_INT4,1,NO_JUST,
               LR,mstr4,MAND_F,lpe);

        movcrc(2,-MAX_COL);
        putstr("DECODEed Subtype [2]: ",LR,"",DISP_F);
        putint(destr,smstr4,ival,PHY_INT4,2,NO_JUST,
               LR,mstr4,MAND_F,lpe);

        setcrc(24,1);
        putstr("Continue? [Yes/No] or [ESCape]: ",LR,"",DISP_F);

        erc = getchar(str,sizeof(str)-1,NO,mtype,LR,inity,MAND_F,NO,
                      &nuexit,&ynchar,1,11,MAND_F,lpe,dvcharyn);

        if (lderc(erc) == 9) break;
        if (ynchar == 'N') break;

        }
```

```
        if ( (lpe == 10) || (lpe == 11) )
                logwrite(6,"QAINT",0,"End Testing");

        blanksc(1,1,MAX_ROW,MAX_COL);
        exit(0);
}
```

- All dvxxxxyy.c functions to be used as function arguments must explicitly be declared in the calling program.
- All masks are declared with outermost field delimiters so that the field limits will always be known regardless of the type of field and video attribute chosen for display.
- All init values are declared to make any necessary revision easy.
- In this case, destr[15] exceeds the nondelimiter size of mask mstr[ ]. The size of a displayed string must not exceed the corresponding number of mask nondelimiter positions.
- Variable lpe is calculated by uprompt.c from runtime user responses and effectively becomes the standard function argument logprerr. (See Chapter 13.)
- Anywhere in the source code where

  if (lderc(erc) = = 9)

  appears, an equivalent statement

  if (nuexit = = −1)

  could have been specified.
- Note that because there were only three possible choices for desubtype, qaint.c simply generates decode 0, 1, and 2 for both INT[2] and INT[4] strings of input.

- Note that hitting the Escape key recycles the program unless performed when the following messages are displayed:

  Enter ENCODE Subtype:

  or

  Continue? [Yes/No] or [ESCape]:

  In either of the above cases, hitting the Escape key exits the program. Hitting Ctrl-Break has no effect in qaxxxx.c functions because Ctrl-Break has been turned off in function _main (see Appendix F).

- Note sample output in Figure 8.1.

```
INTeger Quality Assurance Program

Enter ENCODE Subtype: >0<

Enter INT[2] String : >-123  <

DECODEed Subtype [0]: >  -123<

DECODEed Subtype [1]: >-00123<

DECODEed Subtype [2]: >**-123<


Enter INT[4] String : >-123       <

DECODEed Subtype [0]: >       -123<

DECODEed Subtype [1]: >-0000000123<

DECODEed Subtype [2]: >*******-123<

Continue? [Yes/No] or [ESCape]: >Y<
```

***Figure 8.1**– Qaint.c sample output*

Reals

9

This chapter covers the I/O of real (IEEE floating point arithmetic standard) fields of input that are encoded to and decoded from a storage format as specified by the following statement in ldt.h:

```
typedef union {float f4; double d8;} REAL;
```

Real number fields can therefore be represented as either a float (four bytes) or a double (eight bytes). The maxphys function argument value (either 4 or 8) controls the choice of storage format. Each is often used as a data field in disk record structures, and as a sort field when interfacing to sorting software products.

Each interface definition described in Part 1 of this book is implemented for the real logical data type (xxxx = real). The enreal.c function provided accepts all dereal.c formats and, with the specification of the ensubtype function argument, controls which combination of negative, zero, and positive values is acceptable. The dereal.c function generates floating point character representations under format and number of decimal place control with the specification of a desired desubtype argument value. Data validation functions are provided that validate the allowable encode and decode subtype values discussed above, while function dvrealov.c shows how dvxxxxyy.c functions can provide logic that prompts the user for the confirmation or override (if desired) of a data validation test.

A complete set of utility functions is provided that performs controlled rounding of real numbers, and splits both floats and doubles into their exact constituent whole and fraction parts.

Finally, a testing and quality assurance program (qareal.c) is provided, which allows you to interactively examine and test most of the functions developed in this chapter.

The following chapter index highlights the source code that is provided.

Standard Interface Source Code

A.2.0	Enreal.c:	Encode LDT real
A.3.0	Evreal.c:	Encode and validate LDT real
A.4.0	Getreal.c/ Fgetreal.c:	Combined getstr.c and evreal.c
B.2.0	Dereal.c:	Decode LDT real
B.3.0	Putreal.c/ Fputreal.c:	Combined dereal.c and putstr.c

Data Validation (dvrealyy.c) Functions

C.2.0	Dvrealde.c:	Checks for allowable desubtypes.
C.3.0	Dvrealen.c:	Checks for allowable ensubtypes.
C.4.0	Dvrealov.c:	Checks −1.0 to +1.0 with user override.

Utility (utrealyy.c) Functions

D.2.0	Utrealds.c:	Splits a double into whole and fraction parts
D.3.0	Utrealfs.c:	Splits a float into whole and fraction parts.

D.4.0	Utrealrd.c:	Provides for controlled rounding of reals.

Quality Assurance Programs

F.2.0	Qareal.c:	Standard quality assurance test program

A.0.0 Encode Function Development (enreal.c)

A.1.0 Enreal.c Specifications

A.1.1 Design Objectives

The real logical data type supports the IEEE standard binary floating point formats that are represented by the native C data types of float and double. Refer to Appendix K for complete details.

Both data types are supported because of the following type-def specification for LDT real:

```
union {float f4; double d8;} REAL;
```

This specification allows either component to be addressed as follows:

```
  float val:  = (*pphys).f4;
 double val:  = (*pphys).d8;
```

The valid ranges of float and double are

```
8.43x10^-37<= |FLOAT| <= 3.37x10^38
4.19x10^-307 <= |DOUBLE| <= 1.67x10^308
```

Utilities are provided for the controlled rounding of any real variable. Scientific or exponent notation has not been implemented.

A.1.2 **Field Size (maxin)**

The maximum field size for the float f4 portion of the union specification is MAX_REAL = 12; similarly, the double d8 portion has a maximum field size of MAX_RDBL = 20. These values may be altered and are contained in ldt.h.

A.1.3 **Physical Format (maxphys)**

The C programming language dictates the choice of native C data types for real with (*pphys).f4 corresponding to float and (*pphys).d8 corresponding to double.

Similarly, a maxphys of PHY_REAL = 4 corresponds to the size of a float in bytes, and PHY_RDBL = 8 corresponds to the size of a double.

A.1.4 **Character Set Restrictions**

By design of the getstr.c/fgetstr.c functions, the enreal.c function only "sees" ASCII 0x20 through 0x7E.

For real fields of input this complete range of input is accepted; however, enreal.c processing imposes additional edit checks. (See Sections A.1.6 and A.1.7 below.)

A.1.5 **Subtype Definition (ensubtype)**

The ensubtype parameter provides for immediate data entry editing for negative, zero, and positive floating point values as follows:

0	Any negative, zero, or positive real value
1	Only zero or positive real values
2	Only positive real values
3	Only negative or zero real values
4	Only negative real values

Although the data validation functions can take care of such editing, this editing is so common it is better if the ensubtype function argument encompasses this level of editing and leaves reasonability checks of real fields up to custom data validation functions.

A.1.6 Other Format Controls

Real fields can only consist of numeric digits and a decimal point, without any embedded spaces or other ASCII characters. Leading or trailing blanks are accepted, but they are stripped, and not interpreted in any manner.

The location of a minus sign, if present, is anticipated as follows:

[–][0..0][n..n][.][n..n]

where

[–]	denotes the position of a leading minus sign, if specified.
[0]	denotes a leading zero, if specified.
[n]	indicates a numeric digit.
[.]	indicates an optional decimal point.

A plus sign is acceptable wherever a minus sign is permitted.

A.1.7 Editing

As described in section A.1.5 above, floating point field sign detection has been attributed to the ensubtype parameter.

A.1.8 Default Values

Upon initial entry to the enreal.c function, the appropriate real value, either (*pphys).f4 or (*pphys).d8 as dictated by the maxphys argument value, is initialized to 0.0.

A.1.9 Error Codes

Based upon the ERC_BASE (1000) and ENREAL_E (51) values defined in the ldt.h header file, the following ercs are possible.

1051	Encode Data Entry Error By User
1052	Bad Encode Function Argument
1053	Encode Mandatory Field Not Satisfied

A.2.0 Enreal.c Source Code and Commentary

```
/* file    : enreal.c
** function: int enreal ( pstrin, maxin, pphys, maxphys,
**         :              ensubtype, mflag )
** desc    : encode a logical data type real.
**         : if "maxphys" = 4 == float; = 8 == double;
** test pgm: qareal.c
*/

#include "ctype.h"
#include "ldt.h"

        int enreal (pstrin, maxin, pphys, maxphys, ensubtype, mflag)

        char *pstrin;
        REAL *pphys;
        int maxin, maxphys, ensubtype, mflag;

        {
        double dval, wgt;
        int erc, eerc, size, i, slgth, wslgth, fslgth, digit, pos;
        char str[30], whole[30], fraction[30], sign;

        /*
        ** Table of valid ENCODE subtypes:
        **    0 = any real
        **    1 = 0/+ real only
        **    2 = + real only
        **    3 = 0/- real only
        **    4 = - real only
        */

        /*
        ** Note: whether "pphys" is FLOAT (f4) or
        ** DOUBLE (d8) is controlled by "maxphys"
        **    4 = FLOAT
        **    8 = DOUBLE
        **    otherwise, ENREAL argument error
        */


        /*
        ** Validate the function arguments:
        */

        erc = ERC_BASE + ENREAL_E + 1;

        if (maxphys == 4) size = MAX_REAL;
        else
        if (maxphys == 8) size = MAX_RDBL;
        else
        return(erc);
```

```
if (( maxin < 1 ) || ( maxin > size )) return (erc);
if (( mflag < NO ) || ( mflag > YES )) return (erc);

/*
** validate "ensubtype" and set "default" values
*/

eerc = dvrealen(&ensubtype,PHY_INT);
if (eerc != ERC_OK) return(eerc);

if ( maxphys == 4) (*pphys).f4 = (float)0.0;
else (*pphys).d8 = (double)0.0;

/*
** Validate mandatory field requirement
** OK to check before any other pre-processing
*/

slgth = strlen( pstrin );
if (( mflag ) && ( slgth < 1 )) return(erc+1);

erc = erc - 1;

/*
** encode processing
*/

strcpy(str, pstrin);

/*
** strip leading/trailing blanks.
*/

utcharsb(3,str,C_BLANK);
slgth = strlen(str);
if(slgth < 1) return(erc+2);

sign = C_BLANK;

if ( (str[0] == C_PLUS) || (str[0] == C_MINUS))
{
sign = str[0];
delchr(str,1);
slgth = strlen(str);
if (slgth < 1) return(erc+2);
}


/*
** locate decimal, if any; split into whole/fraction
*/

utcharcb(1,whole,1);
utcharcb(1,fraction,1);

pos = poschr(str,C_PERIOD,LR);
if (pos == 0) strcpy(whole,str);
else
{
for ( i=0; i < (pos-1); i++)
{
inschr(whole,sizeof(whole),str[i],0);
}
for ( i=pos; i < slgth; i++)
{
inschr(fraction,sizeof(fraction),str[i],0);
}
}
```

```
/*
** check that only whole/fraction are digits
*/

wslgth = strlen(whole);
for ( i=0; i < wslgth; i++ )
{
if ( isdigit(whole[i]) == 0 ) return(erc);
}

fslgth = strlen(fraction);
for ( i=0; i < fslgth; i++ )
{
if ( isdigit(fraction[i]) == 0 ) return(erc);
}

/*
** check "sign"
*/

switch ( ensubtype )
{
        case 0: break;
        case 1:
        case 2: if (sign == C_MINUS) return(erc);
                break;
        case 3: break;
        case 4: if (sign != C_MINUS) return(erc);
                break;

}


/*
** process "whole" portion
*/

dval = 0.0;
wgt = 1.0;
for ( i=wslgth-1; i >= 0; i--)
{
digit = whole[i] - C_ZERO;
dval = dval + (double)digit * wgt;
wgt = wgt * (double)10.0;
}

/*
** process "fraction" portion
*/

wgt = 0.1;

for ( i=0; i < fslgth; i++)
{
digit = fraction[i] - C_ZERO;
dval = dval + (double)digit * wgt;
wgt = wgt / (double)10.0;
}

if ( sign == C_MINUS ) dval = -dval;

switch (ensubtype)
{
        case 0: break;
        case 1: if (dval < 0.0) return(erc);
                break;
        case 2: if (dval <= 0.0) return(erc);
                break;
```

```
        case 3: if (dval > 0.0) return(erc);
                break;
        case 4: if (dval >= 0.0) return(erc);
                break;
}

if (maxphys == 4) (*pphys).f4 = (float)dval;
else (*pphys).d8 = dval;

return (ERC_OK);

}
```

- Note that pphys is declared to be of type REAL. Upper-case REAL is a typedef from ldt.h. REAL supports both float and double by virtue of its union specification. Maxphys dictates whether float (maxphys = 4) or double (maxphys = 8) is intended. Any other maxphys value generates an erc.
- For the real LDT, if pstrin contains all blank characters, it does not satisfy the mandatory mflag field requirement.
- Note that pstrin (same as str) locates a decimal point so that the whole and fraction portions of the floating point number can be processed separately. If no decimal point is present, it assumes that only a whole portion has been input.
- Note the use of the cast (float) to transform dval from double to float.

A.3.0 Encode and Validate Source Code and Commentary (evreal.c)

The source code and commentary for function evreal.c parallels evchar.c (Chapter 5, A.3.0). To create function evreal.c, simply copy file evchar.c and edit it as follows:

- Change all occurrences of char to real and CHAR to REAL except for the statement:

  char *pstrin;

- Update the commented function description.

The complete source code is available on disk.

A.4.0 **Advanced Encode Field Processing**

A.4.1 **Getreal.c and Fgetreal.c Error Codes**

See Chapter 5, A.4.1.

A.4.2 **Getreal.c and Fgetreal.c Source Code and Commentary**

The source code and commentary for function getreal.c parallels getchar.c (Chapter 5, A.4.0). To create function getreal.c, simply copy file getchar.c and edit it as follows:

- Change all occurrences of char to real and CHAR to REAL except for the statement:

```
char *string, *mask, *init;
```

The source code and commentary for function fgetreal.c also parallels fgetchar.c (Chapter 5, A.4.0). To create function fgetreal.c, simply copy file fgetchar.c and edit it as follows:

- Change all occurrences of char to real and CHAR to REAL except for the statements:

```
char *string, *mask, *init;
utcharcb(1,string,1);
```

The complete source code is available on disk.

A.4.3 **Associated Mask Utilization Techniques**

Based upon the function argument gmaskflg, mask delimiter characters can be included (YES) from the acquired input string. This facilitates the introduction of character delimiters, which, in this case, would be a decimal point. The delimiter provides a visual cue for the user when entering data, for example,

```
Test Result: "???.??"
```

It is important to remember that enreal.c can be utilized independently of the getstr.c/fgetstr.c and getreal.c/fgetreal.c functions so that some functional redundancy is required to expand the independent use of the enxxxx.c interface definitions developed in this book.

B.0.0 Decode Function Development (dereal.c)

B.1.0 Dereal.c Specifications

B.1.1 Design Objectives

This function provides a real LDT processing function that can display floating point fields stored in either standard IEEE binary floating point format (four-byte float or eight-byte double). Each output format is acceptable to the enreal.c function.

B.1.2 Subtype Definition (desubtype)

The real desubtype is a single integer value consisting of two digits (d2d1). Digit d2 controls the handling of leading zero padding and has the following acceptable digit values:

1 = [−][w..w][.][f..f]
2 = [−][0..0][w..w][.][f..f]

where

[−]	denotes the position of a leading minus sign, if specified.
[0]	denotes a leading zero, if specified.
[w]	indicates a digit representing the whole number portion of a real number.
[.]	indicates an optional decimal point.

[f] indicates a digit representing the fractional number portion of a real number.

Digit d1 specifies the number of desired decimal positions. Digit d1 values can range from 0 through 9.

B.1.3 Default Values

No default is assumed for dereal.c. The output character string pstrout is simply set to a NULL string before processing begins.

B.1.4 Error Codes

Based upon the ERC_BASE (1000) and ENREAL_E (51) values defined in ldt.h, the following erc is possible:

1056	Bad Decode Function Argument

B.2.0 Dereal.c Source Code and Commentary

```
/* file    : dereal.c
** function: int dereal ( pstrout, maxout, pphys, maxphys,
**         :                 desubtype, jflag )
** desc    : decode a logical data type real.
** test pgm: qareal.c
*/

#include "ctype.h"
#include "ldt.h"

        int dereal (pstrout, maxout, pphys, maxphys, desubtype, jflag)

        char *pstrout;
        REAL *pphys;
        int maxout, maxphys, desubtype, jflag;
        {

        int erc, derc, i, slgth, rem, dpos, pos, size, digit2, digit1;
        double value, whole, fraction, div, round, factor;
        double dval, dwhole, dfract;
        float  fval, fwhole, ffract;
        char str[40], digit, ch, sign;
```

```
/*
** Table of valid DECODE subtypes: [digit2|digit1]
**
**      digit2:
**
**      1 = normal [-]nnnn
**      2 = leading zeroes [-]000nnnn
**
**      digit1:
**
**      n = number decimal places (0-9)
**
*/

/*
** Validate the function arguments:
*/

erc = ERC_BASE + ENREAL_E + 5;


if (maxphys == 4) size = MAX_REAL;
else
if (maxphys == 8) size = MAX_RDBL;
else
return(erc);

if (( maxout < 1 ) || ( maxout > size )) return (erc);
if (( jflag < NO_JUST) || ( jflag > R_JUST )) return (erc);


/*
** validate "desubtype" and set "default" values
*/

utcharcb(1,pstrout,1);
utcharcb(1,str,1);

derc = dvrealde(&desubtype,PHY_INT);
if (derc != ERC_OK) return(derc);

digit2 = desubtype / 10;
digit1 = desubtype % 10;

/*
** desubtype processing
*/

round = 0.5;

if (maxphys == 4)
{
fval= (*pphys).f4;
if (fval < (float)0.0) round = -round;
if ( digit1 == 0 ) fval = fval + round;
utrealfs (&fval, &fwhole, &ffract);
value = fval;
whole = fwhole;
fraction = ffract;
}
else
{
dval = (*pphys).d8;
if (dval < (double)0.0) round = -round;
if ( digit1 == 0 ) dval = dval + round;
utrealds (&dval, &dwhole, &dfract);
value = dval;
whole = dwhole;
fraction = dfract;
}
```

```
sign = C_BLANK;

if (value < (double)0.0)
{
sign = C_MINUS;
value = -value;
whole = -whole;
fraction = -fraction;
round = -round;
}

/*
** translate "whole" portion
*/

if (whole == (double)0.0) inschr(str,999,C_ZERO,0);


while ( whole > (double)0.0)
{
div = whole / (double)10.0;
utrealds (&div, &dwhole, &dfract);
rem = whole - (dwhole * (double)10.0);
digit = rem + C_ZERO;

inschr(str,999,digit,1);

whole = dwhole;
}


/*
** translate "fraction" portion
*/

factor = 1.0;
for (i=0; i < digitl; i++)
{
factor = factor * (double)10.0;
}

if (digitl != 0) inschr(str,999,C_PERIOD,0);
pos = strlen(str) + 1;

fraction = (fraction * factor) + round;
utrealds (&fraction, &dwhole, &dfract);
fraction = dwhole;


for (i=0; i < digitl; i++)
{
div = fraction / (double)10.0;
utrealds (&div, &dwhole, &dfract);
rem = fraction - (dwhole * (double)10.0);
digit = rem + C_ZERO;

inschr(str,999,digit,pos);


fraction = dwhole;
}


if (sign == C_MINUS)
{
inschr(str,999,C_MINUS,1);
}
```

```
pos = 1;
switch ( digit2 )
{
        case 1: ch = C_BLANK;
                break;
        case 2: ch = C_ZERO;
                if (sign == C_MINUS) pos = 2;
                break;
}

dpos = maxout - strlen(str);

for (i=0; i < dpos; i++)
{
inschr(str,999,ch,pos);
}

/*
** is pstrout big enough?
*/

utcharcb(3,str,maxout+1);
slgth = strlen(str);
if (slgth > maxout) return(erc);
else strcpy(pstrout,str);

/*
** Justify output string
*/

utcharjs(jflag, pstrout);

return (ERC_OK);

}
```

- Note that both functions utrealfs.c and utrealds.c are used to split fval or dval respectively into a whole and fraction portion. Refer to D.3.0 and D.2.0 for complete details of these functions. They are necessary because a truncation function is not provided for most implementations of C compilers.
- Only the desired number of decimal positions are displayed after proper rounding of the result.
- String justification occurs within the total string field width maxout because of the function call to

  utcharcb (3,str,maxout + 1)

- An erc is generated if the string length of pphys is greater than the maxout string length of pstrout.

B.3.0 Advanced Decode Field Processing

B.3.1 Putreal.c and Fputreal.c Error Codes

See Chapter 5, B.3.1.

B.3.2 Putreal.c and Fputreal.c Source Code and Commentary

The source code and commentary for function putreal.c and fputreal.c parallels putchar.c and fputchar.c (Chapter 5, B.3.0). To create either of these functions copy its parallel function and edit it as follows:

- Change all occurrences of char to real and CHAR to REAL except for the statement:

```
char *pstrout, *mask;
```

The complete source code is available on disk.

B.3.3 Associated Mask Utilization Techniques

- In an analogous manner, putstr.c/fputstr.c and putreal.c/fputreal.c can output a decoded string to a mask field with or without delimiters. The mask itself can also contain the field description:

  ```
  Test Result: "RATIO ??????"
  ```

  Remember that dereal.c can be utilized independently of the putstr.c/fputstr.c and putreal.c/fputreal.c functions so that some functional redundancy is required.

- The getmstr.c function allows the video display to be used as a scratch pad (see Chapter 4) and functionally extends the stand-alone utility of each dexxxx.c. Since the power of masks is only pertinent to video display, getmstr.c retrieves the putxxxx.c string from the video display with mask formatting to enhance the variety of decoded formats that may be created when using dexxxx.c functions in a stand-alone manner.

C.0.0 Data Validation Function Development (dvrealyy.c)

C.1.0 Dvrealyy.c Standard Error Codes

Based upon the ERC_BASE (1000) and ENREAL_E (51) values defined in ldt.h header file, all dvrealyy.c functions report the same ercs:

1054	Data Validation Error
1055	Bad Data Validation Function Argument

C.2.0 Dvrealde.c Function Specification

C.2.1 Dvrealde.c Design Objectives

This function simply validates that an acceptable desubtype argument value has been specified for real.

C.2.2 Dvrealde.c Source Code and Commentary

```
/* file    : dvrealde.c
** function: int dvrealde ( pphys, maxphys )
** desc    : data validation for real; valid decode subtype
** test pgm: qareal.c
*/

#include "ldt.h"

        int dvrealde ( pphys, maxphys )

        INT *pphys;
        int maxphys;
        {
        int erc, val, digit2, digit1;

        erc = ERC_BASE + ENINT_E + 3;

        if (maxphys != PHY_INT) return(erc+1);

        val = (*pphys).i2;
```

```
digit2 = val / 10;
digit1 = val % 10;

if ( (digit2 < 1) || (digit2 > 2) ) return(erc);
if ( (digit1 < 0) || (digit1 > 9) ) return(erc);

return(ERC_OK);

}
```

- Note the use of INT *pphys. The uppercase INT is a typedef from ldt.h which is

  typedef union {int i2; long int i4;} INT;

  The use of the INT typedef allows either int or long int arguments to be passed to dvrealde.c. By design only int types are acceptable to dvrealde.c.

- Note how desubtype is retrieved:

  val = (*pphys).i2;

C.3.0 Dvrealen.c Function Specification

C.3.1 Dvrealen.c Design Objectives

This function simply validates that an acceptable ensubtype argument value has been specified for real.

C.3.2 Dvrealen.c Source Code and Commentary

```
/* file    : dvrealen.c
** function: int dvrealen ( pphys, maxphys )
** desc    : data validation for real; valid encode subtype
** test pgm: qareal.c
*/

#include "ldt.h"

        int dvrealen ( pphys, maxphys )

        INT *pphys;
        int maxphys;
        {
        int erc, val;

        erc = ERC_BASE + ENINT_E + 3;

        if (maxphys != PHY_INT) return(erc+1);

        val = (*pphys).i2;
```

```
if ( ( val < 0 ) || ( val > 4) ) return (erc);
else return(ERC_OK);
}
```

- Note the use of INT *pphys (see C.2.2 commentary).

C.4.0 Dvrealov.c Function Specification

C.4.1 Dvrealov.c Design Objectives

This function checks values between −1.00 and +1.00 for rejection and allows the user to override and accept the value if so desired by responding with either Yes or No.

C.4.2 Dvrealov.c Source Code and Commentary

```
/* file    : dvrealov.c
** function: int dvrealov ( pphys, maxphys )
** desc    : data validation for real; range check with
**         : option to override!
** test pgm: qareal.c
*/

#include "ldt.h"

        int dvrealov ( pphys, maxphys )

        REAL *pphys;
        int maxphys;
        {

        int erc, gerc, nuexit, dvcharyn();
        int row, col;
        double value;
        static char myn[] = ">?<";
        char str[5], ynchar;

        erc = ERC_BASE + ENREAL_E + 3;

        if (maxphys == 4) value = (*pphys).f4;
        else
        if (maxphys == 8) value = (*pphys).d8;
        else
        return(erc+1);

        if ( (value > -1.00) && (value < 1.00) )
        {

        mesende(erc,NO);

        getcrc(&row,&col);

        setcrc(MAX_ROW,1);

        putstr("Override range check <-1.00 to 1.00>? [Yes/No] ",
                LR,"",DISP_F);
```

```
gerc = getchar(str,sizeof(str)-1,NO,myn,LR,"Y",MAND_F,NO,
                &nuexit,&ynchar,1,11,MAND_F,NO,dvcharyn);

blanksc(MAX_ROW,1,MAX_ROW,MAX_COL);
setcrc(row,col);

if (lderc(gerc) != ERC_OK) return(erc);
else
if ( ynchar == 'N' ) return(erc);

}
return(ERC_OK);

}
```

- Note the use of REAL *pphys. The uppercase REAL is a typedef from ldt.h which is

  typedef union {float f4; double d8;} REAL;

  The use of the REAL typedef then permits either float (*pphys).f4 or double (*pphys).d8 variables to be addressed.

- By design, all messaging and data entry is restricted to line 25 (MAX_ROW). Putstr.c displays the text of the message, and getchar.c reads and validates the response with function dvcharyn.c.

- A user response of Yes indicates that the otherwise rejected value is to be accepted (ERC_OK). A response of No indicates that dvrealov.c is to return an erc, indicating that the value entered is unacceptable and has been rejected.

D.0.0 Utility Function Development (utrealyy.c)

D.1.0 Utrealyy.c Standard Error Codes

Based upon the ERC_BASE (1000) and ENREAL_E (51) values defined in ldt.h, all utrealyy.c functions report the following erc:

1057	Utility Function Error

D.2.0 Utrealds.c Specifications

D.2.1 Utrealds.c Design Objectives

This function overcomes the lack of a valid truncation function and is useful with large double values. Normally real numbers can be assigned to an integer number in order to truncate the whole number portion; however, large real numbers generate erroneous results because of the associated integer overflow problem.

The utrealds.c function splits a double variable into two double variables that contain the exact whole and fractional portions of the original double value, thus avoiding overflow.

This is accomplished for IEEE double or eight-byte binary floating point numbers (see Appendix K).

The source code demonstrates the use of the C feature of fields or bit-flags.

D.2.2 Utrealds.c Source Code and Commentary

```
/* file    : utrealds.c
** function: int utrealds (d8, d8w, d8f)
** desc    : convert a double to equivalent whole and fraction
**         : portions of type double
** test pgm: turealds.c
*/

#include "ldt.h"

        int utrealds (d8, d8w, d8f)

        union { double ud8;
        struct {
                unsigned is_sig37 : 1;
                unsigned is_sig38 : 1;
                unsigned is_sig39 : 1;
                unsigned is_sig40 : 1;
                unsigned is_sig41 : 1;
                unsigned is_sig42 : 1;
                unsigned is_sig43 : 1;
                unsigned is_sig44 : 1;
                unsigned is_sig45 : 1;
                unsigned is_sig46 : 1;
                unsigned is_sig47 : 1;
                unsigned is_sig48 : 1;
                unsigned is_sig49 : 1;
                unsigned is_sig50 : 1;
                unsigned is_sig51 : 1;
                unsigned is_sig52 : 1;
                unsigned is_sig21 : 1;
                unsigned is_sig22 : 1;
                unsigned is_sig23 : 1;
                unsigned is_sig24 : 1;
                unsigned is_sig25 : 1;
```

```
                unsigned is_sig26 : 1;
                unsigned is_sig27 : 1;
                unsigned is_sig28 : 1;
                unsigned is_sig29 : 1;
                unsigned is_sig30 : 1;
                unsigned is_sig31 : 1;
                unsigned is_sig32 : 1;
                unsigned is_sig33 : 1;
                unsigned is_sig34 : 1;
                unsigned is_sig35 : 1;
                unsigned is_sig36 : 1;
                unsigned is_sig5  : 1;
                unsigned is_sig6  : 1;
                unsigned is_sig7  : 1;
                unsigned is_sig8  : 1;
                unsigned is_sig9  : 1;
                unsigned is_sig10 : 1;
                unsigned is_sig11 : 1;
                unsigned is_sig12 : 1;
                unsigned is_sig13 : 1;
                unsigned is_sig14 : 1;
                unsigned is_sig15 : 1;
                unsigned is_sig16 : 1;
                unsigned is_sig17 : 1;
                unsigned is_sig18 : 1;
                unsigned is_sig19 : 1;
                unsigned is_sig20 : 1;
                unsigned is_sign  : 1;
                unsigned is_bexp  :11;
                unsigned is_sig1  : 1;
                unsigned is_sig2  : 1;
                unsigned is_sig3  : 1;
                unsigned is_sig4  : 1;
              } sd8; } *d8;

double *d8w, *d8f;

{
int bexp;
double saved8;
int exp;

saved8 = (*d8).ud8;

bexp  = (*d8).sd8.is_bexp;

exp = bexp - 0x3FF;

/*
** eliminate fraction portion of "float"
*/

if (exp > 51) exp = 52;

switch (exp)
{
case  0: (*d8).sd8.is_sig1  = 0;
case  1: (*d8).sd8.is_sig2  = 0;
case  2: (*d8).sd8.is_sig3  = 0;
case  3: (*d8).sd8.is_sig4  = 0;
case  4: (*d8).sd8.is_sig5  = 0;
case  5: (*d8).sd8.is_sig6  = 0;
case  6: (*d8).sd8.is_sig7  = 0;
case  7: (*d8).sd8.is_sig8  = 0;
case  8: (*d8).sd8.is_sig9  = 0;
case  9: (*d8).sd8.is_sig10 = 0;
case 10: (*d8).sd8.is_sig11 = 0;
case 11: (*d8).sd8.is_sig12 = 0;
```

```
case 12: (*d8).sd8.is_sig13 = 0;
case 13: (*d8).sd8.is_sig14 = 0;
case 14: (*d8).sd8.is_sig15 = 0;
case 15: (*d8).sd8.is_sig16 = 0;
case 16: (*d8).sd8.is_sig17 = 0;
case 17: (*d8).sd8.is_sig18 = 0;
case 18: (*d8).sd8.is_sig19 = 0;
case 19: (*d8).sd8.is_sig20 = 0;
case 20: (*d8).sd8.is_sig21 = 0;
case 21: (*d8).sd8.is_sig22 = 0;
case 22: (*d8).sd8.is_sig23 = 0;
case 23: (*d8).sd8.is_sig24 = 0;
case 24: (*d8).sd8.is_sig25 = 0;
case 25: (*d8).sd8.is_sig26 = 0;
case 26: (*d8).sd8.is_sig27 = 0;
case 27: (*d8).sd8.is_sig28 = 0;
case 28: (*d8).sd8.is_sig29 = 0;
case 29: (*d8).sd8.is_sig30 = 0;
case 30: (*d8).sd8.is_sig31 = 0;
case 31: (*d8).sd8.is_sig32 = 0;
case 32: (*d8).sd8.is_sig33 = 0;
case 33: (*d8).sd8.is_sig34 = 0;
case 34: (*d8).sd8.is_sig35 = 0;
case 35: (*d8).sd8.is_sig36 = 0;
case 36: (*d8).sd8.is_sig37 = 0;
case 37: (*d8).sd8.is_sig38 = 0;
case 38: (*d8).sd8.is_sig39 = 0;
case 39: (*d8).sd8.is_sig40 = 0;
case 40: (*d8).sd8.is_sig41 = 0;
case 41: (*d8).sd8.is_sig42 = 0;
case 42: (*d8).sd8.is_sig43 = 0;
case 43: (*d8).sd8.is_sig44 = 0;
case 44: (*d8).sd8.is_sig45 = 0;
case 45: (*d8).sd8.is_sig46 = 0;
case 46: (*d8).sd8.is_sig47 = 0;
case 47: (*d8).sd8.is_sig48 = 0;
case 48: (*d8).sd8.is_sig49 = 0;
case 49: (*d8).sd8.is_sig50 = 0;
case 50: (*d8).sd8.is_sig51 = 0;
case 51: (*d8).sd8.is_sig52 = 0;
case 52: break;
default: break;
}

if (exp < 0)
{
*d8w = 0.0;
*d8f = saved8;
}
else
{
*d8w = (*d8).ud8;
*d8f = saved8 - *d8w;
}

(*d8).ud8 = saved8;

return(ERC_OK);

}
```

- Note that the function arguments d8w and d8f represent the whole and fractional portions of d8 respectively.

- Note the bit numbering scheme used in the structure definition for sd8 within the union structure for the function argument *d8. This reflects the byte and subsequent bit ordering for double found under the physical column in Figure 2.2.
- The fractional portion of *d8 is eliminated by turning off all bits which comprise the fractional portion (as calculated from the biased exponent). This is accomplished by using a switch (exp) expression without any breaks so that all bits from exp on are turned off. This transforms sd8 to the whole number portion of its original value.
- Note that the original values of sd8 and *d8 are restored before this function returns.

D.3.0 Utrealfs.c Specifications

D.3.1 Utrealfs.c Design Objectives

This function, like utrealds.c, overcomes the lack of a valid truncation function but is used with large float variables instead of double variables.

Utrealfs.c uses the IEEE float or four-byte binary floating point numbers as opposed to the eight-byte numbers used by utrealds.c (see D.2.1).

The source code also demonstrates the use of the C feature of fields or bit-flags.

D.3.2 Utrealfs.c Source Code and Commentary

```
/* file    : utrealfs.c
** function: int utrealfs (f4, f4w, f4f)
** desc    : convert a float to equivalent whole and fraction
**         : portions of type float
** test pgm: turealfs.c
*/

#include "ldt.h"

        int utrealfs (f4, f4w, f4f)

        union { float uf4;
        struct {
                unsigned is_sig8  : 1;
                unsigned is_sig9  : 1;
                unsigned is_sig10 : 1;
```

```
            unsigned is_sig11 : 1;
            unsigned is_sig12 : 1;
            unsigned is_sig13 : 1;
            unsigned is_sig14 : 1;
            unsigned is_sig15 : 1;
            unsigned is_sig16 : 1;
            unsigned is_sig17 : 1;
            unsigned is_sig18 : 1;
            unsigned is_sig19 : 1;
            unsigned is_sig20 : 1;
            unsigned is_sig21 : 1;
            unsigned is_sig22 : 1;
            unsigned is_sig23 : 1;
            unsigned is_sign  : 1;
            unsigned is_bexp  : 8;
            unsigned is_sig1  : 1;
            unsigned is_sig2  : 1;
            unsigned is_sig3  : 1;
            unsigned is_sig4  : 1;
            unsigned is_sig5  : 1;
            unsigned is_sig6  : 1;
            unsigned is_sig7  : 1;
           } sf4; } *f4;

    float *f4w, *f4f;

    {
    int bexp;
    float savef4;
    int exp;

    savef4 = (*f4).uf4;

    bexp  = (*f4).sf4.is_bexp;

    exp = bexp - 0x7F;


    /*
    ** eliminate fraction portion of "float"
    */

    if (exp > 22) exp = 23;

    switch (exp)
    {
    case  0: (*f4).sf4.is_sig1  = 0;
    case  1: (*f4).sf4.is_sig2  = 0;
    case  2: (*f4).sf4.is_sig3  = 0;
    case  3: (*f4).sf4.is_sig4  = 0;
    case  4: (*f4).sf4.is_sig5  = 0;
    case  5: (*f4).sf4.is_sig6  = 0;
    case  6: (*f4).sf4.is_sig7  = 0;
    case  7: (*f4).sf4.is_sig8  = 0;
    case  8: (*f4).sf4.is_sig9  = 0;
    case  9: (*f4).sf4.is_sig10 = 0;
    case 10: (*f4).sf4.is_sig11 = 0;
    case 11: (*f4).sf4.is_sig12 = 0;
    case 12: (*f4).sf4.is_sig13 = 0;
    case 13: (*f4).sf4.is_sig14 = 0;
    case 14: (*f4).sf4.is_sig15 = 0;
    case 15: (*f4).sf4.is_sig16 = 0;
    case 16: (*f4).sf4.is_sig17 = 0;
    case 17: (*f4).sf4.is_sig18 = 0;
    case 18: (*f4).sf4.is_sig19 = 0;
    case 19: (*f4).sf4.is_sig20 = 0;
    case 20: (*f4).sf4.is_sig21 = 0;
    case 21: (*f4).sf4.is_sig22 = 0;
```

```
case 22: (*f4).sf4.is_sig23 = 0;
case 23: break;
default: break;
}

if (exp < 0)
{
*f4w = 0.0;
*f4f = savef4;
}
else
{
*f4w = (*f4).uf4;
*f4f = savef4 - *f4w;
}

(*f4).uf4 = savef4;

return(ERC_OK);

}
```

- Note that the function arguments f4w and f4f represent the whole and fractional portions of f4 respectively.

- Note the bit numbering scheme used in the structure definition for sf4 within the union structure for the function argument *f4. This reflects the byte and subsequent bit ordering for float found under the physical column in Figure 2.2.

- The fractional portion of *f4 is eliminated by turning off all bits that comprise the fractional portion (as calculated from the biased-exponent). This is accomplished by using a switch (exp) expression without any breaks, so that all bits from exp on are turned off, transforming sf4 to the whole number portion of its original value.

- Note that the original values of sf4 and *f4 are restored before this function returns.

D.4.0 *Utrealrd.c* Specifications

D.4.1 *Utrealrd.c* Design Objectives

This function can round to whole or decimal places both float and double IEEE standard binary floating point numbers.

D.4.2 Utrealrd.c Source Code and Commentary

```
/* file    : utrealrd.c
** function: int utrealrd ( &pphys, maxphys, npos )
** desc    : round pphys to npos places (+ = .xxx; - = xxx.)
**         : if maxphys = 4, pphys = float;
**         : if maxphys = 8, pphys = double.
** test pgm: turealrd.c
*/

#include "ldt.h"

        int utrealrd (pphys, maxphys, npos)

        REAL *pphys;
        int maxphys, npos;

        {

        double round, factor, dval, dwhole, dfract;
        char sign;
        int i, erc;

        round = 0.5;
        erc = ERC_BASE + ENREAL_E + 6;


        sign = C_BLANK;

        if (maxphys == 4)
        {
        dval = (*pphys).f4;
        }
        else if (maxphys == 8)
        {
        dval = (*pphys).d8;
        }
        else return(erc);

        if (dval < (double)0.0)
        {
        sign = C_MINUS;
        dval = -dval;
        }

        if (npos < 0)
        {
        factor = -1.0;
        npos = -npos;
        }
        else factor = 1.0;

        for (i=0; i < npos; i++)
        {
        factor = factor * (double)10.0;


        }

        utrealds(&dval, &dwhole, &dfract);

        if (factor < (double)0.0)
        {
        factor = -factor;
        dval = (dwhole / factor) + round;
        utrealds(&dval, &dwhole, &dfract);
        dval = dwhole * factor;
        }
```

```
else
{
dval = (dval * factor) + round;
utrealds(&dval, &dwhole, &dfract);
dval = dwhole / factor;
}

if (sign == C_MINUS)
{
dval = -dval;
}

if (maxphys == 4) (*pphys).f4 = (float)dval;
else (*pphys).d8 = dval;

return(ERC_OK);

}
```

- Note that although this is a utility function, the function arguments common to data validation functions, pphys and maxphys, have been used to accommodate both float and double binary floating point numbers. Pphys is a returned value.
- Note that the function argument, npos, can be either a negative, zero, or positive number. A negative npos value rounds to the left of the decimal point, for example:

  123.456 with npos = −3 yields 000.000
  123.456 with npos = −2 yields 100.000
  123.456 with npos = −1 yields 120.000

  A zero npos value rounds to the whole number units position, for example:

  123.456 with npos = 0 yields 123.000

  A positive npos value rounds to decimal number positions to the right of the decimal point, for example:

  123.456 with npos = 1 yields 123.500
  123.456 with npos = 2 yields 123.460
  123.456 with npos = 3 yields 123.456

- Note the use of the split function utrealds.c to assist in the rounding.

E.0.0 LDT Real Application Tips and Reminders

E.1.0 Helpful Notes

Using the real logical data type is again somewhat less complicated than using char. This is because the pphys argument is always passed as an "address of" (&pphys) because pphys is of type REAL (typedef synonymous with union {float f4; double d8;}).

Let's highlight some helpful reminders about using the functions included in this chapter.

1. **Enreal.c and evreal.c**: The maxin function argument should be the sizeof(pstrin) – 1. Maxin is the declared pstrin (size – 1) and does not include the NULL delimiting character. Maxphys should only be PHY_REAL or 4 for type float or PHY_RDBL or 8 for type double.

2. **Getreal.c and fgetreal.c**: The maxstr function argument should be the sizeof(string) – 1. Cltab only controls the very first character read operation performed. Nuexit is a returned value and therefore must be passed as &nuexit.

3. **Dereal.c, putreal.c, and fputreal.c**: The maxout function argument should be the sizeof(pstrin) – 1. Maxout is the declared pstrout (size – 1) and does not include the NULL delimiting character. Maxout must be large enough to receive the decoded pphys or an erc results. Maxphys should only be PHY_REAL or 4 for type float or PHY_RDBL or 8 for type double.

4. **Dvrealyy.c**: When these functions are used as function arguments they must be explicitly declared in the calling program.

5. **General**: Initialize all strings before using them.

E.2.0 Special Uses

We will not present any alternative uses of LDT real.

F.0.0 Testing and Quality Assurance (qareal.c)

F.1.0 Qareal.c Specifications

F.1.1 Qareal.c Design Objectives

The qareal.c test program utilizes enreal.c, evreal.c, getreal.c, fgetreal.c, dereal.c, putreal.c, and fputreal.c as well as dvrealyy.c, utrealyy.c, and supporting functions listed in the linker automatic response file qareal.lnk (Appendix L).

Qareal.c provides runtime control over the resetting of stdlog, the making of stdlog entries, and screen printing upon error detection, as well as the interactive testing of all ensubtype and desubtype values.

Each qaxxxx.c function is not only an excellent example of LDT testing, but also demonstrates techniques for the use of the various standard interfaces portrayed in this book. A close examination of qareal.c reveals a powerful program of 120 statements.

F.1.2 Qareal.c Error Codes

Because qaxxxx.c functions have no reserved ercs of their own, they simply report the ercs detected during processing by the underlying standard interface functions. All ercs detected for LDT real are governed by the following ldt.h values:

```
ERC_BASE        1000
GET_E              1
PUT_E              5
ENREAL_E          51
```

F.2.0 Qareal.c Source Code and Commentary

```
/*
** file   : qareal.c
** desc   : quality assurance test program for LDT real.
** link   : @qareal.lnk,qareal,nul,lcs
*/

#include "ldt.h"

main ()
{
        int dvcharyn(), dvrealen(), dvrealde(), dvrealov();
        int erc;

        static char mtypen[] = ">?<";
        static char mtypde[] = ">??<";
        static char mstrf[] = ">?????????????<";
        static char mstrd[] = ">?????????????????????<";

        static char initen[] = "0";
        static char initde[] = "13";
        static char inity[] = "Y";
        static char initn[] = "N";

        char str[25], destr[25], ynchar;
        int etype, dtype, nuexit, lpe;
        REAL *pphys;
        int smstrf, smstrd;

        smstrf = nondel(mstrf);
        smstrd = nondel(mstrd);

        blanksc(1,1,MAX_ROW,MAX_COL);
        setcrc(1,1);
        putstr("REAL Quality Assurance Program",LR,"",DISP_F);

        /*
        ** Prompt for User Runtime Controls
        */

        uprompt(&lpe);

        if ( (lpe == 10) || (lpe == 11) )
                logwrite(5,"QAREAL",0,"Begin Testing");

        for (;;)
        {

        blanksc(2,1,MAX_ROW,MAX_COL);
        setcrc(1,1);

        movcrc(2,-MAX_COL);
        putstr("Enter ENCODE Subtype: ",LR,"",DISP_F);
        erc = getint(str,sizeof(str)-1,NO,mtypen,LR,initen,MAND_F,YES,
                &nuexit,&etype,PHY_INT,1,MAND_F,lpe,dvrealen);

        if (lderc(erc) == 9) break;

        movcrc(2,-MAX_COL);
        putstr("Enter DECODE Subtype: ",LR,"",DISP_F);

        erc = getint(str,sizeof(str)-1,NO,mtypde,LR,initde,MAND_F,YES,
                &nuexit,&dtype,PHY_INT,1,MAND_F,lpe,dvrealde);

        if (lderc(erc) == 9) continue;
```

```
/*
** FLOAT Testing
*/

        movcrc(2,-MAX_COL);
        putstr("Enter FLOAT String   : ",LR,"",DISP_F);

        erc = getreal(str,sizeof(str)-1,NO,mstrf,LR,"",MAND_F,NO,
                &nuexit,pphys,PHY_REAL,etype,MAND_F,lpe,dvrealov);

        if (lderc(erc) == 9) continue;


        movcrc(2,-MAX_COL);
        putstr("DECODEed FLOAT       : ",LR,"",DISP_F);
        putreal(destr,smstrf,pphys,PHY_REAL,dtype,R_JUST,
                LR,mstrf,MAND_F,lpe);

/*
** DOUBLE Testing
*/

        movcrc(4,-MAX_COL);
        putstr("Enter DOUBLE String : ",LR,"",DISP_F);

        erc = getreal(str,sizeof(str)-1,NO,mstrd,LR,"",MAND_F,NO,
                &nuexit,pphys,PHY_RDBL,etype,MAND_F,lpe,dvrealov);

        if (lderc(erc) == 9) continue;

        movcrc(2,-MAX_COL);
        putstr("DECODEed DOUBLE      : ",LR,"",DISP_F);
        putreal(destr,smstrd,pphys,PHY_RDBL,dtype,R_JUST,
                LR,mstrd,MAND_F,lpe);

        setcrc(24,1);
        putstr("Continue? [Yes/No] or [ESCape]: ",LR,"",DISP_F);

        erc = getchar(str,sizeof(str)-1,NO,mtypen,LR,inity,MAND_F,NO,
                &nuexit,&ynchar,1,11,MAND_F,lpe,dvcharyn);

        if (lderc(erc) == 9) break;
        if (ynchar == 'N') break;
        }

        if ( (lpe == 10) || (lpe == 11) )
                logwrite(6,"QAREAL",0,"End Testing");


        blanksc(1,1,MAX_ROW,MAX_COL);
        exit(0);
}
```

- All dvxxxxyy.c functions to be used as function arguments must be declared explicitly in the calling program.
- All masks are declared with outermost field delimiters so that the field limits can always be known, regardless of the type of field and video attribute chosen for display.

- All init values are declared to make any necessary revision easy.
- In this case destr[25] exceeds the largest nondelimiter size of either mstrf[ ] or mstrd[ ]. The size of a displayed string must not exceed the corresponding number of mask nondelimiter positions if a mask is used for display purposes.
- Variable lpe is calculated by uprompt.c from runtime user responses and effectively becomes the standard function argument logprerr.
- Anywhere in the source code where

  ```
  if (lderc(erc) = = 9)
  ```

  appears, an equivalent statement

  ```
  if ( nuexit = = -1 )
  ```

  can be specified instead.
- Note that because there were many possible choices for both ensubtype and desubtype, qareal.c only allows one ensubtype and desubtype pair to be tested at a time for both float and double.
- Note the use of the function argument dvrealov.c (see C.4.0) for the input of

  Enter FLOAT String:

  and

  Enter DOUBLE String:

  This demonstrates how data validation functions in general can be used to provide range and reasonability checks while also providing the user with the opportunity to override the edit check or perhaps reenter another field value. Data validation functions can become quite sophisticated and complex if necessary and yet fit nicely into our overall structured data entry methodology.

- Note that hitting the Escape key recycles the program unless it is performed at

  Enter ENCODE Subtype:

  or

  Continue? [Yes/No] or [ESCape]:

  where it exits the program. Hitting Ctrl-Break will have no effect in qaxxxx.c functions because Ctrl-Break has been turned off in function _main (see Appendix F).

- Figure 9.1 shows sample output of the qareal.c program.

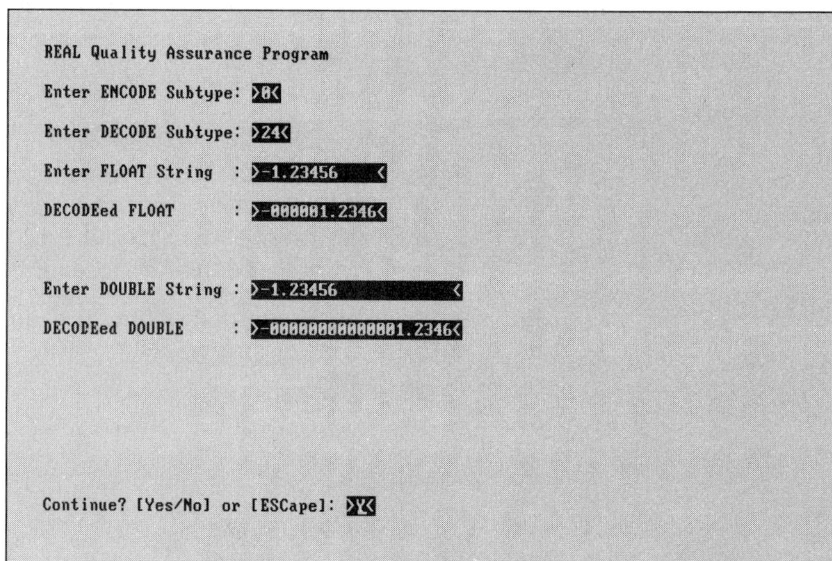

Figure 9.1– *Qareal.c Sample Output*

Telephone Numbers

10

This chapter covers the I/O of telephone fields of input consisting of an area code (e.g., 415) and number (e.g., 848-8233) that are encoded to and decoded from the storage format as specified by the following statement in ldt.h:

```
typedef struct {int tac; long int tnbr;} TELE;
```

LDT tele demonstrates the additional flexibility of our methodology because it accommodates compound data types (structures) as well as the unions and native C data types demonstrated by the other LDTs presented thus far.

The telephone number field is another common data element found in commercial application disk record structures, and is often a key field for interfacing with file management and sorting software packages as described in Chapter 2.

Each interface definition described in Part 1 of this book is implemented for the telephone logical data type (xxxx = tele). The entele.c function accepts all detele.c formats and, with the specification of the ensubtype function argument, controls whether alphabetic telephone exchange identifiers are acceptable as input. The detele.c function generates different telephone number character representations under the format control of a desubtype argument value. Data validation functions validate the allowable encode and decode subtype values discussed above. No utility functions are provided for LDT tele.

Finally, the testing and quality assurance program (qatele.c) allows you to interactively examine and test most of the functions developed in this chapter. Qatele.c also demonstrates how initial values (init) can be used to fill a data entry field only partially (e.g., only the area code portion).

The following chapter index highlights the source code that is provided in this chapter.

Standard Interface Source Code

A.2.0	Entele.c:	Encode LDT tele
A.3.0	Evtele.c:	Encode and validate LDT tele
A.4.0	Gettele.c/ Fgettele.c:	Combined getstr.c and evtele.c
B.2.0	Detele.c:	Decode LDT tele
B.3.0	Puttele.c/ Fputtele.c:	Combined detele.c and putstr.c

Data Validation (dvteleyy.c) Functions

C.2.0	Dvtelede.c:	Checks for allowable desubtypes
C.3.0	Dvteleen.c:	Checks for allowable ensubtypes

Utility (utteleyy.c) Functions

None

Quality Assurance Programs

F.2.0	Qatele.c:	Standard quality assurance test program

A.0.0 Encode Function Development (entele.c)

A.1.0 Entele.c Specifications

A.1.1 Design Objectives

The telephone logical data type accommodates a standard United States area code and telephone number while demonstrating the use of the structure declaration of the C programming language for the pphys argument of a logical data type encode function.

Traditional alphanumeric telephone exchange numbers (e.g., WE6-1212) are acceptable as input, and several related edit checks are included to assure validity of both the area code and telephone number. Given the evolving sophistication in telecommunications, you may need to add components to the construction of the tele LDT to reflect your particular requirements such as:

- International calls: The standard international access code is 011, which must be followed by up to a three-digit country code, up to a three-digit city code, and finally the local telephone number. Clearly, to accommodate international calling, you would have to modify our tele structure declaration.
- Special 10-XXX long distance carrier numbers: With the breakup of the national telephone company, a customer can choose a long distance service from several long distance carriers if equal access service is supported in that area. A customer can select a particular long distance carrier by first dialing 10-XXX followed by the area code and number. Some standardized 10-XXX access codes are listed below:

10-288	AT&T
10-222	MCI
10-777	SPRINT
10-444	ALLNET
10-333	US TEL

Again, modification of the TELE structure outlined in this book will have to be made to accommodate this feature if your application requires it.

- Extensions: It is not uncommon to include a provision for a telephone extension suffix in addition to the area code and number. It is better to make the extension an alphanumeric sequence rather than another numeric sequence.

- Notation: An alphanumeric field can also serve as a general notation to indicate anything from the type of telephone number (e.g., home, business, auto, etc.) to the best time to reach indicator (e.g., am, pm, Sat, Sun, etc.).

Clearly, the structure typedef construction for use with telephone numbers can handle any and all of the above requirements with your customization of the tele LDT. (Refer to Chapter 12 for information about customizing LDTs.)

A.1.2 ***Field Size (maxin)***

The maximum field size for tele variables has been set at 13 character positions (MAX_TELE = 13) to allow for the largest possible input or output display (e.g., (415)848-8233).

A.1.3 ***Physical Format (maxphys)***

The area code portion (tac) of the TELE typedef utilizes int because it must accommodate a range of unique values up to 919. The number portion (tnbr) uses long int. It is always converted to numeric and consists of unique values up to 9999999. Characters are not used because they would need an excessive storage requirement. The combined storage of the area code and number in a double would make it difficult to sort the area code and number separately or to index the area code directly.

The maxphys argument must be set equal to PHY_TELE or 6, or an erc results when using entele.c. The PHY_TELE value is the sum of the size of the int = 2 and long int = 4 portions of the tele structure.

A.1.4 Character Set Restrictions

By design of the getstr.c/fgetstr.c function, the entele.c function only "sees" ASCII 0x20 through 0x7E.

For tele number fields of input this complete range of input is accepted; however, entele.c processing imposes additional edit checks (see sections A.1.6 and A.1.7 below).

A.1.5 Subtype Definition (ensubtype)

0	Accepts alpha telephone exchange if so entered.
1	Accepts only numeric telephone numbers.

A.1.6 Other Format Controls

Any of the detele.c display formats are acceptable as input to the entele.c function such as:

0	(xxx)xxx-xxxx
1	xxx/xxx-xxxx
2	xxx-xxx-xxxx
3	xxxxxxxxxx

No embedded blank characters are allowed. Extraneous leading or trailing blank characters are not permitted; however, the area code, if unknown, may be left blank by the user and is equated to zero. The number portion is also handled in this manner. Zeroed portions of a telephone number field are decoded by detele.c to blanks for consistency.

A.1.7 Editing

All tele LDT components are edited as follows to assure proper area code and telephone number construction:

ABC (area code)	A cannot be 0 or 1. B must be 0 or 1.
DEF-GHIJ (number)	D cannot be 0 or 1. E cannot be 0 or 1. D or E cannot be letters Q or Z.

Other editing is provided to ensure that the syntax of the area code and telephone number conform to the detele.c formats allowed:

- If the (xxx)xxx-xxxx format is used, only one matched pair of parentheses surrounding three digits is allowed.
- If the xxx/xxx-xxxx format is used, only one slash character is permitted.
- Dashes are checked for appropriate location and stripped; otherwise an erc is generated.
- If alphabetic characters are included, they can be either upper- or lowercase, but can only be in the first two positions of the telephone number.
- All remaining characters must be numeric, and must account for ten digits; hence missing components (blank) are converted to zeros.

A.1.8 ***Default Values***

Upon initial entry to the entele.c function, the tele variable components tac and tnbr are initialized to zero.

A.1.9 ***Error Codes***

Based upon the ERC_BASE (1000) and ENTELE_E (61) values defined in ldt.h, the following ercs are possible:

1061	Encode Data Entry Error by User
1062	Bad Encode Function Argument
1063	Encode Mandatory Field Not Satisfied

A.2.0 ***Entele.c Source Code and Commentary***

```
/* file    : entele.c
** function: int entele ( pstrin, maxin, pphys, maxphys,
**         :                ensubtype, mflag )
** desc    : encode a logical data type tele.
**         : maxphys = 6 == struct { int; long int };
** test pgm: qatele.c
*/
```

```
#include "ctype.h"
#include "ldt.h"

        int entele (pstrin, maxin, pphys, maxphys, ensubtype, mflag)

        char *pstrin;
        TELE *pphys;
        int maxin, maxphys, ensubtype, mflag;
        {

        int erc, eerc, i, j, slgth, loc, ftele, digit;
        long int vtnbr, wgt;
        char str[15], mstr[15];

        /*
        ** Table of valid ENCODE subtypes:
        **     0 = accept "alpha" telephone number
        **     1 = do NOT accept "alpha" telephone number
        */

        /*
        ** Validate the function arguments:
        */

        erc = ERC_BASE + ENTELE_E + 1;

        /*
        ** validate "maxphys"
        */

        if (maxphys != PHY_TELE) return(erc);

        if (( maxin < 1 ) || ( maxin > MAX_TELE)) return (erc);

        /*
        ** validate "ensubtype" and set "default" values
        */

        eerc = dvteleen(&ensubtype,PHY_INT);
        if (eerc != ERC_OK) return(eerc);

        (*pphys).tac = 0;
        (*pphys).tnbr = (long)0;

        /*
        ** validate "mflag" for TRUE/FALSE
        */

        if (( mflag < NO ) || ( mflag > YES ))
                return (erc);

        /*
        ** Validate mandatory field requirement
        ** OK to check before any other pre-processing
        */

        slgth = strlen( pstrin );
        if (( mflag ) && ( slgth < 1 ))
                return(erc + 1);

        erc = erc - 1;

        /*
        ** encode processing
        */

        strcpy(str, pstrin);

        if(slgth < 10) return(erc);
```

```
/*
** check for "(xxx)" TELE format; matched pair only!
** containing only 3-digits
*/

ftele = FALSE;

if (str[0] == C_LPAR)
{
delchr(str,1);
slgth = strlen(str);
if (slgth < 10) return(erc);

loc = poschr(str,C_RPAR,RL);
if (loc != 4) return(erc);
else
{
ftele = TRUE;
delchr(str,loc);
slgth = strlen(str);
if (slgth < 10) return(erc);
}
}

/*
** check for single "/" "TELE" format
*/

loc = poschr(str,C_SLASH,LR);
if ( (ftele == FALSE) && (loc != 0) )
{
ftele = TRUE;
if (loc != 4) return(erc);
delchr(str,loc);
slgth = strlen(str);
if (slgth < 10) return(erc);
}

/*
** check for single "-" "TELE" format
*/

loc = poschr(str,C_DASH,LR);
if ( (ftele == FALSE) && (loc != 0) )
{
ftele = TRUE;
if (loc != 4) return(erc);
delchr(str,loc);
slgth = strlen(str);
if (slgth < 10) return(erc);
}

/*
** find/delete last  AC '-' NBR
*/

loc = poschr(str,C_DASH,RL);
if (loc != 0)
{
if (loc != 7) return(erc);
delchr(str,loc);
slgth = strlen(str);
if (slgth < 10) return(erc);
}
```

```
/*
** final Mandatory field check
*/

strcpy(mstr,str);
utcharsb(3,mstr,C_BLANK);
slgth = strlen(mstr);
if((mflag) && (slgth < 1)) return(erc+2);
slgth = strlen(str);

/*
** get Area Code
*/

ftele = TRUE;
if ( (str[0] == C_BLANK) && (str[1] == C_BLANK) &&

   (str[2] == C_BLANK) )
{
ftele = FALSE;
str[0] = C_ZERO;
str[1] = C_ZERO;
str[2] = C_ZERO;
}

for ( i=0; i < 3; i++ )
{
if ( isdigit(str[i]) == 0 ) return(erc);
}

if (ftele == TRUE)
{
if ((str[0] == C_ZERO) || (str[0] == C_ONE) ) return(erc);
if ((str[1] != C_ZERO) && (str[1] != C_ONE) ) return(erc);
}

(*pphys).tac = ((str[0] - C_ZERO) * 100) +
               ((str[1] - C_ZERO) * 10) +
                (str[2]- C_ZERO);

delchr(str,1);
delchr(str,1);
delchr(str,1);

slgth = strlen(str);
if(slgth < 7) return(erc);

ftele = FALSE;
for (i=0;i<7;i++)
{
if (str[i] != C_BLANK)
{
ftele = TRUE;
break;
}
}

if (ftele == FALSE)
{
for (i=0;i<7;i++)
{
str[i] = C_ZERO;
}
}
```

```
utcharsb(2,str,C_BLANK);
slgth = strlen(str);
if( slgth < 7) return(erc);

if (ensubtype == 0)
{
if (isalpha(str[0]) != 0)
{
if (isalpha(str[1]) == 0) return(erc);

for (j=0; j<2; j++)
{

str[j] = toupper(str[j]);

switch (str[j])
{
        case 'A':
        case 'B':
        case 'C': str[j] = '2';
                  break;
        case 'D':
        case 'E':
        case 'F': str[j] = '3';
                  break;
        case 'G':
        case 'H':
        case 'I': str[j] = '4';
                  break;
        case 'J':
        case 'K':
        case 'L': str[j] = '5';
                  break;
        case 'M':
        case 'N':
        case 'O': str[j] = '6';
                  break;
        case 'P':
        case 'R':
        case 'S': str[j] = '7';
                  break;
        case 'T':
        case 'U':
        case 'V': str[j] = '8';
                  break;
        case 'W':
        case 'X':
        case 'Y': str[j] = '9';
                  break;

        default: return(erc);

}
}
}
}


if (ftele == TRUE)

{
if ((str[0] == C_ZERO) || (str[0] == C_ONE)) return(erc);
if ((str[1] == C_ZERO) || (str[1] == C_ONE)) return(erc);
}


wgt = 1;
vtnbr = 0;
```

```
for ( i= (slgth - 1); i >=0; i--)
{
if (isdigit(str[i]) == 0) return(erc);
digit = str[i] - C_ZERO;
vtnbr = vtnbr + wgt * (long)digit;
wgt = wgt * (long)10;
}

(*pphys).tnbr = vtnbr;

return (ERC_OK);

}
```

- Note that pphys is declared to be of type TELE. Uppercase TELE is a typedef from ldt.h. TELE is the following structure definition:

  struct {int tac; long int tnbr;} TELE;

  Maxphys is always equal to PHY_TELE = 6, the sum of the component sizes of int and long int. Any other maxphys value generates an erc.
  The area code component of the tele LDT is accessed as follows:

  (*pphys).tac;

  and the number portion is accessed in a similar fashion:

  (*pphys).tnbr;

- For the tele LDT, if pstrin contains all blank characters, it will not satisfy the mandatory mflag field requirement.
- The macros isalpha and toupper are provided by the header file ctype.h (see Appendix G).

A.3.0 Evtele.c Source Code and Commentary

The source code and commentary for function evtele.c parallels evchar.c (Chapter 5, A.3.0). To create function evtele.c, simply copy file evchar.c and edit it as follows:

- Change all occurrences of char to tele and CHAR to TELE except for the statement

  char *pstrin;

- Update the commented function description.

The complete source code is available on disk.

A.4.0 Advanced Encode Field Processing

A.4.1 Gettele.c and Fgettele.c Error Codes

See Chapter 5, A.4.1.

A.4.2 Gettele.c and Fgettele.c Source Code and Commentary

The source code and commentary for function gettele.c parallels getchar.c (Chapter 5, A.4.0). To create function gettele.c, copy file getchar.c and edit it as follows:

- Change all occurrences of char to tele and CHAR to TELE except for the statement

```
char *string, *mask, *init;
```

The source code and commentary for function fgettele.c also parallels fgetchar.c (Chapter 5, A.4.0). To create function fgettele.c, copy file fgetchar.c and edit it as follows:

- Change all occurrences of char to tele and CHAR to TELE except for the statements

```
char *string, *mask, *init;
utcharcb(1,string,1);
```

The complete source code is available on disk.

A.4.3 Associated Mask Utilization Techniques

Based upon the function argument gmaskflg, mask delimiter characters are either included (YES) or excluded (NO) from the acquired input string. This facilitates the introduction or elimination of character separators that allow the user to enter lengthy telephone numbers without having to key in the separators, for example:

Standard USA telephone number: "???-???-????"

As with the other encode functions, it is important to remember that entele.c can be used independently of the getstr.c/fgetstr.c and gettele.c/fgettele.c functions so that some functional redundancy is required to expand the independent use of the enxxxx.c interface definitions developed in this book.

B.0.0 **Decode Function Development (detele.c)**

B.1.0 **Detele.c Specifications**

B.1.1 **Design Objectives**

This function provides a facility for the display of a TELE variable in a variety of commonly needed commercial phone number display formats.

B.1.2 **Subtype Definition (desubtype)**

0	(xxx)xxx-xxxx
1	xxx/xxx-xxxx
2	xxx-xxx-xxxx
3	xxxxxxxxxx

B.1.3 **Default Values**

No default is assumed for detele.c. The output character string pstrout is simply set to a NULL string before processing begins.

B.1.4 **Error Codes**

Based upon the ERC_BASE (1000) and ENTELE_E (61) values defined in the ldt.h header file, the following erc is possible:

1066	Bad Decode Function Argument

B.2.0 Detele.c Source Code and Commentary

```
/* file    : detele.c
** function: int detele ( pstrout, maxout, pphys, maxphys,
**         :                desubtype, jflag )
** desc    : decode a logical data type tele
** test pgm: qatele.c
*/

#include "ctype.h"
#include "ldt.h"

        int detele (pstrout, maxout, pphys, maxphys, desubtype, jflag)

        char *pstrout;
        TELE *pphys;
        int maxout, maxphys, desubtype, jflag;
        {

        int erc, derc, i, slgth, rem, fvalue;
        int vtac;
        long int vtnbr, value;
        char digit, str[15];

        /*
        ** Table of valid DECODE subtypes:
        **    0 = format: (xxx)xxx-xxxx
        **    1 = format: xxx/xxx-xxxx
        **    2 = format: xxx-xxx-xxxx
        **    3 = format: xxxxxxxxxx
        */

        /*
        ** Validate the function arguments:
        */

        erc = ERC_BASE + ENTELE_E + 5;

        /*
        ** validate "maxphys"
        */

        if (maxphys != PHY_TELE) return(erc);

        /*
        ** validate "maxout"
        */

        if (( maxout < 1 ) || ( maxout > MAX_TELE)) return (erc);

        /*
        ** validate "desubtype" and set "default" values
        */

        utcharcb(1,pstrout,1);
        utcharcb(1,str,1);

        derc = dvtelede(&desubtype,PHY_INT);
        if (derc != ERC_OK) return(derc);

        /*
        ** validate "jflag" for (NO_JUST, L_JUST, C_JUST, R_JUST)
        */

        if (( jflag < NO_JUST) || ( jflag > R_JUST ))
            return (erc);
```

```
/*
** desubtype processing
*/

vtac = (*pphys).tac;
vtnbr = (*pphys).tnbr;

/*
** put "tnbr" then "tac"
*/

value = vtnbr;
fvalue = TRUE;
if (value == (long)0) fvalue = FALSE;

for (i = 0; i < 7; i++)
{
rem = value % (long)10;
digit = rem + C_ZERO;

if (fvalue == FALSE) digit = C_BLANK;
inschr(str,999,digit,1);

if ((i == 3) && (desubtype != 3))
inschr(str,999,C_DASH,1);

value = value / (long)10;
}

if (desubtype == 0) inschr(str,999,C_RPAR,1);
if (desubtype == 1) inschr(str,999,C_SLASH,1);
if (desubtype == 2) inschr(str,999,C_DASH,1);

value = vtac;
fvalue = TRUE;
if (value == (long)0) fvalue = FALSE;

for (i=0; i < 3; i++)
{

rem = value % (long)10;
digit = rem + C_ZERO;

if (fvalue == FALSE) digit = C_BLANK;
inschr(str,999,digit,1);

value  = value / (long)10;
}

if (desubtype == 0) inschr(str,999,C_LPAR,1);

/*
** check if "pstrout" big enough?
*/

utcharcb(3,str,maxout+1);
slgth = strlen(str);
if (slgth > maxout) return(erc);
else strcpy(pstrout,str);

/*
** Justify output string
*/

utcharjs(jflag, pstrout);

return (ERC_OK);

}
```

- Note the extensive use of function inschr.c to build str and hence pstrout from left to right based upon the effective desubtype value. The inschr.c function argument value, 999, was arbitrarily chosen as a large value to override the possibility that a character insertion attempt would be rejected.
- String justification occurs within the total string field width maxout because of the function call to

```
utcharcb (3,str,maxout+1)
```

- An erc is generated if the string length of pphys is greater than the maxout string length of pstrout.

B.3.0 Advanced Decode Field Processing

B.3.1 Puttele.c and Fputtele.c Error Codes

See Chapter 5, B.3.1.

B.3.2 Puttele.c and Fputtele.c Source Code and Commentary

The source code and commentary for function puttele.c and fputtele.c parallels putchar.c and fputchar.c (Chapter 5, B.3.0). To create either of these functions, copy its parallel function and edit it as follows:

- Change all occurrences of char to tele and CHAR to TELE except for the statement

```
char *pstrout, *mask;
```

The complete source code is available on disk.

B.3.3 Associated Mask Utilization Techniques

- In an analogous manner, putstr.c/fputstr.c and puttele.c/fputtele.c can be used to output a decoded string to a mask field with or without delimiters. Remember that detele.c can be utilized independently of the putstr.c/fputstr.c and puttele.c/fputtele.c functions so that some functional redundancy is required to expand the independent use of the dexxxx.c interface definitions.

- The getmstr.c function allows use of the video display as a scratch pad (see Chapter 4) and functionally extends the stand-alone utility of each dexxxx.c. Since the power of masks is only pertinent to video display, getmstr.c retrieves the putxxxx.c string from the video display with mask formatting to enhance the variety of decoded formats that can be created when using dexxxx.c functions in a stand-alone manner.

C.0.0 Data Validation Function Development (dvteleyy.c)

C.1.0 Dvteleyy.c Standard Error Codes

Based upon the ERC_BASE (1000) and ENTELE_E (61) values defined in the ldt.h header file, all dvteleyy.c functions report the following ercs:

1064	Data Validation Error
1065	Bad Data Validation Function Argument

C.2.0 Dvtelede.c Function Specification

C.2.1 Dvtelede.c Design Objectives

This function validates that an acceptable desubtype argument value has been specified for the tele LDT.

C.2.2 Dvtelede.c Source Code and Commentary

```
/* file    : dvtelede.c
** function: int dvtelede ( pphys, maxphys )
** desc    : data validation for tele; valid decode subtype
** test pgm: qatele.c
*/

#include "ldt.h"

        int dvtelede ( pphys, maxphys )

        INT *pphys;
        int maxphys;
        {
        int erc, val;

        erc = ERC_BASE + ENINT_E + 3;

        if (maxphys != PHY_INT) return(erc+1);

        val = (*pphys).i2;

        if (( val < 0 ) || ( val > 3)) return (erc);

        else return(ERC_OK);

        }
```

- Note the use of INT *pphys. The uppercase INT is a typedef from the ldt.h header file which is

  typedef union {int i2; long int i4;} INT;

  The use of the INT typedef allows either int or long int arguments to be passed to dvtelede.c. By design, only int types are acceptable to detelede.c.

- Note how desubtype is retrieved:

  val = (*pphys).i2;

C.3.0 Dvteleen.c Function Specification

C.3.1 Dvteleen.c Design Objectives

This function simply validates that an acceptable ensubtype argument value has been specified for the tele LDT.

C.3.2 Dvteleen.c Source Code and Commentary

```
/* file    : dvteleen.c
** function: int dvteleen ( pphys, maxphys )
** desc    : data validation for tele; valid encode subtype
** test pgm: qatele.c
*/

#include "ldt.h"

        int dvteleen ( pphys, maxphys )

        INT *pphys;
        int maxphys;
        {
        int erc, val;

        erc = ERC_BASE + ENINT_E + 3;

        if (maxphys != PHY_INT) return(erc+1);

        val = (*pphys).i2;

        if (( val < 0 ) || ( val > 1)) return (erc);

        else return(ERC_OK);

        }
```

- For commentary, see C.2.2.

D.0.0 Utility Function Development (utteleyy.c)

D.1.0 Utteleyy.c Standard Error Codes

Based upon the ERC_BASE (1000) and ENTELE_E (61) values defined in the ldt.h header file, all utteleyy.c functions report the following erc:

1067	Utility Function Error

D.2.0 Uttele Function Specifications

We will not present any utility functions for tele.

E.0.0 **LDT Tele Application Tips and Reminders**

E.1.0 **Helpful Notes**

The standard interface function definitions for the tele logical data type are less complicated than for LDT char. This is because the pphys argument is always passed as an "address of" (&pphys) because pphys is of type TELE (typedef synonymous with "struct {int tac; long int tnbr;}").

Let's highlight some helpful reminders about the functions included in this chapter.

1. **Entele.c and Evtele.c:** The maxin function argument should be the sizeof(pstrin) − 1. Maxin is the declared pstrin (size − 1) and does not include the NULL delimiting character. Maxphys should always be PHY_TELE.
2. **Gettele.c and Fgettele.c:** The maxstr function argument should be the sizeof(string) − 1. Cltab only controls the very first character read operation performed. Nuexit is a returned value and therefore must be passed as &nuexit.
3. **Detele.c, Puttele.c, and Fputtele.c:** The maxout function argument should be the sizeof(pstrin) − 1. Maxout is the declared pstrout (size − 1) and does not include the NULL delimiting character. Maxout must be large enough to receive the decoded pphys or an erc will result. Maxphys should always be PHY_TELE.
4. **Dvteleyy.c:** When these functions are used as function arguments they must be declared explicitly in the calling program.
5. **General:** Initialize all strings before using them.

E.2.0 **Special Uses**

We will not present any alternative uses of LDT tele.

F.0.0 Testing and Quality Assurance (qatele.c)

F.1.0 Qatele.c Specification

F.1.1 Qatele.c Design Objectives

Like all other qaxxxx.c functions, qatele.c utilizes entele.c, evtele.c, gettele.c, fgettele.c, detele.c, puttele.c, and fputtele.c as well as dvteleyy.c, utteleyy.c, and supporting functions listed in the linker automatic response file qatele.lnk (Appendix L).

Qatele.c provides runtime control over the resetting of stdlog, making of stdlog entries, and screen printing upon error detection, as well as the interactive testing of all entele.c and detele.c subtypes.

Each qaxxxx.c function is not only an excellent example of LDT testing, but also demonstrates techniques for the use of the various standard interfaces. A close examination of qatele.c reveals a powerful program of only 100 statements.

F.1.2 Qatele.c Error Codes

Qaxxxx.c functions do not have any reserved ercs of their own; they simply report the ercs detected during processing by the underlying standard interface functions.

All ercs detected for LDT tele, however, are governed by the following ldt.h header file values:

ERC_BASE	1000
GET_E	1
PUT_E	5
ENTELE_E	61

F.2.0 Qatele.c Source Code and Commentary

```
/*
** file    : qatele.c
** desc    : quality assurance test program for LDT tele
** link    : @qatele.lnk,qatele,nul,lcs
*/
```

```
#include "ldt.h"

main ()
{
        int dvcharyn(), dvteleen(), dvdummy();
        int erc;

        static char mtype[] = ">?<";
        static char mstrin[] = ">(???)???-????<";
        static char mstr[] = ">?????????????<";

        static char initi[] = "0";
        static char initac[] = DEF_AC;
        static char inity[] = "Y";
        static char initn[] = "N";

        char str[15], destr[15], ynchar;
        int etype, nuexit, lpe;
        TELE *pphys;
        int smstr;

        smstr = nondel(mstr);

        blanksc(1,1,MAX_ROW,MAX_COL);
        setcrc(1,1);
        putstr("TELEphone Quality Assurance Program",LR,"",DISP_F);

        /*
        ** Prompt for User Runtime Controls
        */

        uprompt(&lpe);

        if ( (lpe == 10) || (lpe == 11) )
                logwrite(5,"QATELE",0,"Begin Testing");

        for (;;)
        {

        blanksc(2,1,MAX_ROW,MAX_COL);
        setcrc(1,1);

        movcrc(2,-MAX_COL);
        putstr("Enter ENCODE Subtype    : ",LR,"",DISP_F);

        erc = getint(str,sizeof(str)-1,NO,mtype,LR,initi,MAND_F,YES,
                     &nuexit,&etype,PHY_INT,1,MAND_F,lpe,dvteleen);

        if (lderc(erc) == 9) break;

        movcrc(2,-MAX_COL);
        putstr("Enter Telephone String : ",LR,"",DISP_F);

        erc = gettele(str,sizeof(str)-1,NO,mstrin,LR,initac,MAND_F,NO,
                      &nuexit,pphys,PHY_TELE,etype,MAND_F,lpe,dvdummy);

        if (lderc(erc) == 9) continue;

        movcrc(2,-MAX_COL);
        putstr("DECODEed Subtype [0]    : ",LR,"",DISP_F);
        puttele(destr,smstr,pphys,PHY_TELE,0,NO_JUST,
                LR,mstr,MAND_F,lpe);

        movcrc(2,-MAX_COL);
        putstr("DECODEed Subtype [1]    : ",LR,"",DISP_F);
        puttele(destr,smstr,pphys,PHY_TELE,1,NO_JUST,
                LR,mstr,MAND_F,lpe);
```

```
        movcrc(2,-MAX_COL);
        putstr("DECODEed Subtype [2]    : ",LR,"",DISP_F);
        puttele(destr,smstr,pphys,PHY_TELE,2,NO_JUST,
                LR,mstr,MAND_F,lpe);

        movcrc(2,-MAX_COL);
        putstr("DECODEed Subtype [3]    : ",LR,"",DISP_F);
        puttele(destr,smstr,pphys,PHY_TELE,3,NO_JUST,
                LR,mstr,MAND_F,lpe);

        setcrc(24,1);
        putstr("Continue? [Yes/No] or [ESCape]: ",LR,"",DISP_F);

        erc = getchar(str,sizeof(str)-1,NO,mtype,LR,inity,MAND_F,NO,
                    &nuexit,&ynchar,1,11,MAND_F,lpe,dvcharyn);

        if (lderc(erc) == 9) break;
        if (ynchar == 'N') break;

        }

        if ( (lpe == 10) || (lpe == 11) )
                logwrite(6,"QATELE",0,"End Testing");

        blanksc(1,1,MAX_ROW,MAX_COL);
        exit(0);
}
```

- All dvxxxxyy.c functions used as function arguments must be declared explicitly in the calling program.
- All masks are declared with outermost field delimiters so that the field limits are always known, regardless of the type of field and video attributes chosen for display.
- All init values are declared to make any necessary revision easy. Note the assignment of

  initac[ ] = DEF_AC

  Header file ldt.h contains the constant initial value 215. The DEF_AC value can be either altered or simply equated to a NULL string.
- In this case destr[15] exceeds the nondelimiter size of mask (mstr[ ]). The size of a displayed string must not exceed the corresponding number of mask nondelimiter positions, if a mask is used for display purposes.
- Note how TELE *pphys is defined as a pointer to the structure TELE named pphys. By this definition, function argument use of pphys does not require that the "address of" &pphys notation be used, rather only pphys.

- Variable lpe is calculated by uprompt.c from runtime user responses and effectively becomes the standard function argument logprerr.
- Anywhere in the source code where

  ```
  if (lderc(erc) == 9)
  ```

  appears, an equivalent statement

  ```
  if (nuexit == -1)
  ```

  can be specified instead.
- Note that because there were only four possible choices for desubtype, qatele.c simply generates decode 0,1,2, and 3 for either ensubtype value chosen.
- Note that hitting the Escape key recycles the program unless it is performed at

  Enter ENCODE Subtype:

  or

  Continue? [Yes/No] or [ESCape]:

  where it exits the program. Hitting Ctrl-Break has no effect in qaxxxx.c programs because Ctrl-Break has been turned off in function _main (see Appendix F).
- Note the sample output of the qatele.c program shown in Figure 10.1.

```
TELEphone Quality Assurance Program

Enter ENCODE Subtype    : >0<

Enter Telephone String : >(215)WE6-1212<

DECODEed Subtype [0]    : >(215)936-1212<

DECODEed Subtype [1]    : >215/936-1212 <

DECODEed Subtype [2]    : >215-936-1212 <

DECODEed Subtype [3]    : >2159361212   <




Continue? [Yes/No] or [ESCape]: >Y<
```

***Figure** 10.1–* *Qatele.c sample output*

Times

11

This chapter covers the I/O of time fields that are encoded to and decoded from a storage format as specified by the following statement in ldt.h:

```
typedef int TIME;
```

The integer value for a time field is the number of minutes from 12:00 midnight (e.g., 12:30am = 30; 12:30pm = 750; 11:30pm = 1410). To accommodate both am/pm time and military time formats, allowable time values range from 0 through 1440 (24:00 hours military). Many commercial applications require time to be recorded (with minutes accuracy) and math operations to be performed using time fields of input. Time fields are found in disk record structures, and are often used as key fields when interfacing with file management and sorting software packages as described in Chapter 2.

Each interface definition described in Part 1 of this book is implemented for the time logical data type (xxxx = time). The entime.c function accepts all detime.c formats and, with the specification of the ensubtype function argument, controls which time format is anticipated, either am/pm or military. The detime.c function similarly generates time character representations for either format under the control of the desubtype argument value. Data validation functions validate the allowable encode and decode subtype values discussed above.

The included uttimesi.c function acquires the system time (systime) in standard time LDT format.

Finally, a testing and quality assurance program (qatime.c) allows you to interactively examine and test most of the functions developed in this chapter.

The following chapter index highlights the source code that is provided.

Standard Interface Source Code

A.2.0	Entime.c:	Encode LDT time
A.3.0	Evtime.c:	Encode and validate LDT time
A.4.0	Gettime.c/ Fgettime.c:	Combined getstr.c and evtime.c
B.2.0	Detime.c:	Decode LDT time
B.3.0	Puttime.c/ Fputtime.c:	Combined detime.c and putstr.c

Data Validation (dvtimeyy.c) Functions

C.2.0	Dvtimede.c:	Checks for allowable desubtypes.
C.3.0	Dvtimeen.c:	Checks for allowable ensubtypes.

Utility (uttimeyy.c) Functions

D.2.0	Uttimesi.c:	Encode System Time (systime)

Quality Assurance Programs

F.2.0	Qatime.c:	Standard quality assurance test program

A.0.0 Encode Function Development (entime.c)

A.1.0 Entime.c Specifications

A.1.1 Design Objectives

The time logical data type provides a compact means of storing time fields to an accuracy of minutes for common commercial use in scheduling applications using standard am/pm format or military format. The proposed time int format, in contrast to other possible floating point or alphanumeric formats, also facilitates mathematical operations with time variables in a normal manner.

A.1.2 Field Size (maxin)

The maximum field size for time variables has been set at 6 character positions (MAX_TIME = 6) to allow for the largest possible input or output display (e.g., 12:00A).

A.1.3 Physical Format (maxphys)

Since we wanted to store time in minutes (24 hours × 60 minutes/hr = 1440 minutes), we used the int data type because it can most compactly accommodate up to 32767 while supporting any necessary mathematical operations.

The maxphys argument must be set to PHY_TIME or 2, which equals the byte size of an int, or an erc would result.

A.1.4 Character Set Restrictions

By design of the getstr.c/fgetstr.c function, the entime function only "sees" ASCII 0x20 through 0x7E. For time fields of input, this complete range of input is acceptable; however, entime.c processing imposes additional edit checks. (See A.1.6 and A.1.7 below.)

A.1.5 Subtype Definition (ensubtype)

0	Standard am/pm time (hh:mm) (A/P/N/M)
1	Military time (hh:mm)

where

hh = hours
mm = minutes
A = am
P = pm
N = noon
M = midnight

A.1.6 Other Format Controls

The enforced format varies by ensubtype. Both formats conform to the following rules:

1. One colon separator must be present. No other separator is acceptable.
2. No embedded blanks are allowed.
3. The hour (hh) portion can consist of either one or two digits.
4. The minute (mm) portion must consist of two digits.

For standard am/pm time format, the following additional rule applies:

5. Only alpha suffixes (A = am, P = pm, N = noon, and M = midnight) are acceptable. Either upper- or lowercase characters are acceptable.

A.1.7 Editing

The selected ensubtype value determines which type of editing is used. The standard am/pm time format is edited as follows:

1 <= hh <= 12
0 <= mm <= 59

The military time format is edited as follows:

0 <= hh <= 23
0 <= mm <= 59

(24:00 is an acceptable alternative for 0:00.)

A.1.8 ***Default Values***

Upon initial entry to the entime.c function, the time variable is initialized to zero.

A.1.9 ***Error Codes***

Based upon the ERC_BASE (1000) and ENTIME_E (71) values defined in the ldt.h header file, the following ercs are possible:

1071	Encode Data Entry Error By User
1072	Bad Encode Function Argument
1073	Encode Mandatory Field Not Satisfied

A.2.0 ***Entime.c Source Code and Commentary***

```
/* file    : entime.c
** function: int entime ( pstrin, maxin, pphys, maxphys,
**         :                ensubtype, mflag )
** desc    : encode a logical data type time.
** test pgm: qatime.c
*/

#include "ctype.h"
#include "ldt.h"

        int entime (pstrin, maxin, pphys, maxphys, ensubtype, mflag)

        char *pstrin;
        TIME *pphys;
        int maxin, maxphys, ensubtype, mflag;
        {

        int erc, eerc, i, slgth, floc, lloc, hr, mn, addhr, twelve;
        char str[10], hh[10], mm[10], ampm;

        /*
        ** Table of valid ENCODE subtypes:
        **     0 = Standard AM/PM time format
        **     1 = Military time format
        */
```

```
/*
** Validate the function arguments:
*/

erc = ERC_BASE + ENTIME_E + 1;

/*
** validate "maxin" & "maxphys"
*/

if (( maxin < 1 ) || ( maxin > MAX_TIME)) return (erc);

if (maxphys != PHY_TIME) return(erc);

/*
** validate "ensubtype" and set "default" values
*/

eerc = dvtimeen(&ensubtype,PHY_INT);
if (eerc != ERC_OK) return(eerc);

*pphys = 0;

/*
** validate "mflag" for YES/NO
*/

if (( mflag < NO ) || ( mflag > YES ))
        return (erc);

/*
** Validate mandatory field requirement
** OK to check before any other pre-processing
*/

slgth = strlen( pstrin );
if (( mflag ) && ( slgth < 1 ))
        return(erc + 1);

erc = erc - 1;

/*
** encode processing
*/

strcpy(str, pstrin);

/*
** strip leading/trailing blanks
*/

utcharsb(3,str,C_BLANK);
slgth = strlen(str);
if( (mflag ) && (slgth < 1)) return(erc+2);

/*
** force any alpha to upper case
*/

for (i=0; i < slgth; i++)
{
*(str+i) = toupper(*(str+i));
}

/*
** locate "colon" separator; check that only 1 exists;
** remove ':' from "str"
*/
```

```
floc = poschr(str,C_COLON,LR);
if (floc == 0) return(erc);

lloc = poschr(str,C_COLON,RL);
if (floc != lloc) return(erc);

delchr(str,floc);

/*
** if AM/PM type save/remove last char
** check if [A,P,N,M] only
*/

slgth = strlen(str);
if (slgth < 1) return(erc);

if ( ensubtype == 0 )
{
ampm = *(str+slgth-1);
delchr(str,slgth);
slgth = strlen(str);
if (slgth < 1) return(erc);
}
else ampm = C_BLANK;

switch (ampm)
{
        case C_A:
        case C_P:
        case C_M:
        case C_N:
        case C_BLANK: break;
        default : return(erc);
}
/*
** check for all digits (no embedded blanks)
*/

for (i=0; i < slgth; i++)
{
if ( isdigit(*(str+i)) == 0 ) return(erc);
}

/*
** strip "hh" and "mm" from digit string
*/
strcpy(hh,str);
hh[floc-1] = C_NUL;

slgth = strlen(hh);
if ( (slgth < 1) || (slgth > 2) ) return(erc);

hr = hh[0] - C_ZERO;
if (slgth == 2) hr = (hr * 10) + (hh[1] - C_ZERO);

switch(ensubtype)
{
        case 0: if ( (hr < 1) || (hr > 12) ) return(erc);
                break;
        case 1: if ( hr > 24 ) return(erc);
                break;
}

strcpy(mm,str);
for (i=0; i < (floc-1); i++)
{
delchr(mm,1);
}
```

```
slgth = strlen(mm);
if (slgth != 2) return(erc);

mn = mm[0] - C_ZERO;
mn = (mn * 10) + (mm[1] - C_ZERO);

if ( mn > 59 ) return(erc);
if ((ensubtype == 1) && (hr == 24) && (mn > 0)) return (erc);
if ( (hr == 12) && (mn == 0) ) twelve = TRUE;
else twelve = FALSE;

switch (ampm)
{
        case C_BLANK: addhr = 0;
                    break;
        case C_A:   if (hr == 12) addhr = -12;
                    else addhr = 0;
                    break;
        case C_P:   if (hr == 12) addhr = 0;
                    else addhr = 12;
                    break;
        case C_M:   if (twelve == TRUE) addhr = -12;
                    else return(erc);
                    break;
        case C_N:   if (twelve == TRUE) addhr = 0;
                    else return(erc);
                    break;
}

*pphys = ((hr + addhr) * 60) + mn;

return (ERC_OK);

}
```

- Note that pphys is declared to be of type TIME. Uppercase TIME is a typedef from the ldt.h header file. TIME is therefore equivalent to int.
- For the time LDT, if pstrin contains all blank characters, it will not satisfy the mandatory mflag field requirement.
- Note the use of function poschr.c to locate one and only one colon. Poschr.c first checks LR then RL.
- The variable addhr is used to adjust hr according to the effects of am, pm, noon, and midnight.

A.3.0 ***Evtime.c Source Code and Commentary***

The source code and commentary for function evtime.c parallels evchar.c (Chapter 5, A.3.0). To create function evtime.c, simply copy file evchar.c and edit it as follows:

- Change all occurrences of char to time and CHAR to TIME except for the statement

```
char *pstrin;
```

- Update the commented function description.

The complete source code is available on disk.

A.4.0 Advanced Encode Field Processing

A.4.1 Gettime.c and Fgettime.c Error Codes

See Chapter 5, A.4.1.

A.4.2 Gettime.c and Fgettime.c Source Code and Commentary

The source code and commentary for function gettime.c parallels getchar.c (Chapter 5, A.4.0). To create function gettime.c, simply copy file getchar.c and edit it as follows:

- Change all occurrences of char to time and CHAR to TIME except for the statement

```
char *string, *mask, *init;
```

The source code and commentary for function fgettime.c also parallels fgetchar.c (Chapter 5, A.4.0). To create function fgettime.c, copy file fgetchar.c and edit it as follows:

- Change all occurrences of char to time and CHAR to TIME except for the statements

```
char *string, *mask, *init;
utcharcb(1,string,1);
```

The complete source code is available on disk.

A.4.3 Associated Mask Utilization Techniques

Based upon the function argument gmaskflg, mask delimiter characters can be included (YES) in the acquired input string. This facilitates the introduction of a character delimiter, which in this case would be a colon. When included, this delimiter aids the user in entering data by providing a visual cue:

Time mask: "??:??A"

Remember that entime.c can be utilized independently of the getstr.c/fgetstr.c and gettime.c/fgettime.c functions so that some functional redundancy is required to expand the independent use of the enxxxx.c interface definitions developed in this book.

B.0.0 Decode Function Development (detime.c)

B.1.0 Detime.c Specifications

B.1.1 Design Objectives

This function provides a facility for the display of a time variable in standard am/pm format or military format.

B.1.2 Subtype Definition (desubtype)

See section A.1.5.

B.1.3 Default Values

No default is assumed for detime.c. The output character string pstrout is simply set to a NULL string before processing begins.

B.1.4 Error Codes

Based upon the ERC_BASE (1000) and ENTIME_E (71) values defined in ldt.h, the following erc is possible:

1076	Bad Decode Function Argument

B.2.0 Detime.c Source Code and Commentary

```
/* file    : detime.c
** function: int detime ( pstrout, maxout, pphys, maxphys,
**         :              desubtype, jflag )
** desc    : decode a logical data type time.
** test pgm: qatime.c
*/

#include "ctype.h"
#include "ldt.h"

        int detime (pstrout, maxout, pphys, maxphys, desubtype, jflag)

        char *pstrout;
        TIME *pphys;
        int maxout, maxphys, desubtype, jflag;
        {

        TIME value;
        int erc, derc, i, slgth, hr, mn;
        char str[8], ch, h1, h2, m1, m2, ampm;

        /*
        ** Table of valid DECODE subtypes:
        **    0 = Standard AM/PM format
        **    1 = Military Time format
        */

        /*
        ** Validate the function arguments:
        */

        erc = ERC_BASE + ENTIME_E + 5;

        /*
        ** validate "pphys"
        */

        value = *pphys;

        if ( (value < 0) || (value > 1440) ) return(erc);

        /*
        ** validate "maxphys"
        */

        if (maxphys != PHY_TIME) return(erc);

        /*
        ** validate "maxout"
        */

        if (( maxout < 1 ) || ( maxout > MAX_TIME)) return (erc);

        /*
        ** validate "desubtype" and set "default" values
        */

        utcharcb(1,pstrout,1);
        utcharcb(1,str,1);

        derc = dvtimede(&desubtype,PHY_INT);
        if (derc != ERC_OK) return(derc);
```

```
/*
** validate "jflag" for (NO_JUST, L_JUST, C_JUST, R_JUST)
*/

if (( jflag < NO_JUST) || ( jflag > R_JUST ))
        return (erc);

/*
** desubtype processing
*/

hr = value / 60;
mn = value % 60;

switch (desubtype)
{
        case 0: if ( hr == 0 )
                {
                ampm = C_A;
                if (mn == 0) ampm = C_M;
                hr = hr + 12;
                break;
                }

                if ( hr < 12 )
                {
                ampm = C_A;
                break;
                }

                if (hr == 12)
                {
                ampm = C_P;
                if (mn == 0) ampm = C_N;
                break;
                }

                if ( hr < 24 )
                {
                ampm = C_P;
                hr = hr - 12;
                break;
                }

                if ( hr == 24 )
                {
                ampm = C_M;
                hr = 12;
                break;
                }

        case 1: ampm = C_BLANK;
                break;
}

h1 = (hr / 10) + C_ZERO;
h2 = (hr % 10) + C_ZERO;

m1 = (mn / 10) + C_ZERO;
m2 = (mn % 10) + C_ZERO;

inschr(str,999,h1,0);

inschr(str,999,h2,0);

inschr(str,999,C_COLON,0);

inschr(str,999,m1,0);
```

```
inschr(str,999,m2,0);

if ( ampm != C_BLANK )
{
inschr(str,999,ampm,0);
}

/*
** check if "pstrout" big enough?
*/

utcharcb(3,str,maxout+1);
slgth = strlen(str);
if (slgth > maxout) return(erc);
else strcpy(pstrout,str);

/*
** Justify output string
*/

utcharjs(jflag, pstrout);

return (ERC_OK);

}
```

- Desubtype controls the bulk of the processing in detime.c. Clearly, standard am/pm time conversion is more complicated than military time.
- An erc will be generated if the string length of pphys is greater than the maxout string length of pstrout.
- String justification occurs within the total string field width maxout because of the function call to

  utcharcb (3,str,maxout + 1).

B.3.0 Advanced Decode Field Processing

B.3.1 Puttime.c and Fputtime.c Error Codes

See Chapter 5, B.3.1.

B.3.2 Puttime.c and Fputtime.c Source Code and Commentary

The source code and commentary for function puttime.c and fputtime.c parallels putchar.c and fputchar.c (Chapter 5, B.3.0). To create either of these functions, copy its parallel function and edit it as follows:

- Change all occurrences of char to time and CHAR to TIME except for the statement

```
char *pstrout, *mask;
```

The complete source code is available on disk.

B.3.3 Associated Mask Utilization Techniques

- In an analogous manner, putstr.c/fputstr.c and puttime.c/fputtime.c can be utilized to output a decoded string to a mask field with or without delimiters. For example,

  Time mask: "The current time is ??????"

  Again, remember that detime.c can be used independently of the putstr.c/fputstr.c and puttime.c/fputtime.c functions so that some functional redundancy is required to expand the independent use of the dexxxx.c interface definitions.

- Use of the getmstr.c function allows the video display to be used as a scratch pad (see Chapter 4) and functionally extends the stand-alone utility of each dexxxx.c. Since the power of masks is only pertinent to video display, getmstr.c retrieves the putxxxx.c string from the video display with mask formatting to enhance the variety of decoded formats that may be created when using dexxxx.c functions in a stand-alone manner.

C.0.0 Data Validation Function Development (dvtimeyy.c)

C.1.0 Dvtimeyy.c Standard Error Codes

Based upon the ERC_BASE (1000) and ENTIME_E (71) values defined in ldt.h, all dvtimeyy.c functions report the following ercs.

1074	Data Validation Error
1075	Bad Data Validation Function Argument

C.2.0 Dvtimede.c Function Specification

C.2.1 Dvtimede.c Design Objectives

This function validates that an acceptable desubtype argument value has been specified for the time LDT.

C.2.2 Dvtimede.c Source Code and Commentary

```
/* file    : dvtimede.c
** function: int dvtimede ( pphys, maxphys )
** desc    : data validation for time: valid decode subtypes
** test pgm: qatime.c
*/

#include "ldt.h"

        int dvtimede ( pphys, maxphys )

        INT *pphys;
        int maxphys;
        {
        int erc, val;

        erc = ERC_BASE + ENINT_E + 3;

        if (maxphys != PHY_INT) return(erc+1);

        val = (*pphys).i2;

        if (( val < 0 ) || ( val > 1)) return (erc);

        else return(ERC_OK);

        }
```

- Note the use of INT *pphys. The uppercase INT is a typedef from ldt.h which is

  typedef union {int i2; long int i4;} INT;

  The use of the INT typedef allows either int or long int arguments to be passed to dvtimede.c. By design, only int types are acceptable to detimede.c.

- Note how desubtype is retrieved:

  val = (*pphys).i2;

C.3.0 Dvtimeen.c Function Specification

C.3.1 Dvtimeen.c Design Objectives

This function validates that an acceptable ensubtype argument value has been specified for the time LDT.

C.3.2 Dvtimeen.c Source Code and Commentary

```
/* file    : dvtimeen.c
** function: int dvtimeen ( pphys, maxphys )
** desc    : data validation for time: valid encode subtypes
** test pgm: qatime.c
*/

#include "ldt.h"

        int dvtimeen ( pphys, maxphys )

        INT *pphys;
        int maxphys;
        {
        int erc, val;

        erc = ERC_BASE + ENINT_E + 3;

        if (maxphys != PHY_INT) return(erc+1);

        val = (*pphys).i2;

        if (( val < 0 ) || ( val > 1)) return (erc);

        else return(ERC_OK);

        }
```

- For commentary, see C.2.2.

D.0.0 Utility Function Development (uttimeyy.c)

D.1.0 Uttimeyy.c Standard Error Codes

Based upon the ERC_BASE (1000) and ENTIME_E (71) values defined in ldt.h, all uttimeyy.c functions report the following erc.

1077 Utility Function Error

D.2.0 Uttimesi.c Function Specifications

D.2.1 Uttimesi.c Design Objectives

This function acquires the system time (systime) and converts it to LDT time standard internal format.

D.2.2 Uttimesi.c Source Code and Commentary

```
/*
** file    : uttimesi.c
** function: TIME uttimesi()
** desc    : convert DOS system time to LDT TIME format
** test pgm: (none) See: ttime.c APPENDIX B
*/

#include "dos.h"
#include "ldt.h"

        TIME uttimesi()
        {

        union REGS ir, or;
        int hours, minutes;
        TIME itime;

        ir.h.ah = DOS_TIME;
        int86 (INT_DOS, &ir, &or);
        hours = or.h.ch;
        minutes = or.h.cl;

        itime = (hours * 60) + minutes;

        return(itime);
        }
```

- Note that function uttimesi.c is of type TIME, the typedef equivalent to int.
- Refer to Appendix D for a discussion of DOS interrupts.
- Note that no rounding of the minutes portion of time is performed.

E.0.0 LDT Time Application Tips and Reminders

E.1.0 Helpful Notes

Using the standard interface function definitions for the time logical data type is less complicated than for LDT char. This is because the pphys argument is always passed as an "address of" (&pphys) because pphys is of type TIME (typedef synonymous with int).

Let's highlight some helpful reminders about using the functions in this chapter.

1. **Entime.c and evtime.c:** The maxin function argument should be the sizeof(pstrin) − 1. Maxin is the declared pstrin (size − 1) and does not include the NULL delimiting character. Maxphys should always be PHY_TIME.

2. **Gettime.c and fgettime.c:** The maxstr function argument should be the sizeof(string) − 1. Cltab only controls the very first character read operation performed. Nuexit is a returned value and therefore must be passed as &nuexit.

3. **Detime.c, puttime.c, and fputtime.c:** The maxout function argument should be the sizeof(pstrin) − 1. Maxout is the declared pstrout (size − 1) and does not include the NULL delimiting character. Maxout must be large enough to receive the decoded pphys or an erc results. Maxphys should always be PHY_TIME.

4. **Dvtimeyy.c:** When these functions are used as function arguments they must be declared explicitly in the calling program.

5. **General:** Initialize all strings before using them.

E.2.0 Special Uses

We will not present any alternative uses of LDT time.

F.0.0 Testing and Quality Assurance (qatime.c)

F.1.0 Qatime.c Specification

F.1.1 Qatime.c Design Objectives

Like all other qaxxxx.c functions, qatime.c utilizes entime.c, evtime.c, gettime.c, fgettime.c, detime.c, puttime.c, and fputtime.c as well as dvtimeyy.c, uttimeyy.c, and supporting functions listed in the linker automatic response file qatime.lnk (Appendix L).

Qatime.c provides runtime control over the resetting of stdlog, the making of stdlog entries, and screen printing upon error detection, as well as the interactive testing of all entime.c and detime.c subtypes.

Each qaxxxx.c function is not only an excellent example of LDT testing, but also demonstrates techniques for the use of the various standard interfaces portrayed in this book. A close examination of qatime.c reveals a powerful program of only 90 statements.

F.1.2 Qatime.c Error Codes

Qaxxxx.c functions do not have any reserved ercs of their own; rather, they simply report the ercs detected by the underlying standard interface functions during processing.

All ercs detected for LDT time, however, are governed by the ldt.h header file values in effect for

ERC_BASE	1000
GET_E	1
PUT_E	5
ENTIME_E	71

F.2.0 Qatime.c Source Code and Commentary

```
/*
** file   : qatime.c
** desc   : quality assurance test program for LDT time
** link   : @qatime.lnk,qatime,nul,lcs
*/

#include "ldt.h"

main ()
{
        int dvcharyn(), dvtimeen(), dvdummy();
        int erc;

        static char mtype[] = ">?<";
        static char mstr[] = ">??????<";

        static char initi[] = "0";
        static char inity[] = "Y";
        static char initn[] = "N";

        char str[15], destr[15], ynchar;
        int etype, nuexit, lpe;
        TIME ival;
        int smstr;

        smstr = nondel(mstr);

        blanksc(1,1,MAX_ROW,MAX_COL);
        setcrc(1,1);
        putstr("TIME Quality Assurance Program",LR,"",DISP_F);

        /*
        ** Prompt User for Runtime Controls
        */

        uprompt(&lpe);

        if ( (lpe == 10) || (lpe == 11) )
                logwrite(5,"QATIME",0,"Begin Testing");

        for (;;)
        {

        blanksc(2,1,MAX_ROW,MAX_COL);
        setcrc(1,1);

        movcrc(2,-MAX_COL);
        putstr("Enter ENCODE Subtype: ",LR,"",DISP_F);

        erc = getint(str,sizeof(str)-1,NO,mtype,LR,initi,MAND_F,YES,
                     &nuexit,&etype,PHY_INT,1,MAND_F,lpe,dvtimeen);

        if (lderc(erc) == 9) break;


        movcrc(2,-MAX_COL);
        putstr("Enter TIME String    : ",LR,"",DISP_F);

        erc = gettime(str,sizeof(str)-1,NO,mstr,LR,"",MAND_F,NO,
                 &nuexit,&ival,PHY_TIME,etype,MAND_F,lpe,dvdummy);

        if (lderc(erc) == 9) continue;
```

```
            movcrc(2,-MAX_COL);
            putstr("DECODEed Subtype [0]: ",LR,"",DISP_F);
            puttime(destr,smstr,&ival,PHY_TIME,0,NO_JUST,
                    LR,mstr,MAND_F,lpe);

            movcrc(2,-MAX_COL);
            putstr("DECODEed Subtype [1]: ",LR,"",DISP_F);
            puttime(destr,smstr,&ival,PHY_TIME,1,NO_JUST,
                    LR,mstr,MAND_F,lpe);

            setcrc(24,1);
            putstr("Continue? [Yes/No] or [ESCape]: ",LR,"",DISP_F);

            erc = getchar(str,sizeof(str)-1,NO,mtype,LR,inity,MAND_F,NO,
                          &nuexit,&ynchar,1,11,MAND_F,lpe,dvcharyn);

            if (lderc(erc) == 9) break;
            if (ynchar == 'N') break;

            }

            if ( (lpe == 10) || (lpe == 11) )
                    logwrite(6,"QATIME",0,"End Testing");

            blanksc(1,1,MAX_ROW,MAX_COL);
            exit(0);
}
```

- All dvxxxxyy.c functions used as function arguments must be declared explicitly in the calling program.

- All masks are declared with outermost field delimiters so that the field limits are always known regardless of the type of field and video attributes chosen for display.

- All init values are declared to make any necessary revision easy.

- In this case destr[15] exceeds the nondelimiter size of mask (mstr[ ]). The size of a displayed string must not exceed the corresponding number of mask nondelimiter positions if a mask is used for display purposes.

- Variable lpe is calculated by uprompt.c from runtime user responses and effectively becomes the standard function argument logprerr.

- Anywhere in the source code where

  if (lderc(erc) = = 9)

  appears, an equivalent statement

  if (nuexit = = −1)

  could have been specified instead.

- Note that because there were only two possible choices for both ensubtype and desubtype, qatime.c simply generates decode 0 and 1 for the specified time encode subtype.

- Note that hitting the Escape key recycles the program unless it is performed at

  Enter ENCODE Subtype:

  or

  Continue? [Yes/No] or [ESCape]:

  where it exits the program. Hitting Ctrl-Break has no effect in qaxxxx.c programs because Ctrl-Break has been turned off in function _main (see Appendix F).

- Note the sample output of the qatime.c program shown in Figure 11.1.

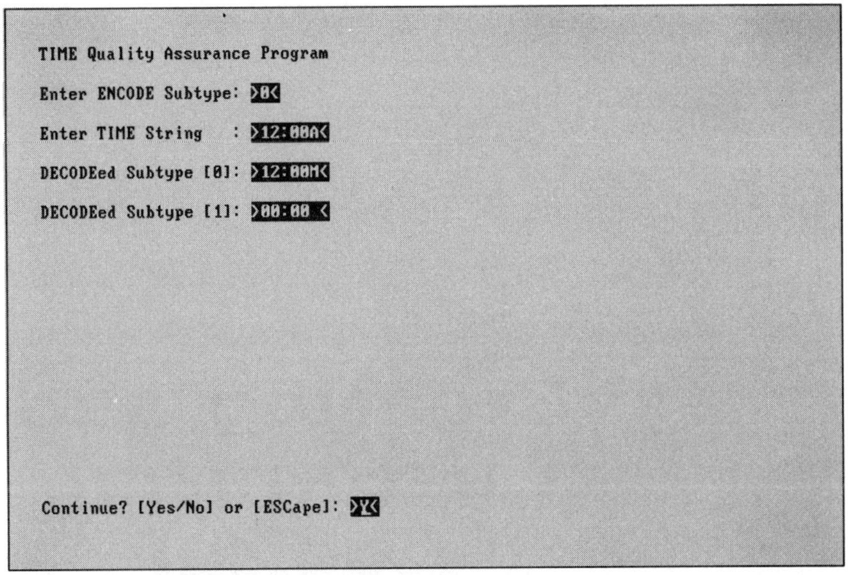

***Figure** 11.1–* *Qatime.c sample output*

Creating and Customizing Logical Data Types

12

It is possible that the LDTs implemented in this book (char, date, dolr, int, real, tele, and time) may not conform exactly to your own project requirements. This chapter will help you adapt our structured methodology and source code to your specific needs by providing guidelines for

1. Modifying underlying features common to all LDTs
2. Modifying any LDT included in this book
3. Creating new LDTs

We will not attempt to provide any guidelines for the modification of the standard interface definitions presented in Chapters 3 and 4 for enxxxx.c, dvxxxxyy.c, evxxxx.c, dexxxx.c, getstr.c/fgetstr.c, getxxxx.c/fgetxxxx.c, putstr.c/fputstr.c, or putxxxx.c/fputxxxx.c. We will, however, address the alteration of any of the source code implementations found in Chapter 5–11, and any of the other underlying support functions found throughout this book. You will find that, due to the standardized structure of our methodology, making revisions is fairly simple.

We have provided checklists and guidelines that will help you use the source code and documentation presented so far to modify our LDTs or create any new ones that you may require.

Modifying Common LDT Features

There are many common assumptions that underlie all the LDTs developed in this book. Our assumptions, however, may vary slightly from your specific needs. If you want to use our LDTs in your application, first check the following features and change any that need modification to work better for you. Next, edit the affected files and then be certain to recompile all source code that includes any header files (.h) you have modified.

1. Review the ASCII and scan code interpretations implemented by fgetstr.c (Chapter 4). Remember that fgetstr.c handles all user data entry interaction. You may want to alter the overall allowable range of ASCII characters (presently 0x20–0x7E), the use of F1 for Help, F2 for Copy, and the various keystrokes recognized for normal field exiting: Return, Forward tab, Up arrow, PgUp, Tab, Down arrow, PgDn, and Back tab. For example, to remove the recognition of PgUp and PgDn, edit file fgetstr.c and delete the following lines of source code:

```
case 73: *nuexit = 5;
         userexit = TRUE;
         continue;

case 81: *nuexit = 6;
         userexit = TRUE;
         continue;
```

You may also wish to implement functionality for the Ins key (scan code 82). Fgetstr.c currently assumes that all data entry is in insert mode, and the Ins key does not toggle data entry between insert mode and overwrite mode. In order to make the Ins key functional, you could set a boolean flag (int variable ins_key for example) in fgetstr.c to reflect which Ins key mode is in effect: either TRUE (insert mode), or FALSE (overwrite mode). In turn, you would have to modify the logic of processing all case statements for data entry (versus control) to check for the boolean flag ins_key. It should be clear to you that handling the Ins key introduces additional logic into fgetstr.c.

2. Verify that the MAX_ROW and MAX_COL #define items in ldt.h match the size of your video display. It is presently set at 25 rows and 80 columns.

3. Verify that the video attributes, assigned in ldt.h to connote field type (ftype) throughout our methodology, are appropriate for use with your particular video hardware (V_PSWD = nondisplay password field, V_NMAN = underlined nonmandatory field, V_MAND = reverse video mandatory field, and V_DISP = normal display field). The assigned hexadecimal values are more fully described in the comments of function putchs.c (see Chapter 4). They are appropriate for a monochrome (black and white) video display. If you are using a color video monitor, you may wish to alter these hexadecimal values to reflect your use of color and to distinguish between field types.

4. Verify that each LDT field width (MAX_xxxx) #define item in ldt.h matches your field width requirements. If not, simply edit ldt.h and modify any associated LDT MAX_xxxx field size values accordingly. Remember that these values only represent maximum allowable field width input or output values. You can use smaller field size masks in your source code, but if you use a larger size, an erc will be generated.

5. Check that the #define items YYYY_MIN, YYYY_MAX, and DEF_AC found in ldt.h match your requirements for the minimum and maximum allowable calendar dates used by LDT date (see Chapter 6), and the default telephone area code which is used by LDT tele (see Chapter 10).

6. Verify that the speaker port assignment (BEL_PORT in dos.h) is valid for your particular microprocessor. Function beep.c uses this feature (see Chapter 4).

7. Calibrate the delay.c function for your microprocessor. Use test program tbeep.c to adjust the defined item DEL_ITER found in dos.h, so that the unit of 1/10th of a second for the assignment of the delay.c function argument is correct. Refer to the commented source code for function delay.c and test program tbeep.c found in Chapter 4.

8. Verify that the block of error return codes reserved for our structured methodology (1001–1077) does not conflict with your operating system or applications software. If a conflict exists, you can alter the value of ERC_BASE in ldt.h by shifting the block of ercs to an unused range of ercs. Remember that in this book, all ercs have the following form:

   erc = ERC_BASE + error + constant

   The #define item ERC_BASE can be assigned any zero or positive integer number. Be certain that your reassignment of ERC_BASE does not create an integer overflow problem for any possible ercs. We strongly advise against assigning a negative number to ERC_BASE. Our overall system of using lderc.c, the least significant digit of an erc, would be invalidated if ERC_BASE was negative because of the way in which each erc is computed. Lastly, be certain to fully document your new ercs.

9. Review the implemented error control and recovery features described in Chapter 13. Consider whether to retain or disable the use of stdlog, automatic screen printing, and video error messaging. If you want to disable stdlog

   - Use the standard _main function supplied with the Lattice C compiler, not the _main version noted in Appendix F.

   - Remove the reference to stdlog in header file stdio.h.

- Eliminate the reference to logreset.c in function uprompt.c (Chapter 4).
- Eliminate all references to function logwrite.c found in functions mesgsps.c and mesende.c.
- Alter all qaxxxx.c programs to remove any references to function logwrite.c.

To disable automatic screen printing, simply restrict the assignment value of function argument logprerr (equivalent to pflag for functions mesgsps.c and mesende.c) to either 0 or 10. Refer to the specification of logprerr found in the interface definition for getxxxx.c/fgetxxxx.c (in Chapter 4) or to pflag found in the commented source code for functions mesgsps.c (in Chapter 4) and mesende.c (in Chapter 3).

To disable or modify the handling of all video error and warning messages, you must alter functions mesgsps.c and mesende.c accordingly. For example, presently an error message is displayed, two audible beeps are generated, and then the message is erased from the video. If you wished to have the error message remain on the screen until the problem is resolved by the user, it would be necessary to modify mesgsps.c, mesende.c, and all fgetxxxx.c functions. To edit both mesgsps.c and mesende.c, delete the last occurrence of the following statement from each file:

```
blanksc(MAX_ROW,1,MAX_ROW,MAX_COL);
```

Also edit and modify each LDT fgetxxxx.c function so that it reads as follows:

```
erc = fgetstr( ....as stated.... );

mesgsps(erc,prnerr);
if (lderc(erc) = = 9) break;

erc = evchar( .....as stated.... );
.
.
.
else
```

```
{
mesende(erc,prnerr);
break;
}
}
return(erc);
```

When these revised functions are linked into any qaxxxx.c program, they leave warning or error messages displayed until the user resolves them.

10. Implement or eliminate the Help feature. All Help is presently initiated by function fgetstr.c. Function key F1 initiates a function call to help.c. To disable the help feature, simply edit file fgetstr.c and delete the following lines of source code:

```
case 59: help();
         continue;
```

The implementation of a complete help feature would involve establishing a systemwide coding convention for setting and resetting a series of global variables. These variables would fully identify where a user is located at any point in time, so that messaging could be keyed for retrieval when F1 (Help) is requested by the user.

11. Besides carefully examining the contents of the ldt.h header file, which is uniquely associated with our LDT methodology, recognize that we have altered the dos.h and stdio.h files normally distributed with the Lattice C compiler. Use the header (.h) files that we provide in Appendix G, or modify your files to conform to the additions and changes we have made.

Modifying Existing LDTs

Your specific project requirements may call for the modification of some or all of the LDTs presented in Part 2. When thinking about what kind of modifications you might need to make, consider the following possibilities:

- Alteration of #define items in header file ldt.h

- Alteration of the specified LDT typedefs (associated native C data types) found in ldt.h
- Removal or addition of ensubtype and desubtype values
- Addition of more specific data validation routines
- Addition of handy utility routines
- Alteration of qaxxxx.c and development of any additional test programs that may be necessary to ensure source code integrity. There are about 30 test programs, which are not included in the text of this book, but are available on disk (see back page); these may also be helpful to you.

LDT Modification Checklist

Making revisions to the LDTs included in this book is simplified by the checklist we have created for you. As an example of the LDT modification process, we have outlined a suggested modification to the Telephone Number LDT that provides for a combined telephone extension/note field. It conforms to the following input mask definition:

Telephone number: "(???)???-???? EXT ?????"

For example,

(415)848-8233 EXT David

It also sets a default telephone area code to 415. Let's carefully examine each step in our checklist.

Step 1

Go through each of the subheadings in the chapter of the LDT you want to modify and develop a list of specific changes you want to make under each heading. For the extension/note field modification, we reviewed Chapter 10 and made the following list of changes:

A.1.1 Add a five-character (alphanumeric) array to handle our extension/note field (defined as char ext[6]).

A.1.2 MAX_TELE becomes 23 (13 + " EXT " + 5 input characters).

A.1.3 Modify the existing TELE typedef to

```
struct {int tac; long int tnbr; char ext[6];} TELE;
```

PHY_TELE becomes 12 (2 + 4 + 6 bytes).

A.1.6 Add the display of extension to all formats shown. A missing extension is handled as a blank string.

A.1.7 Provide for editing the input string to detect a missing or partially filled extension component of the telephone number (e.g., 10 digits followed by an optional " EXT " and then the five-character extension/note component).

A.1.8 Default the extension component as noted by

```
TELE *pphys;
utcharcb(1,&(*pphys).ext,6);
```

A.2.0 Revise the entele.c function source code.

A.4.3 Revise the mask as described above.

B.1.1 Add the extension component.

B.2.0 Revise the detele.c function source code.

F.2.0 Modify qatele.c accordingly.

Step 2

Modify any affected items in the ldt.h header file, for example, #define MAX_xxxx value, #define PHY_xxxx value, typedef definition, and any other #define items. For our extension/note field modifications, the following changes are required:

```
#define MAX_TELE 23
#define PHY_TELE 12
typedef struct {int tac; long int tnbr; char ext[6];} TELE;
#define DEF_AC "415"
```

Note that we have kept the ext character string allocation to an even number of bytes as we recommended in Chapter 2. Also note the quotations around the DEF_AC value 415, making it a character string, not an integer value, which is required.

Step 3

Edit the ldt.h header file and any other included files so that they incorporate all additional #define items that may be required by an encode, decode, data validation, or utility function. Be certain these new #define values do not conflict with any previous #defines in ldt.h or any other included files. Restrict all new #define variable names to eight characters or less; otherwise, duplicate defined items will be generated because only the first eight characters are considered by the compiler. No additional #define items are required by our extension/note modification.

Step 4

Modify the enxxxx.c function as necessary. To accomodate our extension/note component of the telephone LDT, edit file entele.c as follows.

1. Delete the following group of statements:

```
utcharsb(2,str,C_BLANK);
slgth = strlen(str);
if ( slgth < 7) return(erc);
```

2. Modify the following statements by changing

```
char str[15], mstr[15];
```

to

```
char str[24], mstr[24];
```

Change

```
if (slgth < 10) return(erc); /* all occurrences */
```

to

```
if (slgth < 15) return(erc);
```

Change

```
if (slgth < 7) return(erc);
```

to

```
if (slgth < 12) return(erc);
```

Change

```
for ( i= (slgth - 1); i >=0; i--)
```

to

```
for (i=6; i>=0; i--)
```

3. Add the following group of statements just prior to the last statement of the program:

```
for (i=0; i<7; i++)
{
delchr(str,1);
}

slgth = strlen(str);
if ((slgth != 5) && (slgth != 10)) return(erc);

utcharcb(1,&(*pphys).ext,1);

if (slgth == 5) strcat(&(*pphys).ext,str);
else strcat(&(*pphys).ext,str[5]);
```

Note that the reference /* all occurrences */ above indicates that the noted change should be made consistently throughout the file. The construction

```
&(*pphys).ext
```

used in the above source code is intended to stress the fact that although character strings are normally passed as pointers when used as function arguments, if a character string is embedded within a structure, as with character string ext, the address of (&) must be specified explicitly.

Step 5

Modify the dexxxx.c function as necessary. To accommodate our extension/note component of the telephone LDT, edit file detele.c as follows:

1. Modify the following statement by changing

   ```
   char digit, str[15];
   ```

   to

   ```
   char digit, str[24];
   ```

2. Modify the following comment lines to read as follows:

   ```
   ** 0 = format: (xxx)xxxx-xxxx EXT xxxxx
   ** 1 = format: xxx/xxx-xxxx EXT xxxxx
   ** 2 = format: xxx-xxx-xxxx EXT xxxxx
   ** 3 = format: xxxxxxxxxxxxxxx
   ```

3. Add the following statements after the statement "if (desubtype = = 0) inschr(str,999,C_LPAR,1);"

   ```
   /*
   ** put the extension/note component
   */

   if (desubtype != 3) strcat(str," EXT ");

   for (i=0; i < 5; i++)
   {
   inschr(str,999,(*pphys).ext[i],0);
   }
   ```

Step 6

Modify or develop any required dvxxxxyy.c functions. If the ensubtype values have changed, revise dvxxxxen.c; if the desubtype values have changed, revise dvxxxxde.c. Since we have not introduced any additional ensubtype or desubtype values, no changes to dvteleen.c and dvtelede.c must be made; and there is no need for additional dvteleyy.c functions.

Step 7

Modify the qaxxxx.c routine as necessary. Only three lines of source code need to be modified in program file qatele.c to accomodate our addition of an extension/note component to the telephone number LDT. Change

```
static char mstrin[] = ">(???)???-????<";
```

to

```
static char mstrin[] = ">(???)???-???? EXT ?????<";
```

Change

```
static char mstr[] = ">?????????????<";
```

to

```
static char mstr[] = ">???????????????????????<";
```

Change

```
char str[15], destr[15], ynchar;
```

to

```
char str[16], destr[24], ynchar;
```

Note that initac[] is set equal to DEF_AC and is used along with the input mask mstrin[] by the following statement:

```
erc = gettele(str,sizeof(str) - 1,NO,mstrin,LR,initac,
              MAND_F,NO,&nuexit,pphys,PHY_TELE,etype,
              MAND_F,lpe,dvdummy);
```

Also note that the third function argument (gmaskflg) is set equal to NO, thereby telling fgetstr.c to acquire only the nondelimiter character positions from mask mstrin. Hence the string str passed to entele.c has no delimiter characters present. For our example above, str would contain "4158488233David", the smallest possible input string description for the tele LDT. Str is then transformed by entele.c into the internal typedef form of

int tac	:	415
long int tnbr	:	8488233
char ext[6]	:	"David"

The input string str of 16 bytes is reduced internally to a size of PHY_TELE, or 12 bytes. Str could have been as large as MAX_TELE, or 23.

Step 8

Using qaxxxx.c and other test programs as needed, thoroughly test the encode, decode, and data validation functions and subtypes of your modified LDT.

Step 9

Develop and test any required utxxxxyy.c functions. None is required by our modification.

Step 10

Release the revised LDT object modules (.obj) and test programs (.exe) for Beta site testing. Make any final code revisions based upon the results of field testing and finalize documentation.

Step 11

Move all revised source (.c), object (.obj), and run (.exe) files into their respective libraries.

Step 12

Release the modified LDT libraries to your staff for system-wide use.

Creating New LDTs

Because the source code for functions evxxxx.c, getxxxx.c/fgetxxxx.c, and putxxxx.c/fputxxxx.c is parallel for all LDTs (see Chapters 5–11), the production of a new LDT rests primarily in the development of an enxxxx.c and dexxxx.c function that conforms to the standard interface definitions, together with any necessary dvxxxxyy.c and utxxxxyy.c functions. Finally, you should construct a qaxxxx.c program along with any other test programs for quality assurance and control purposes.

To demonstrate this process, we will explore the creation of an LDT for handling the I/O of feet-inches-fractions (e.g. 125'10-3/4"), measurements common to all construction trades and many inventory control problems. Such measurements, along with many others (e.g., weight measured in pounds-ounces, angles measured in degrees-minutes-seconds, and even time measured in hours-minutes-seconds) belong to a field of mathematics called mixed numbers. Such measurements are not readily or normally expressed in decimal (base10) form, and inaccuracies result when such conversions are made.

A classic example of an application using mixed-number arithmetic would be the creation of an interactive computer program to teach children how to perform math with fractions, for example, (3 5/8) + (2 2/3) = (6 7/24). Mixed numbers often take the form of A:B/C. In this example, A represents the whole number, B represents the numerator of the fraction and C represents the denominator of the fraction.

We will use the feet-inches-fractions example of mixed numbers throughout the LDT creation checklist that follows to further demonstrate the flexibility of our structured methodology, and to provide better insight into the thought process involved in creating new LDTs.

LDT Creation Checklist

Because of our structured methodology, the steps for creating an entirely new LDT are similar to those you would consider if you were simply modifying an existing LDT. We will call our new LDT field "feet" and it will conform to the following input mask definition:

```
Measurement: "???'??-??/??\"";
```

For example, 125'10-11/16" is interpreted as 125 feet, 10 and 11/16th inches.

Note that the input mask described above demonstrates how to construct a mask that must contain a double quotation mark (representing the common notation for inches). In a C string, a double quote character must be preceded by a backslash (\). Let's proceed to study each step in our checklist.

Step 1

Develop a complete specification for the new LDT by following the standard chapter outline established for all LDTs and establish a new four-character-or-less acronym "xxxx" for the logical data type that does not conflict with any existing LDTs. For our new LDT, we have selected an acronym "feet," and after reviewing Chapter 10 (Telephone Numbers) we have prepared the following list of specifications.

A.1.1 The most crucial decisions that must be made when creating a new LDT are the choices of typedef and standard input mask. We have elected to use the input mask described above and to establish a minimum field width of 9 for the case when gmaskflg is NO, and the maximum field width of 13 if gmaskflg is YES. Assuming these would suffice for I/O, a MAX_FEET value of 13 would be set. To set PHY_FEET, select a typedef from the following alternatives:

1. With the imposition of a smallest allowable denominator, say 1/32nds of an inch, we could handle this LDT the same way we handled the time LDT; that is, by storing the internal value as a long int representation of the number of component 1/32nds of an inch.

   ```
   typedef long int FEET;
   ```

   This would not prevent data entry in 1/16ths or 1/8ths; however, an ultimate conversion to 1/32nds would have to be made. Because of the maximum allowable long int of 2147483647 the largest possible value would exceed 5,500,000 feet. This approach is useful when performing math operations, but it would not suffice for the children's teaching example noted above, for we would not want to restrict the largest denominator to 32 or an integral multiple of 32.

2. To handle the children's teaching example, true mixed number arithmetic would have to be performed, and thus the integer portions A:B/C would have to be

stored as integers, for example:

```
typedef struct { int A; int B; int C; } MIX;
typedef struct { long int A; int B; int C; } MIX;
```

The choice of such a typedef would immediately necessitate the development of a complete group of math utility (utfeetyy.c) functions.

Let's assume that we elect to use the typedef long int FEET.

A.1.2 MAX_FEET becomes 13 characters.

A.1.3 Implement the following typedef from among those we discussed:

```
struct long int FEET;
```

PHY_FEET becomes four bytes.

A.1.5 Assign ensubtype values for the different fraction denominators:

2: 1/2"
4: 1/4"
8: 1/8"
16: 1/16"
32: 1/32"

A.1.6 All output formats produced by desubtype are acceptable as input by enfeet.c. I/O can either be reduced to 9 consecutive characters conforming to the nondelimiter positions of the standard mask defined above, or 13 characters including the delimiters. The delimiters in the mask must appear as shown, and are simply stripped. All blank component characters are transformed to the character zero.

A.1.7 Provide for editing the input string to accept only numerics.

A.1.8 Default the encoded variable to zero:

```
FEET pphys;
pphys = 0;
```

A.1.9 Assign ENFEET_E the yet unassigned value of 81 in the ldt.h header file, which sets up the error codes of 1081, 1082, and 1083.

A.2.0 Create the enfeet.c function source code according to the specifications noted above using entele.c as a guideline.

A.3.0 Create evfeet.c from evchar.c as described for the LDTs in Chapters 6–11.

A.4.0 Create getfeet.c/fgetfeet.c from getchar.c/fgetchar.c as described for the LDTs in Chapter 6–11.

B.1.1 Create function defeet.c so that it can produce either a formatted display conforming to the mask specified, or simply nine contiguous characters intended for use with a mask.

B.1.2 The desubtype values consist of two components (d2d1), where d2 is identical to the ensubtype values and d1 is either equal to 0 (9 character contiguous display) or 1 (13 character formatted display). Since the fractional base used to encode a number is unknown because it has not been stored as part of the number itself, we must rely on the specification of the desubtype value. We could have reserved the two least significant digits of the long int FEET to store the fraction used for encoding, but that would reduce our maximum allowable value to just over 55,000 feet, and would require a set of math utility functions (utfeetyy.c) to perform all math operations. This way we can rely upon C's intrinsic ability to perform integer arithmetic.

B.1.3 No default, set to a NULL string.

B.1.4 From ENFEET_E of 81, assign the 1086 error code.

B.2.0 Create the defeet.c function source code to the specifications noted above using detele.c as a guideline.

B.3.0 Create putfeet.c/fputfeet.c from putchar.c/fputchar.c as described for the LDTs in Chapter 6–11.

C.1.0 From ENFEET_E of 81, assign the 1084 and 1085 error codes.

C.2.0 Create dvfeetde.c to validate allowable desubtype values (d2d1).

C.3.0 Create dvfeeten.c to validate allowable ensubtype value as d1.

D.1.0 From ENFEET_E of 81, assign the error code 1087.

D.2.0–n.0 Create utfeetyy.c functions as required for math operations or for other purposes. None is required due to our choice of typedef. Utdolryy.c functions can be used if necessary.

F.1.2 Set up ERC_BASE 1000, GET_E 1, PUT_E 5, and ENFEET_E 81.

F.2.0 Create qafeet.c, which will prompt for an allowable ensubtype value and produce two standard output string displays. This function would be similar to qatele.c.

Step 2

Edit the ldt.h header file to include the following new items: #define ENxxxx_E value, #define MAX_xxxx value, #define PHY_xxxx value, and typedef definition. For our example, you must edit ldt.h to include the following new statements:

```
#define ENFEET_E 81
#define MAX_FEET 13
#define PHY_FEET 4

typedef long int FEET;
```

Step 3

Edit the ldt.h header file to include any additional #define items that may be required by an encode, decode, data validation, utility, or quality assurance function. Be certain these new #define values do not conflict with any previous #defines in ldt.h or any other header file. As noted above, restrict all new #define variable names to eight characters or less. None is required by LDT feet.

Step 4

Develop the enxxxx.c function. Conform to the standard encode interface definition explained in Chapter 3. To create a new enxxxx.c function, you can follow the flow of logic common to all enxxxx.c functions: error code assignment, function argument validation, ensubtype validation, mandatory field checking, encode algorithm implementation, and return. If possible, use the encode source code for an existing LDT as a starting point. Use entele.c as a guideline for LDT feet.

Step 5

Develop the dexxxx.c function. Conform to the standard decode interface definition explained in Chapter 3. As with enxxxx.c, you can follow the flow of logic common to all dexxxx.c functions: error code assignment, function argument validation, desubtype validation, decode algorithm implementation, output string justification, and return. If possible, use the decode source code for an existing LDT as a starting point. Use detele.c as a guideline for LDT feet.

Step 6

Develop dvxxxxen.c, dvxxxxde.c, and any other dvxxxxyy.c functions required, conforming to the standard interface definition found in Chapter 3. For LDT feet, create function dvfeetde.c and dvfeeten.c to validate the allowable desubtype and ensubtype values described in B.1.2 and A.1.5

Step 7

Develop a qaxxxx.c test program. Simply copy the source code for one of the qaxxxx.c programs in Part 2 that most closely parallels your requirements, and edit the program file as required to create qafeet.c. Use qatele.c as a guideline for developing the source code for qafeet.c

Step 8

Follow steps 8–12 in the LDT modification checklist above.

Error Control and Recovery

13

Error control and recovery, like comprehensive system testing, are critical design components for all commercial applications; however, they seem to be considered of less importance by project managers today. Lately, because of the increased pace and competitive demand of the computer market, management has less and less time to discover and solve bugs. Also, because software is now widely understood to be evolutionary in nature, management is more accepting of software that has bugs. Apparently it is believed that the marketplace will continue to purchase software that does not perform as intended. We believe that this perception has become a crutch that is being grossly abused. As the microcomputer software industry matures, comprehensive testing along with error control and recovery will again become fashionable as it was prior to the age of microcomputers. Due to our belief in this phenomenon, and in anticipation of an impending shift in sentiment, we are promoting the inclusion of both comprehensive system testing and adequate error control and recovery features in all microcomputer-based software development projects.

In keeping with this belief, we have made the following features integral to the development of all the standard interface definitions and source code included in this book:

1. The standard practice of assigning error return codes (ercs) as function return values
2. The standard use of lderc.c for error trapping and the role that checkerc-like functions can play
3. The creation of stdlog as a systemwide error and message logging file
4. The standardized access and control of stdlog by functions logwrite.c and logreset.c
5. The uniform screen error messaging provided by mesende.c and mesgsps.c
6. The consistent use of audibles (beep.c) throughout the system
7. The implementation of optional screen printing controlled by function argument logprerr (or pflag)
8. The deliberate choice to create a comprehensive qaxxxx.c testing mechanism for each LDT
9. The development of other quality assurance related test programs to facilitate the complete testing of underlying support functions (see Index of Source Code: any program prefaced with a T is a test program and available on disk)

We will show that the implementation of these features not only reduces the number and severity of software bugs, but also significantly benefits project management in several other ways.

The Role of Function Return Values

Functions, which are the building blocks of all programs written in C, facilitate the implementation of sound error control and recovery procedures. We prefer to use the function return value to pass error return codes (ercs as we call them) rather than relying on a designated function argument. For most of the routines developed in this book we declare functions to be of type integer (default type), and thereby they become candidates to return an integer value or status code. We reserve the return code value of zero (ERC_OK) to signify the function performed without error; and positive or negative return values (ranging from −32767 to +32767) to indicate error conditions.

The reader is familiar with the general form of a function in C:

```
[type] name([argument list])
   [argument declarations]
   {
      declarations and statements
      return(erc);
   }
```

where:

[type]	is an optional type specification for the function return value. The default is int.
name	is a required function name.
(	is a required parenthesis.
[argument list]	is an optional argument list.
)	is a required parenthesis.
[argument declarations]	is an optional argument declaration list that corresponds with [argument list]
{	is a required left brace for the body of the function.
declarations and statements	is the body of the function.
return(erc)	is the erc (error return code) returned by the function call.
}	is a required right brace for the body of the function.

By employing a programming technique that consistently interrogates the erc returned by function calls, an effective error control and recovery mechanism can be implemented. Let's take a closer look at some techniques that can be used to interrogate ercs.

Methods of Trapping Ercs

Several techniques for error detection are possible that trap function return values:

1. The most widely used technique in this book, lderc.c (least significant digit of an erc), is described in Chapter 3 and is used for switching purposes as follows:

```
int erc;
erc = myfunction(arg0, arg1, ...);
switch ( lderc(erc) )
{
   case 0: return(ERC_OK);
   case 1: . . . break;
   case 2: . . . break;
   case 3: . . . break;
   case 4: . . . break;
   case 5: . . . break;
   case 6: . . . break;
   case 7: . . . break;
   case 8: . . . break;
   case 9: . . . break;
}
```

This method is used by mesgsps.c and mesende.c and necessitates the use of a structured system of assigning ercs. Note that for this technique to function correctly, all ENxxxx_E values must be assigned in increments of ten. Provisions are made to allow for the customized assignment of these error codes for the functions we have developed (see ldt.h: ERC_BASE, GET_E, PUT_E, and ENxxxx_E). For more information on the inferred meaning of lderc(erc), refer back to Chapters 3 and 4: Summaries of Possible Error Return Codes.

2. The "if-else technique" is an alternative to the lderc.c method described above:

```
int erc;
erc = myfunction (arg0, arg1, . . .);
if (erc = = ERC_OK) { . . . . };
   else if (erc = = e1val) { . . . . };
      else if (erc = = e2val) { . . . . };
         else ckerc(erc);
```

3. Lastly, the ckerc.c (or checkerc-like) function normally surrounds the function to be interrogated and provides for program branching. Ckerc.c is useful when it is not only necessary to trap the error condition, but you also want the function to make a log entry, and branch to initiate error recovery. For example,

```
ckerc(erc);
```

or

```
ckerc(myfunction(arg0, arg1, . . .));
```

A Closer Look at Ckerc.c

No use of the ckerc.c function has been made in this book; however, such a function may be of use to you. Checkerc-like functions are generally used to capture all nonzero ercs, which by design are understood to be unanticipated and indicative of a significant flaw in the expected sequence of events. As such, checkerc-like functions are usually used to perform user messaging, error logging, and screen printing as well as to initiate branching to another program.

We have not used this technique because it is so closely tied to a software project's overall design that its use is better left to the discretion of a system designer. Typically, if an error condition is detected in a large and diverse menu-driven software environment, a checkerc-like function would initiate branching to the last safe logic node in the overall design of the system. In such an environment, a global variable might be used to reflect the current program-id in use, and another global variable or stack would reflect the last safe program-id. Such a design would permit ckerc.c always to know where it is for error logging purposes, and where control should pass to if the function detects an error condition. Unlike our use of lderc.c, which always continues processing within the same program environment, checkerc-like functions are best thought of as transfer of control functions. The source code of such a checkerc-like function should perform the following activities:

1. Detect the error condition
2. Write screen message to user
3. Write stdlog entry (optional)
4. Copy screen to printer (optional)
5. Link to another program

The activities of user messaging, error return code logging, error screen printing, and program branching constitute the error recovery process. Such a checkerc-like function, ckerc.c, is included as a guide to the construction of such a function.

Ckerc.c Source Code and Commentary

```
/*
** file    : ckerc.c
** function: int ckerc(erc);
** desc    : interrogate an erc: if ( erc != 0 ) message user,
**         : write stdlog, print screen, and branch.
** test pgm: tckerc.c
*/

#include "ldt.h"

        int ckerc(erc)
        int erc;
        {

        int irow, icol;
        char str[7];

        if ( erc != ERC_OK )
        {
        /*
        ** write screen message to line 25 = MAX_ROW;
        */

        getcrc(&irow,&icol);
        setcrc(MAX_ROW,1);
        blanksc(MAX_ROW,1,MAX_ROW,MAX_COL);
```

```
putstr("Unrecoverable Error Detected!",LR,"",DISP_F);
deint(str,MAX_INT,&erc,PHY_INT,0,NO_JUST);
movcrc(0,MAX_COL);
movcrc(0,-11);
putstr("ERC = ",LR,"",DISP_F);
putstr(str,LR,"",DISP_F);

beep(1);
delay(2);
beep(1);

/*
** write stdlog with writelog message;
** if global variables exist for present program
** and last safe program, modify following
** log entry accordingly to provide an audit
** trail for software maintenance purposes.
*/

logwrite(1,"CKERC",erc,"Branch to DOS");

/*
** print the current screen
*/

pscreen();

/*
** optionally chain to the operating system or
** to another program (special "chaining" or
** "linking" functions may be required)
*/

blanksc(MAX_ROW,1,MAX_ROW,MAX_COL);
setcrc(irow,icol);
exit(0);

}

else return(0);
}
```

- According to our predetermined screen design standards, MAX_ROW (line 25) is set aside for user error messaging purposes in this book. Note the stand-alone use of deint.c to convert erc into an ASCII character string for display purposes using putstr.c. The system standard sequence, beep(1), delay(2), beep(1), has been adopted to establish a uniform audible user alert when error conditions are detected and messaging occurs.
- Note that the fourth function argument of logwrite.c is a variable length note string.
- Each function argument can be dynamically assigned by ckerc.c if global variables exist for the logwrite.c arguments pgmid, erc, and mesgtype.

- Note that branching control in this instance is accommodated by exit(0). Again, in practice, a transfer of control or link function would normally be performed to relinquish program control. Such link functions are generally available from software vendors such as those listed in Appendix C.
- Note that if erc = = ERC_OK, the ckerc.c function simply returns, and performs no other logic.
- A test program tckerc.c which resets stdlog and tests the performance of ckerc.c is available on disk.

The Use of Log Files in Error Control

Once a disciplined approach to error trapping is adopted, it is possible to produce an ongoing chronology of error conditions by the implementation of a log file.

In a commercial application environment, a log file can reveal a wealth of information if analyzed (sorted and reported) properly. By its very existence, a log file is an audit trail or chronology of events. By simple selection, sorting, and listing, you can prepare reports that have importance to operational, software maintenance, and development staff. We will not focus upon the operational uses of log files, for these are traditional and widely understood; however, we would like to emphasize their software development and maintenance use.

With a log file, software developers do not have to passively wait until users report the difficulties they are encountering; nor do they have to be brow-beaten with phantom stories of the problems users are experiencing. The automatic printing of the video display upon the detection of an error can provide a hard-copy record on which the user can jot any additional notes or comments that may be helpful when documenting what caused the error condition to be generated. By implementing optional screen printing and aggressively studying reports from log files, software developers can immediately know what happened, when, and where. All that needs to be done to fix the bug is to figure out why it occurred. Aggressive use of a log file can avert much user frustration resulting from application software that fails to perform as expected.

Similarly, weaknesses in system documentation and training can also be inferred from the analysis of log file reports that cover a longer period (month/quarter/year) of system operation. Whether a small or large organization, problem solving must rely upon management's review of facts and not fiction. The implementation of a log file and error screen printing is an important step towards the establishment of an audit trail of facts. Careful use of these facilities can result in effective problem solving and will begin to overcome the poor software quality image that persists with most microcomputer-based software today.

Stdlog

Let's look closely at how we have elected to implement our standard error and message logging file called stdlog. Every C program automatically allocates three files: stdin, stdout, and stderr. These correspond to the standard input, standard output, and standard error files that are normally assigned to the console. Both stdin and stdout can be reassigned from the console by the command line argument list (argc, argv) constructed by the function called _main found in file main.c (see Appendix F). The function _main has the unique property of being automatically linked into every Lattice C program. Because _main already assigns stdin, stdout, and stderr, it makes an ideal place for the assignment of an additional file called stdlog—our system-wide standard message and error log file. A version of _main, modified to include the allocation of stdlog, is shown in Appendix F. Stdlog is opened in append mode, so that log entries can be continually added to the end of the file. To make stdlog global to all functions, it has been defined as stdlog in stdio.h, along with stdin, stdout, and stderr (see Appendix G).

Stdlog Utility Functions

Let's consider what capabilities are needed to make the stdlog file work in a commercial programming environment:

1. The ability to clear and reset stdlog, which is opened in append mode when assigned in _main (see the logreset.c function in Chapter 3).
2. The ability to create and write a record entry to stdlog (see function logwrite.c in Chapter 3).

Comments on Logreset.c

Stdlog must provide an ongoing audit trail of all message and error activity. In a production environment, it is important not to permit users to bypass using stdlog. Typically, daily or weekly clearing of the stdlog file should occur to minimize the growth of the stdlog file and to allow for archiving and analysis of the contents. This restricted activity should be performed only by an assigned individual.

One interesting method for handling this process would be to append stdlog to an ongoing dBASE database. As designed, stdlog can automatically be used as a file that can be loaded directly into dBASE by using the APPEND FROM command, thus archiving stdlog and providing an immediate sorting and reporting capability. After completing this dBASE append step, stdlog would be reset using function logreset.c.

Comments on Logwrite.c

Logwrite.c controls and standardizes the writing of all record entries to the stdlog file, whether they are errors or simply messages. All entries to stdlog that are not error related must be made by an explicit call to function logwrite.c.

Prototype Stdlog Record Structure

Now that we have a convenient mechanism for assigning, writing, and maintaining stdlog, let's develop a standardized record structure for the text data log file. If it is structured in a standard format it can be independently sorted and listed to make the information in the log file more useful. At a minimum, it is important to include the following:

Field	Bytes	Description
Date	8	Log entry sysdate (yyyymmdd)
Time	6	Log entry systime (hh:mmx where x is A, P, N, or M)
Message type	8	Standard type of message entry
Erc	6	Error return code value

Program ID	8	Program identification
Note	n	Variable length text (fixed if used with dBASE)

Because it is desirable to use a text file with the record structure outlined above, we created stdlog instead of altering the assignment of stderr in _main. Because PC-DOS uses stderr for all its error messaging, a uniform record structure could not be implemented for the combined use of stderr by PC-DOS and our application program environment. Without strict record formatting, we would not be able to create sorted reports from the stdlog file. You can, of course, alter the proposed record layout of stdlog to suit your specific requirements.

To assure better management use of stdlog, we have established standard message type categories in function logwrite.c with the following case statement integer values:

Case	**Type**	**Description**
1	ERROR	Error condition
2	WARNING	Warning condition or reminder
3	SECURITY	Sign on rejections and logoff
4	INSTALL	Software installation and updates
5	ENTRY	Program initiation
6	EXIT	Program departure
7	GENERAL	Standard messaging
8	MISC	Non-standard messaging

Clearly these categories can be modified to satisfy your needs, but standard categories should be established so that analysis of the stdlog file is possible.

Error Messaging and Screen Printing

Typically, as shown in functions mesgsps.c (Chapter 4) and mesende.c (Chapter 3), all error or warning messages are displayed to the user, but only some categories are logged to stdlog.

These functions are solely responsible for error logging, display, and printing. Their function argument pflag controls whether stdlog is written and whether the video display is printed if an error is detected.

These functions, together with help.c, enforce our design decision to use MAX_ROW of the video display for all user messaging and the standard use of audibles (beep.c) to alert the user that an error condition has been detected and a message will be displayed.

Quality Assurance Testing and Stdlog

Each qaxxxx.c program (Chapters 5–11, section F.2.0) implements the features outlined in this chapter for stdlog. All messages are written directly to stdlog by logwrite.c itself, or indirectly by calls to logwrite.c from mesgsps.c and mesende.c. A typical stdlog record entry generated by any qaxxxx.c program would appear as follows:

Entry	Description	
19851101	Date of log entry	November 1, 1985
08:01A	Time of log entry	08:01AM
ERROR	Type of log entry	ERROR
001041	Erc value	1041; Bad INT Encode
QAINT	Program ID	Program qaint.c
NULL	Notation	(none)

Because of the uprompt.c function, all the qaxxxx.c test programs (and the demo.c programs in Chapter 2) present the following choices to the user at run time:

Reset stdlog?
Write stdlog?
Print screen?

A **Yes** response to each of these prompts instructs qaxxxx.c to

1. Reset stdlog by calling logreset()

2. Set standard interface function argument logprerr equal to 11, which instructs mesgsps.c and mesende.c to issue a logwrite.c function call for writing stdlog and to issue a pscreen.c function call for error screen printing.

We have elected to include these features for the test environment created for LDTs using the qaxxxx.c programs.

In the development phase of a software project it is often desirable to disable these features. The error log and screen printing are less helpful in the debugging process while errors are plentiful. They play a more significant role in a production environment when errors are more critical, and are the exception, not the rule. When fully operational, stdlog resetting is handled by a restricted operational procedure, and error logging and screen printing is mandatory.

After exiting any qaxxxx.c LDT test session, use the PC-DOS TYPE command to examine the contents of file stdlog. Another test program tckerc.c, which independently tests logreset.c and ckerc.c, is also available on disk.

Appendixes

Appendix A
Glossary

The following definitions are by no means intended to be universal, but pertain only to the material presented in this book.

Access method Any algorithm used with respect to a given storage structure to retrieve or place it into storage.

Alt-Ctrl-Del A keyboard sequence that causes the PC-DOS BIOS to reboot the computer (interrupt 0x19). Since there is no hardware reset button on the IBM-PC, Alt-Ctrl-Del must be used instead.

ASCII **A**merican **S**tandard **C**ode for **I**nformation **I**nterchange. ASCII consists of seven-bit coded characters used for information exchange between data processing, data communications, and associated equipment (see Appendix E).

Attribute Generally associated with video display. Video attributes control such display features as underline, reverse video, nondisplay, blinking, and full or normal intensity.

Backout The removal of the effects of any partially completed file transaction that may be caused by a hardware or software malfunction.

Benchmark A test program designed to highlight the performance characteristics of a given combination of computer hardware, system software, and application software.

Beta test The field testing of a software product that precedes widespread distribution.

Binary key An unsigned byte or word. The interpretation of the physical ordering of bytes in a word varies depending on how each software product defines binary key.

BIOS **B**asic **I**nput **O**utput **S**ystem. BIOS provides low level PC-DOS device services (see Appendix D).

Bit **B**inary Dig**it**.

Boundary alignment The assignment of a starting address for arithmetic data types dictated by hardware design and language compiler standards (see Chapter 2).

B-tree A balanced tree implementation of an indexing scheme.

Characteristic Analogous to the term exponent, it is used to describe a component of floating point numbers on some computers. *See also* Exponent.

Check digit The additional digit(s) carried along with a numeric or alphabetic field for error detection purposes (see Appendix J).

Checkerc Generic name for any function that interrogates a status or error return code of a function (see Chapter 13).

Composite key Key specifications that span fields of a record.

Concatenation The joining of two or more character strings into a larger string.

Ctrl-Break Keyboard sequence that causes the PC-DOS BIOS to generate a 0x23 interrupt terminating the present program (see Appendix D).

DAM file **D**irect **A**ccess **M**ethod. Records are written and retrieved by their relative record position number in the file (from 1 to n).

Data bus A network of common electrical paths within an electronic system. The bus width is equal to the number of parallel circuits (bits).

Data validation Any logical tests that are applied after a logical data type has been encoded.

De The standard decode function name prefix, generically spoken of as dexxxx.c functions.

Decode A function that converts a native C data type representation of a logical data type and produces an ASCII string of characters.

Delimiter A character with special significance for separating or bounding other characters of input or output in a mask.

DOS device names Names reserved for specific I/O devices, for example:

Console: CON
Printer: PRN, LPT, LPT1, LPT2, LPT3, LST
Aux Port: AUX, COM, COM1, COM2, RDR, PUN

Null Device: NUL

Driver routine Any testing or quality assurance program.

Dv The standard data validation function name prefix, generically spoken of as dvxxxxyy.c functions.

En The standard encode function name prefix, generically spoken of as enxxxx.c functions.

Encode A function that accepts an ASCII character string and performs a conversion to a native C data type representing a logical data type.

EOF End-of-file indicator, normally −1 or 0x1A; also end-of-field.

Erc An error return code or status value returned by a function.

ERC_OK The erc of zero (0)—a status code indicating that a function has not detected an error.

Esc Shorthand for Escape, the Escape key.

Ev The standard encode and validation function name prefix, generically spoken of as evxxxx.c functions.

Exponent Standard IEEE binary floating point arithmetic component that locates the binary point within the significant digits (see Appendix K).

Fget The standard getstr.c and evxxxx.c function name prefix identifier. The F connotes a function interface definition that has full coordinates; e.g., win(dow), row, and col(umn) arguments.

Field Field of input, as in standard commercial programming. It does not mean bit isolation in a structure as in Kernighan and Ritchie (p.196).

Filter program Reads data from a standard input device, modifies the data, and writes the results to a standard output device.

Fput The Standard dexxxx.c and putstr.c function name prefix. The F connotes a function interface definition that has full coordinates; e.g., win(dow), row, and col(umn) arguments.

Functions Equivalent to a subroutine or function in FORTRAN or a procedure in PASCAL: a black-box encapsulation of a unit of computation.

Functionality The documented responsibilities and conditions attributed to a function.

F1 Function key #1; used as the help key.

F2 Function key #2; used for screen printing.

Get The standard getstr and evxxxx.c function name prefix. Getxxxx.c functions do not have arguments for coordinates win(dow), row, and col(umn).

Header file A compact control file intended to be included in a C source program that contains system and program constants and macro definitions of functions referred to as (.h) files (see Appendix G).

IEEE Institute for **E**lectrical and **E**lectronic **E**ngineers.

Implementation The operating system and language compiler specific source code for an interface. Several implementations can exist for a single interface definition.

Indexed file Broadly used to describe a B-tree file management implementation.

Interface A widely used black box function with clearly documented arguments. The standard interface definition defines the characteristics of the arguments, but not the actual source code (*see also* Implementation).

ISAM file **I**ndexed **S**equential **A**ccess **M**ethod.

I/O **I**nput/**O**utput.

Justification The process of aligning character strings on the left or right, while ignoring leading or trailing blanks, respectively, to provide for columnar readability (see cjust.c ljust.c, and rjust.c, Chapter 3).

Key The ordered, access pathways defined for an indexed file.

LDT *See* **l**ogical **d**ata **t**ype.

Ldt.h The logical data type header file.

Least significant digit The rightmost digit, often called the low-order position.

Linker file A linker automatic response file (.lnk), conforming to IBM's linker for creating run files (.exe). We supply a .lnk file for each test program (see Appendix L).

Logical data type Abstractions that facilitate computer program development of such fields of input as dates, dollars, time, etc.

Magnitude The bits comprising a char or int data type exclusive of the sign bit.

Mandatory field A data entry field of input that must be comprised of one or more nonwhite space characters.

Mantissa Analogous to significand; used to describe a component of floating point numbers on some computers (*see also* Significand).

Mapping Translating between ASCII character strings and native C data types.

Mask Used to control the display and retrieval of characters from the video display; a character string consisting of delimiter and nondelimiter positions (see Chapter 4).

Most significant digit The leftmost nonzero digit, often called the high-order position.

Native data type Part of the C language data type specification itself. We speak of the native C data types of char, int, float, and double.

Nibble Half of a byte (normally four bits). The high-order nibble corresponds to bits 7, 6, 5, and 4 of a byte.

Nonmandatory field A data entry field of input that can be skipped and yet be considered acceptable.

Nonsegmented key A key that physically represents a contiguous, ascending range of bytes within a record.

No-op No operation. Although dvdummy is a data validation function, it never performs data validation and always returns ERC_OK, making it, in effect, a no-op.

NUL The bit bucket PC-DOS device name. As an input device it generates an immediate EOF (−1). As an output device, the write operations are simulated, but no data are actually written.

NULL ASCII representation of hexadecimal 0 (i.e., 0x00), not to be confused with DOS device NUL, which is the bit bucket. Character strings are terminated by a trailing NULL character.

One's complement In binary arithmetic express a binary quantity (dec 27 = 00011011) as (dec 228 = 11100100) or simply change all 0s to 1s and 1s to 0s. This mathematically is spoken of as the "radix-minus-one complement n' of an m-digit number n in radix r" expressed as

n′ = [(r^m) − 1] − n

where

```
r   = 2
m   = 8
n   = 00011011 (dec 27)
r^m          =    100000000  (dec 256)
[(r^m)−1]    =    011111111  (dec 255)
 − n         =  −  00011011  (dec 27)
n'           =     11100100  (dec 228)
```

Overflow The generation of a number larger than a computer's arithmetic capacity can handle.

Packed decimal Also called BCD (binary coded decimal or 8-4-2-1 code) whereby each byte consists of two four-bit digits (nibbles). For example, (dec 385) = (bcd 0000 0011 1000 0101 = 0385).

Pad byte *See* Padding.

Padding The insertion of bytes to satisfy boundary alignment of native C data types for pointers, structures and unions (see Chapter 2).

Physical data type Analogous term for native data type, in contrast to a logical data type.

Piping The chaining of programs with the automatic redirection of standard input and output.

Portability A measure of ease with which software can be moved between computers of different architecture or operating system software.

Precision The smallest reliably measured portion of a numeric value; e.g., for 1.001 the precision is 1/1000.

Pseudocode Jargon for outline of a function's logical structure.

Put The standard dexxxx.c and putstr.c function name prefix, without coordinates win(dow), row, col(umn).

qa The standard quality assurance driver program name prefix, generically spoken of as qaxxxx.c programs.

Radix A number system with r symbols is said to be of radix r. The base10 (radix 10) number system consists of symbols 0–9. The binary (radix 2) number system consists of symbols 0–1 (see utcharrx.c: Chapter 5, E.5.0).

Relational model A theoretical approach to database management based on tables and their manipulation proposed by E.F. Codd and others. It supports a relational view of data such as flat files (a relation in normal form) and data sublanguages (for data interrogation and updating).

RSAM file **R**ecord **S**equential **A**ccess **M**ethod.

Scratch space Disk storage space required, from time to time, for intermediate files of information. It is allocated as required and released or deallocated when no longer required. Scratch space is a major component of disk storage space planning beyond permanent files and operating and application system space.

Segmented key A key that physically represents an unordered series of nonoverlapping, ascending ranges of bytes of a record.

Shift-PrtSc A keyboard sequence that causes the PC-DOS BIOS to perform interrupt 0x05 to print the video.

Significand Standard IEEE binary floating point arithmetic component that holds the numbers significant digits in binary notation (see Appendix K)

Significant digits The number of digits of a numeric quantity that can be represented reliably by the internal storage format of that data type; e.g., 1.23456789 for float would have only six significant digits and would be represented as 1.23456(789)—the (789) shown would be questionable (see Appendix K).

Slack byte Same as pad byte. *See* Padding.

Stderr The standard error file assigned to a C program, typically the console.

Stdin The standard input file assigned to a C program, typically the keyboard.

Stdio.h The standard I/O header file.

Stdlog The standard error and message logging file (see Chapter 13).

Stdout The standard output file assigned to a C program, typically the video, but often a printer or disk file.

Sysdate System **date.**

Systime System **time.**

Text file A file of contiguous ASCII characters, some of which have special control meanings such as tab, line feed, carriage return, and end with a 0x1A (EOF) character.

Token A computer language (lexical) element. In C there are six classes of tokens: identifiers, constants, strings, operators, and other separators.

Transaction A sequence of file processing operations defined as a group by a begin and end transaction command.

Transparency Data character translations that occur without knowledge of the user and without any adverse effect. For example, standard C I/O emits a carriage return (0x0D) whenever it encounters a single line feed character (0x0A). This ensures that all I/O is CR/LF (0x0D/0x0A).

Two's complement In binary arithmetic express a binary quantity (dec 27 = 00011011) as (dec 229 = 11100101) or simply add 1 to the one's complement (n'). Mathematically, this is spoken of as the "radix complement n" of an m-digit number n in radix r" expressed as

$$n'' = n' + 1$$

where

r	=	2
m	=	8
n	=	00011011 (dec 27)
n'	=	11100100 (dec 228: *see* One's Complement)
+ 1	=	00000001
n"	=	11100101 (dec 229)

Underflow The generation of a number smaller than a computer's arithmetic capacity can handle.

Ut The standard utility function name prefix, generically called utxxxxyy.c functions.

White space In C, blanks (0x20), tabs (\t), newlines (\n) and comments (/* */) are considered white space and are collectively ignored unless they serve to separate tokens.

xxxx The standard logical data type function name suffix identifiers: char, date, dolr, int, real, tele, time, and any others you may create.

yy A standard data validation or utility function suffix identifier.

Zoned decimal Each byte contains one eight-bit digit representation. The low order nibble contains the digit, and the high order nibble contains the zone. In punched card format, the zone, if over-punched, is for a minus (−) sign.

8087 A single chip hardware implementation of the proposed IEEE standard for floating point binary arithmetic. The 8087 is also commonly referred to as an NPX or NPE—numeric processor extension.

8088/86/186 INTEL's series of 8088, 8086, 80186 microprocessors.

Appendix B
Bibliography

Association for Computing Machinery, Inc. (ACM). *Collected Algorithms of the ACM.* Volume 1: Algorithms 1–220. New York: ACM, 1980.

The Chemical Rubber Company. *Handbook of Chemistry and Physics.* 47th Edition. Cleveland, Ohio: 1966–1967.

Clifton, Harold D., *Systems Analysis for Business Data Processing.* Princeton, NJ: Auerbach Publishers, Inc., 1969.

Codd, E.F., "A Relational Model of Data for Large Shared Data Banks." *Communications of the ACM.* 13:6(1970).

Coonen, J.; Kahan, W.; Palmer, J.; Pittman, T.; and Stevenson, D. "A Proposed Standard for Binary Floating Point Arithmetic." *ACM SIGNUM Newsletter.* Special Issue (October 1979).

Galitz, Wilbert O. *Handbook of Screen Format Design.* Wellesley, MA.: Q.E.D. Information Sciences, Inc., 1981.

Galitz, Wilbert O. *Human Factors in Office Automation.* Chicago: Life Office Management Association, Inc., 1980.

Hellerman, Herbert. *Digital Computer System Principles.* New York: McGraw-Hill Book Company, 1967.

Hunt, William J. "Drop-in Modules for C." *PC Tech Journal* 3:6 (1985), pp.100–117; 3:7(1985), pp.135–146.

Hunter, Bruce H. *Understanding C.* Berkeley: SYBEX Inc., 1984.

IBM Corporation. *Disk Operating System Reference, Version 3.10.* Boca Raton, FL: 1985.

IBM Corporation. *Disk Operating System Technical Reference, Version 3.10.* Boca Raton, FL: 1985.

IBM Corporation. *PC-XT Technical Reference Manual,* Boca Raton, FL: 1983.

Intel Corporation. *iAPX 86/88, 186/188 Programmer's Reference.* Santa Clara, CA: May 1983: #210911-001.

Kernighan, Brian W., and Ritchie, Dennis M. *The C Programming Language.* Englewood Cliffs, NJ: Prentice-Hall, 1978.

Kreithen, Alexander. *Data Communications Consultant.* St. Paul, MN: Data Tactics, Inc., 1976.

Lincoln, Thomas L. *The Elegant Automation of Everyday Clerical Procedures: A Scheduling Example.* Strasbourg, France: World Association for Medical Informatics, 1981.

Martin, James. *Introduction to Teleprocessing.* Englewood Cliffs, NJ: Prentice-Hall, Inc., 1972.

National Archives and Record Service. *Getting Started Beginning Your Genealogical Research in the National Archives.* Washington, DC: U.S. General Services Administration, 1983.

Osborne/McGraw-Hill. *Some Common Pascal Programs.* Berkeley: 1982

Sand, Paul A. *Advanced Pascal Programming Techniques.* Berkeley: Osborne/McGraw-Hill, 1984.

Sawin III, Dwight H. *Microprocessors and Microcomputer Systems.* Lexington, MA: D.C. Heath & Co., 1977.

Uspensky, J.V., and Heaslet, M.A. *Elementary Number Theory.* New York: McGraw Hill Book Co., 1939.

Appendix C
Vendors of C Products

This Appendix contains vendors that supply C language compilers and C software utility products. Each utility product extends the capabilities of the C language by providing libraries of useful functions that are not a part of the standard libraries distributed with the C compiler itself.

We have segmented the products into the following groups for your convenience: C compilers, general utility libraries, indexed file processing, sorting, and screen/window management. They are listed in alphabetical order by the vendor's company name. There has been no attempt to rate or recommend the listed products. Each vendor will be happy to supply you with promotional literature or demo disk with which you can evaluate the strengths and weaknesses of the products that interest you. Any vendor omissions or errors in these lists are by no means intentional.

C Compilers

These products are available for most 16 bit microprocessors.

Computer Innovations, Inc. 980 Shrewsbury Avenue #310 Tinton Falls, NJ 07724 201/542-5920	C86: $395
C WARE Corporation P.O. Box C Sunnyvale, CA 94087 408/720-9696	DeSmet C: $109
C-Systems P.O. Box 3253 Fullerton, CA 92634 714/637-5362	C: $199
Datalight, Inc. 11557 Eighth Avenue NE Seattle, WA 98125 206/367-1803	Datalight C: $60

Digital Research, Inc. P.O. Box DRI 60 Garden Court Monterey, CA 93942 408/649-3896	DRC: $350
Lattice, Inc. P.O. Box 3072 Glen Ellyn, IL 60138 312/858-7950	LATC: $500
MANX Aztec C Box 55 Shrewsbury, NJ 07701 201/530-7997	Aztec C: $499
Mark Williams Company 1430 West Wrightwood Avenue Chicago, IL 60614 312/472-6659	MWC86: $495
MicroSoft Corporation Box 97200 10700 Northup Way Bellevue, WA 98009 206/828-8088	C Version 3: $395
MIX Software 2116 East Arapaho Suite 363 Richardson, TX 75081 214/783-6001	MIX C: $40
Rational Systems, Inc. P.O. Box 480 Natick, MA 01760 617/653-6194	Instant-C: $495
Supersoft, Inc. 1713 S. Neil Street P.O. Box 1628 Champaign, IL 61820 217/359-2112	SS-C: $350
Wizard Systems Software, Inc. 11 Willow Court	C: $450

Arlington, MA 02174
617/641-2379

General Utility Libraries

These products provide one or more of the following types of utilities: access to PC-DOS services, control of keyboard input, cursor control of text output, a screen graphics facility, asynchronous communications support, broader printer support, control of audible speaker, and better string processing functions.

Blaise Computing Inc. 2034 Blake Street Berkeley, CA 94704 415/540-5441	C Tools: $125 C Tools 2: $100
Computer Application Engineers, Inc. c/o Robert A. Radcliffe 517 North 19th Street Philadelphia, PA 19130 215/988-9378	LDT: $30 LDT-C: $20
Creative Programming Box 112097 Carrollton, TX 75011 214/783-9388	Vitamin C: $150
Entelekon Software Systems 12118 Kimberley Houston, TX 77024 713/468-4412	C Libraries: $100
Essential Software, Inc. 29 Salter Place Maplewood, NJ 07040 914/762-6605	C Utility Library: $149
Greenleaf Software, Inc. 2101 Hickory Drive Carrollton, TX 75006 214/446-8641	Greenleaf Functions: $185
Lattice, Inc. P.O. Box 3072 Glen Ellyn, IL 60138 213/858-7950	TopView Toolbasket: $250

Lifeboat Associates 1651 Third Avenue New York, NY 10128 212/860-0300	C-Food Smorgasbord: $150
MEF Environmental, Inc. P.O. Box 26537 Austin, TX 78755 512/251-5543	No-Limit: $129
OES Systems 1906 Bruschcliff Road Pittsburgh, PA 15221 412/243-7365	The Hammer: $110
Polytron Corporation P.O. Box 787 Hillsboro, OR 97123 503/684-3000	C Library I: $99
Shaw American Technologies 830 South Second Street Louisville, KY 40201 502/583-5527	APT: $395
Software Horizons, Inc. 165 Bedford Street Burlington, MA 01803 617/273-4711	Building Blocks I: $149
Software Labs 1221 Matisse Street Sunnyvale, CA 94087 408/730-8108	C Utilities: $119
XOR Corporation 5421 Opportunity Court Minnetonka, MN 55343 612/938-0005	C TOOLS: $100

Indexed File Processing

These products generally provide the following utilities: multi-key access to records, single or multiple user record access control, and transaction processing with file recovery for backup/backout.

Computer Control Systems,Inc. 298 - 21st Terrace, S.E. Largo, FL 33541 813/586-1886	FABS: $150
Digital Research, Inc. 60 Garden Court Monterey, CA 93942 408/649-3896	Access Manager: $400
FairCom 2606 Johnson Drive Columbia, MO 65203 314/445-6833	C-Tree: $395
Johnson Associates Software P.O. Box 3069 Redding, CA 96049 916/221-0740	ISAM 300: $190
Lifeboat Associates 1651 Third Avenue New York, NY 10128 212/860-0300	db-c ISAM: $250
PHACT Associates, Ltd.. 225 Lafayette Street Suite 1005 New York, NY 10012 212/420-1512	PHACT ISAM: $250
Raima Corporation 11717 Rainier Avenue South Seattle, WA 98178 206/772-1515	db-Vista: $495
Relational Data Base Systems 2471 East Bayshore Road Suite 600 Palo Alto, CA 94303 415/424-1300	C-ISAM: $225
SoftCraft, Inc. 3624 North Hills Drive Austin, TX 78371 512/346-8380	Btrieve: $245 Btrieve/N: $595

SoftFocus 1277 Pallatine Drive Oakville, Ontario, Canada L6H 1Z1 416/844-2610	Btree Library: $75
Software Horizons, Inc. 165 Bedford Street Burlington, MA 01803 617/273-4711	Power Pack II: $149
Trio Systems 2210 Wilshire Boulevard Suite 289 Santa Monica, CA 90403 213/394-0796	C-Index+: $400

Sorting

These products provide utilities that handle stand-alone and C-language callable sorting of fixed and variable length record files, and the sorting of multiple fields in ascending or descending order.

Computer Control Systems,Inc. 298 - 21st Terrace, S.E. Largo, FL 33541 813/586-1886	AutoSort: $150
Opt-Tech Data Processing P.O. BOX 2167 Humble, TX 77347 713/454-7428	Opt-Tech Sort: $99

Screen/Window Management

These products generally provide utilities for the creation and library maintenance of screens for data entry and display, support of on-line help, and documentation.

Amber Systems, Inc. 1171 S. Saratoga- Sunnyvale Road San Jose, CA 95129 408/996-1883	VSI: $60

Blaise Computing, Inc. 2034 Blake Street Berkeley, CA 94704 415/540-5441	View Manager: $275
Computer Application Engineers, Inc. c/o Robert A. Radcliffe 517 North 19th Street Philadelphia, PA 19130 215/988-9378	LDT: $30.00 LDT-C: $20.00
Creative Solutions 21 Elm Avenue Richford, VT 05476 802/848-7738	Windows for C: $195
Entelekon Software Systems 12118 Kimberley Houston, TX 77024 713/468-4412	C Windows: $100
Lattice, Inc. P.O. BOX 3072 Glen Ellyn, IL 60138 312/858-7950	Lattice Windows: $295.
LRM Systems 4438 Donna Drive Cleveland, OH 44143 216/383-9831	CRIOS: $50
Roundhill Computer Systems Axholme-London Road Marlborough, Wiltshire England (SN8 1LR)	PANEL: $295
Social & Scientific Systems 7101 Wisconsin Avenue Suite 610 Bethesda, MD 20814 301/986-4870	S3-Screen: $30
Softron, Inc. 109 E. Scenic Drive Pass Christian, MS 39571 800/824-3609	OH->Windows: $75

Software Horizons, Inc. 165 Bedford Street Burlington, MA 01803 617/273-4711	BB2:Pack4: $149
Softway, Inc. 500 Sutter Street Suite 222T San Francisco, CA 94102 415/397-4666	MATIS: $50
Vance Info Systems 2818 Clay Street San Francisco, CA 94115 415/922-6539	C-lib: $145
Vermont Creative Software 21 Elm Avenue Richford, VT 05476 802/848-7738	Windows for C: $245

Appendix D Performing PC-DOS Interrupt Functions from Lattice C

The standard function used to generate a PC-DOS function call from the Lattice C environment is as follows:

```
int86( intno, &ir, &or);
```

where:

```
intno;               /*indicates interrupt number*/
union REGS ir;       /*indicates input registers*/
union REGS or;       /*indicates output registers*/
```

The following partial list of interrupt calls is grouped by hexadecimal interrupt number (intno):

Intno	Description
0x00	Divide by zero
0x01	Single step
0x02	Nonmaskable
0x03	Breakpoint
0x04	Overflow
0x05	*Print screen (dos.h: INT_PSC)
0x06	Reserved
0x07	Reserved
0x08	Time of day
0x09	Keyboard
0x0A	Reserved
0x0B	Communications
0x0C	Communications
0x0D	Disk
0x0E	Diskette
0x0F	Printer
0x10	*Video (dos.h: INT_VID)
0x11	Equipment check

0x12	Memory
0x13	Diskette/Disk
0x14	Communications
0x15	Cassette
0x16	Keyboard
0x17	Printer
0x18	Resident BASIC
0x19	Bootstrap
0x1A	Time of day
0x1B	Keyboard break
0x1C	Timer tick
0x1D	Video initialization
0x1E	Disk parameters
0x1F	Video graphics chars
0x20	Program terminate
0x21	*DOS function request (dos.h: INT_DOS)
0x22	Terminate address
0x23	Ctrl-break exit address
0x24	Critical error handler vector
0x25	Absolute disk read
0x26	Absolute disk write
0x27	Terminate but stay resident
0x28	Used internally by DOS
0x29–2E	Reserved by DOS
0x2F	Used internally by DOS
0x30–3F	Reserved for DOS

The asterisks above denote the interrupts that are implemented in this book.

Refer to your most current PC-DOS manual for a complete list of available PC-DOS interrupt calls and for the proper register usage for each function call. The REGS structures are defined in the dos.h header file as follows:

```
struct XREG {short ax,bx,cx,dx,si,di;};
struct HREG {byte al,ah,bl,bh,cl,ch,dl,dh;};
union REGS {struct XREG x; struct HREG h;};
```

Interrupt 0x05: Print Screen

It is possible to invoke the special keyboard handling of Shift-PrtSc by invoking an Interrupt 0x05 [INT_PSC] using function int86. We have provided the function pscreen.c to improve upon the keyboard effect of Shift-PrtSc by adding a printer form feed after completion of printing. This function is used in Chapter 13. See the end of Chapter 4 for pscreen.c source code.

Interrupt 0x10: BIOS Video Control

The following partial list of video control function calls is grouped by call number:

Call	Description
0x00	Set CRT type
0x01	Set cursor type
0x02	*Set cursor position (dos.h: VID_SETC)
0x03	*Read cursor position (dos.h: VID_GETC)
0x04	Read light pen position
0x05	Select active display page
0x06	*Scroll active page up (dos.h: VID_SCUP)
0x07	Scroll active page down
0x08	*Read char/attr at cursor (dos.h: VID_GETA)
0x09	*Write char/attr at cursor (dos.h: VID_WRCA)
0x0A	*Write character only at cursor (dos.h: VID_WRCO)
0x0B	Set color palette
0x0C	Write dot
0x0D	Read dot
0x0E	Write teletype to active page
0x0F	Get current video state

Again, the asterisks denote the functions that are implemented in this book.

Refer to your most current PC-DOS BIOS manual for a complete list of available [INT_VID] video control function calls and for the proper register usage for each function.

For two examples of the use of interrupt 0x10, see the functions getcrc.c, which gets the current cursor position, and setcrc.c, which sets the current cursor position. You will find these functions in Chapter 4.

Interrupt 0x21: PC-DOS Function Calls

The following partial list of PC-DOS function calls is grouped by call number:

Call	Description
0x01–0C	Traditional character device I/O
0x0D–24	Traditional file management
0x25–26	Traditional non-device functions
0x27–29	Traditional file management
0x2A–2E	Traditional non-device functions
0x2F–38	Extended function group
0x39–3B	Directory group
0x3C–46	Extended file management group
0x47–47	Directory group
0x48–4B	Extended memory management group
0x4C–57	Extended function group
0x59–5C	Extended function group
0x5E–5F	Network function group
0x62–62	Extended function group

Refer to your most current PC-DOS Manual for a complete list of available [INT_DOS] function calls for the proper register usage for each function call.

For two examples of the use of interrupt 0x21 see the functions utdatesg.c (Chapter 6, D.16.0), which gets the DOS system date, and uttimesi.c (Chapter 11, D.1.0), which gets the DOS system time. You may also want to look at tdate.c and ttime.c which are available on disk only.

The above interrupt calls were reprinted by permission of IBM Corp. from the IBM Disk Operating System Technical Reference Manual #6138536, 1985, *and the* IBM PC-XT Technical Reference Manual #1502237, 1983.

Appendix E
ASCII Character Set

The following table gives the ASCII (American Standard Code for Information Interchange) character set.

Dec	Hex	Character	Binary	Description
00	00	NUL	0000 0000	NULL; \0 delimiter
01	01	SOH (^A)	0000 0001	Start of heading
02	02	STX (^B)	0000 0010	Start of text
03	03	ETX (^C)	0000 0011	End of text
04	04	EOT (^D)	0000 0100	End of transmission
05	05	ENQ (^E)	0000 0101	Inquiry
06	06	ACK (^F)	0000 0110	Affirmative acknowledgement
07	07	BEL (^G)	0000 0111	Audible bell
08	08	BS (^H)	0000 1000	Backspace
09	09	TAB (^I)	0000 1001	Horizontal tab
10	0A	LF (^J)	0000 1010	Line feed
11	0B	VT (^K)	0000 1011	Vertical tab
12	0C	FF (^L)	0000 1100	Form feed
13	0D	CR (^M)	0000 1101	Carriage return
14	0E	SO (^N)	0000 1110	Shift out
15	0F	SI (^O)	0000 1111	Shift in
16	10	DLE (^P)	0001 0000	Data link escape
17	11	DC1 (^Q)	0001 0001	Device control 1
18	12	DC2 (^R)	0001 0010	Device control 2
19	13	DC3 (^S)	0001 0011	Device control 3
20	14	DC4 (^T)	0001 0100	Device control 4
21	15	NAK (^U)	0001 0101	Negative acknowledgement
22	16	SYN (^V)	0001 0110	Synchronous/Idle
23	17	ETB (^W)	0001 0111	End of transmission block
24	18	CAN (^X)	0001 1000	Cancel
25	19	EM (^Y)	0001 1001	End of medium
26	1A	SUB (^Z)	0001 1010	Substitute
27	1B	ESC	0001 1011	Escape
28	1C	FS	0001 1100	File separator
29	1D	GS	0001 1101	Group separator
30	1E	RS	0001 1110	Record separator
31	1F	US	0001 1111	United separator

Dec	Hex	Character	Binary	Description
32	20	SPACE	0010 0000	Space/Blank character
33	21	!	0010 0001	Exclamation point
34	22	“	0010 0010	Double quotation mark
35	23	#	0010 0011	Pound sign
36	24	$	0010 0100	Dollar sign
37	25	%	0010 0101	Percent sign
38	26	&	0010 0110	Ampersand sign
39	27	‘	0010 0111	Single quotation mark
40	28	(	0010 1000	Left parenthesis
41	29	)	0010 1001	Right parenthesis
42	2A	*	0010 1010	Asterisk
43	2B	+	0010 1011	Plus sign
44	2C	,	0010 1100	Comma
45	2D	-	0010 1101	Hyphen/minus/dash
46	2E	.	0010 1110	Period
47	2F	/	0010 1111	Slash
48	30	0	0011 0000	
49	31	1	0011 0001	
50	32	2	0011 0010	
51	33	3	0011 0011	
52	34	4	0011 0100	
53	35	5	0011 0101	
54	36	6	0011 0110	
55	37	7	0011 0111	
56	38	8	0011 1000	
57	39	9	0011 1001	
58	3A	:	0011 1010	Colon
59	3B	;	0011 1011	Semicolon
60	3C	<	0011 1100	Less-than sign
61	3D	=	0011 1101	Equal-to sign
62	3E	>	0011 1110	Greater-than sign
63	3F	?	0011 1111	Question mark
64	40	@	0100 0000	“At” sign
65	41	A	0100 0001	
66	42	B	0100 0010	
67	43	C	0100 0011	
68	44	D	0100 0100	
69	45	E	0100 0101	
70	46	F	0100 0110	
71	47	G	0100 0111	

Dec	Hex	Character	Binary	Description
72	48	H	0100 1000	
73	49	I	0100 1001	
74	4A	J	0100 1010	
75	4B	K	0100 1011	
76	4C	L	0100 1100	
77	4D	M	0100 1101	
78	4E	N	0100 1110	
79	4F	O	0100 1111	
80	50	P	0101 0000	
81	51	Q	0101 0001	
82	52	R	0101 0010	
83	53	S	0101 0011	
84	54	T	0101 0100	
85	55	U	0101 0101	
86	56	V	0101 0110	
87	57	W	0101 0111	
88	58	X	0101 1000	
89	59	Y	0101 1001	
90	5A	Z	0101 1010	
91	5B	[	0101 1011	Left bracket
92	5C	\	0101 1100	Back slash
93	5D	]	0101 1101	Right bracket
94	5E	^	0101 1110	Caret
95	5F	_	0101 1111	Underline
96	60	‘	0110 0000	Reverse accent
97	61	a	0110 0001	
98	62	b	0110 0010	
99	63	c	0110 0011	
100	64	d	0110 0100	
101	65	e	0110 0101	
102	66	f	0110 0110	
103	67	g	0110 0111	
104	68	h	0110 1000	
105	69	i	0110 1001	
106	6A	j	0110 1010	
107	6B	k	0110 1011	
108	6C	l	0110 1100	
109	6D	m	0110 1101	
110	6E	n	0110 1110	
111	6F	o	0110 1111	

Dec	Hex	Character	Binary	Description
112	70	p	0111 0000	
113	71	q	0111 0001	
114	72	r	0111 0010	
115	73	s	0111 0011	
116	74	t	0111 0100	
117	75	u	0111 0101	
118	76	v	0111 0110	
119	77	w	0111 0111	
120	78	x	0111 1000	
121	79	y	0111 1001	
122	7A	z	0111 1010	
123	7B	{	0111 1011	Left brace
124	7C	¦	0111 1100	Broken vertical bar
125	7D	}	0111 1101	Right brace
126	7E	~	0111 1110	Tilde
127	7F	DEL	0111 1111	Delete/Rubout

For a comprehensive description of character codes (0x00–0x1F) refer to *Introduction to Teleprocessing* by James Martin, p. 71.

Appendix F _main Preprocessing Function for a Lattice C Program

Function _main is found in the file main.c. Main.c is supplied with the Lattice C compiler in source form and in object code format in the lc"x".lib series of libraries, where x corresponds to the memory model being used. In the case of this book, lcs.lib is always used. To override the lcs.lib version of _main when linking programs, you must

1. Use a librarian product to lib a revised main.obj into lcs.lib, or
2. Specifically include main.obj in the list of object modules for the PC-DOS link command.

It is preferable to use a librarian product to put main.obj into lcs.lib; however, to keep this book from depending upon a particular vendor's librarian product, we have elected to specifically include main.obj and all other .objs when linking in the linker automatic response files (.lnk) listed in Appendix L.

For this book we have customized _main (file main.c) to allocate stdlog—our standard message and error logging file—and to disable the Ctrl-Break interrupt normally detected by the PC-DOS BIOS. It is recommended that Ctrl-Break be disabled in the production version of most commercial application software products.

The source code corresponding to the revised _main function follows.

Main.c Source Code

```
/*
** file    : main.c
** function: int _main(line)
**           char *line
** desc    : process command line, open files and call main.
**           This function is a custom version of _main that
**           performs the standard preprocessing of the DOS command
**           line for the main module of a C program. It accepts a
**           command line of the form
**
**            C arg1 arg2 ...
```

```
**
**          and builds a list of pointers to each argument. The first
**          pointer is to the program name C. The standard I/O files
**          stdin, stdout, and stderr are also opened, using file names
**          that were set up by the cx.obj. An additional special file
**          stdlog - standard error and message log file - is opened in
**          Append mode. Ctrl-Break recognition is also turned off.
** test pgm: tmain.c
*/

#include "dos.h"
#include "stdio.h"
#include "ctype.h"
#include "iosl.h"

extern int _stack;
extern char _iname[], _oname[];
extern struct UFB _ufbs[];

#define MAXARG 32               /* maximum command line arguments
*/

int argc;                       /* arg count */
char *argv[MAXARG];             /* arg pointers */

_main(line)

char *line;

{

char c;
FILE *fp0, *fp1, *fp2, *fp3;
extern int _bufsiz;
char *getmem();

union REGS ir, or;          /* Register Setup for DOS call */
byte cbkflag;

/*
** Build argument pointer list
*/

for (argc = 0; argc < MAXARG; )
{
while (isspace(*line)) line++;
if (*line == '\0') break;
argv[argc++] = line;
while ((*line != '\0') && (isspace(*line) == 0)) line++;
c = *line;
*line++ = '\0';
if (c == '\0') break;
}

/*
** Open standard files
**
** fp2 = STDERR
** fp0 = STDIN
** fp1 = STDOUT
*/


/*
** STDERR
*/

fp2 = freopen ("","a",stderr);
if (fp2 == NULL) _exit(1);      /* Note use of _exit vs. exit */
```

```
stderr->_file = 2;
stderr->_flag = _IOWRT | _IONBF;

_ufbs[2].ufbfh = 2;
_ufbs[2].ufbflg = UFB_OP | UFB_WA;


/*
** STDIN
*/

fp0 = freopen (_iname,"r",stdin);
if (fp0 == NULL)
   {
   fputs ("Can't open STDIN file\n", fp2);
   exit(1);
   }

setbuf (fp0, getmem(_bufsiz)); /* set stdin buffered */
fp0->_flag &= ~_IOMYBUF;      /* allow rlsmem if later set
unbuff'd */

stdin->_file = 0;
stdin->_flag = _IOREAD;


 _ufbs[0].ufbflg = UFB_OP | UFB_RA;


 /*
 ** STDOUT
 **
 ** If Command line used a >> (append) redirection to stdout,
 ** open stdout in Append mode otherwise Write mode.
 */

 if (_oname[0] != '>')
      fp1 = freopen (_oname,"w",stdout);
      else
      fp1 = freopen (&_oname[1],"a",stdout);

 if (fp1 == NULL)
    {
    fputs ("Can't open STDOUT file\n", fp2);
    exit(1);
    }

 stdout->_file = 1;
 stdout->_flag = _IOWRT;

 _ufbs[1].ufbfh = 1;
 _ufbs[1].ufbflg = UFB_OP | UFB_WA;

 if (_fgdi(1) & 0x80) stdout->_flag |= _IONBF;



 /*
 ** Open "custom" STDLOG: Standard Error and Message Log File
 */

 fp3 = fopen ("stdlog","a");
 if (fp3 == NULL)
      {
      fputs ("Can't open STDLOG file\n",fp2);
      exit(1);
      }
```

```
/*
** Perform other application system initializations:
** Turn off Ctrl-Break system recognition. There
** should be no need to Ctrl-Break from an application
** system environment!
*/

ir.h.ah = DOS_CTLB;    /* DOS function call */
ir.h.al = 0x01;        /* Set the CTRL-BREAK State */
ir.h.dl = 0x00;        /* Turn CTRL-BREAK OFF */

int86 (INT_DOS, &ir, &or);

cbkflag = or.h.dl;

if (cbkflag != 0x00)
     {
     fputs ("Can't turn OFF CTRL-BREAK\n", fp2);
     exit(1);
     }

/*
** Call user's main program
*/

main(argc,argv);                /* call main function */

exit(0);

}
```

Using _main with Your C Program

To more clearly understand why we have chosen to assign stdlog and disable Ctrl-Break in function _main, it is necessary to understand how and where _main fits into the overall flow of events related to the execution of a C program, the Lattice C compiler, and the PC-DOS environment.

When executing a Lattice C program from PC-DOS, command line arguments can be provided as follows:

DOS: pgname arg1 arg2 . . .

where the pgname is considered as arg0. By using the piping feature, stdin may be redirected with <myinput and stdout may be redirected with >myoutput. <myinput is any valid input device name or file specification and >myoutput is any valid output device name or file specification. (Possible PC-DOS device names are listed in the glossary under DOS device names.)

When using Lattice C, the preprocessing of the command line for the detection of

< (stdin redirection),
= (stack override value)

and

> (stdout redirection)

is performed by cx.obj (where x is s, d, p, or l, depending on the memory model chosen for Lattice C). Cx.obj is linked into every Lattice C program. Any command line arguments for the redirection of standard I/O must precede any other program arguments.

To specify stdin and stdout redirection use the following command line as a guide:

DOS: pgname <myinput >myoutput argx argy . . .

From the example line above, cx.obj sets up the Lattice C environment, drops the pgname and standard I/O redirection arguments, and passes the following command line to _main:

C argx argy . . .

_main actually performs the assignment of stdin, stdout, and stderr, creates the argument list (argc, argv), and then passes control to your main program, which can then access any of the remaining function arguments (argx, argy).

_main is therefore always executed just prior to your program, and is an excellent point at which to ensure that the assignment of stdlog and disabling of Ctrl-Break always occurs.

The information presented in this appendix is provided by permission of Lattice Inc.

Appendix G
Standard C Header Files

The following header files (.h) are included in this book:

Ldt.h:	Logical data type header file
Dos.h:	Operating system and C-compiler flags
Stdio.h:	Standard I/O package
Ctype.h:	ASCII character manipulation macros
Ios1.h:	File block structure for level 1 I/O

The Ldt.h Header File Source Code

```
/* This is the ldt.h header file.
**
** This header file defines all constants used by the
** structured data entry methodology. All global values
** required for the use of logical data type encode,
** decode, data validation, encode and validate, utility,
** and quality assurance functions are found here.
*/

/*
** Error Codes
*/

#define ERC_OK          0
#define ERC_BASE        1000

#define GET_E           1
#define PUT_E           5

#define ENCHAR_E        11
#define ENDATE_E        21
#define ENDOLR_E        31
#define ENINT_E         41
#define ENREAL_E        51
#define ENTELE_E        61
#define ENTIME_E        71
```

```
/*
** Boolean Flags
*/

#define FALSE           0
#define TRUE            1

#define NO              0
#define YES             1

#define LR              0           /* Left ==> Right */
#define RL              1           /* Right ==> Left */

/*
** DECODE Justification Flags
*/

#define NO_JUST         0
#define L_JUST          1
#define C_JUST          2
#define R_JUST          3

/*
** Video Dimensions: assume [1,1] Top/Left Corner
*/

#define MAX_ROW 25
#define MAX_COL 80

/*
** Video Attributes
*/

#define V_PSWD 0x00
#define V_NMAN 0x01
#define V_MAND 0x78
#define V_DISP 0x07


/*
** Other Field Flags
*/
#define PSWD_F  -1      /* Password Field */
#define NMAN_F  0       /* Non-Mandatory Field */
#define MAND_F  1       /* Mandatory Field */
#define DISP_F  2       /* Display Only Field */

/*
** Frequently used character constants
*/
```

```
#define C_NUL       0x00  /* Nul character */
#define C_FF        0x0C  /* Form Feed character */
#define C_CR        0x0D  /* Carriage Return */
#define C_LF        0x0A  /* Line Feed */
#define C_EOF       0x1A  /* End-Of-File Marker = CTRL-Z */
#define C_BLANK     0x20  /* Blank character */
#define C_SPACE     0x20  /* Blank character */
#define C_DQUOTE    0x22  /* Double Quotation */
#define C_DSIGN     0x24  /* Dollar Sign */
#define C_AMPER     0x26  /* Ampersand */
#define C_LPAR      0x28  /* Left Parenthesis */
#define C_RPAR      0x29  /* Right Parenthesis */
#define C_AST       0x2A  /* Asterisk */
#define C_PLUS      0x2B  /* Plus Sign */
#define C_COMMA     0x2C  /* Comma */
#define C_MINUS     0x2D  /* Minus Sign */
#define C_HYPHEN    0x2D  /* Hyphen */
#define C_DASH      0x2D  /* Dash */
#define C_PERIOD    0x2E  /* Period */
#define C_SLASH     0x2F  /* Slash */
#define C_ZERO      0x30  /* Numeric 0 */
#define C_ONE       0x31  /* Numeric 1 */
#define C_NINE      0x39  /* Numeric 9 */
#define C_COLON     0x3A  /* Colon */
#define C_QUEST     0x3F  /* Question Mark */
#define C_A         0x41  /* Character A */
#define C_M         0x4D  /* Character M */
#define C_N         0x4E  /* Character N */
#define C_P         0x50  /* Character P */
#define C_Z         0x5A  /* Character Z */
#define C_UL        0x5F  /* Underline character */

/*
** Maximum field width specifications by LDT
** i.e. char string[n+1] where n = MAX-XXXX below:
*/

#define MAX_CHAR    80
#define MAX_DATE    30
#define MAX_DOLR    20
#define MAX_INT      6
#define MAX_INT4    11
#define MAX_REAL    12
#define MAX_RDBL    20
#define MAX_TELE    13
#define MAX_TIME     6
```

```
/*
** Physical (native C) data type size in bytes
** associated with each logical data type. Refer
** to typedefs defined below!
*/

#define PHY_CHAR        80  /* Defined string[n+1]
                               where n=PHY_CHAR */
#define PHY_DATE         4
#define PHY_DOLR         4
#define PHY_INT          2
#define PHY_INT4         4
#define PHY_REAL         4
#define PHY_RDBL         8
#define PHY_TELE         6
#define PHY_TIME         2
/*
** Typedefs for logical data types:
**
** Note that with the seven logical data types included in this
** book, every C data type and construction (union and structure)
** has been included. This demonstrates the versatility
** of this methodology in handling every C data type, unions of
** C data types, and structures of C data types!
*/

typedef char CHAR;
typedef long int DATE;
typedef long int DOLR;
typedef union { int i2; long int i4; } INT;
typedef union { float f4; double d8; } REAL;
typedef struct { int tac; long int tnbr; } TELE;
typedef int TIME;

/*
** LDT "DATE" min/max Calendar Years
*/

#define YYYY_MIN 1885
#define YYYY_MAX 2020

/*
** LDT "TELE" default Telephone Area Code
*/
#define DEF_AC "215"
```

Source Code for Other Header Files

Dos.h Header File

```
/* This is the dos.h header file.
**
** This header file supplies information needed to interface MSDOS
** Version 2.0+ with the Lattice C compiler for the IBM PC computer
**
*/

/*
** The following symbol defines which computer is being used.
**
**      IBMPC   IBM Personal Computer
*/

#define IBMPC 1

/*
** The following symbol defines which processor is being used
**
**      I8086   Intel 8086 or 8088
*/

#define I8086 1

/*
** The following symbol defines which memory addressing model
** is in use for chips of the Intel 8086 variety.
**
**      I8086S          64K program, 64K data
*/

#define I8086S 1

/*
** The following definitions indicate which type of integer
** has the same size as a pointer.
**
**      SPTR    defined if sizeof(pointer) == sizeof(short int)
*/

#define SPTR 1

/*
** The following symbols define which operating system is being used.
**
**      MSDOS           Microsoft's MSDOS
**      MSDOS2          MSDOS Version 2
**
**      Note: CPM will be set to 1 for any of the above.
*/

#define MSDOS 1

#define MSDOS2 1

#define CPM 1
```

```
/*
** The following symbols define which particular C compiler is being used.
**
**      LATTICE         Lattice C compiler
*/

#define LATTICE 1


/*
** The following type definitions take care of the particularly nasty
** machine dependency caused by the unspecified handling of sign
** extension in the C language.  When converting char to int, some
** compilers will extend the sign, while others will not. Both are
** correct, and the unsuspecting programmer is the loser. For
** situations where it matters, the new type byte is equivalent
** to unsigned char.
*/

#ifdef LATTICE

typedef char byte;

#endif

/*
** Miscellaneous definitions
*/

#define SECSIZ 128              /* disk sector size */

#ifdef CPM

#define DMA (char *)0x80        /* disk buffer address */

#endif


/*
** The following structure is a file control block.  Operating systems
** with CPM-like characteristics use the FCB to store information about
** a file while it is open.
*/

struct FCB
{
char fcbdrv;                    /* drive code */
char fcbnam[8];                 /* file name */
char fcbext[3];                 /* file name extension */


#ifdef MSDOS

short fcbcb;                    /* current block number */
short fcblrs;                   /* logical record size */
long fcblfs;                    /* logical file size */
short fcbdat;                   /* create/change date */
char fcbsys[10];                /* reserved */
char fcbcr;                     /* current record number */
long fcbrec;                    /* random record number */

#else

char fcbexn;                    /* extent number */
char fcbsl;                     /* reserved */
char fcbs2;                     /* reserved */
char fcbrc;                     /* record count */
char fcbsys[16];                /* reserved */
```

```
char fcbcr;                    /* current record number */
short fcbrec;                  /* random record number */
char fcbovf;                   /* random record overflow */

#endif
};

#define FCBSIZ sizeof(struct FCB)


/*
** The following symbols define the sizes of file names and node names.
*/

#ifdef CPM

#define FNSIZE 16              /* maximum file node name size */
#define FMSIZE 16              /* maximum file name size */

#endif

#ifdef MSDOS2

#define FNSIZE 16
#define FMSIZE 64

#endif


/*
** The following structures define the 8086 registers that are passed to
** various low-level operating system service functions.
*/

#ifdef I8086

struct XREG
{
short ax,bx,cx,dx,si,di;
};

struct HREG
{
byte al,ah,bl,bh,cl,ch,dl,dh;
};

union REGS
{
struct XREG x;
struct HREG h;
};

struct SREGS
{
short es,cs,ss,ds;
};

#endif

/*
** The following interrupt numbers are used by function
**      int86 ( intno, inregs, outregs )
** "intno" values used in this book follow:
*/

#ifdef MSDOS

#define INT_PSC  0x05          /* Print Screen */
#define INT_VID  0x10          /* BIOS CRT Control */
#define INT_DOS  0x21          /* DOS Function Call Access */
```

```
#endif

/*
** The following symbols define the code numbers for
** the various VID service functions.
*/
#ifdef MSDOS

#define VID_SETC  0x02          /* Set cursor position */
#define VID_GETC  0x03          /* Get cursor position */
#define VID_SCUP  0x06          /* Scroll active page up */
#define VID_GETA  0x08          /* Get char/attribute */
#define VID_WRCA  0x09          /* Write char/attribute */
#define VID_WRCO  0x0A          /* Write character only */

#endif

/*
** The following symbols define the code numbers for
** the various DOS service functions.
*/

#ifdef MSDOS

#define DOS_PCON 0x02           /* put character to console */
#define DOS_PPRN 0x05           /* put character to printer */
#define DOS_GKBC 0x07           /* get character from keyboard */
#define DOS_CTAB 0x0C           /* clear kbd type ahead buffer */
#define DOS_DATE 0x2A           /* get system date */
#define DOS_TIME 0x2C           /* get system time */
#define DOS_CTLB 0x33           /* setoff CTRL-BREAK */
#define DOS_EXEC 0x4B           /* execute (chain to) a program
*/

#endif


/*
** The following codes are used to open files in various modes.
*/

#ifdef LATTICE

#define OPENR 0x8000            /* open for reading */
#define OPENW 0x8001            /* open for writing */
#define OPENU 0x8002            /* open for read/write */
#define OPENC 0x8001            /* create and open for writing */

#else

#define OPENR 0
#define OPENW 1
#define OPENU 2

#endif


/*
** The following codes are returned by the low-level operating
** system service calls.  They are usually placed into _oserr
** by the OS interface functions.
*/

#if MSDOS2

#define E_FUNC  1       /* invalid function code */
#define E_FNF   2       /* file not found */
#define E_PNF   3       /* path not found */
#define E_NMH   4       /* no more file handles */
```

```
#define E_ACC    5        /* access denied */
#define E_IFH    6        /* invalid file handle */
#define E_MCB    7        /* memory control block problem */
#define E_MEM    8        /* insufficient memory */
#define E_MBA    9        /* invalid memory block address */
#define E_ENV   10        /* invalid environment */
#define E_FMT   11        /* invalid format */
#define E_IAC   12        /* invalid access code */
#define E_DATA 13         /* invalid data */
#define E_DRV   15        /* invalid drive code */
#define E_RMV   16        /* remove denied */
#define E_DEV   17        /* invalid device */
#define E_NMF   18        /* no more files */

#endif

/*
** Miscellaneous defined items for application system use.
*/

/*
** constant defining the equivalent of 1/10th second
** timing for the expression: for (i=0; i < DEL_ITER; i++)
*/

#define DEL_ITER 1250

/*
** port for the speaker (bell) on the IBM PC
*/

#define BEL_PORT 0x61
```

Stdio.h Header File

```
/* This is the stdio.h header file.
**
** This header file defines the information used by the standard
I/O
** package.
**
*/

#define _BUFSIZ 512               /* standard buffer size */
#define BUFSIZ 512                /* standard buffer size */
#define _NFILE 20                 /* maximum number of files */

struct _iobuf
{
char *_ptr;                       /* current buffer pointer */
int _rcnt;                        /* current byte count for reading
*/
int _wcnt;                        /* current byte count for writing
*/
char *_base;                      /* base address of I/O buffer */
char _flag;                       /* control flags */
char _file;                       /* file number */
int _size;                        /* size of buffer */
char _cbuff;                      /* single char buffer */
char _pad;                        /* (pad to even number of bytes)
*/
};
```

```
extern struct _iobuf _iob[_NFILE];

#define _IOREAD 1             /* read flag */
#define _IOWRT 2              /* write flag */
#define _IONBF 4              /* non-buffered flag */
#define _IOMYBUF 8            /* private buffer flag */
#define _IOEOF 16             /* end-of-file flag */
#define _IOERR 32             /* error flag */
#define _IOSTRG 64
#define _IORW 128             /* read-write (update) flag */

#define NULL 0                /* null pointer value */
#define FILE struct _iobuf    /* shorthand */
#define EOF (-1)              /* end-of-file code */

#define stdin (&_iob[0])      /* standard input file pointer */
#define stdout (&_iob[1])     /* standard output file pointer
*/
#define stderr (&_iob[2])     /* standard error file pointer */

/*
** Additional assignment of standard system log file pointer
** as allocated in _main (Appendix E).
*/

#define stdlog (&_iob[3])

#define getc(p) (--(p)->_rcnt>=0? *(p)->_ptr++:_filbf(p))

/*
** The following macro getchar has been renamed to getchars
** as not to conflict with the structured data entry methodology
** function getchar!
*/

#define getchars() getc(stdin)

#define putc(c,p) (--(p)->_wcnt>=0? ((int)(*(p)->_ptr++=(c))):
                _flsbf((c),p))

/*
** The following macro putchar has been renamed to putchars
** as not to conflict with the structured data entry methodology
** function putchar!
*/

#define putchars(c) putc(c,stdout)

#define feof(p) (((p)->_flag&_IOEOF)!=0)
#define ferror(p) (((p)->_flag&_IOERR)!=0)
#define fileno(p) (p)->_file
#define rewind(fp) fseek(fp,0L,0)
#define fflush(fp) _flsbf(-1,fp)

FILE *fopen();
FILE *freopen();
long ftell();
char *fgets();

#define abs(x) ((x)<0?-(x):(x))
#define max(a,b) ((a)>(b)?(a):(b))
#define min(a,b) ((a)<=(b)?(a):(b))
```

Ctype.h Header File

```
/* This is the ctype.h header file.
**
** This header file defines various ASCII character manipulation macros,
** as follows:
**
**        isalpha(c)    non-zero if c is alpha
**        isupper(c)    non-zero if c is upper case
**        islower(c)    non-zero if c is lower case
**        isdigit(c)    non-zero if c is a digit (0 to 9)
**        isxdigit(c)   non-zero if c is a hexadecimal digit (0 to 9,
**                                                          A to F,
**                                                          a to f)
**        isspace(c)    non-zero if c is white space
**        ispunct(c)    non-zero if c is punctuation
**        isalnum(c)    non-zero if c is alpha or digit
**        isprint(c)    non-zero if c is printable (including blank)
**        isgraph(c)    non-zero if c is graphic (excluding blank)
**        iscntrl(c)    non-zero if c is control character
**        isascii(c)    non-zero if c is ASCII
**        iscsym(c)     non-zero if valid character for C symbols
**        iscsymf(c)    non-zero if valid first character for C symbols
**
*/

#define _U 1           /* upper case flag */
#define _L 2           /* lower case flag */
#define _N 4           /* number flag */
#define _S 8           /* space flag */
#define _P 16          /* punctuation flag */
#define _C 32          /* control character flag */
#define _B 64          /* blank flag */
#define _X 128         /* hexadecimal flag */

extern char _ctype[];   /* character type table */

#define isalpha(c)      (_ctype[(c)+1]&(_U|_L))
#define isupper(c)      (_ctype[(c)+1]&_U)
#define islower(c)      (_ctype[(c)+1]&_L)
#define isdigit(c)      (_ctype[(c)+1]&_N)
#define isxdigit(c)     (_ctype[(c)+1]&_X)
#define isspace(c)      (_ctype[(c)+1]&_S)
#define ispunct(c)      (_ctype[(c)+1]&_P)
#define isalnum(c)      (_ctype[(c)+1]&(_U|_L|_N))
#define isprint(c)      (_ctype[(c)+1]&(_P|_U|_L|_N|_B))
#define isgraph(c)      (_ctype[(c)+1]&(_P|_U|_L|_N))
#define iscntrl(c)      (_ctype[(c)+1]&_C)
#define isascii(c)      ((unsigned)(c)<=127)
#define iscsym(c)       (isalnum(c)||(((c)&127)==0x5f))
#define iscsymf(c)      (isalpha(c)||(((c)&127)==0x5f))

#define toupper(c)      (islower(c)?((c)-('a'-'A')):(c))
#define tolower(c)      (isupper(c)?((c)+('a'-'A')):(c))
#define toascii(c)      ((c)&127)
```

Ios1.h Header File

```
/* This is the iosl.h header file.
**
** The following structure is a UNIX file block that retains
** information about a file being accessed via the
** level 1 I/O functions.
*/
```

```
struct UFB
{
char ufbflg;            /* flags */
char ufbtyp;            /* device type */

#if MSDOS

#if MSDOS2

int ufbfh;              /* file handle */

#else

struct FCB ufbfcb;      /* file control block */

#endif

#else

struct FAB
        {
        struct FCB fcb;         /* file control block */
        char wf;                /* buffer write flag */
        long fpos;              /* file position */
        long eof;               /* end of file */
        long peof;              /* previous end of file */
        int bn;                 /* block number */
        char b[128];            /* block buffer */
        }
    ufbfcb;

#endif
};

#define NUFBS 20        /* number of UFBs defined */

/*
** UFB.ufbflg definitions
*/

#define UFB_OP 0x80     /* file is open */
#define UFB_RA 0x40     /* reading is allowed */
#define UFB_WA 0x20     /* writing is allowed */
#define UFB_NT 0x10     /* access file with no translation */
#define UFB_AP 8        /* append mode flag */


/*
** UFB.ufbtyp definitions
*/

#define D_DISK 0
#define D_CON 1
#define D_PRN 2
#define D_AUX 3
#define D_NULL 4
```

The dos.h, stdio.h, ctype.h, and ios1.h header files are included with permission from Lattice, Inc. Dos.h has been extensively edited; stdio.h has been slightly modified; and ctype.h and ios.h are exactly as distributed.

Appendix H
Utility Routines for Byte Reordering of C Data Types

The following utility routines are useful for altering the physical storage order of the C data types shown in Chapter 2, Figure 2.2.

Function [INT]	
RI2 (INT);	Reverses integer two bytes
Function [LONG]	
RI4 (LONG);	Reverses integer four bytes
Function [FLOAT]	
RF4 (FLOAT);	Reverses float four bytes
Function [DOUBLE]	
RD8 (DOUBLE);	Reverses double eight bytes

Each routine is presently designed to reverse the byte order of each data type. Out intent is to create physical representations that agree with the logical representations shown in Figure 2.2 and therefore become true binary representations.

Alteration may be necessary to offset the features (or lack of) of a particular indexed file or sorting package. You can use these functions to alter the physical storage for C data types fields of a data structure defined as either key fields or sort fields. Since the utility routines are designed to return the transformed data type by value, they can conveniently be used to surround the normal data type variable names.

Remember, however, that each program utilizing these functions must specifically declare each function type, since they all do not return a default data type of integer. For example:

```
int ri2();
long ri4();
float rf4();
double rd8();
```

The source code for these functions, grouped together in file rbcdt.c, is found in the listing that follows.

Rbcdt.c Source Code and Commentary

```
/*
** file    : rbcdt.c
** function: int ri2();
**         : long int ri4();
**         : float rd4();
**         : double rd8();
** desc    : functions to alter C arithmetic data type physical
**           storage characteristics on the INTEL 8088/86/186
** test pgm: trbcdt.c
*/
/*
**      Function ri2: Reverse INTEGER 2 bytes
*/
        int ri2 (ival)
        int ival;
        {
        struct S1 { int i2; };
        struct S2 { char b1;
                    char b2;
                    char b3; };
        union U1  { struct S1 _int;
                    struct S2 _byte; } u1;
        u1._int.i2 = ival;
        u1._byte.b3 = u1._byte.b2;
        u1._byte.b2 = u1._byte.b1;
        u1._byte.b1 = u1._byte.b3;
        u1._int.i2 = u1._int.i2;
        return ( u1._int.i2 );
        }
/*
**      Function ri4: Reverse LONG INTEGER 4 bytes
*/
        long ri4 (lval)
        long lval;
        {
        struct S3 { long i4; };
        struct S4 { char b1;
                    char b2;
                    char b3;
                    char b4;
                    char b5; };
        union U2  { struct S3 _long;
                    struct S4 _byte; } u2;
        u2._long.i4 = lval;
        u2._byte.b5 = u2._byte.b1;
        u2._byte.b1 = u2._byte.b4;
        u2._byte.b4 = u2._byte.b5;
        u2._byte.b5 = u2._byte.b2;
        u2._byte.b2 = u2._byte.b3;
        u2._byte.b3 = u2._byte.b5;
        return ( u2._long.i4 );
        }
/*
**      Function rf4: Reverse FLOAT 4 bytes
*/
        float rf4 (fval)
        float fval;
        {
        struct S5 { float f4; };
        struct S6 { char b1;
                    char b2;
                    char b3;
                    char b4;
                    char b5; };
```

```
        union U3  { struct S5 _float;
                    struct S6 _byte; } u3;
        u3._float.f4 = fval;
        u3._byte.b5 = u3._byte.bl;
        u3._byte.bl = u3._byte.b4;
        u3._byte.b4 = u3._byte.b5;
        u3._byte.b5 = u3._byte.b2;
        u3._byte.b2 = u3._byte.b3;
        u3._byte.b3 = u3._byte.b5;
        return ( u3._float.f4 );
        }
/*
**      Function rd8: Reverse DOUBLE 8 bytes
*/
        double rd8 (dval)
        double dval;
        {
        struct S7 { double d8; };
        struct S8 { char bl;
                    char b2;
                    char b3;
                    char b4;
                    char b5;
                    char b6;
                    char b7;
                    char b8;
                    char b9; };
        union U4  { struct S7 _double;
                    struct S8 _byte; } u4;
        u4._double.d8 = dval;
        u4._byte.b9 = u4._byte.bl;
        u4._byte.bl = u4._byte.b8;
        u4._byte.b8 = u4._byte.b9;
        u4._byte.b9 = u4._byte.b2;
        u4._byte.b2 = u4._byte.b7;
        u4._byte.b7 = u4._byte.b9;
        u4._byte.b9 = u4._byte.b3;
        u4._byte.b3 = u4._byte.b6;
        u4._byte.b6 = u4._byte.b9;
        u4._byte.b9 = u4._byte.b4;
        u4._byte.b4 = u4._byte.b5;
        u4._byte.b5 = u4._byte.b9;
        return ( u4._double.d8 );
        }
```

- Note that each function is declared as a different type. This is necessary because values other than int are being returned.
- Note the use of _variable names. Underlining variable names is a convenient way of avoiding compiler keyword conflicts while promoting self-documenting source code.
- Note the use of structures and unions to facilitate the transformation of the argument values. It is critical that Lattice C compiler option -a be used for these functions to work properly. The selection of option -a for pass one (lc1) is critical when using unions, for real time applications, and when making memory mapped I/O assignments. The choice of option -a prevents code

optimization in pass two (lc2), which may alter the intent or sequence of your code. All C source code included in this book has been compiled with option -a.

- A test program, trbcdt.c, is available on disk.

Appendix I
Powers of 2 ^ n Table

This table has been rounded and truncated at the least (rightmost) significant digit to accommodate photocomposition.

This table is useful in developing the binary representations of int, float, and double C data types.

2^n	n	2^-n
1	0	1.0
2	1	0.5
4	2	0.25
8	3	0.125
16	4	0.062 5
32	5	0.031 25
64	6	0.015 625
128	7	0.007 812 5
256	8	0.003 906 25
512	9	0.001 953 125
1 024	10	0.000 976 562 5
2 048	11	0.000 488 281 25
4 096	12	0.000 244 140 625
8 192	13	0.000 122 070 312 5
16 384	14	0.000 061 035 156 25
32 768	15	0.000 030 517 578 125
65 536	16	0.000 015 258 789 062 5
131 072	17	0.000 007 629 394 531 25
262 144	18	0.000 003 814 697 265 625
524 288	19	0.000 001 907 348 632 812 5
1 048 576	20	0.000 000 953 674 316 406 25
2 097 152	21	0.000 000 476 837 158 203 125
4 194 304	22	0.000 000 238 418 579 101 562 5
8 388 608	23	0.000 000 119 209 289 550 781 25
16 777 216	24	0.000 000 059 604 644 775 390 625
33 554 432	25	0.000 000 029 802 322 387 695 312 5
67 108 864	26	0.000 000 014 901 161 193 847 656 25
134 217 728	27	0.000 000 007 450 580 596 923 828 125
268 435 456	28	0.000 000 003 725 290 298 461 914 062 5
536 870 912	29	0.000 000 001 862 645 149 230 957 031 25
1 073 741 824	30	0.000 000 000 931 322 574 615 478 515 625
2 147 483 648	31	0.000 000 000 465 661 287 307 739 257 812 5
4 294 967 296	32	0.000 000 000 232 830 643 653 869 628 906 3
8 589 934 592	33	0.000 000 000 116 415 321 826 934 814 453 1
17 179 869 184	34	0.000 000 000 058 207 660 913 467 407 226 6
34 359 738 368	35	0.000 000 000 029 103 830 456 733 703 613 3
68 719 476 736	36	0.000 000 000 014 551 915 228 366 851 806 6
137 438 953 472	37	0.000 000 000 007 275 957 614 183 425 903 3
274 877 906 944	38	0.000 000 000 003 637 978 807 091 712 951 7
549 755 813 888	39	0.000 000 000 001 818 989 403 545 856 475 8
1 099 511 627 776	40	0.000 000 000 000 909 494 701 772 928 237 9
2 199 023 255 552	41	0.000 000 000 000 454 747 350 886 464 119 0
4 398 046 511 104	42	0.000 000 000 000 227 373 675 443 232 059 5
8 796 093 022 208	43	0.000 000 000 000 113 686 837 721 616 029 7
17 592 186 044 416	44	0.000 000 000 000 056 843 418 860 808 014 9
35 184 372 088 832	45	0.000 000 000 000 028 421 709 430 404 007 4
70 368 744 177 664	46	0.000 000 000 000 014 210 854 715 202 003 7
140 737 488 355 328	47	0.000 000 000 000 007 105 427 357 601 001 9
281 474 976 710 656	48	0.000 000 000 000 003 552 713 678 800 501 0
562 949 953 421 312	49	0.000 000 000 000 001 776 356 839 400 250 5
1 125 899 906 842 624	50	0.000 000 000 000 000 888 178 419 700 125 2
2 251 799 813 685 248	51	0.000 000 000 000 000 444 089 209 850 062 6
4 503 599 627 370 496	52	0.000 000 000 000 000 222 044 604 925 031 3

Appendix J
Check Digit Error Detection Algorithms

Check digits can be used as a means of detecting human errors that sometimes occur when transcribing identification fields of information from one document or medium to another. Such errors generally fall into three categories: transcription (87%), transposition (8%), and other (5%). Check digits are used in addition to the identification field itself and carry no meaning other than assurance of the correctness of an identification field. Check digits relate to the value of an identification field in such a way that any change in the identification field is reflected in a change in the check digits.

Various modulus check digit methods exist to control and detect common human transcription and transposition errors. Modulus *n* schemes produce $n-1$ check digits. Therefore modulus 10 produces a single check digit of value 0 through 9. The popular modulus 11 produces two check digits, 00 through 10, or a single alphabetic check digit, A through L (omitting I).

Check digits can be calculated from identification fields that are strictly alphabetic, strictly numeric, or a combination of alphabetic and numeric. Typically, characters in an identification field other than the set of blank, hyphen, ampersand, and slash (which are ignored in the modulus calculation) result in a blank check digit.

Let's examine two common check digit algorithms.

Modulus 10 Check Digits

Calculation

1. The units position and every alternating digit of the number are multiplied by 2. Each other position is multiplied by 1.

2. The digits of the resulting products are then added together.
3. This total is subtracted from the next higher number ending in zero; the difference is the check digit.

Sample Calculation

ID field	75264
Code number	7 5 2 6 4
Weights	2 1 2 1 2
Products	14 5 4 6 8 = 37
Check digit	40 − 37 = 3
Code number	75264–3

Verification

1. The check digit position and every alternating digit is multiplied by 1. All other digits are multiplied by 2.
2. The digits of the resulting product are all added together.
3. This total is divided by the modulus 10. If the remainder is zero, the identification number is correct; otherwise it is an error.

Sample Verification

ID field	75264–3
Code number	7 5 2 6 4 3
Weights	2 1 2 1 2 1
Products	14 5 4 6 8 3 = 40
Remainder	40/10 = 0 OK!

Examples

Shown below are a number of different types of errors that can occur using the code number 75264–3 where 3 is the check digit.

Type of error	Example	Products	Sum	Rem
Transcription	753643	14 05 06 06 08 03	42	2
Transposition	752463	14 05 04 04 12 03	42	2
Double transposition	762543	14 06 04 05 08 03	40	0*
Left shift	52643_	10 02 12 04 06 --	34	4
Right shift	_75264	-- 07 10 02 12 04	35	5
Omission right move	_75243	-- 07 10 02 08 03	30	0**
Omission left move	75243_	14 05 04 04 06 --	33	3
Insertion	7526643	07 10 02 12 06 08 03	48	2

* This line demonstrates an imperfection in the system. A code number of zero indicates an acceptable value. Double transposition is not detected because the alternating weights of 1 and 2 do not alter the product sum. Modulus 11 below detects this error.

** This line demonstrates an imperfection in the system. A code number of zero indicates an acceptable value. It must be remembered that in this case, the number would be taken to be 7524 with a check digit of 3. This imperfection also applies to other types of errors and check digit systems.

Modulus 11 Check Digits

Calculation

1. Multiply each digit by its weight; the digit in the rightmost (or least significant position) has a weight of 2, the next position a weight of 3, and so on.
2. Add together the products of these multiplications.
3. Divide this sum by 11.
4. Subtract the remainder of step 3 from 11; the result is the modulus 11 check digit.

Sample Calculation

ID field	75264						
Code number	7	5	2	6	4		
Weights	6	5	4	3	2		
Products	42	25	8	18	8	=	101
Remainder	101/11 = 2						
Check digit	11 − 2 = 9						
Code number	75264–9						

Verification

1. Multiply each digit by its weight; the check digit in the rightmost (or least significant position) has a weight of 1, the next position a weight of 2, and so on.
2. Add together the products of these multiplications.
3. This total is divided by the modulus 11. If the remainder is zero the identification number is correct; otherwise it is an error.

Sample Verification

ID field	75264–9							
Code number	7	5	2	6	4	9		
Weights	6	5	4	3	2	1		
Products	42	25	8	18	8	9	=	110
Remainder	110/11 = 0 OK!							

Examples

Shown below are a number of different types of errors that can occur using the code number 75264–9 where 9 is the check digit.

Type of error	Example	Products	Sum	Rem
Transcription	753649	42 25 12 18 08 09	114	4
Transposition	752469	42 25 08 12 12 09	108	9
Double transposition	762549	42 30 08 15 08 09	112	2
Left shift	52649_	30 10 24 12 18 --	94	6
Right shift	_75264	-- 35 20 06 12 04	77	0*
Omission right move	_75249	-- 35 20 06 08 09	78	1
Omission left move	75249_	42 25 08 12 18 --	105	6
Insertion	7526649	49 30 10 24 18 08 09	148	5

* This line demonstrates an imperfection in the system. A code number of zero indicates an acceptable value. It must be remembered that in this case, the number would be taken to be 7526 with a check digit of 4. This imperfection also applies to other types of errors and check digit systems.

Modulus 11 is 100% secure for transcription, transposition, and double transposition errors. Together these errors account for 95% of all errors made. It is 91% secure for all other types of errors (5% of all errors made). The overall efficiency of modulus 11 for error detection is 99.55%. Only about one error in 200 escapes detection.

Appendix K Value Range Computations for Native C Data Types

Char

All char constants are of the ASCII (seven-bit) character set. The numeric value of a character is its ordinal position in the ASCII character set ranging from 0x00 = 0 to 0x7F = 127. Mathematically this range can be expressed as

0 <= char <= [2^(n−1)] − 1

where n = 8 for an eight-bit byte. ASCII character constants are always positive.

The logical and physical bit patterning for char is shown in Figure 2.2 for the INTEL 8088/86/186.

Int

All 16-bit ints have a signed range of −32,767 to +32,767. (Normally, the allowable range would be −32,768 to +32,768 but, for portability reasons, we have chosen to further limit this range.) Ints are composed of one high order sign bit and 15 magnitude bits. Mathematically this can be expressed as

−[2^(n−1)] + 1 <= int <= +[2^(n−1)] − 1

where n = 16 for two eight-bit bytes. All negative values are stored in two's complement form.

The number of significant digits is determined from 2^15 magnitude bits giving 4–5 significant digits.

If all 16-bits are treated as a binary unit, the following ascending sorted sequence results for a number range from −Nmin through +Nmax:

0 . . . +Nmax, −Nmin . . . −1

Unsigned int data types are always positive and range from 0 to +65,536. Mathematically this can be expressed as

$$0 <= \text{unsigned int} <= +[2\hat{}(n)]$$

The logical and physical bit patterning for ints is shown in Figure 2.2 for the INTEL 8088/86/186.

Long Int

All 32-bit long ints have a signed range from −2,147,483,647 to + 2,147,483,647. (Normally, the allowable range would be −2,147,483,648 to +2,147,483,648 but again, for portability reasons, we have chosen to further limit this range.) Long ints are composed of one high order sign bit and 31 magnitude bits. Mathematically this can be expressed as

$$-[2\hat{}(n-1)] + 1 <= \text{long int} <= +[2\hat{}(n-1)] - 1$$

where n = 32 for four eight-bit bytes. All negative values are stored in two's complement form.

The number of significant digits is determined from 2^31 magnitude bits giving 9–10 significant digits.

If all 32-bits are treated as a binary unit, the following ascending sorted sequence results for a number range from −Nmin through +Nmax:

0 . . . +Nmax, −Nmin . . . −1

Unsigned long int data types are always positive and range from 0 to +4,294,967,296. Mathematically this can be expressed as

$$0 <= \text{unsigned long int} <= +[2\hat{}(n)]$$

The logical and physical bit patterning for long ints is shown in Figure 2.2 for the INTEL 8088/86/186.

Float

All 32-bit floating point numbers in the IEEE (8087) format have an absolute value range of $8.43 \times 10\hat{}-37$ to

3.37 × 10 ^ 38. Float type numbers are composed of one high order sign bit, an 8-bit biased exponent, and 23 significand bits. The biased exponent represents the number of bit-shifts applied to the significand to locate the decimal point. The bias shift is 0x7F = 127 and forces all biased exponent field values to be positive ([2 ^ 8]/2 − 1 or 2 ^ 7 − 1). One high order bit is always assumed. Therefore, for very large numbers, there can be 127 + 1 bit shifts, which, in binary, can represent a number as large as 2 ^ 128 (3.37 × 10 ^ 37). For very small numbers, there can be (127 − 1) bit shifts, which in binary can represent a number as small as 2 ^ 126 (8.43 × 10 ^ − 37). The number of significant digits is determined from 2 ^ 23 magnitude bits, giving 6–7 significant digits.

To further clarify how C float numbers are represented, let's convert the positive decimal number (511.375).

1. Represent 511 in binary: 0x1FF = 1 1111 1111 (Appendix I).
2. The number of bit shifts necessary to retain one high-order (leftmost) bit is eight.
3. Compute the biased exponent value: 0x7F + 0x08 = 0x87.
4. Represent the biased exponent in binary: 1000 0111 (see Appendix I).
5. Represent 0.375 in binary: 0110 . . . . . (Appendix I).
6. Construct the binary representation of this float:

Positive sign bit	:	0
Biased exponent	:	1000 0111
Significand	:	
Integer (511)	:	1111 1111
Fraction(.375)	:	0110 0000 0000 000

7. Reconstruct four eight-bit bytes:

0100 0011	1111 1111	1011 0000	0000 0000
4 3	F F	B 0	0 0

8. The IEEE float representation of 511.375 in hexadecimal is

x 43 FF B0 00

For additional clarity, let's convert (−511.375).

1-5. These steps are the same as above.

6. Construct the binary representation of this float:

```
=> Negative sign bit  :  1
   Biased exponent    :  1000 0111
   Significand        :
     Integer (511)    :  1111 1111
     Fraction(.375)   :  0110 0000 0000 000
```

7. Reconstruct four eight-bit bytes:

```
1100 0011   1111 1111   1011 0000   0000 0000
  C    3      F    F      B    0      0    0
```

8. The IEEE float representation of −511.375 in hexadecimal is

x C3 FF B0 00

Because of the biased exponent form of representing real numbers, two float numbers of the same sign can be compared as if they are unsigned binary integers. By comparing them bitwise from left to right (starting at the high order biased exponent bit), the first bit position that differs orders the two numbers.

If all 32-bits are treated as a binary unit, the following ascending sorted sequence would result for a number range from −Rmin to +Rmax:

0, 0+ . . . +Rmax, 0− . . . −Rmin

The logical and physical bit patterning for float is shown in Figure 2.2 for the INTEL 8088/86/186.

Double

All 64-bit floating point numbers in the IEEE (8087) format have an absolute value range from 4.19×10^−307 to +1.67×10^308. Double type numbers are composed of one high order sign bit, an 11 bit biased exponent, and 52 significand bits. The biased exponent represents the number of bit-shifts applied to the significand to locate the decimal point. The bias shift is 0x3FF (1023) and forces all biased exponent field values to be positive ([2^11]/2 − 1 or 2^10 − 1). One high order bit is always assumed. Therefore, for very large numbers, there can be 1023 + 1 bit shifts, which in binary can represent a number as large as 2^1024 (1.67×10^308). For very small numbers there can be 1023 − 1 bit shifts, which in binary can represent a number as small as 2^1022 (4.19 ×10^−307). The number of significant digits is determined from 2^52 magnitude bits giving 15–16 significant digits.

To further clarify how C double numbers are represented, lets convert the positive decimal number (511.375).

1. Represent 511 in binary: 0x1FF = 1 1111 1111 (see Appendix I).
2. The number of bit shifts necessary to retain one high-order (leftmost) bit is eight.
3. Compute the biased exponent value: 0x3FF + 0x08 = 0x407.
4. Represent the biased exponent in binary: 100 0000 0111 (see Appendix I).
5. Represent 0.375 in binary: 0110 . . . . . (Appendix I).
6. Construct the binary representation of this double:

Positive sign bit	:	0
Biased exponent	:	100 0000 0111
Significand	:	
Integer (511)	:	1111 1111
Fraction(.375)	:	0110 0000 0000 000

7. Reconstruct eight eight-bit bytes:

0100 0000	0111 1111	1111 0110	0000 0000	...
4 0	7 F	F 6	0 0	...

8. The IEEE double representation of 511.375 in hexadecimal is

x 40 7F F6 00 00 00 00 00

For additional clarity, let's convert –511.375.

1-5. These steps are the same as above.

6. Construct the binary representation of this double:

=>Negative sign bit	:	1
Biased exponent	:	100 0000 0111
Significand	:	
Integer (511)	:	1111 1111
Fraction(.375)	:	0110 0000 0000 000

7. Reconstruct eight eight-bit bytes:

1100 0000	**0111 1111**	**1111 0110**	**0000 0000**	...
C 0	**7 F**	**F 6**	**0 0**	...

8. The IEEE double representation of –511.375 in hexadecimal is

x C0 7F F6 00 00 00 00 00

Because of the biased exponent form of representing real numbers, two double numbers of the same sign can be compared as if they are unsigned binary integers. By comparing them bitwise from left to right (starting at the high order biased exponent bit), the first bit position that differs orders the two numbers.

If all 64-bits are treated as a binary unit, the following ascending sorted sequence would result for a number range from –Rmin to +Rmax:

0, 0+ . . . +Rmax, 0– . . . –Rmin

The logical and physical bit patterning for double is shown in Figure 2.2 for the INTEL 8088/86/186.

Appendix L
Linker Automatic Response Files (.lnk)

This appendix lists all the link files that are necessary to run the test programs included in this book. Each of the test programs begins with the following comment lines for identification purposes:

```
/*
** file  : tfunct.c <diskette file name for this program>
** desc: <brief program description>
** link  : link instructions (without use of librarian)
*/
```

In order to use a test program, you must follow the link instructions listed in the third comment line. These instructions indicate which of the following link programs to use for that particular test program.

File Name	Contents
DEMO.LNK	beep + blanksc + cjust + clrtab + cs + dechar + dedate + dedolr + deint + delay + delchr + demo + dereal + detele + detime + dvcharqc + dvcharqs + dvcharyn + dvdatede + dvdateen + dvdolrde + dvdolren + dvdummy + dvintde + dvinten + dvrealde + dvrealen + dvtelede + dvteleen + dvtimede + dvtimeen + enchar + endate + endolr + enint + enreal + entele + entime + evchar + evdate + evdolr + evint + evreal + evtele + evtime + fgetchar + fgetdate + fgetdolr + fgetint + fgetreal + fgetstr + fgettele + fgettime + fputchar + fputdate + fputdolr + fputint + fputreal + fputstr + fputtele +

File Name	Contents
	fputtime + getcha + getchar + getchr + getcrc + getdate + getdolr + getint + getreal + gettele + gettime + help + inschr + lderc + ljust + logreset + logwrite + main + mesende + mesgsps + movcrc + nondel + poschr + pscreen + pstdprn + putchar + putchr + putchs + putdate + putdolr + putint + putmask + putreal + putstr + puttele + puttime + rjust + setcrc + snlbntb + utcharcb + utcharcm + utcharjs + utcharrs + utcharsb + utdatedd + utdatedm + utdatedn + utdatedw + utdategi + utdateig + utdately + utdatemm + utdatemy + utdatesg + utdatesi + utrealds + utrealfs + uttimesi
QACHAR.LNK	beep + blanksc + cjust + clrtab + cs + dechar + deint + delay + delchr + detime + dvcharqc + dvcharqs + dvcharyn + dvdummy + dvintde + dvinten + dvtimede + enchar + enint + evchar + evint + fgetchar + fgetint + fgetstr + fputchar + fputstr + getcha + getchar + getchr + getcrc + getint + help + inschr + lderc + ljust + logreset + logwrite + main + mesende + mesgsps + movcrc + nondel + poschr + pscreen + pstdprn + putchar + putchr + putchs + putmask + putstr + qachar + rjust + setcrc + snlbntb + uprompt + utcharcb + utcharcs + utcharjs + utcharrs + utcharsb + utdategi + utdatesg + utdatesi + uttimesi
QACHARV1.LNK	beep + blanksc + cjust + clrtab + cs + dechar + deint + delay + detime + delchr + dvcharqc + dvcharqs + dvcharyn + dvdummy + dvintde + dvinten + dvtimede + enchar + enint

File Name	Contents
	+ evchar + evint + fgetstr + fputstr + getcha + getchr + getcrc + getstr + help + inschr + lderc + ljust + logreset + logwrite + main + mesende + mesgsps + movcrc + nondel + poschr + pscreen + pstdprn + putchr + putchs + putmask + putstr + qacharv1 + rjust + setcrc + snlbntb + utcharcb + utcharcs + utcharjs + utcharrs + utcharsb + utdategi + utdatesg + utdatesi + uttimesi
QADATE.LNK	beep + blanksc + cjust + clrtab + cs + dedate + deint + delay + delchr + detime + dvcharqc + dvcharqs + dvcharyn + dvdatede + dvdateen + dvdummy + dvintde + dvinten + dvtimede + enchar + endate + enint + evchar + evdate + evint + fgetchar + fgetdate + fgetint + fgetstr + fputdate + fputint + fputstr + getcha + getchar + getchr + getcrc + getdate + getint + help + inschr + lderc + ljust + logreset + logwrite + main + mesende + mesgsps + movcrc + nondel + poschr + pscreen + pstdprn + putchr + putchs + putdate + putint + putmask + putstr + qadate + rjust + setcrc + snlbntb + uprompt + utcharcb + utcharcm + utcharjs + utcharrs + utcharsb + utdatedd + utdatedm + utdatedn + utdatedw + utdategi + utdateig + utdately + utdatemm + utdatemy + utdatesg + utdatesi + uttimesi
QADOLR.LNK	beep + blanksc + cjust + clrtab + cs + dedolr + deint + delay + delchr + detime + dvcharqc + dvcharqs + dvcharyn + dvdolrde + dvdolren + dvdummy + dvintde + dvinten +

File Name	Contents
	dvtimede + enchar + endolr + enint + evchar + evdolr + evint + fgetchar + fgetdolr + fgetint + fgetstr + fputdolr + fputint + fputstr + getcha + getchar + getchr + getcrc + getdolr + getint + help + inschr + lderc + ljust + logreset + logwrite + main + mesende + mesgsps + movcrc + nondel + poschr + pscreen + pstdprn + putchr + putchs + putdolr + putint + putmask + putstr + qadolr + rjust + setcrc + snlbntb + uprompt + utcharcb + utcharjs + utcharrs + utcharsb + utdategi + utdatesg + utdatesi + uttimesi
QAINT.LNK	beep + blanksc + cjust + clrtab + cs + deint + delay + delchr + detime + dvcharqc + dvcharqs + dvcharyn + dvdummy + dvintde + dvinten + dvtimede + enchar + enint + evchar + evint + fgetchar + fgetint + fgetstr + fputint + fputstr + getcha + getchar + getchr + getcrc + getint + help + inschr + lderc + ljust + logreset + logwrite + main + mesende + mesgsps + movcrc + nondel + poschr + pscreen + pstdprn + putchr + putchs + putint + putmask + putstr + qaint + rjust + setcrc + snlbntb + uprompt + utcharcb + utcharjs + utcharrs + utcharsb + utdategi + utdatesg + utdatesi + uttimesi
QAREAL.LNK	beep + blanksc + cjust + clrtab + cs + deint + delay + delchr + dereal + detime + dvcharqc + dvcharqs + dvcharyn + dvdummy + dvintde + dvinten + dvrealde + dvrealen +

File Name	Contents
	dvrealov + dvtimede + enchar + enint + enreal + evchar + evint + evreal + fgetchar + fgetint + fgetreal + fgetstr + fputreal + fputstr + getcha + getchar + getchr + getcrc + getint + getreal + help + inschr + lderc + ljust + logreset + logwrite + main + mesende + mesgsps + movcrc + nondel + poschr + pscreen + pstdprn + putchr + putchs + putmask + putreal + putstr + qareal + rjust + setcrc + snlbntb + uprompt + utcharcb + utcharjs + utcharrs + utcharsb + utdategi + utdatesg + utdatesi + utrealds + utrealfs + uttimesi
QATELE.LNK	beep + blanksc + cjust + clrtab + cs + deint + delay + delchr + detele + detime + dvcharqc + dvcharqs + dvcharyn + dvdummy + dvintde + dvinten + dvtelede + dvteleen + dvtimede + enchar + enint + entele + evchar + evint + evtele + fgetchar + fgetint + fgetstr + fgettele + fputstr + fputtele + getcha + getchar + getchr + getcrc + getint + gettele + help + inschr + lderc + ljustlogreset + logwrite + main + mesende + mesgsps + movcrc + nondel + poschr + pscreen + pstdprn + putchr + putchs + putmask + putstr + puttele + qatele + rjust + setcrc + snlbntb + uprompt + utcharcb + utcharjs + utcharrs + utcharsb + utdategi + utdatesg + utdatesi + uttimesi
QATIME.LNK	beep + blanksc + cjust + clrtab + cs + deint + delay + delchr + detime + dvcharqc + dvcharqs + dvcharyn +

File Name	Contents
	dvdummy + dvintde + dvinten + dvtimede + dvtimeen + enchar + enint + entime + evchar + evint + evtime + fgetchar + fgetint + fgetstr + fgettime + fputstr + fputtime + getcha + getchar + getchr + getcrc + getint + gettime + help + inschr + lderc + ljust + logreset + logwrite + main + mesende + mesgsps + movcrc + nondel + poschr + pscreen + pstdprn + putchr + putchs + putmask + putstr + puttime + qatime + rjust + setcrc + snlbntb + uprompt + utcharcb + utcharjs + utcharrs + utcharsb + utdategi + utdatesg + utdatesi + uttimesi
TBEEP.LNK	beep + cs + delay + tbeep
TGETSTR.LNK	beep + blanksc + clrtab + cs + delay + fgetstr + fputstr + getcha + getchr + getcrc + getstr + help + inschr + main + movcrc + nondel + poschr + pscreen + pstdprn + putchr + putchs + putmask + putstr + setcrc + snlbntb + tgetstr + utcharcb + utcharrs
TJUST.LNK	cjust + cs + ljust + rjust + snlbntb + tjust

Index of Source Code Files

The source code index provides an alphabetical listing of all the source code available in the book and on disk. The index uses the following conventions:

1. All filenames conform to PC-DOS standards (filename.ext) where the filename is 1–8 characters long, and the extension is 1–3 characters long.

2. The filename prefixes typically denote the following types of files (xxxx is a logical data type identifier and yy is a suffix identifier):

de	Decode xxxx function
dv	Data validation xxxxyy function
en	Encode xxxx function
ev	Encode xxxx and validate xxxxyy function
fget	Getstring and ev xxxx function with coordinates
fput	Decode xxxx and putstring with coordinates
get	Getstring and ev xxxx function without coordinates
put	Decode xxxx and putstring without coordinates
qa	Quality assurance xxxx function
t	Test program
ut	Utility xxxxyy function

3. The filename suffixes denote the following types of files:

.c	C source code file
.h	Header file source code

4. The symbols in the Flag column denote the following:

*	indicates functions that are dependent upon special DOS or Lattice C compiler features.
+	indicates functions that are *not* of function type integer.
d	indicates a function that is available only on disk, and not listed in the text.

File Name	Flag	Page	Description
evdate.c		206	Encodes and validates date LDT.
evdolr.c		264	Encodes and validates dollar LDT.
evint.c		299	Encodes and validates integer LDT.
evreal.c		327	Encodes and validates real LDT.
evtele.c		365	Encodes and validates telephone LDT.
evtime.c		388	Encodes and validates time LDT.
fgetchar.c		144	Combines getstr and evchar with coordinates.
fgetdate.c		207	Combines getstr and evdate with coordinates.
fgetdolr.c		265	Combines getstr and evdolr with coordinates.
fgetint.c		299	Combines getstr and evint with coordinates.
fgetreal.c		328	Combines getstr and evreal with coordinates.
fgetstr.c		81	Performs all user keyboard interaction and gets a string under mask control with coordinates.
fgettele.c		366	Combines getstr and evtele with coordinates.
fgettime.c		389	Combines getstr and evtime with coordinates.
fputchar.c		150	Combines dechar and putstr with coordinates.
fputdate.c		216	Combines dedate and putstr with coordinates.
fputdolr.c		271	Combines dedolr and putstr with coordinates.
fputint.c		304	Combines deint and putstr with coordinates.
fputreal.c		334	Combines dereal and putstr with coordinates.
fputstr.c		92	Puts a string under mask and video attribute control with coordinates.
fputtele.c		370	Combines detele and putstr with coordinates.
fputtime.c		393	Combines detime and putstr with coordinates.
getcha.c	*	115	Gets character/attribute from the video.
getchar.c		143	Combines getstr and evchar without coordinates.
getchr.c	* +	113	Gets a character from the keyboard.
getcrc.c	*	114	Gets cursor row/column from the video.
getdate.c		207	Combines getstr and evdate without coordinates.
getdolr.c		265	Combines getstr and evdolr without coordinates.
getint.c		299	Combines getstr and evint without coordinates.
getmstr.c		105	Gets a string under mask control.
getreal.c		328	Combines getstr and evreal without coordinates.
getstr.c		81	Performs all user keyboard interaction and gets a string under mask control without coordinates.
gettele.c		366	Combines getstr and evtele without coordinates.
gettime.c		389	Combines getstr and evtime without coordinates.
help.c		108	Simulates system-wide dummy Help feature.
inschr.c		123	Inserts character in a string.
ios1.h	*	482	Provides UFB level 1 file I/O information used by _main (main.c).
lderc.c		54	Returns least significant digit of erc.

File Name	Flag	Page	Description
utcharcm.c		165	Compares strings.
utcharcs.c		166	Converts between characters and strings.
utcharjs.c		167	Justifies strings.
utcharmd.c		172	Computes modulus 10/11 check digits for LDT char.
utcharna.c	+	174	Formats names.
utcharrs.c		168	Reverses strings.
utcharrx.c	+	176	Converts between different radix number systems.
utcharsb.c		169	Strips string characters.
utcharsx.c		179	Computes a soundex code given a surname.
utdatedd.c	+	227	Gets a three-character day name.
utdatedm.c		223	Computes the days in a month.
utdatedn.c	+	228	Gets full day name.
utdatedw.c		224	Computes day of week number.
utdatega.c		238	Computes age from gregorian date.
utdategd.c	+	241	Computes delta days from gregorian date.
utdategi.c	+	231	Converts from gregorian to encoded date.
utdategj.c	+	231	Converts gregorian to julian date.
utdateia.c		239	Computes age from encoded date.
utdateid.c	+	242	Computes delta days from encoded date.
utdateig.c		232	Converts encoded date to gregorian date.
utdateij.c	+	233	Converts encoded date to julian date.
utdateja.c		240	Computes age from julian date.
utdatejd.c	+	243	Computes delta days from julian date.
utdatejg.c		234	Converts julian to gregorian date.
utdateji.c	+	235	Converts julian to encoded date.
utdatejy.c		225	Computes number of days this year.
utdately.c		226	Computes leap year adjustment for February.
utdatemm.c	+	229	Gets three-character month name.
utdatemy.c	+	230	Gets full month name.
utdateng.c		243	Computes next gregorian day, given offset.
utdateni.c	+	244	Computes next encoded date, given offset.
utdatenj.c	+	245	Computes next julian date, given offset.
utdatesg.c	*	236	Converts system date to gregorian.
utdatesi.c	+	237	Converts system date to encoded date.
utdatesj.c	+	237	Converts system date to julian date.
utdolrad.c		275	Adds dolr LDT fields.
utdolrcw.c	+	281	Provides a complete checkwriter capability to whole cents with range checking (calls utdolrda.c).
utdolrda.c		282	Expands (using recursion) a whole dollar amount to an equivalent work expression for checkwriting purposes.
utdolrdv.c		276	Divides dolr LDT fields.
utdolrml.c		277	Multiplies dolr LDT fields.
utdolrsb.c		279	Subtracts dolr LDT fields.

Index

SYBEX COMPUTER BOOKS

are different.

Here is why . . .

At SYBEX, each book is designed with you in mind. Every manuscript is carefully selected and supervised by our editors, who are themselves computer experts. We publish the best authors, whose technical expertise is matched by an ability to write clearly and to communicate effectively. Programs are thoroughly tested for accuracy by our technical staff. Our computerized production department goes to great lengths to make sure that each book is well-designed.

In the pursuit of timeliness, SYBEX has achieved many publishing firsts. SYBEX was among the first to integrate personal computers used by authors and staff into the publishing process. SYBEX was the first to publish books on the CP/M operating system, microprocessor interfacing techniques, word processing, and many more topics.

Expertise in computers and dedication to the highest quality product have made SYBEX a world leader in computer book publishing. Translated into fourteen languages, SYBEX books have helped millions of people around the world to get the most from their computers. We hope we have helped you, too.

For a complete catalog of our publications:

SYBEX, Inc. 2344 Sixth Street, Berkeley, California 94710
Tel: (415) 848-8233 Telex: 336311

DATA HANDLING UTILITIES IN C

Programs Available on Disk

If you'd like to use the programs in this book but don't want to type them in yourself, you can send for disks containing the source files for every function in the book and for additional test programs not included in the book. The disks (double-sided, double density) contain all programs listed in the source code index of this book. There are two sets of disks you can choose from:

1. **LDT-C:** Includes all .c, .h, and .lnk source code files in this book—$20.00.
2. **LDT:** Includes everything in LDT-C *plus* all corresponding .obj files—$30.00.

To obtain these disks, complete the order form and return it along with the appropriate amount. There is no additional charge for postage and handling. Please allow 10 days for delivery.

Computer Application Engineers, Inc.
c/o Robert A. Radcliffe
517 North 19th St.
Philadelphia, PA 19130

Name____________________________________

Address__________________________________

City/State/ZIP_____________________________

LDT-C $20.00 ☐ LDT $30.00 ☐

Enclosed is my check or money order (in U.S. dollars).
(Make check payable to *Computer Application Engineers, Inc.*)

SYBEX is not affiliated with Computer Application Engineers, Inc. *and assumes no responsibility for any defect in the disk or program.*